COUNSELS *of* IMPERFECTION

COUNSELS of IMPERFECTION

Thinking Through Catholic Social Teaching

EDWARD HADAS

The Catholic University of America Press
Washington, DC

Copyright © 2021
The Catholic University of America Press
All rights reserved
The paper used in this publication meets the minimum requirements of American
National Standards for Information Science—Permanence of Paper for Printed
Library Materials, ANSI Z39.48–1984.
∞

Library of Congress Cataloging-in-Publication Data

Names: Hadas, Edward, author.
Title: Counsels of imperfection : thinking through Catholic social teaching / Edward
Hadas.
Description: Washington, DC : The Catholic University of America Press, 2021. |
Includes bibliographical references and index. | Summary: "The book is aimed
especially to curious newcomers, especially people who do not want to be told
that there are simple Catholic answers to the complicated problems of the modern
world. The goal is not only to explain what the Church really says, but also how it
got to its current position and who it is arguing with. For each topic, Counsels of
Imperfection provides biblical, historical and a broad philosophical background.
In the spirit of a doctrine always in development, Counsels of Imperfection points
out both strong-points and imperfections in the teaching. The book is divided
into 11 chapters. First comes an introduction to ever-changing modernity and the
unchanging Christian understanding of human nature and society. Then come two
chapters on economics, including a careful delineation of the Catholic response to
socialism and capitalism. The next topic is government (Church and State, War,
and democracy and related topics). Next two chapters on ecology. The last topic is
the family teaching, which presents the social aspects of the Church's sexual teaching as relates to society. A brief concluding chapter looks at the teaching's changing
response to the modern world, and at the ambiguous Catholic appreciation of the
modern idea of progress"—Provided by publisher.
Identifiers: LCCN 2020043683 (print) | LCCN 2020043684 (ebook) | ISBN
9780813233314 (paperback) | ISBN 9780813233321 (ebook)
Subjects: LCSH: Catholic Church—Doctrines. | Christian sociology—Catholic
Church. | Christian ethics—Catholic authors.
Classification: LCC BX1753 .H2235 2021 (print) | LCC BX1753 (ebook) | DDC
261/.1—dc23
LC record available at https://lccn.loc.gov/2020043683
LC ebook record available at https://lccn.loc.gov/2020043684

Contents

Introduction   1

Explanations and Acknowledgments

Chapter 1: Background and Key Ideas   9

Idea 1: Human Nature Is Real and Comes in Three Types   15

Idea 2: People Naturally Search for the Supernatural   19

Idea 3: People Are Fundamentally Social   20

Idea 4: Love Is the Foundation of All Human Communities   21

Idea 5: Societies Are Always Imperfect   23

Idea 6: Authority Is a Necessary Part of Social Life   24

Idea 7: The Only Historical Story That Really Matters Is the Story of Redemption   25

Idea 8: Catholics Have Responded to Modernity but Not Very Successfully   27

Idea 9: The Catholic Social Teaching Is a Response to Huge Changes   33

Idea 10: Most of the Catholic Social Teaching Is Universal   35

Idea 11: The Catholic Social Teaching Can Only Offer Counsels of Imperfection   37

Idea 12: The Church Always Calls People to Perfection   40

Chapter 2: Economic Issues in an Industrial Age   42

The Biblical Base   48

The Philosophical Base   55

Five Principles   58

Chapter 3: Economics Ideas, New and Old   96

The Virtues and Vices of Technical Ingenuity   96

The Fading Challenge of Poverty and the New Challenges of
Affluence   99

Free Markets   104

A Better Way   117

Chapter 4: Government—Church and State   127

The Biblical Base   129

Philosophical Tensions   134

Historical Perspective   143

What Now?   153

Chapter 5: Government—War and Peace   163

The Biblical Background   164

The Philosophical Background   168

The Historical Background   174

The Just War Doctrine   181

The Current Teaching—The War against War   185

Chapter 6: The Church Adrift in a Secular World   191

Democracy   193

Human Rights   202

The Welfare State   210

Crimes and Punishment   216

Anti-Semitism   227

Migration   235

Looking Forward   245

Chapter 7: The Care of Creation   246

The Biblical and Theological Base   247

The Teaching in Context   252

Catholics against the Mainstream—Four Issues   259

Chapter 8: Integral Ecology   276

The Big Old Idea—Misguided Anthropocentrism   277
The Big New Idea—The Technocratic Paradigm   280
Food Production—People in Nature   286
The Life of Cities—The Poor and the Rich   291
The Life of Leisure   296
The Denigration of the Domestic   302
Cautionary Conclusion   309

Chapter 9: The Human Family—I   311

The Family in the Bible   313
The Modern Shift, in Practice   320
The Modern Shift, in Theory   334

Chapter 10: The Human Family—II   345

The Catholic Response   345
The Catholic Response in More Detail   354
A Brief Cheerful Conclusion   375

Chapter 11: Three Concluding Thoughts   376

Light and Shadows   376
From Frightened Pride to Confident Humility   381
Progress and Its Discontents   388

Bibliography   393

Index   421

Introduction

OUTSIDE OF A RELATIVELY SMALL group of specialists, the Social Teaching of the Catholic Church is rarely studied in great detail. The only plausible answer to John Paul II's rhetorical question, posed in 1994, "It must be asked how many Christians really know and put into practice the principles of the Church's social doctrine" is "not very many."[1] If I did not regret this state of affairs, I would not have taken the trouble of lecturing on the topic, let alone expanding the lectures into a fairly substantial book. Still, it is worth admitting at the very beginning that the lack of interest is in some ways quite reasonable.

One problem is cultural. The basic tenor of the teaching is alien to modern readers. The strangeness should not be surprising. The teaching is distinctly Christian and frequently imbued with a particularly Catholic coloring, while modern thinking is almost always post-Christian, frequently anti-Christian, and often distinctly anti-Catholic. (I explain my broad understanding of "the modern" in chapter 1, under idea 8.) These modern thinkers have come in many varieties: rationalist, materialist, scientific, deist, Kantian, Hegelian, liberal (in any of the many ways that word is used), democratic, Romantic, anti-Semitic, socialist, Utilitarian, Darwinian, fascist, totalitarian, nihilist, or moral relativist, Some were avowedly progressive and some claimed to be conservative. They disagree about many things, but almost all of them have considered the Catholic view of society to be fundamentally

---

1. John Paul II, Apostolic Letter *Tertio Millennio Adveniente* (November 10, 1984), 36. Unless otherwise noted in the bibliography, magisterial texts are taken from the Vatican website (Vatican.va). Quotes from John Paul II's catechesis on human sexuality are taken from the Michael Waldstein translation (full details in the bibliography).

wrongheaded. They see the Church as opposed to much of what they consider to be good, whether that be true freedom, emotional expressions, moral autonomy, worldly pleasure, tolerance, radical equality, just government, national traditions, the free development of culture, the glory of races and nations, the will of the people, or any of the other modern virtues. When the Catholic Church has been praised by a modern thinker, it was usually for some anti-Christian pseudovirtue. For example, the nineteenth-century positivist Auguste Comte dismissed Christianity and considered the Church an outmoded relic but admired its manipulative ability to centralize power.[2] Such cynical compliments have become rarer, but they linger, further weakening secular respect for any thinking labeled as Catholic.

Since the Catholic Social Teaching that this book describes is part of that widely rejected Catholic world and worldview, it is hardly surprising that its influence on nominal and practicing Catholics is limited and has probably declined since 1994. Today's Catholics, after all, live in the modern world. They will inevitably fall into the common ways of thinking, unless the conventional wisdom is countered by serious efforts from both them and their teachers in the faith. Such effort is scarce enough that most Catholics share their non-Catholic peers' attitude about most of life, from shopping and sports to divorce and the nature of freedom. An almost instinctive distrust of portentous Church pronouncements is on the list of shared values. For many jaded Catholics, the corpus of social teaching, if they have heard of it at all, amounts to nothing more than another set of would-be authoritative Church teachings to ignore.

This clash of cultures discourages interest in the Social Teaching, but it does not invalidate it. On the contrary, the Catholic discussion provides fruitful challenges to many widely held modern ideas. However, I fear that too many of the teaching's promoters downplay the fundamental conflict between Christian values and modern secular thinking. Too often, they seem to secularize teachings that are essentially religious, manipulating the doctrines and documents to squeeze them into conformity with a partisan political agenda. There are several conflicting thinly veiled secularisms—consider, for example, the bitter intra-Catholic debates about migration and the proper role of government—but their adherents share a tendency to make

---

2. For a distinctly Catholic appreciation of Comte's efforts see Henri de Lubac, *Le Drame de l'humanisme athée,* 6th ed. (Paris: Éditions du Cerf, 2000 [1959]), 141–288.

the Catholic Social Teaching sound like a refuge for people who want to preach what they think to be the truth with a too strong emphasis on seasonally appropriate elements.[3]

The case for paying attention to the teaching is further weakened by a second problem, of apparent historical inconsistency. Many specific policy recommendations have shifted or even been reversed since 1891, when Pope Leo XIII's *Rerum Novarum*—or "On the new things"—is conventionally said to have inaugurated the Catholic Social Teaching, also known as Catholic Social Doctrine. (The date is somewhat arbitrary, but later popes have steadily used this encyclical as a reference point.) The Church used to be highly skeptical about democracy, now it is tremendously enthusiastic (see chapter 6). It used to have no problem with the death penalty, now it is totally opposed (also see chapter 6). It has, to some extent and in some significant aspects, changed its judgments on, to give a few prominent examples, the fundamental injustice of waging war (chapter 4), conscientious objection to military service (chapter 4), freedom of religious belief and practice (chapter 3), church-state relations (chapter 3), the role of Jews in society (chapter 6), and the appropriateness of state funding for education and health care (touched on in chapter 6).

Fundamentally, the appearances are deceptive or at least misleading. The guiding principles in all these disputed questions are constant. The evolution of judgments as circumstances change is better seen as a sign of a responsive and maturing intellectual life than of weak-minded inconsistency. However, there is a tendency among Catholic apologists to gloss over the genuine changes in practical teachings. Whether motivated by ignorance or by foolish pride, the denial of the development of the actual counsels can leave the Church looking intellectually dishonest.

It is worth noting that the changes in the teaching have all pushed the Church in the same direction, closer to the current secular consensus. Religious reasoning is always provided, but the trend can suggest another weakness, a too great willingness to offer a meek "baptism" of a secular agenda that was not in obvious need of religious validation. Indeed, I have heard cogent critics of all or part of the teaching complain that many of the revisions amount to inept efforts to catch up with the times, a surrender to the secular spirit. The critics sometimes say that the weakness and worldliness are too

---

3.   cf. 2 Tm 4:2.

far from the consistency that Jesus demanded. Did he not tell his followers simply to be perfect, as "your heavenly father is perfect"?[4] All people always fall short of that goal, of course, but at least Jesus gave Christians a pretty good idea of what perfection consists of—renunciation of property and social position for the sake of the gospel, total love of God and neighbor, total forgiveness. In contrast to such counsels of perfection, the critics conclude, the Social Teaching can sound more like counsels of cowardice and confusion. They might as well be called counsels of imperfection.

As the title of this book suggests, I agree with that conclusion, although I certainly dissent from the critics' sneering tone. The Social Teaching does indeed consist of counsels of imperfection, but imperfection is entirely appropriate for teaching about practical matters in the fallen world. The Social Teaching is less like the Catholic Church's unchanging teachings on faith and morals and more like human-made laws, which Thomas Aquinas, following Augustine, declares can be changed, both because "it seems natural to human reason to advance gradually from the imperfect to the perfect" and "on account of the changed condition of man, to whom different things are expedient according to the difference of his condition."[5] I say more about the imperfections of the Social Teaching in chapter 1.

The imperfections and changes are inevitable, but I believe that the Catholic Social Teaching provides the most profound analysis of almost all the substantial controversies of contemporary society. The success is not surprising. After all, the Church forms its doctrine from the best raw material—the revelation of divine love in the life, death, and resurrection of Jesus Christ; the revelation-aided philosophical study of human nature; and the worldly experience of preaching the gospel for two millennia in a wide variety of cultures.

Yes, the Church changes its mind, but that only shows that the institution and its leaders learn from experience and respond to changes in social reality. Yes, current judgments are subject to debate and revision, but they are never totally irrational or foolish. Indeed, I believe that after centuries of reflection on the value and implications of a long procession of modern notions, the Church's prudential judgments on every aspect of the modern world are now almost

---

4. Mt 5:48.

5. Thomas Aquinas, *Summa* Theologica, trans. Fathers of the English Dominican Province, 5 vols. (London: Sheed & Ward, 1920 [1274]), II.1.97.1 *corpus*.

always the best available. They should be, because each one emerges from the same timeless truths—a view of people as good but weak in their nature, transcendental in their aspirations but all too easily confused in their thinking, and all too often wrong in their actions. (I also explain these principles in the first chapter.) In the words of Pope Benedict XVI, the teaching has an inner "coherence." This "does not mean a closed system: on the contrary, it means dynamic faithfulness to a light received."[6] Because of this inner coherence, the whole is far greater than the sum of its parts. Each of the disparate teachings, on economics, government, the environment, and so forth, is reasonable and insightful on its own, but what is best and most helpful about the teaching is the comprehensive Catholic approach to all aspects of society. I will necessarily be dealing with the teachings separately but will try throughout to show how it all fits together.

Explanations and Acknowledgments

My own interest in the Catholic Social Teaching started in 1991, with the appearance of John Paul II's encyclical *Centesimus Annus*. At the time, I was a fairly new convert to Catholicism. While most of the immediate American responses to the encyclical were concerned with Saint John Paul II's judgment on "capitalism," I was struck at a more basic level, by the Church's wisdom about so many pressing social, economic, and political issues. (As a finance professional, I was less delighted by how many commentators ignored his sophisticated mixed judgment on the prevalent economic system.) The initial pleasure has not faded. Rather, as I have studied the teaching over the years, my appreciation has only increased. I hope this book exudes some of that enthusiasm.

Mine is hardly the only available introduction to this teaching. There is an official document, *The Compendium of Catholic Social Doctrine*, as well as many more or less orthodox and more or less complete books. Why add to the pile? I hope for five unique selling propositions (to use the jargon of marketing). First is the attention to historical, cultural, and intellectual context. Second is an unusually broad view of what the Catholic Social Teaching includes. Third is the attempt to balance the teaching's unchanging and changing aspects. Fourth, although it is dangerous to boast of impartiality, I

---

6. Benedict XVI, Encyclical Letter *Caritas in Veritate* (June 29, 2009), 12.

have certainly striven to avoid twisting authoritative words to buttress my own political and cultural opinions. Finally, while treating all current teachings with respect, I have included some hopefully constructive commentary, both laudatory and critical, and some suggestions for improvement, most notably in the discussions of economics and integral ecology. I offer these personal contributions in a faithful spirit. I hope they can be examples of the sort of dialogue that can help the teaching develop.

The book is aimed at many audiences. I want to help enthusiastic Catholics understand the doctrine's depths; to persuade less committed Catholics that the teaching is insightful and helpful; to point out to excessively confident Catholics that it has significant limits; to offer the shepherds of the teaching some suggestions for improvement; to demonstrate to non-Catholic Christians that this teaching is not parochially Catholic; and to invite non-Christians to enter into a way of thinking that will help them respond better to the modern world. That list is obviously extremely ambitious. I am sure that the book, like the teaching it describes, is not completely satisfactory. Still, I hope that my basic approach—trying to show Catholics how the teaching looks to outsiders and to show outsiders how the teaching looks to Catholics—proves helpful.

Some of my desired readers would probably have been happier to see more quotations from the rich treasury of official Church documents. Others might think that I have given too much space to such texts, many of which are awkward in style or partly superseded in content. I can only say that I have done my best to balance authority-based and universal approaches to the teaching, and that I have striven to differentiate clearly between what the Church always teaches, what it has taught in the past, what it teaches now, and what I think it should consider teaching in the future.

The book is divided into eleven chapters. The first and last are general, starting the series with the historical and intellectual foundations of the teaching and concluding it with a few remarks about the Church's overall judgment of modern society. In between are nine chapters, two each on economics, family, the environment, and government and one, the sixth, which is a bit of a medley. In comparison to many similar works, I have given relatively little space to economic matters. This weighting reflects my judgment of relative current importance. The Magisterium, Latin for *teaching* and the technical word for the ever-expanding collection of the Church's official teaching documents, was right to focus on the economy at the end of the nineteenth century. At that time, the struggles over industrial labor and the social control of productive property were pressing and socially extremely divisive. Their resolution would determine some of the most important contours of modern societies. Other issues have become more challenging over the subsequent one hundred and thirty years, both for society as a whole and for Christians trying to deal with the contemporary world.

A brief introduction to so big a topic inevitably requires a harsh triage. I particularly regret one omission, the social morality of health care. Catholics are especially well placed to help meet the tremendous ethical questions in this area: among them, what resources to dedicate to health and illness; how to balance investments in prevention, cure, and care; and how to decide which patients should receive what sort of treatments. The need is great now, as the controversies over the response to the covid-19 pandemic have made painfully clear. Unfortunately, the official commentary on these issues has been relatively scanty and I lack the expertise needed to help out.

The original chapters were five hour-long informal talks to parishioners and a few curious visitors at St. Mary Moorfields parish church in London's financial district. That was back in 2007. In the long process of turning notes into a coherent text, five fairly casual lectures have somehow ended up as eleven chapters with many quotes and footnoted sources. The footnotes are there both to provide some supporting evidence for controversial claims and to help curious readers follow my thinking and the church's back to the sources.

Warm thanks are due to Father Peter Newby, then parish priest of St. Mary Moorfields, who arranged the initial talks, to the Maryvale Institute in Birmingham, whose teachers and students encouraged me in this project and clarified my thinking, and to everyone connected with Blackfriars Hall at Oxford University, which has provided me an intellectual and institutional home. I thank the anonymous readers for the Catholic University of America Press and four volunteer readers of various versions of the manuscript: Lucy Sheaf, Lucy Traves, Stephen Bullivant, and Ruth Kelly—whose comments and complaints led, I hope, to a more cogent text. I also thank my professional colleagues over the years at Reuters Breakingviews, who have provided friendship, intellectual challenges, and frequent reality checks. I am grateful to everyone connected with the Catholic University of America Press for their moral support and practical help. More personally, Fathers Hugh Mackenzie and Richard Finn, the Kelly and Sheehy families, Leonie Caldecott, and the late Stratford Caldecott have all provided various sorts of valuable assistance. Finally, my children have never failed to protect, promote, and provoke me as I worked through the many aspects of this rich teaching. To them and to all the others who have knowingly and unknowingly helped me along the way, deepest thanks.

CHAPTER 1

Background and Key Ideas

BEFORE DESCRIBING THE Catholic Church's Social Teaching, it is worth discussing whether the whole project makes any sense. Many people think not. They can present three skeptical arguments. Fortunately (for my purposes and those of the Catholic Church), none of them is persuasive.

The first and most fundamental claim is that social problems, like all the other things of this world, are the responsibility of the secular and worldly government, not of religion, which should be entirely and eternally oriented toward heaven. Christians in particular have no business messing with government, according to this line of thought, since Jesus himself told his disciples to "[r]ender therefore to Caesar the things that are Caesar's, and to God the things that are God's."[1] However, a more likely interpretation of that saying is that Jesus is explaining that there need be no contradiction between obedience to worldly authority and attention to the things of God, just as a little later in the same chapter he sees no contradiction between the love of "your neighbor as yourself" and the total love of God.[2]

---

1. Mt 22:21. All Bible quotations are taken from the Revised Standard Version, 1966 Catholic edition.

2. Mt 22:39. For a modern commentary on this "relatively cryptic" command, see *A Critical and Exegetical Commentary on the Gospel According to Saint Matthew*, W. D. Davies and Dale C. Allison Jr., vol. 3, *Commentary on Matthew XIX–XXVIII* (London: Bloomsbury 2004 [1997]), 218. Also, Ulrich Luz, *Matthew 21–28; A Commentary*, trans. James E. Crouch, (Minneapolis: Fortress Press, 2005): 67: "It is not the case, therefore, that Jesus thinks that one half of a person belongs to the emperor (for example, the material or cultural or the external that deal with the kingdom of the world) and the other to God (for example, the spiritual, the person or the inner life)."

The Lord's approach to worldly responsibilities is more thoroughly expressed in the final discourse recounted in the gospel of Matthew, when he tells his disciples that their eternal judgment will be based on whether they served "the least of my brothers." The service is to be rendered in remarkably tangible, this-world ways—feeding the hungry, clothing the naked, and visiting the imprisoned.[3] Still, although this injunction is firmly worldly, it also sounds individualistic. It says nothing directly about the social responsibility, whether of society as a whole or of the Christian Church within it, to promote social justice or social reform. There is, though, a logical connection. Communal arrangements can help ensure the feeding, clothing, and visiting of the least of Christ's brothers; the Church is supposed to encourage and provide Christian charity to these needy people; so the Church has an obligation to provide a moral evaluation of actual and potential social arrangements.

The same point can be made more theologically. Jesus was fully human as well as fully divine. He was a man who lived in a particular society, cured people who suffered from the miseries of this world, and praised such this-worldly social virtues as generosity and obedience. He set up a community of men and women to propagate his love in the world and to offer his salvation to the world. This community is the Church, which Saint Paul called the body of Christ.[4] Catholics believe that the earthly representatives of Jesus, the pope speaking for the bishops and the people, have the responsibility to help and guide all the members of this body in their worldly lives so they can best follow Jesus' injunction to love their neighbors as themselves. Since those lives are always lived in societies (as I explain shortly), practical Christian love is not only expressed person-to-person but also in social arrangements. The body of Christ has a duty to help spread and secure this social love, and the leaders of that body are obliged to determine how best to go about this central Christian task.

The biblical-philosophical and theological-sociological arguments are buttressed by an unchanging tradition. For the Church's Magisterium, which can be considered the authoritative statement of the Christian tradition as it develops, the correct way of living in society has been a concern from the very beginning. Peter, the

---

3. Mt 25:31–46.

4. e.g., 1 Cor 12:27.

leader of the archetypal Christian community described in the Acts of the Apostles, condemned believers who refused to share all their assets with the community so they could be used to help the needy.[5] He also instituted the diaconate with the specific mission of exercising physical works of charity.[6] Paul expressed the obligation in his concluding exhortation in the Letter to the Galatians, "So then, as we have opportunity, let us do good to all men, and especially to those who are of the household of faith."[7] From the beginning of the Church, this scriptural injunction was fully integrated into the Christian tradition. The leaders of both the whole Catholic Church and of nearly every other Christian community have always instructed members and implored rulers to promote virtue in society, often in quite specific ways.

The second objection is more practical. How can the Church actually teach anything substantial about society? Catholics believe that the pope can speak infallibly about matters of faith and morals and that the Church as a whole is infallibly guided by the Holy Spirit, if only it would listen. However, neither pope nor bishop can expect to understand the Spirit's precise explication of the maze of currently available arguments about such complicated technical and transient topics as the value of labor unions, the justice of different types of taxes, or the relative desirability of kingdoms and democracies. Without reliable divine help, it looks like the Catholic Social Teaching can amount only to more or less informed human opinions. Rather than write and promote bold encyclicals (the standard form of official teaching document), perhaps popes should merely encourage the formation of consciences. Moral sharpening can help people who have the relevant expertise better address social issues, without asking clerics to become experts.

Such a hands-off approach is neither necessary nor advantageous. It is not required because popes do not work alone. They can and do ask any number of people for help. At their best, the encyclicals and other less authoritative documents express the whole Church's considered thinking. Their arguments are gleaned from the most thoughtful observers and knowledgeable experts, purified with prayer, enlightened by revelation, leavened with the wisdom of the

---

5. Acts 5:1–11.

6. Acts 6:1–7.

7. Gal 6:10. Cf. Benedict XVI, Encyclical Letter *Deus Caritas Est* (December 25, 2005), 20–25.

ages, and sensitive to the signs of the times. An excessively scrupulous avoidance of detail is also not advantageous, because specific advice from the Church can be more insightful, both morally and practically, than can similarly detailed suggestions from even the most thoughtful and virtuous secular specialist. Future priests typically study philosophy and theology for five or more years. Those who pay some attention should have insights that are not as easily available to more narrowly educated specialists in economics, politics, or any other secular study.

In particular, the Catholic approach to social science is far more oriented to the common good than are its more secular rivals. This philosophical-sociological term is defined in various ways, both inside and outside of the Catholic tradition. Roughly and broadly, regarding the Social Teaching, the common good describes the overarching, shared, and lasting flourishing of the divine-human covenant, the ordered and disordered elements of creation, every society, every community, and each person within it. More theologically, it is the human mirror of the shared good of the Trinity, in which the infinite gifts of love among the divine Persons are the distinct and united good of each person and of the whole Trinity.

The concept of common good is central in the Catholic Social Teaching, so it is worth lingering on it. The phrase is ancient, and its meaning has changed as societies have become more secular and individualistic. Over the past century, Catholic thinkers have argued about how to express the idea in appropriately modern terms. Disputed questions include whether the common good is inherently transcendental or can also or only be found in some purely worldly form, whether there is actually a common good that is distinct from the combined individual goods of all the members of a community, whether the common good exists only to promote those individual goods or is actually a separate good pertaining to the community, and under what circumstances the common good takes precedence over real or apparent individual goods. I am not persuaded that all of these debates are fruitful.

My own description is an amplification of the definition given by the Second Vatican Council, which has become canonical in discussions of the Social Teaching, "the totality of those conditions of social life that allow social groups and their individual members relatively

BACKGROUND AND KEY IDEAS

thorough and ready access to their own fulfilment."[8] The definition is vague, I think suitably so. Narrower descriptions, such as the raison d'être of the state or the social counterpart to "private gain" in economic matters, both provided by John XXIII,[9] are helpful but miss the concept's ambition and breadth. A better starting point is to think of a communal expression of Jesus' purpose, "I came that they may have life, and have it abundantly."[10] The common good encompasses the transcendental and creaturely flourishing of individuals, of various social groupings, of entire societies, and of all humanity, present and future. In society, the common good is both created and enjoyed communally, with each member and each organization both responsible to contribute appropriately and able to benefit abundantly. It reflects the truth that each person's flourishing relies on the flourishing of all and the sometimes-painful corollary of that truth, that this shared flourishing sometimes requires that some members of the community give up on elements of what might appear to be their individual good. The common good that enhances, supports, and sometimes seems to sacrifice each individual's good—this good is at the heart of the Christian vision of society. Its promotion is the guiding principle for the distinctly social teaching of the Catholic Church.[11]

Returning to the question of clerical involvement in the teaching, priests, bishops, and popes cannot be expected always to identify the common good correctly in any particular situation, even with expert help. Their weaknesses, though, do not disqualify them from commenting. Even when they are in error, they can advance the debate, because their training points them in the right direction, toward the breadth and depth of human virtue, seen in the light of eternity. The popes, who produce the encyclicals that define the current teaching,

---

8. Vatican Council II, *Gaudium et Spes* (December 7, 1965), 26, translation altered.

9. John XXIII, Encyclical Letter *Mater et Magistra* (May 15, 1961), 20, 40.

10. Jn 10:10.

11. This description of the common good follows chapter 4 of Jacques Maritain, *La personne et le bien commun* (Paris: Desclée de Brouwer, 1947), a book that influenced John XXIII and the fathers of the Second Vatican Council. For further background, see Mary Keys, *Aquinas, Aristotle, and the Promise of the Common Good* (Cambridge: Cambridge University Press, 2006); the essays by Jean Porter, Dennis P. McCann, and William T Cavanaugh in Dennis P. McCann and Patrick D. Miller, eds., *In Search of the Common Good* (New York: T&T Clark, 2005); Patrick Riordan, *A Grammar of the Common Good: Speaking of Globalisation* (London: Continuum, 2008). A theologically unambitious vision is presented with helpful historical and philosophical background in David Hollenbach, *The Common Good and Christian Ethics* (Cambridge: Cambridge University Press, 2002).

have enough authority to provide what the *Compendium of the Social Doctrine of Church* calls an "authentic Magisterium, which obligates the faithful to adhere to it." These encyclicals, my primary source of the doctrine in this book, are supplemented by less authoritative papal, episcopal, and curial documents and statements. The mass of detailed commentary and instructions cannot be infallible, because each official statement of the Social Teaching, even the weightiest declarations from the Second Vatican Council or the most finely drafted statements in the *Catechism*, is filled with what the *Compendium* calls "contingent and variable elements" that mitigate the "doctrinal weight of the different teachings and the assent required."[12] However, the Church does know enough and speak with enough authority to provide a compelling—and for Catholics a somewhat binding—teaching.[13]

The third sort of incomprehension is even more pragmatic. It seems pointless for the Catholic Church to pronounce judgment on societies that, as I pointed out in the Introduction, are almost always unsympathetic, and often hostile, to the Catholic understanding of the world. If no one is listening, there is no reason to bother talking.

Actually, it is not quite that bad. The media in countries with large Catholic populations or with strong Christian traditions still take note of social encyclicals and papal pronouncements. Within the Church, the Social Teaching is covered in many catechetical programs, and Catholic charities often use its documents as practical guides. Sadly, there is often much more incomprehension than interest. Promulgators and proponents of the Social Teaching should cling to the cardinal virtue of hope, starting with the hope that people

---

12. Pontifical Council for Justice and Peace, *Compendium of the Social Doctrine of the Church* (Vatican City: Libreria Editrice Vaticana, 2004), 80.

13. There is a controversy over how authoritative the Social Teaching is for Catholics. The *Compendium*'s text is ambiguous, quite possibly on purpose. "Insofar as it is part of the Church's moral teaching, the Church's social doctrine has the same dignity and authority as her moral teaching" (*Compendium of the Social Doctrine of the Church*, 80). It is not clear how to assign the various parts of the social teaching to permanent moral or to possibly changing prudential teaching. Some of the fundamental principles discussed in chapter 2 (e.g., the preferential option for the poor) may well have enough authority to be considered "non-definitive authoritative doctrine" (the infelicitous phrase in Richard R. Gaillardetz, *Teaching with Authority: A Theology of the Magisterium in the Church* (Collegeville, Minn.: Liturgical Press, 1997), 102, but that claim adds little to any debate on how an authoritative doctrine should be applied in specific circumstances. In my analysis of the nature and limits of magisterial authority, I basically follow Avery Dulles, *Magisterium: Teacher and Guardian of the Faith* (Naples, Fla: Sapientia Press, 2007), 63–64.

will notice well-made arguments. The hope is not irrational, since it relies on the confidence that the social teachings of the Magisterium are not only wise enough to be worth listening to but compelling enough to attract attention, sooner or later, even in a hostile age. In turn, the confidence is based on a basic claim of Catholic anthropology (the Catholic view of how people are by nature) that "[t]he truth is that only in the mystery of the incarnate Word does the mystery of man take on light."[14] The truth revealed by Jesus Christ is "in harmony with the most secret desires of the human heart."[15] It satisfies all human cravings and is in accord with human reason. Since the natural reasoning of humankind and the revealed truth are the basis of the Social Teaching, the teaching will have both natural and supernatural appeal. "He who has ears to hear, let him hear."[16]

Without abandoning hope, we can see that it is true that the Social Teaching is in many ways fundamentally opposed to many dominant modern values. As I suggested, that is ultimately one of its most compelling characteristics, because culture that can be called modern deserves to be opposed in many domains. (I discuss the relevant understanding of modern later in this chapter.) However, the distance between magisterial and conventional thinking is wide enough that untrained people may struggle to follow the Church's approach. It is all too likely that without some intellectual or spiritual enticement they will find the magisterial documents—the words, style, and basic ideas—surprising, strange, or even awful. The rest of this chapter is dedicated to helping and comforting those outsiders. I introduce, and try briefly to justify, twelve foundational ideas on which the edifice of the Catholic Social Teaching is built.

Idea 1: Human Nature Is Real and Comes in Three Types

You do not have to be Catholic or Christian or religious to accept the reality of human nature, humankind's universally shared collection of essential qualities. Philosophers of all sorts have endorsed the idea, suggesting such defining human characteristics as wisdom (we are *Homo sapiens* after all*)*, reason, love, friendship, worship, play, morality, and tool use. For Christians and Jews, the core of human

---

14.   Vatican Council II, *Gaudium et Spes*, 22.

15.   Vatican Council II, *Gaudium et Spes*, 21.

16.   Mk 4:9.

nature is described in the book of Genesis[17]—people, man and woman, are made in the image and likeness of God. That statement is bold but not conclusive. It immediately leads to questions about the nature of "image" and "likeness"–and about the nature of God.

Everyday language is a good place to start answering them. "That's just human nature, I'm afraid" is a common excuse for bad behavior, while "that's totally unnatural" is a common exclamation of disgust about particularly bad behavior. These apparently contradictory usages—both "nature" and "unnatural" are used to describe bad actions—hint at the distinctly Christian understanding. Our nature includes both an unsatisfactory "is"—the way people actually think and behave—and an ideal "ought"—the way people should think and behave. This is-ought duality has been described, from Saint Paul to the present, in three types or stages: God-created humanity, fallen humanity, and redeemed humanity.

Start with God-created humanity, who are made in the image and likeness of their Creator. This likeness describes the basic "ought" of human nature. A little philosophical reflection shows that the simple description implies three bold claims about that nature.

First, since men and women are in the likeness of God, all people have something godly at their core. People are like God in their desire to create, control, and understand everything in their world. More profoundly, they touch the divine in their longing for perfection, glory, and freedom of action and thought and in their dissatisfaction with the sad contours of death-limited life. Most profoundly, since Christians believe that "God is love,"[18] people touch the divine in their ability to love one another and to live in God's love. This multifaceted godliness gives each person an ineradicable worth and dignity.

Second, God, not humanity, is the measure of all things. People are most as they ought to be when they live up to their original likeness to God, when they live according to God's standard of goodness.

Third, people are naturally good, or virtuous, because God is complete goodness and people are like God. Since God and his goodness do not change, human goodness, in the image and likeness of the ultimate divine goodness, is also absolute. All people want to live in accord with the good that is unchanging and divine.

---

17.   Gn 1:27.

18.   1 Jn 4:8.

These statements of the fundamental godliness and goodness of human nature sit well with the description of some abhorrent acts as being "unnatural," but poorly with the use of human "nature" as an excuse for bad behavior. The difference is explained by the second sort of human nature, the fallen. It is a sad fact that people-as-they-were-created are no longer available for study. The "is" of humanity is sinful "de-natured" men and women.

The account of Adam's transgression (in the third chapter of Genesis) and the first theological-historical explanation of its inevitable hereditary nature (in the fifth chapter of Romans) are in the Bible, but for practical purposes Scripture is only confirming the obvious—the unavoidable ubiquity of evil and suffering. No one always strives solely after the truly good; nor does anyone always crave truth, long for the beautiful, or live for eternity. (Catholics believe that Jesus and his mother are exceptions to this otherwise universal truth.) Motivations and actions are at best morally mixed, and lives pass in conditions that hardly seem divine—hard-to-bear sorrow, pain, and doubt. This, too, is human nature.

How deeply does the wickedness of fallen nature cut into the goodness of created nature? Are people good but a little weak or perhaps very weak with merely some traces or possibilities of goodness? Christians discuss this question explicitly, but the argument also lies behind most discussions about social issues. Can laws be mild, to respect of basic human goodness, or must they be strict, to discipline the terrible weakness of humanity? The official Catholic teaching does not answer such questions precisely, saying of people in general only, "He still desires the good, but his nature bears the wound of original sin. He is now inclined to evil and subject to error."[19] Fortunately, it is not necessary to determine the exact moral calibration of fallen humanity to understand the Catholic Social Teaching. All that is required is recognition of this paradoxical duality—people are both truly good and truly bad. They always wish for what they think is good, but they are always tempted by false visions of the good—by sin. Because no one can always resist that temptation, societies are always both good and sinful.

The third sort of nature, the redeemed, is an exclusively Christian concept, because it cannot be articulated completely outside of

---

19.   *Catechism of the Catholic Church* (Vatican City: Libreria Editrice Vaticana, 1993 [for Latin text, English text revised in 1997]), 1707.

the Christian mystery of salvation. Jesus Christ, through his passion, death, and resurrection, offers all who follow him the possibility of full freedom from the pain and penalties of sin. He gives Christians, the people who accept this grace of salvation, the potential of overcoming all sin and death, which is the final fruit of sin.

Although Christians believe that redemption comes only from Jesus Christ and Catholics believe that it comes only through his Church, God's generosity is not limited to baptized Christians, let alone to Catholics in good standing. The Savior's grace overflows out of his visible Church and reaches invisibly toward everyone who strives for God. That group includes all men and women, since all people, made in the image of the loving God, always want to resemble their Creator. All people and all societies have the potential for, and the seeds of, redemption. In the words of the Second Vatican Council, "Nor is God far distant from those who in shadows and images seek the unknown God, for it is He who gives to all men life and breath and all things. . . . Those also can attain to salvation who through no fault of their own do not know the Gospel of Christ or His Church."[20] This universality allows the concept of redeemed nature (if not that phrase) to be understood and applied in every society.[21]

The reality of potential redemption has a practical effect on life, both for each person and in communities. With and through the grace of God, the balance in the fundamental human struggle against evil can be tipped more toward the good. Sin will always be too potent for societies to be organized on the expectation that everyone will always or almost always be good, but redemption is near enough that everyone should always be offered the freedom to be virtuous. Redeemed human nature, the nature glimpsed in the saints, is capable of remarkable accomplishments, even in a fallen world. The social order should respond to that capacity. It should

---

20.   Vatican Council II, Dogmatic Constitution *Lumen Gentium* (November 21, 1964), 16.

21.   The universality of the call to, and possibility of, redemption might seem to contradict the doctrine that there is no salvation outside of the Church. Some Catholics have undoubtedly believed this, in effect damning the overwhelming majority of humanity. The magisterial teaching on the subject was clarified in 1949 in a document approved by Pius XII. "[F]or a person to obtain his salvation, it is not always required that he be de facto incorporated into the Church as a member, but he must at least be united to the Church through desire or hope. However, it is not always necessary that this hope be explicit. . . . When one is in a state of invincible ignorance, God accepts an implicit desire." Holy Office, "Statement by the Holy Office Approved by Pius XII on 28 July 1949," cited in letter from Cardinal F. Marchetti-Selvaggiani to the Cardinal Archbishop of Boston (August 8, 1949).

Idea 2: People Naturally Search for the Supernatural

be built to allow and to encourage the good, not merely to hold the bad in check.

Idea 2: People Naturally Search for the Supernatural

It is natural for people to wonder at the mysterious depths of the created world, from the starry skies above to the incomprehensible reality of human consciousness and conscience. The yearnings of the heart for something beyond the endless cycle of birth, thriving, suffering, and death are also natural. So are the searches for beauty in the world, for meaning in experiences, for truth in reasoning, and for goodness in actions. In other words, it is natural to search for the supernatural. The higher reality, the divine world, God himself beckons us forward. Always and everywhere, we crave something more than the everyday. (God's answer to this craving, the revelation of the supernatural, is gratuitous, not natural, but that theological mystery is not directly relevant to social teaching.)

The worldly and the heavenly orientation of human nature are both present in every person; Christians recognize the higher orientation, which permeates all human thinking and desiring, as a yearning for the divine grace that "does not destroy nature but perfects it," as Thomas Aquinas declared at the beginning of his summary of theology.[22] Significantly, this *Summa Theologicae* includes not only discussions of God but also discussions of all aspects of worldly life. The natural and supernatural lives are also present and intermingled in every society. In other words, the religious, spiritual, or grace-infused life is social as well as private, while the political life is both worldly and, to some degree and in some ways, divine.

The transcendental search is natural, but fallen people often fight their created nature. They are easily tempted to allow the cares and pleasures of this world to crowd out their higher calling. This temptation can be resisted with the help of the grace offered by the crucified and risen Christ (which grace, remember, reaches well beyond the visible Church, into every human heart and each human society). The divine calling is ultimately personal, but societies can and should be organized to welcome the transcendental. They can and should advertise to all the possibility and reality of God's grace. A spiritually well-ordered community will

---

22. Thomas Aquinas, *Summa Theologicae*, I.8 ad 2.

offer reminders, markers, and celebrations of the higher things of life and of the things higher than life. It will have shared rituals to respect the moments when life touches infinity—birth, marriage, and death. It will promote religion, art, grandeur, virtue, wisdom, and whatever else brings people closer to the divine. It will not leave these most important matters solely to private lives. I come back to the great difficult modern societies have in living up to their spiritual responsibilities in chapter 4.

Idea 3: People Are Fundamentally Social

Until the advent of modern individualism, almost all philosophers took it for granted that human nature, both created and fallen, was naturally social. It was assumed that people naturally lived as members of communities of various sorts. One of the first new things of modern thinking was the reversal of that assumption. The meaning of this historic discovery of "the self"[23] is not a simple matter, as it touches many modern ideas. The typical modern conclusion, however, is straightforward—people are by nature isolated individuals who live for themselves. Each individual man, woman, and child naturally searches for his or her own way in life, and social control of any sort is an imposition on true human nature. In the distinction of the eighteenth-century German philosopher Immanuel Kant, autonomy (self-lawgiving) is "the ground of the dignity of human nature," while heteronomy (the uncritical reliance on any outside authority) is unfree and never universal.[24]

Christians reject this radical modern individualism. People were created in community, man and woman together,[25] and the many ties of all societies spring naturally from the human likeness to the Trinitarian God who "is love."[26] Just as the Father can only be who he is with the infinite love for and from the Son, a mutual divine love that is the person of the Holy Spirit, any individual person can only be who he or she is in the love for and from neighbors. The primordial

---

23. For a good summary of the development of the modern individual, see Charles Taylor, *Sources of the Self, The Making of the Modern Identity* (Cambridge, Mass.: Harvard University Press, 1992).

24. For Kant's simplest exposition, see Immanuel Kant, *Groundwork of the Metaphysic of Morals*, trans. H. J. Paton (London: Hutchinson's University Press, 3rd ed., 1956 [1785]), 103.

25. Gn 1:26.

26. 1 Jn 4:8.

and universal human love is expressed in personal relationships, but it also takes many social forms—the groups that tie people to each other by varying bonds of affection, dependence, responsibility, and commonality of concerns or beliefs. These groups should all be loving. Within them, justice, social justice, should be the rule.

The family is the most basic and intimate of social groups. This community combines the voluntary and complementary bond of man and woman, a bond that is both personal and social, with the involuntary and inevitably dependent bonds of children to parents. What can be considered family is not necessarily limited to those united by close romantic, emotional, or even biological ties. It can extend to unfriendly parents, unrelated servants, more distant relatives, and perhaps even to all those who are mythically tied together by common tribal ancestors, "race," or "nationality." I say more about families in chapters 9 and 10.

The family may be the model community, but there are many others: small (a few coworkers in a department or workshop) and large (a billion Christians or Chinese citizens); spiritual (a monastery) and worldly (a tax collectors' lobbying organization); simple (speakers of the same language) and almost incredibly complex (an army bound by extensive rules and mutual obligations). Tribes, races, and nations may not actually be related by "blood," but they are certainly social groups. So are trade unions, corporations, departments, guilds, schools, classes, confraternities, churches, parishes, political parties, clubs, and teams.

Idea 4: Love Is the Foundation of All Human Communities

The orientation to goodness and communion in all communities is profound, so much so that it deserves to be restated in the strongest possible terms. All communities, from the smallest family to the whole of humankind, are constituted from fundamentally loving relationships. People basically love each other as they grow up, flourish, and decline. They are essentially bound by love in their work, play, misery, joy, study, and worship. Sadly, this love is not always obvious and it is never unclouded, because the brambles and weeds of sin hide and weaken the foundation of love. Underneath, though, love remains the essential base of all communities. Without love, there can be no unity among people and thus no society whatsoever.

This Christian claim is distinctly antimodern. Thomas Hobbes, one the founders of modern thinking, claimed that societies were constituted only to stop people from their natural total hostility, "a perpetual war of every man against his neighbor."[27] Contemporary individualists may have a draw a less belligerent picture of human nature but share with Hobbes the presumption of the priority of each person's self-promotion in the organization of societies. They do not see communities in which the good is primarily common. Rather, all group efforts are explained as mere contracts of mutually beneficial self-interest. To these individualists, cooperation and sacrifice are not noble principles but only deceptive or temporary strategies. When people steeped in individualistic values do think of love, it is all too often imagined as a temporary and largely narcissistic emotion, not as a defining and inherently sacrificial human bond.

From the perspective of Catholic anthropology, the modern belief in individual self-interest and the concomitant denial of the intrinsic value of the common good are wrong, unpleasant, and profoundly inaccurate. They are wrong because people all actually do want what is good (however poorly they understand what is truly good). They are unpleasant because they disfigure the virtue of cooperation into a vice of hidden selfishness and they discredit people's own understanding of their motivations. They are inaccurate because communities would not flourish, as they generally do, if each member were always secretly looking only for her or his own individual gain.

As I explain in more detail in chapter 9, the Christian idea of love, the love that supports societies, is far more encompassing than the romantic love that is almost idolized in modern societies. For now, I will just say that the incarnation of Jesus Christ gives the perfect example of the qualities of the full and true love that binds together all human groups. This love is humble, as Jesus "emptied himself"[28] out of love for fallen humankind. It is expressed concretely in ordered relationships, as the Son does the will of the Father. It is communal, as Jesus expresses his love by gathering disciples into what would become a Church. It is generous, as Jesus gives himself to his community. This love is glorious, that is it shows something of the divine, as Jesus glorifies the Father. It is a mission, as the Son strives to bring people to the Father's kingdom. It responds to sin with sacrifice, as

---

27.   Thomas Hobbes, *Leviathan*, ed. Edwin Curley (Indianapolis: Hackett, 1994 [1660]), chap. 20.

28.   Phil 2:7.

BACKGROUND AND KEY IDEAS 23

the Son willingly endured the crucifixion. And this love is realistic. It recognizes the value of the world that God so loved that he sent his only Son to redeem it,[29] but it also recognizes the world's great need of redemption, transformation, and transcendence. Jesus answers all three needs—"I have said this to you, that in me you may have peace. . . . I have overcome the world."[30]

In his revelation and redemption, Jesus Christ illuminates the love that underlies all societies, not merely those with a Christian orientation or heritage. The most violent and unjust pagan society is just as much founded on love as was the most peaceful and pious land of Christendom, the once explicitly Christian territories of Europe. The difference is only the thickness of the sin covering. Some societies are undoubtedly more imperfect than others, but as I am about to explain, in our fallen world all societies fall far short of perfection.

Idea 5: Societies Are Always Imperfect

Societies cannot escape the curse of sin. They are all marred by each member's transgressions, by the hostility of nature (related to sin because the human fall leaves "creation" is "bondage to decay"[31]), and by the moral distortions found in every human organization. All types of social relations are scarred by all types of sin—between men and women, parents and children, rulers and governed, our tribe and their tribe, the elite and the wretched, the strong and the weak. Sin sows enmity and mistrust. It tempts people to put themselves before others, to cheat friends, and to treat strangers as enemies. It turns the expansive pleasures of love into unwelcome duty or cruel oppression. Sin creates social injustice.

It is idle and dangerous to think sin can be eliminated. The only perfect societies are imaginary—either some long-lost mythological golden age or some long-in-coming utopia. In any attempt to create a perfect society in this world—whether communist, capitalist, or Christian—the goal will always be receding, the leaders will eventually abuse their power, and most followers will be reduced to a combination of despair and rebellion.

---

29. Jn 3:16.
30. Jn 16:33.
31. Rom 8:22.

Rather than aim for total perfection, the Catholic Social Teaching tries to reduce the most flagrant imperfections. It is particularly concerned to identify and to fight against what Pope John Paul II called "structures of sin."[32] He was describing moral disorders that are embedded in laws, rules, customs, and unspoken expectations of behavior. Structures of sin can exist in all societies, from the most "primitive" to the most advanced. John Paul II gave the modern examples of the "idolatry" of "money, ideology, class, technology."[33] This false worship distorts economic and political judgments. I think the concept helps illuminate many deeply flawed features of modern societies, from welfare systems that replace charity with demeaning human-mechanical arrangements to health care systems that treat the ill as little more than malfunctioning machines.

Idea 6: Authority Is a Necessary Part of Social Life

I have already mentioned modern individualism's antipathy to all social authority. To Catholics, there is something unnatural about this. To say that people must not blindly take directions about what to think or do is not actually to call for the self-creation of authentic selves. Rather, it is to deny human nature. People can only exist, let alone thrive, inside of communities and societies, all of which have authorities and hierarchies. Those words—authority and hierarchy—do not deserve the almost inevitable pejorative sense they have in modern discourse. No community can survive without some sort of authority, because the mutual responsibilities of love are never perfectly symmetrical. Even in the Trinity, in which all the Persons are totally united and equally God, the Son's obedient relation to the Father is not identical to the Father's generating relation to the Son. As Jesus says, "The Father is greater than I."[34] The human analogy to the Trinity is of course deeply imperfect, but it is clear that some people naturally have the capacity to lead, that all people naturally have some willingness to obey, and that without some authority societies fall apart.

All communities and organizations have some sort of hierarchical authority. A chain of command is obviously essential to any

---

32. John Paul II, Encyclical Letter *Sollicitudo Rei Socialis* (December 30, 1987), 36–38.

33. John Paul II, *Sollicitudo Rei Socialis*, 37.

34. Jn 14:28.

BACKGROUND AND KEY IDEAS 25

bureaucratic organizations, and bureaucracies of some sort—more or less dependent on traditional or modern ideas of order, purpose, propriety, and efficiency—are not only the musculoskeletal system of all modern organizations but also one of the key features of any complex society.[35] Structures of authority, whether bureaucratic, hereditary, or relying on some other mark of social position, are found in all societies and organizations, from the most complex to the simplest. Ordered relations, without any bureaucratic features, are inherent to the life of families, in which children naturally depend on, learn from, and obey their parents. In schools, teachers naturally have authority over students. In polities, the members of government naturally have authority over the governed. In many premodern societies, men were thought naturally to have authority over women in various parts of life.

If human nature had remained in its created state, authority would always be offered graciously, exercised justly, and received gratefully. In the reality of fallen nature, however, authority is always tainted by sin. Harsh obligations and tight restrictions too often take the place of generous and sympathetic love, while injustice too often permeates the rules, their interpretations, and the various relations of superiority and dependency. Authority is often received with hostility, even when it is mostly enforced with justice and charity. Societies can and do strive to purify structures and promote virtue, but power attracts sin and resentment just as certainly as candles attract moths.

The Catholic Social Teaching can be seen as an effort to restore some fragments of the originally created justice and love in society. It aims to help in God's work of redeeming the tangled and sometimes sinful webs by which people are tied to each other.

Idea 7: The Only Historical Story That Really Matters Is the Story of Redemption

Philosophers argue about the patterns of history. Perhaps it is fundamentally cyclical (empires do seem to rise and fall in succession),

---

35. The classic text on the importance of bureaucracy is Max Weber, *Economics and Society: An Outline of Interpretive Sociology*, eds. Guenther Roth and Claus Wittich (Berkeley: University of California Press, 1968 [1914–1920]). David Beetham, *Bureaucracy* (Buckingham, UK: Open University Press, 2nd ed. 1996) packs a great deal of helpful theory into a small number of pages. Tellingly, it makes no mention of Catholic thinking on the topic. There are many interesting thoughts in the essays in Peter Crooks and Timothy H. Parsons, *Empires and Bureaucracy in World History: From Late Antiquity to the Twentieth Century* (Cambridge: Cambridge University Press, 2016).

maybe linear (knowledge of agriculture, writing, or technology has largely been increasing), or perhaps follows some other consistent rules. As I explain in several subsequent chapters, the Catholic Social Teaching is often directly opposed to two popular claims about the direction of history. It rejects the progressive "Enlightenment" view of inevitable, unadulterated, and continuing improvements, both in everyday life and in human behavior and morality. It also rejects the thesis of a "dialectical" pattern that leads, inevitably but through a much more crooked journey, to the integration of everything in the world into a single, quasi-mystical state. This pattern with its extensive ramifications was first expounded by the early nineteenth-century German philosopher G. W. F. Hegel (his name and ideas come up frequently in this book).

For Christians, the only certainly about history is its Christian meaning—everything takes place in the shadow of the Cross. Starting from creation and continuing until the Last Judgment, the story of all civilizations in all epochs is always the working out of the history of salvation. The God-given social task always remains the same. We are called to make the City of Man conform as closely as possible to the City of God (in the terminology of Saint Augustine), to create a "civilization of love," in the words of Paul VI.[36] In other words, people are always called to do God's will on earth as it is done in heaven. Since the devil always "prowls around like a roaring lion,"[37] anything less than full attention to virtue within the City of Man will allow sin to gain ground in society.

As I have said, however long history may last, this essential human effort will never succeed completely. It is necessary to fight against evil, but suffering cannot be eliminated. Full redemption—full freedom from the effects of the Fall—comes only with the end of history, when the City of God is established in "a new heaven and a new earth."[38] This eschatological perspective allows Catholics to be more realistic than is possible for followers of a more rigid model of history. Unlike believers in the necessity and virtue of continuing progress, Catholics do not need to welcome all innovations. (I talk about the Catholic idea of progress in chapter 11.) Unlike Hegelians, Catholics do not have to accept conflict in the working out of the World Spirit. Unlike the

---

36. Paul VI, Angelus Message *Regina Caeli* (May 17, 1970).

37. 1 Pt 5:8.

38. Rv 21:1.

followers of Hegel's disciple Karl Marx, they do not see history as a series of inevitable economic battles. Rather, Catholics see no particular social arrangement, accomplishment, or failure as either historically predestined or clearly desirable. This open-mindedness applies to the modern world as a whole and to each of its many historically unprecedented features. There is no need either simply to condemn or unequivocally to endorse. There is merely a responsibility to discern what should be weakened, what fortified, and what changed.

Idea 8: Catholics Have Responded to Modernity but Not Very Successfully

I have already mentioned the modern world several times . The Catholic Social Teaching can be understood as a response to that world, one part of the Church's effort to live up the responsibility articulated by John XXIII: "The Church today is faced with an immense task: to humanize and to Christianize this modern civilization of ours."[39] That statement needs interpretation, since the phrases "modern world" and "modern civilization" (I mostly use the former one) can refer to many things. For the purposes of this book, modernity includes everything connected with the increasingly firm turn away from the values of what was once a predominantly Catholic world, values that were, among other things, strongly Christian. In that civilization, born and nurtured in the decline and division of the Roman Empire and gradually coming to dominate much of the territory around the Mediterranean and farther north in Europe, Christianity was the nearly universal religion. Rulers and almost all the ruled assumed that their societies were naturally and essentially Christian. Christendom, as that world came to be known, has disappeared into the past, and the modern world is what replaced it. The modern values were born and nurtured in the decline and division of Christendom.

Scholars debate when modern ideas started to undermine the old order. The seeds are certainly ancient. The eighteenth-century English writer Samuel Johnson half-seriously called the devil "the first Whig" (at the time the leading English party representing the modern spirit), because he counseled resisting traditional authority.[40] The

---

39. John XXIII, *Mater et Magistra*, 256.

40. From James Boswell, *The Life of Samuel Johnson*, eds. George Birkbeck, Norman Hill, and L. F. Powell (Oxford: Oxford University Press Scholarly Editions Online 2014 [1791]), 3: 326.

nineteenth-century English radical poet Percy Bysshe Shelley gave a more positive prehistory to this ever-searching and ever-dominating human spirit, this confident desire for "the alleviations of his state." The ancient Titan Prometheus "gave man speech, and speech created thought, / Which is the measure of the universe."[41] The temptation or tendency may be rooted in human nature, whether as fallen or as created, but the first visible shoots only appeared much later. Suggested first sightings include the importation of Aristotle into Europe in the twelfth century, the development of nominalist philosophy a few centuries later, the Franciscan teaching on property, trade relations with the East, and the first stirrings of experimental science.

For the purposes of understanding the Church's Social Teaching, later dates are more helpful. The political-religious beginning of the modern age is arguably the sixteenth-century Reformation, which divided the Christians of Europe. Intellectually, one reasonable starting place is the somewhat later development of the philosophical school known as empiricism, which postulated wide gulfs between the individual and the world and between the world and anything transcendent. Another closely related intellectual milestone was the roughly contemporaneous creation of social contract theory, which claimed that governments gained their legitimacy only from the governed and only indirectly or not at all from God.[42] Eventually, those political thoughts became known as "liberal," but that word has added and shifted meanings over the centuries. I use it frequently, following the popes and other Catholics. They have used it to express both specific objectionable beliefs and the general wrong-headed and anti-Catholic spirit of the modern world.[43]

---

41. Percy Bysshe Shelley, "Prometheus Unbound: A Lyrical Drama in Four Acts" (London: C & J Ollier, 1820), act 2, scene 1, lines 98, 72–73. Accessed at http://knarf.english.upenn.edu /PShelley/prom2.html.

42. Here are three sample intellectual histories of modernity: Louis Dupré, *Transition to Modernity: An Essay in the Hermeneutics of Nature and Culture* (New Haven, Conn.: Yale University Press, 1993); Charles Taylor, *A Secular Age* (Cambridge, Mass.: Harvard University Press, 2007); David C. Schindler, *Freedom from Reality: The Diabolical Character of Modern Liberty* (Notre Dame, Ind.: Notre Dame University Press, 2017). For a technological-intellectual analysis, see Joel Mokyr, *A Culture of Growth: The Origins of the Modern Economy* (Princeton, N.J.: Princeton University Press, 2017).

43. Some thinkers do not see "liberalism," as they define it, as inherently opposed to true Christianity. Larry Siedentop, *The Origins of Western Liberalism* (London: Allen Lane, 2014) emphasizes the Christian origins of some of the liberal values associated with modern individualism. Chapter 4 of Reinhard Hütter, *Dust Bound for Heaven: Explorations in the Theology of Thomas Aquinas* (Grand Rapids, Mich.: Eerdmans, 2012), postulates the existence of a "genuine

Anti-Catholicism was probably inherent in the liberal approach, but at first the new ideas were in many ways Christian—in expression, moral orientation, and sentiment. This is not surprising, as these ideas were developed in Christian societies, almost entirely by people who were either believing Christians themselves or at least raised in Christian families. (Baruch Spinoza, who grew up in a Jewish community, is an obvious exception.) The Christian influence on modern thinking is so profound that the conflict between moderns and the original Christians, the Catholics, has what Freudians would call an Oedipal element. Much of the modern mindset, in particular its approach to equality, freedom, peace, economic activity, and love, can justly be characterized as the rebellious offspring of a Christian parent, a parent that the child resembles and emulates even while wishing to overthrow and surpass this obstacle to full development.

The explicitly Christian formulation of modern ideas waned gradually. Some scholars think the age of exploration, which brought the gigantic non-Christian world into clearer focus, sped the process. The discoveries undoubtedly spurred a huge Christian missionary effort, but they may also have gradually reduced Christians' confidence in the universal authority of their creed. Then came scientific, political, and eventually economic revolutions, which stripped away much of the religious infrastructure of society while creating powerful secular rivals to the premodern Christian worldview. The momentum of de-Christianization and de-Catholicizing increased from the eighteenth century onward as the many seedlings of new thought became tall trees with abundant intellectual foliage. Some of the new ideas were eventually gathered into a collection of "-isms": deism, rationalism, materialism, scientism, Utilitarianism, romanticism, the already-mentioned protean liberalism, Freudianism, consumerism, environmentalism, authoritarianism, antiauthoritarianism, and

---

liberalism"—"the Christian understanding of the human being . . . is presupposed in the tenets and program of genuine liberalism" (p. 105). For more standard histories of what has been called liberal thinking, see Pierre Manent, *Cours familier de philosophie politique* (Paris: Gallimard 2006); Richard Bellamy, *Rethinking Liberalism* (London: Pinter, 2000); from a radical socialist perspective, Anthony Arblaster, *The Rise and Decline Western Liberalism* (Oxford: Basil Blackwell, 1984); Irene Collins, *Liberalism in Nineteenth-Century Europe*, (London: Historical Association, 1957); Guido de Ruggiero, *The History of European Liberalism*, trans. R. G. Collingwood (Oxford: Oxford University Press, 1927); T. H. Green, *Lectures on the Principles of Political Obligations and Other Writings*, ed. Paul Harris and John Morrow (Cambridge: Cambridge University Press, 1986); Alan Ryan, "Liberalism 1900–1940" in *The Cambridge Companion to Liberalism*, ed. Steven Wall, 59–84 (Cambridge: Cambridge University Press, 2015).

nihilism. These streams still flow. Postmodernism is the latest "ism," while the levelling of sexual differences is waiting for a good descriptive noun. What I think of as the dominant non-Christian notion so far in the twenty-first century, or perhaps antinotion, also does not yet have a generally accepted "ism" name but can be described as a dull and cynical apathy.

By now, modern and distinctly non-Christian categories of thought have replaced premodern ones as the standard framework for thinking about most parts of the human experience. Speaking very broadly, the predominant focus in one domain after another has moved from the transcendental to the worldly, from the dispassionate and objective to the emotional and subjective, from the descriptive to the mathematical, from the purposeful to the random, and from the praise of the old and entrenched to the praise of the new and free. Over time, this ever-enlarging collection of modern ideas has been expressed in many new social forms: bourgeois, autocratic, totalitarian, democratic, and bureaucratic governments; bureaucratic profit-seeking companies; incredibly productive industrial economies; academic specialization in huge research universities; growing cities and burgeoning suburbs; cultural and economic globalization; romantic marriages and sexual liberation. Over time, also, many of these modern ideas have spread far from their European and North American origins. Some of them are now nearly global, and almost no peoples are sufficiently isolated to be totally untouched by the modern worldview and its practical manifestations.

The Social Teaching is far from the only Catholic response to the multicentury spread of this multifaceted modernity. In every domain and through all of the last half-millennium, the Magisterium has tried to discern which religious, cultural, intellectual, and technological innovations were totally unacceptable, which were clearly valuable, and which were possibly helpful. The Church and its teachers have responded in many ways, not always consistent over time or with each other. Protestant criticisms of superstitious practices were answered with various reforms, including improvements in priestly formation. The reply to Protestant austerity was baroque exuberance. Protestant individualistic piety was easily Catholicized, while the Protestant rejection of the authority of tradition and the tradition of authority was steadily condemned.

The new natural sciences were sometimes accepted and sometimes resisted, with the resistance sometimes confusing untenable intellectual traditions with pertinent philosophical doubts. The Catholic-secular split was gradual. Catholics participated fully in the lively interdenominational intellectual life of the sixteenth century, although not always with the full support of the hierarchy (the or a collection of bishops). Later, the Church and most of its leading thinkers became more hostile to the European intellectual mainstream, often in ways that now may appear unduly uncomprehending. In contrast, the Romanticism and individualism of the nineteenth and twentieth centuries have been Christianized, perhaps at some cost to Christianity. Industrialization and the technological culture have been welcomed in part and firmly rejected in part.

Not just the substance but the tone of the Catholic responses has varied over time, place, and challenge. The Magisterium has been almost everything—fiercely hostile, bitterly resigned, grudgingly accommodating, and almost naively enthusiastic. It has cheerfully baptized some developments and hastily anathematized others. There have been some notable bad patches, for example, the long delay in accepting both Copernican astronomy and modern techniques of biblical study,[44] but overall and especially where it matters most, the Church has made a steady, although almost never speedy, effort to purify its own teachings and express them in terms that modern people can understand. The popes and approved teachers have explained—thoughtfully, carefully, beautifully, sympathetically—that the modern idol of pure freedom, a supposedly empowering freedom that denies the existence of any unchanging truth about human nature, is an illusion. The Church has warned—steadily, sometimes hysterically, sometimes timidly, sometimes elegantly—that freedom that is not grounded in truth is only a pseudofreedom. Such a "freedom" can only be guided by irrational willfulness and has no defense against the lure of irresponsible and destructive desires. It ultimately can lead only to confusion, misery, and enslavement to some tempting lie. Further, the Church has elegantly diagnosed (as I explain in chapter 8) and firmly criticized the modern era's misplaced trust in the human ability to control everything in the world, including not only the earth and all it contains but human biology and behavior.

---

44. The two Church errors were intimately related, since the scientific reluctance was based on the mandated "literalist" approach to the Scriptures. See the relevant chapters of Ernan McMullin, ed., *The Church and Galileo* (Notre Dame, Ind.: University of Notre Dame Press, 2005).

It is not surprising that the Church's many enemies have sneered at most of its responses to the challenges of modernity, but many believers have also winced when the Magisterium tried to hold onto some of the traditional formulations, practices, and privileges that had been undermined by new thinking and the course of history. In the domain of the Social Teaching, an outstanding example of pigheadedness dressed up as high theology was the Vatican refusal to recognize the legitimacy of the Italian state for sixty years. Another embarrassing historical fact is the persistence of the Index of Prohibited Books, a list that was supposed to ensure that Catholics were not corrupted by, among other things, modern ideas. It was officially abandoned only in 1966.[45]

The 1960s were a turning point for the Church. Before then, the typical Church error was to resist modern thinking too blindly, and the typical Church recounting of its history was triumphalist—win or lose the battles of history, the Magisterium was always on the right side. Since then, the leading error has been to embrace any new ideas and practices without adequate caution. Bishops, priests, and laypeople have all too often crudely simplified and wildly exaggerated the mostly balanced and wise responses of the Second Vatican Council to the modern world. Conversely, a healthy humility about past mistakes has all too often been exaggerated into a willing renunciation of all past teachings that might conflict with new secular orthodoxies. The gushing enthusiasm for modern thinking is as cringeworthy as the previous blind resistance.

For all of these weaknesses, in my judgment, the Church has done the world a great favor in expressing the timeless truth in modern language and in offering practical counsel to troubled modern people. However, the world is certainly not grateful for this illumination. Indeed, the dominant culture has paid ever less attention to Catholic responses to modern challenges. The pope is still a media personality, but the Church has clearly not found a way to beat back the tide of non-Christian modernity. Catholics have been left on the defensive—more changed and challenged by the modern world than

---

45. The index had become almost totally ineffective well before it was abolished, in Congregation for the Doctrine of the Faith. *"Notificatio" and "Decretum" Concerning the Index of Prohibited Books* (June 14, 1966, and November 15, 1966), but a revised list of forbidden books had been published as recently as 1938, *Index Librorum Prohibitorum* (Vatican City: Typis Polyglottis, 1938), including such threats to the faith as John James Blunt's 1827 *Vestiges of Ancient Manners and Customs Discoverable in Modern Italy*, Lord Acton's *History of the Vatican Councils* (listed only in German), and Victor Hugo's *Notre Dame de Paris* and *Les Misérables*.

BACKGROUND AND KEY IDEAS   33

changing and challenging it. The same judgment—more changed and challenged than changing and challenging—applies to the Church's Social Teaching. The teaching has had some successes but far more in the battle of ideas than in the actual policies and practices of societies. I discuss how this history of failure has changed the tone of the Catholic Social Teaching in the final chapter.

Idea 9: The Catholic Social Teaching Is a Response to Huge Changes

In the second half of the nineteenth century, social issues, as they had come to be called, were one the crucial points of Catholic-modern contact. Catholics had to deal with a remarkable collection of unprecedented innovations that had profoundly changed societies in most of the Catholic world. By the 1880s, when Leo XIII came to write *Rerum Novarum*, the list included the decline of family farming; the spread of hugely productive industrial enterprises; vastly expanded cities teeming with the wretchedly poor but increasingly led by a rapidly expanding bourgeoisie; government mostly by appointed bureaucracies and elected assemblies (rather than by hereditary hierarchies); widespread literacy and nearly universal primary education; easy transport of material, people, and ideas over long distances; rapidly increasing life expectancies; and the decline of aristocratic prestige that accompanied the modern judgment that hierarchical social orders were human constructions of dubious moral value (rather than somehow natural to the human condition). It can be debated whether all the social changes, taken as a whole, were more or less dramatic than the modern spiritual and intellectual shifts that preceded and accompanied them. What can hardly be doubted is that both the many social novelties and the new intellectual systems presented a tremendous challenge to the Catholic Church.

Leo's first distinctly social encyclical did not take on everything new in society. *Rerum Novarum* deals largely with socialism, economic liberalism, and urban poverty. The then-prevalent socialism was an obvious enemy. It was avowedly atheistic and anticlerical. It offered an apparently full alternative world system to Catholicism: its own creed (worldly and messianic), its own freedom (economic), and its own unified worldview (nontranscendental). The liberal form of capitalism was hardly less opposed to Christian values, especially when it was presented as an excuse for the rich to mistreat the poor in the name of supposed laws of the market or in a supposed battle for survival. Leo and his successors felt obliged to offer a Catholic counterattack against the ideologies and the conditions that allowed such intellectual and social weeds to flourish.

The initial criticisms of the tolerance of poverty still have value, especially in poor countries, but the condemnations of ideological fervor have become a bit dated. Economic organizations in prosperous countries have become too successful, complex, and pragmatic to inspire much ideological fervor of any sort. There are still significant economic problems, but they no longer pose the preeminent modern challenge to Catholic values (as I explain in chapter 3). Economic progress, though, has not lessened the pressure on more recent popes to respond to new social developments. If anything, the stream of faith-challenging social novelties has become wider, faster, and more treacherous for the Church.

The most recent list of "new things" includes the jettisoning of marriage as the standard framework for sexual relations and child rearing; the expectation that only about half of life will be spent in paid labor and an even smaller proportion in full-time child rearing, with increased proportions dedicated to education, retirement, and poor health; the expectation of tremendous universal prosperity in rich countries; the development of a ubiquitous secular bureaucratic welfare state; the creation of a massive gap in prosperity between rich and poor countries; the possibility of immediate massive destruction in nuclear war; and the lack of acceptance of human responsibility for maintaining the natural world in good condition. In addition, the early modern explorers' discovery of the bigness of the world has been in some way reversed. Tourism, telecommunications, and peaceful migration have made the earth smaller, so that both the diversity and the unity of humanity have become matters of experience rather than of theory.

The Vatican has done its best to respond to as many as possible of these social changes, with a series of encyclicals and with the establishment of various offices dedicated to particular problems. Some of the answers provided may be incomplete or even inappropriate, but the Vatican deserves some sympathy. The challenge is tremendous and, while the Church's spiritual resources are infinite, its intellectual capital is not.

Idea 10: Most of the Catholic Social Teaching Is Universal

The Catholic Social Teaching is not just for Catholics. That statement might be surprising. It is not obviously supported by reading the relevant magisterial documents, which have many distinctly intra-Catholic features. They generally include numerous and not always obviously relevant citations of earlier documents. They are mostly studded with laborious, although sometimes veiled, efforts to criticize, support, or reconcile different groups within the Church. They have been known to contain ample doses of what can uncharitably be called a Catholic form of pious bureaucratic waffle.

The older documents also have a distinctly parochial feeling for the concrete reason that their principle audience was Catholics who accepted, or were expected to accept, that the Church was "Mother and Teacher of all nations," as John XXIII explained in 1961.[46] While the popes wrote in universal terms about natural law, human nature, and secular modern trends, until some years after the Second World War the actual advice was directed primarily if not exclusively to leaders and residents of European countries that had traditionally had been part of Catholic Christendom. As the Church's direct authority faded, the approach shifted. The popes and bishops became more aware of their moral authority—completely unlike the days of Christendom, they were respected for *not* searching for worldly glory—and of their moral responsibility to support, instruct, and inspire everyone for whom Christ had died, that is everyone. The trend toward universality reached its peak in 1965, when *Gaudium et Spes*, the Second Vatican Council's leading social document, declared that the Church "now addresses itself without hesitation, not only to the sons of the Church and to all who invoke the name of Christ, but to the whole of humanity."[47]

The whole of humanity includes nonpracticing Catholics, non-Catholic Christians, and numerous varieties of non-Christians. Many members of all these groups could struggle with the document's social teaching. Christians should not blanch at the numerous biblical quotes, and everyone might endorse in principle the Second Vatican Council's goal of helping "the world conform more closely to the surpassing dignity of the human person,"[48] although the understanding of "dignity" in that phrase is distinctly Catholic.

---

46. John XXIII, *Mater et Magistra*, 1.

47. Vatican Council II, *Gaudium et Spes*, 2.

48. Vatican Council II, *Gaudium et Spes*, 93, my translation.

However, only Catholics who are at home in the doctrinal and intellectual tradition of the Church will be really comfortable with the understanding of the world presupposed in the Catholic Social Teaching. It assumes the primacy of love in all things human, the stubborn ubiquity of sin, the unceasing obligations of service and forgiveness, the supreme importance of the divine in the orientation of people and societies, the power of the Cross and Resurrection, the reality and finality of truth, and the authority and limits of the human position in creation. To the modern mindset, all of these claims are likely to seem hopelessly Christian—extravagant, irrational, and unjustified.

The strangeness should not be a stumbling block. Christians, of course, are called to further study, but non-Christians need not be afraid. While Christian revelation and faith are wonderful and welcome in the discernment of the truth about society, neither is required to grasp the basic ideas of the Catholic Social Teaching. The doctrine is logical, and its truth is naturally accessible to all. Specifically, it can be explained and defended in terms that anyone might accept—the way human nature is, the way societies work, the evidence of history, and the rudiments of natural law. Of course, modern people will often have to suspend various types of nonbelief to see the force of some arguments. However, if that suspension can be managed, non-Christians will appreciate the plausibility of Catholic understanding of the nature of human nature and of societies. Once understood properly, the Social Teaching fits with personal experience, social observation, and many modern people's intuitive ideas of justice. Recent popes have tried to make the bridge between the faith world and the modern world easier to cross by citing secular authors and adopting a more modern voice in their writing. I will follow their lead.

Not everything in the contemporary teaching is universal, though. Parts are still aimed primarily at the Catholic audience. In particular, believers will be much more interested than will outsiders in the question of how to respond to social prejudice against Catholic teachings or persecution of those who adhere to these teachings. As I discuss in chapter 11, as the world becomes more distant from Catholic values, such counsels of resistance are likely to take up a larger proportion of future documents. For now, though, the predominant theme remains universal as well as Catholic—to teach everyone to discern the values of the age and to transcend them when they are debased and false.

Idea 11: The Catholic Social Teaching Can Only Offer Counsels of Imperfection

The universality, depth, and variability of social imperfection ensures that the magisterial effort to provide guidance in social virtue will always be, as suggested in the introduction (and by the title of this book), counsels of imperfection. The imperfection is found first of all in the necessarily narrow range of interests. Societies cannot fight against all their evils with all their strength all at once. Indeed, one of the most important tasks of the teaching is to identify which social evils are currently most egregious and which virtues right now need most urgently to be promoted.

The necessity to limit the range of the teaching has the unfortunate effect of ensuring that all documents will eventually appear inadequate, because some evils are always being downplayed, or in practice tolerated, and some virtues are always being downplayed, or in practice ignored. Throughout the book, I provide examples of such excessively one-sided past analysis in the Social Teaching and I write in full awareness that similar accusations about the current judgments will justly be made in the future.

The teachings must also suffer from a different imperfection, an imperfect fit with any particular part of the current world. It is true, as I just said, that all of today's societies are modern in some ways, but they differ greatly in their preeminent moral challenges and the most pertinent practical solutions. The appropriate approach varies in societies that are predominantly rich or poor, rising or declining, well-led or ill-led, ex-Christian or never-Christian, and so forth. No single social doctrine, no matter how carefully crafted, can ever fit everywhere effortlessly and exactly. Also, whatever might fit today is unlikely to fit tomorrow, as societies are always changing.

The popes have tried to find the best balance between social counsels that are quite universal but too vague to be applied easily and counsels that are specific and clear but not applicable in many situations or not optimal for a long time. Vague teachings spawn sharp disputes as to how they can best be applied here and now. At the other extreme, specific advice generates sharp disputes about which recommendations are actually most relevant here and now and how exactly to apply them. Whatever the advice, the applications require a great deal of what theologians and moral philosophers sometimes call prudential judgments. In the spirit of imperfection, people have to do their best to discern and judge each situation.

As an example of the difficulties with specific counsels, consider the question of parental responsibility for religious and moral education. The *Compendium* endorses a particular policy, "The refusal to provide public economic support to non-public schools that need assistance and that render a service to civil society is to be considered an injustice."[49] Translated from the Vatican's somewhat lofty vocabulary, the advice is fairly specific: parents should have access to religious schools at the state's expense.

The Church's view was once quite different. In the late nineteenth century, Catholic authorities took a dim view of all tax-funded education, partly in response to the secular criticism of Catholic-supervised education by Jules Ferry, a pioneer of French state education, and his allies. The magisterial recommendation changed, largely in response to a more accommodating attitude from many secular authorities. The actual teaching—that children should be educated in the faith— was not altered, but the preferred policy implication of that teaching evolved in response to a new reading of the signs of the times.

In recent decades, the political environment surrounding education has changed again. Many contemporary states hinder truly Christian instruction. For example, state-supported Catholic schools in France and the United Kingdom are required follow a curriculum imbued with a worldview that is always non-Catholic and often anti-Catholic. On the other side of the educational divide, it has been hard to develop schools with little or no state control of the curriculum to offer young people a more fully Catholic education. Catholic parents in almost every country have been reluctant to forgo state schools that charge no tuition.

Under such circumstances, Catholic education might be better protected by returning to a variation of the earlier view: states should not necessarily control education and religious schools should reject financial support from the state. In that way, the ecclesial hierarchy and Catholic parents, rather than the government, would have full control of young Catholics' education. This is the practice in the

---

49. *Compendium of the Social Doctrine of the Church*, 241.

United States, where Catholic schools mostly have less money than state schools but can to a large extent teach what and how they want.

In short, the decisions to condemn and then to endorse tax-funded Catholic education may have been wise when they were made, and a further revision might also be prudent. The alterations can be disconcerting, but the alternative of merely stating that children need a Catholic education would have brought its own problems. Such statements give Catholic legislators no guidance on whether to ask for fully independent Catholic schools, government-backed Catholic schools, or merely guaranteed time for non-school Catholic education. It also leaves Catholic parents and educators without any clues about how much to cooperate with secular educational authorities. The issue is increasingly pressing, and I regret that the Vatican commentary has not moved far past the *Compendium*'s increasingly superseded advice. (I discuss the Catholic Social Teaching on education briefly at the end of chapter 10.)

The Magisterium may sometimes seem clumsy, but its task is truly difficult and delicate. To continue with the educational example, Catholic parents should ensure their children's education does not isolate them from the non-Catholic world, because Christians should always be "the light of the world."[50] However, parents should also not let the often anti-Catholic secular society corrupt and seduce their children. While Catholic schools should not be pawns of the state's misguided intentions, neither should they be pointlessly uncooperative with the state's legitimate demands for academic quality. The best way to resolve such dilemmas in a particular society depends on many factors, including the degree of antagonism from the non-Catholic world, the relations of state and church, and the society's history and social structures. The best way it is likely to change is over time, and it is always going to be deeply imperfect.

Two opposite systematic errors always lurk in the Social Teaching's counsels of imperfection. On one side is the danger of asking too much of the faithful—of expecting something close to heroic virtue. In the educational example, it would be excessively ambitious to require all parents in contemporary Europe to find or found excellent Catholic schools that are loyal to the Magisterium. On the other side is the danger of asking too little—of compromising with objective error rather than fighting or uneasily tolerating it. It would be

---

50. Mt 5:14.

excessively weak to permit Catholic parents to trust unquestioningly the education offered by the state or in nominally Catholic schools.

The range of imperfect counsels between these two undesirable extremes is wide. In many cases, there is not so much a single right way as a range of more or less morally acceptable approaches. Magisterial judgment can often limit and frame all debates, but it cannot fully and finally resolve very many of them. The exceptions are debates over objectively sinful acts such as the sexual and family practices discussed in chapter 10. Even in the discussion of how to respond to these sins, much of the teaching is necessarily prudential—there is no infallible way to reorganize any society or community to reduce sinful practices.

Idea 12: The Church Always Calls People to Perfection

Imperfection, toleration, uncomfortable compromises, irresolvable questions—such weak terms threaten to end this discussion with the wrong tone. The Church is the very body of "the Way, and the Truth, and the Life,"[51] and the last word about its approach to the world should not belong to the pragmatic institutional Church of sinners, of people who stumble in ignorance. Rather, it belongs to the prophetic Church awaiting heaven, which calls everyone to nothing less than perfection and which promises nothing less than eternal life with God. Compromises may be inevitable in the Catholic Social Teaching, but people are called to do more than make the best of a bad situation. Jesus calls them to be perfect, as "your heavenly Father is perfect."[52] The Catholic Social Teaching must be realistic, but it should also be shot through with the burning desire for perfection.

The dethronement of the Church from its previous position at the institutional center of many Western societies has given it greater freedom to live up to its transcendental calling. For example, when the papacy was a military power fully participating in endless disputes over the control of the different cities and regions of the Italian peninsula, it was probably too compromised by fighting military enemies and finding military allies to offer a credible condemnation of all war on principle. Now that it has lost its direct worldly sway, it can speak with a strong prophetic voice. On war, it has. The modern Church's teaching can be reduced to a few crystalline sentences of Paul VI, "No more war, war never again. It is peace, peace which must

---

51. Jn 14:6.

52. Mt 5:48.

guide the destinies of peoples and of all mankind."[53] Such a prophetic exhortation is of course impractical—I introduce the Church's quite practical views on threatened and actual military conflicts in chapter 5—but it sets the right tone for a Church founded by the divine Prince of Peace.

Indeed, in entering into sin-stained social questions, the Church must always follow Jesus Christ, whose love for sinful humanity led him to strip off his divine glory and become one of us.[54] This same divine love inspires the Magisterium to walk along the shifting, muddy ground of actual social arrangements, always with its eyes on heaven. Some worldly slime will always cling to the Church; whenever and wherever any missionary walks through the world, his or her feet will end up dirty. The missionary Church of Catholic Social Teaching can take comfort from Jesus himself, who washed clean the soiled feet of his disciples.[55]

---

53. Paul VI, *Address to the United Nations* (October 4, 1965).

54. cf. Phil 2:7

55. Jn 13:1–12

CHAPTER 2

Economic Issues in an Industrial Age

THE PRIMARY CONCERNS OF *Rerum Novarum* were economic. The encyclical's title, which translates as "Of New Things," was apt for that, because in 1891 the modern economy was a very new thing indeed. The old socioeconomic order, based on agriculture, was largely shattered, but the new manufacturing-based economy did not yet have institutions that were just and adequate to its needs. The economic newness was reflected in the world of ideas. Neither "socialism" nor "liberalism," Leo's great economic enemies, was more than a century old. As suited the new secular age, both movements were ideologically opposed to organized religion (itself a very modern notion), especially to the hierarchical Catholic Church with its socially conservative episcopal hierarchy.

The academic discipline of economics was much newer than was either of these ideologies but shared their nonreligious assumptions. To some extent, Leo entered into on this new worldview in his formative encyclical, for example by accepting its entirely non-Christian categories of "capital," "labor," and "working classes."[1] Most significantly, his understanding of "private property"[2] was strongly influenced by interpretations of both "private" and "property" that were quite new and quite distant from any intellectual tradition that could be considered deeply Christian, as I explain in chapter 3.

Of course, the economy was not an entirely new field for the Catholic Church. Besides interpreting biblical teachings, which I

---

1. Leo XIII, Encyclical Letter *Rerum Novarum* (May 15, 1891), 1, 2.
2. Leo XIII, *Rerum Novarum*, 2.

ECONOMIC ISSUES IN AN INDUSTRIAL AGE 43

discuss shortly, the Church had accompanied the everyday economic lives of all sorts of believers for almost two millennia. This responsibility led to many lively interactions with the earliest manifestations of what would become the modern economy. In trying to find the best Christian response to these new things, Leo might have looked as far back as the thirteenth century, when Saint Francis of Assisi, repelled by the newly acquired monetary wealth of Italian merchants, offered extravagant praise for voluntary poverty.[3] If there was any Franciscan influence on papal thinking, it was quite indirect, but Leo and his advisors had certainly studied some of the centuries-long Christian debates on such economic topics as the permissibility of usury,[4] the existence and determination of just prices,[5] and the justifications of different types of slavery.[6] Also, they had presumably read the vaguely economic portions

---

3. The social context and theological meaning of Saint Francis's enthusiasm for poverty is discussed, in a knowledgeable if perhaps overly critical way, in Kenneth Baxter Wolf, *The Poverty of Riches: St. Francis of Assisi Reconsidered* (New York: Oxford University Press, 2003).

4. On the remarkably controversial topic of the Church's teaching on usury, see Brian M. McCall, *The Church and the Usurers: Unprofitable Lending for the Modern Economy* (Ave Maria, Fla.: Sapientia Press, 2013); John T. Noonan Jr., *The Scholastic Analysis of Usury* (Cambridge, Mass.: Harvard University Press, 1957); D. Stephen Long and Nancy Ruth Fox, *Calculated Futures: Theology, Ethics, and Economics* (Waco, Tex.: Baylor University Press, 2007), chap. 6; Odd Langholm, *The Legacy of Scholasticism in Economic Thought: Antecedents of Choice and Power* (Cambridge: Cambridge University Press, 1998), chap. 4. All scholarly discussions of this long-standing debate are marred by historical anachronisms, whether a love of free markets, a hatred of free markets, a romantic vision of the Middle Ages, or a modern understanding of the social and economic role of commerce. The historical sections of the McCall book are the least biased, and his biases on modern issues are in line with the Catholic tradition.

5. On the Church and the just price, see the discussion in Noonan, *Scholastic Analysis of Usury*; Juan Manuel Elegido, "The Just Price: Three Insights from the Salamanca School," *Journal of Business Ethics* 90, no. 1 (2009): 29–46; and Raymond de Roover, "The Concept of the Just Price: Theory and Economic Policy," *The Journal of Economic History* 18, no. 4 (1958): 418–34. The discussions of just prices are even more marred by various sorts of historical false consciousness than are the discussions of usury.

6. On the Church and slavery, see John Francis Maxwell, *Slavery and the Catholic Church: The History of Catholic Teaching Concerning the Moral Legitimacy of the Institution of Slavery* (Chichester, UK: Barry Rose Publishers, 1975). He points out (p. 123) the condemnation in *Rerum Novarum* was not clear and direct enough to prevent at least seven (cited) subsequently published Catholic handbooks of moral theology from defending the justice of slavery under certain conditions. The first unconditional condemnation of all types of slavery came in the Vatican Council II, *Gaudium et Spes* (December 7, 1965), 27. See also Herbert S. Klein, "Anglicanism, Catholicism, and the Negro Slave," *Comparative Studies in Society and History* 8, no. 3 (1966): 295–327; and the rather narrow condemnation in Pope Gregory XVI, Papal Bull *In Supremo Apostolatus* (December 3, 1839).

of more recent papal writings.[7] Less intellectually, Leo was well aware of the efforts of the mostly new lay Christian groups and religious orders to promote the material and spiritual good of the rapidly expanding masses of the urban poor.[8]

Still, while the Church's existing intellectual and spiritual treasures were substantial, they were not enough to provide a full Christian answer to the main antagonists in *Rerum Novarum*, the socialists. Leo needed something more, something new, to counter fully their claims of promoting earthly justice for the wretched of the earth. Indeed, he needed to absorb what was good and ultimately Christian in the teaching of the people and groups that were so hostile to Catholicism. The Catholic Church could not promote justice for the poor, the least of Christ's brothers,[9] without giving full Christian assent to one of the central premises of socialist thinking: the social dignity and spiritual value of the everyday economic activity of every person.

It is often hard to learn from ideological opponents, but Christians should have had relatively little trouble with this particular borrowing. They could easily understand that the socialists' interest in the material dignity of the poor was a legitimate application of a fundamental and timeless truth of the Christian faith: the equal dignity of all people before God. From a more worldly perspective, though, the recognition of a fundamental human equality in the economy and in society was still a relatively new thing, one that was somewhat hard to manage. The new thinking about social equality, which was first taken seriously as a political notion during the most extreme phase of the French Revolution, required a revision of an often-unspoken assumption of almost all premodern philosophers and theologians, pagan and Christian alike. They agreed that activities performed under physical or instinctual compulsion are less in the image of the totally free God than are activities that require the leisurely cultivation of intellectual and psychological excellences.[10]

---

7. On pre-Leo XIII "proto-social teaching" in general, see chap. 1 of Michael J Schuck, *That They Be One: The Social Teaching of the Papal Encyclicals 1740–1989* (Washington, DC: Georgetown University Press, 1991) and the relevant sections of Joe Holland, *Modern Catholic Social Teaching: The Popes Confront the Industrial Age 1740–1958* (Mahwah, N.J.: Paulist Press, 2003).

8. See Paul Misner, *Social Catholicism in Europe: From the Onset of Industrialisation to the First World War* (London: Darton, Longman and Todd, 1991).

9. cf. Mt 25:40.

10. On Aristotle's hierarchy, with references to Plato and the later philosophical tradition, see Tom Angier, "Aristotle on Work," *Revue international de philosophie* 278, no. 4 (2016): 435–50.

The social prejudice against those who toil at these basic economic activities was equally uniform. "Nobles" joined philosophers and theologians in holding "the people" in something like disdain.

The history of the Church's gradual absorption of the modern egalitarian and universalist approach to society is fascinating and perhaps not yet complete, but it is beyond the scope of this book. Here I will only provide three examples of the change, all taken from within the Church itself. The first is the presentation of the life of Jesus. During the course of the nineteenth century, Catholic writers increasingly described the incarnate savior as a lowly common man who grew up in a humble family of rural craftsman. The full humanity of his person was far from elitist or aristocratic. Rather, teachers of the faith emphasized that he spoke of such everyday matters as commercial fishing, the quality of wine at wedding feasts, merchants' trading practices, and the skills of vinedressers.

The idea of the worker Jesus was not entirely new, but the portrayal of the humble Holy Family definitely was. Leo XIII drew the social moral of this vision in 1889, when he introduced Saint Joseph as a patron of laborers. In Catholic devotion, the husband of Mary had previously been noted largely for his descent from King David. The pope expounded on an almost contradictory characteristic, his lowly social condition. "For Joseph, of royal blood . . . passed his life in labor, and won by the toil of the artisan the needful support of his family. It is, then, true that the condition of the lowly has nothing shameful in it, and the work of the laborer is not only not dishonoring, but can, if virtue be joined to it, be singularly ennobled. . . . Through these considerations, the poor and those who live by the labor of their hands should be of good heart and learn to be just."[11]

If the prose sounds a little condescending, that is a sign of the persistence of old thinking. Almost a century later John Paul II expressed the same idea in a purely positive way. "[T]he eloquence of the life of Christ is unequivocal: he belongs to the 'working world,' he has appreciation and respect for human work. It can indeed be said that he looks with love upon human work and the different forms that it takes, seeing in each one of these forms a particular facet of man's likeness with God, the Creator and Father. Is it not he who says: 'My Father is the vinedresser'?"[12]

---

11. Leo XIII, Encyclical Letter *Quamquam Pluries* (August 15, 1889), 4, 5.

12. John Paul II, Encyclical Letter *Laborem Exercens* (September 14, 1981), 26, citing Jn 15:1.

My second example, the interpretation of the phrase "pray and work" (*ora et labora*), shows how difficult it is for today's Catholics to recognize just how new the things of *Rerum Novarum* were at the time. In the twenty-first century, this word pairing is commonly taken to mean that the life of prayer should not be separated from, and has equal spiritual value with, the daily toil of manual, caring, or office labor. The saying is frequently thought to express a basic and long-standing principle of the full Christian life. It is often associated with the entire Benedictine order, and sometimes attributed to Saint Benedict himself. Pope Francis does so in *Laudato Si'*.[13]

Such thinking is anachronistic. The phrase *ora et labora* was rarely used before the modern era, its premodern application was exclusively monastic, and the "labor" in question was assumed to be the study of religious matters, often the copying of manuscripts. The current universal meaning was first popularized in a book by a Benedictine monk published in 1880, a little more than a decade before *Rerum Novarum*.[14]

The late arrival of the phrase does not invalidate the spiritual wisdom of the currently accepted meaning. On the contrary, this understanding of *ora et labora* exemplifies the new wise and holy understanding of the role of labor and of simple laborers in what used to be called the "economy of salvation." The most basic Catholic Social Teaching about the economy ties together the old and new meanings of "economy," as can be seen in John Paul II's discussion of human labor. "Man has to subdue the earth and dominate it, because as the 'image of God' he is a person, that is to say, a subjective being capable . . . of deciding about himself . . . [T]here is no doubt that human work has an ethical value of its own, which clearly and directly remains linked to the fact that the one who carries it out is a person."[15]

---

13. Francis, Encyclical Letter *Laudato Si'* (May 24, 2015), 126.

14. Some history is provided in Oliver J. Kaftan, "Ora et labora—(k)ein benediktinisches Motto Eine Spurensuche," *Erbe und Auftrag* 14, no. 4 (2014): 415–42. Thomas Aquinas specifically rejects the claim that the "religious are bound to manual labor," citing only long gone "Egyptian monasteries" as demanding that all members "work or labor . . . lest [the soul] be led astray by wicked thoughts." (*Summa theologica* II.II.187.3, corpus).

15. John Paul II, *Laborem Exercens*, 6. For a helpful introduction to John Paul II's understanding of the dignity of labor, explained in the context of the Marxist understanding of action, see Angela Franks, "A Body of Work: Labor and Culture in Karol Wojtyła and Karl Marx," in *Leisure and Labor: Essays on the Liberal Arts in Catholic Higher Education*, ed. Anthony P. Coleman (Lanham, Md.: Rowman & Littlefield, 2019).

ECONOMIC ISSUES IN AN INDUSTRIAL AGE 47

The Church's universalist economic affirmation eventually blended almost seamlessly into a social one, a rejection of the traditional "differentiation of people into classes according to the type of work done."[16] However, the transition to a more universalist approach to social organization was quite gradual. My final example, the hierarchy within the religious life, demonstrates that sharp social divisions still seemed normal decades after Leo wrote. Consider the 1926 British pamphlet, *A Manual for Dominican Lay Brothers*. It explained that the nonclerical members of the community performed "manual labor" so "[t]hat the Friars might apply themselves without hindrance to preaching." The lay brothers' "hard laborious work" did not leave "abundant leisure for prayer," but that was not a problem, since for them "to work is to pray."[17] The social ranking taken for granted in this manual is not determined by the ability of the various brothers, and the hierarchical social life that is assumed is far from the modern ideals of universal education and social opportunities for all. It is a simple class structure.

The religious houses, like the Catholic Church as a whole, eventually caught up with the modern, more egalitarian approach to social organization. In 1965, the Second Vatican Council suggested that these "class" lines in the religious life should be blurred. "Those who are called lay-brothers, assistants, or some similar name should be drawn closely in to the life and work of the community."[18] Now, a half century after the Council, the idea that there could be lesser religious who were destined to lesser work is almost incomprehensible, as is the idea that manual labor is less valuable in the eyes of God than is spiritual labor.

The idea that spiritual equality should be reflected in all worldly affairs has implications that extend far past the economy. Indeed, the assertion that all humanity is equally called to sanctify everything in the world can be considered the founding principle of most of the Catholic Social Teaching. The full Christian implications of this incarnational principle of social justice were certainly not clear to Leo XIII. They may not be fully clear yet, but the Magisterium has been working them out for 130 years, often in a tense dialogue

---

16. John Paul II, *Laborem Exercens*, 6.

17. Hugh Pope, *A Manual for Dominican Lay-brothers* (Woodchester Priory , 1926): 1, 26.

18. Vatican Council II, Decree on the Adaptation and Renewal of Religious Life *Perfectae Caritatis* (October 28, 1965), 15. For a sample of the social history in the religious life, see Augustine Thomson, *Dominican Brothers: Conversi, Lay, and Cooperator Friars* (Chicago: New Priory Press, 2017).

with secular thinkers. The results of this thinking and rethinking will be found in many of this book's chapters, for the new social vision affects the conduct of governments, the relations of peoples and of social classes, and the stewardship of Creation.

Needless to say, Catholics have not always responded perfectly to the magisterial call to find holiness in everyday experience. Instead of sanctifying the secular, some of them end up secularizing the sacred. In economics, well-intentioned believers have fairly often "baptized" an essentially nonreligious approach. "Liberation theologians" sometimes claim that Christians should endorse an almost unadulterated Marxism, while standard Western liberals (in the American, big-government sense of the latter word) often offer too-enthusiastic endorsements of undignified and intrusive government welfare programs. Some self-styled "conservative" lovers of "free markets" promote fundamentally non-Catholic understandings of both freedom and markets. (I discuss liberation theology briefly in this chapter and free markets at slightly more length in the next one. Big government is a major theme of chapter 6.)

These misguided interpretations should not be held against the Church's economic Magisterium. In my opinion, the popes' economic analysis and counsel is the most well-thought-out branch of the whole Social Teaching. I will try to justify that judgment after introducing both the biblical background and a Catholic philosophy of economic activity.

The Biblical Base

The Catholic Social Teaching, like all things truly Catholic, is both reasonable (in accordance with natural law) and inspired (in accordance with revelation). All of the various doctrines can be developed from first principles and, at least in their rudiments, from faithful analysis of the text of sacred Scripture. The interaction of the two is particularly fruitful. From Leo XIII's day on, popes have used a mix of revelation and reason to explain social doctrines. I follow that tradition throughout the book, always starting with the biblical base. Christians believe that the Bible, from the earliest books onward, reveals the truth about God, people, and the world. Non-Christians may not accept the truth of revelation, but they can appreciate many strands of biblical wisdom, including the economic.

A caution is necessary, one that applies to almost all the Social Teaching (migration, discussed in chapter 6, may be the only exception). All modern social exegesis of both the Old and New Testaments requires great prudence. While the Bible's truth is eternal, the books were all written in the premodern world. Their writers cannot be expected to provide the practical reason needed to deal with the modern world's many historically unprecedented features. Even when the Bible does have a great deal to say about a social topic, as it does about government, the connection between the ancient texts and contemporary reality is often tenuous. For most of the subjects I discuss, there are only scriptural indications, not injunctions— gleanings, not a rich harvest.

Economic biblical analysis certainly fits that description. Basically, the Bible shows relatively little interest in economic matters. Still, there is enough in both the Old and New Testaments to help shape the Christian approach to economic activity in every age. The most fundamental economic revelation comes at the beginning. When men and women are created, God makes it clear that their labor is an essential part of the human condition. In the first creation account in the book of Genesis, the deity says that humanity's role in this "very good"[19] creation is to "fill the earth and subdue it; and have dominion . . . over every living thing that moves upon the earth."[20] Similarly, in the following chapter's account of Adam and Eve, the man's task in the Garden of Eden is to "till it and keep it."[21] Significantly, this injunction is stated both before the Fall and afterward, when our first ancestors were expelled from Paradise.[22] For people, labor is part of the goodness of life in the fallen world, still a divinely approved and noble activity. Of course, toil, the hard labor of necessity, comes with pain and hardship. Although the harshness may stain the intrinsic nobility of labor, it does not fully remove the divine approbation.

These biblical texts on labor mention only male agricultural labor. That may seem a bit narrow for the purposes of the Social Teaching, but most exegetes believe it is appropriate to expand the meaning of taking care of the earth to include everything that people do to keep

---

19. Gn 1:31.

20. Gn 1:28.

21. Gn 2:15.

22. Gn 3:23.

the world in human order. In that sense, the subduing of the created world certainly encompasses the necessarily feminine labor of bearing children and the traditionally feminine labor of raising them. In general, women's labor receives little attention in the Scriptures (as in all other spiritual and literary traditions), probably because it was simply assumed that women are responsible primarily for childbearing, child rearing, and much of the hard slog of running premodern households. However, the lovely description of the admirable wife in chapter 31 of the book of Proverbs suggests that women's work might also include some sort of trading and buying a vineyard.[23]

The entry of sin into the world, described in the third chapter of Genesis, does not change either the goodness of responsible labor or the earth's ability to satisfy human desires. It does, however, poison the human relationship with the material world. Human nature as first created includes labor but not toil. In our fallen nature, however, the two are inseparable. "Cursed is the ground because of you; in toil you shall eat of it all the days of your life. . . . In the sweat of your face you shall eat bread."[24]

Overall, the moral economics expressed in the biblical account of the Creation and the Fall reflect the moral position of humanity. As part of created human nature, labor is good. It allows people, creatures who are loved by God, to thrive. Labor also expresses the goodness of the human likeness to God, in their control of and responsibility to the created world. Sadly, as part of fallen human nature, labor is distorted by evil. This taint leads directly to pain, and indirectly, as I discuss in the next section of this chapter, to all sorts of bad behavior. From the perspective of the created world, the Fall is also bad, because it breaks the harmony of people and the world in which they live. The human labor that subdues the earth no longer necessarily also takes care of it. (The human responsibility to the created world is the topic of chapter 7.)

Along with this fundamental mix of labor, domination, and toil, I would suggest five other leading biblical economic concerns. The first is the relationship between material wealth and spiritual excellence. The God of the Old Testament, who "satisfiest the desire of every living thing,"[25] is sometimes said to provide prosperity as a

---

23. Prv 31:10–31.

24. Gn 3:17–19.

25. Ps 145:16.

direct reward for religious virtue, while giving poverty as a punishment for disobedience. "And the LORD will make you abound in prosperity . . . bless all the work of your hands . . .if you obey the commandments of the LORD your God . . . But if you will not obey . . . the LORD will send upon you curses, confusion, and frustration in all that you undertake to do."[26] The simplistic equivalence of this "prosperity gospel" requires some modification. To start, the biblical writers were not stupid. They could see that prosperity was not always and only a divine reward for virtue, since bad people were sometimes wealthy, wealthy people were often bad, and virtuous people were far too often poor.

The story of Job brings out another aspect of the tension between goodness and riches. When God praises the rich Job for his virtue, Satan sneers at the compliment. "Does Job fear God for naught . . .Thou hast blessed the work of his hands, and his possessions have increased in the land."[27] The biblical book's author seems to be asking whether wealth is a reward for piety or whether piety is merely an all-too-easy response to God's favor. The book of Job does not answer that question. Indeed, the best Old Testament explanation of the worldly rewards for bad behavior is a vague claim that the balance will eventually be righted. "[T]hough the wicked sprout like grass / and all evildoers flourish, / they are doomed to destruction forever"[28]

The New Testament completely rejects the simple equivalence of wealth and divine favor for virtue. Jesus treats all earthly treasures not as rewards but as suspect, because they take people away from God. "You cannot serve God and Mammon."[29] The danger of affluence is so great that "[i]t is easier for a camel to go through the eye of a needle than for a rich man to enter the kingdom of God."[30] The epistle of James takes an even stronger antiwealth line: "Come now, you rich, weep and howl for the miseries that are coming on you."[31]

The Gospels do not condemn all wealthy people unconditionally. Salvation comes to the rich tax collector Zacchaeus, who climbs a tree in his fervor to see Jesus.[32] Joseph of Arimathea, "a rich man"

---

26. Dt 28:11–20.

27. Jb 1:9–10.

28. Ps 92:7, cf. Mal 3:14–15.

29. Lk 16:13.

30. Lk 18:24.

31. Jas 5:1.

32. Lk 19:1–10.

and a disciple of Jesus,[33] takes charge of the burial of Jesus. Still, Jesus never recognizes money as a reward and frequently classes it as a threat to true religion—"For where your treasure is, there will your heart be also."[34] Conversely, Jesus praises those who lack earthly treasure, the humble and poor, because they are free to treasure God. "Blessed are you poor, for yours is the kingdom of God."[35]

The mix of messages in the New Testament does not reverse the Old Testament teaching. Rather, Jesus perfects that teaching in perhaps unexpected ways. The consistent underlying lesson is that God watches over and takes a moral interest in people's actions in worldly matters. Wealth and poverty should both always be considered God-given, and both come with responsibilities to their divine donor.

A second biblical economic principle is that economic action should be just. Most directly, dealing should be fair. "You shall have just balances, just weights, a just ephah and a just hin."[36] True economic justice, however, goes beyond honest commerce; it includes generosity. "You shall not harden your heart or shut your hand against your poor brother, but you shall open your hand to him, and lend him sufficient for his need, whatever it may be."[37] "When you reap your harvest in your field, and have forgotten a sheaf in the field . . . it shall be for the sojourner, the fatherless, and the widow."[38] The ethical standard of fairness and generosity is high. To judge from the intensity and frequency of prophetic condemnations, the Israelites often did not live up to it.

In the New Testament, Jesus reiterates and intensifies the command of generosity. In the previous chapter, I mentioned the Lord's injunction of what came to be called corporal acts of mercy.[39] Three of them are economic: feeding the hungry, giving drink to the thirsty, and clothing the naked. (The others are welcoming the stranger, visiting the sick, and coming to the prisoner.) The charitable act of the rich giving to the poor is theologically significant. Just as Jesus, the Son of God, "offered up himself"[40] in sacrifice for the good of the spir-

---

33.   Mt 27:57.

34.   Mt 6:21.

35.   Lk 6:20.

36.   Lv 19:36.

37.   Dt 15:7–8.

38.   Dt 24:19.

39.   Mt 25:31–46.

40.   Heb 7:27.

ECONOMIC ISSUES IN AN INDUSTRIAL AGE 53

itually impoverished world, the followers of Jesus must offer what they have to the needy.[41] That theological model is always seen as having practical economic applications. Even while Jesus was alive, his disciples engaged in organized charity; otherwise Judas could not have argued that money spent on costly ointment should have been "given to the poor."[42]

Judas is on the wrong track in this case, but Jesus clearly teaches that Christian charity, like God's love for humanity, should be excessive by the standards of the world. He tells the disciples[43] and later the rich young man to go past measured generosity by embracing the total sacrifice of worldly goods: "sell all that you have and distribute to the poor."[44] The appointment of deacons described in the Acts of the Apostles demonstrates that organized charity, the specific labor of the diaconate, was considered an integral part of the Church's mission from the very beginning.

A third theme is the cautious biblical approach to what would now be called technology. Like the teaching on wealth, the attitude evolved. In the Old Testament, God is often hostile to mechanical hubris. He tears down the brick-and-mortar tower of Babel,[45] causes the high-tech Egyptian chariots to get stuck in the mud,[46] and uses David's low-tech sling-and-rock contraption to overcome the sophisticated bronze armor of Goliath.[47] This distrust of clever worldliness is not taken up in the New Testament. If anything, the willingness of Jesus to suggest as models both the crafty steward ("make friends for yourselves by means of unrighteous mammon"[48]) and the merchants who multiply rather than hide away their talents implies a respect for those who make good use of whatever God provides as raw economic material.

If there is a contradiction, it is only superficial. Jesus is not in favor of high tech or of trying to speed up the pace of economic

---

41. Gary A. Anderson, *Sin: A History* (New Haven, Conn.: Yale University Press, 2009) provides some helpful background on how almsgiving fit in with the early Christian (and contemporary Jewish) theology of atonement.

42. Jn 12:6.

43. Lk 12:33.

44. Lk 18:22.

45. Gn 11:3.

46. Ex 14:25.

47. 1 Sm 5:6.

48. Lk 16:9.

development. Rather, he is perfecting the Old Testament teaching that people should not rely on human ingenuity but should entrust all their economic lives to God.[49] He explains that there is no point in worrying about "'what shall we eat?' . . . or 'what shall we wear?'" because "your heavenly father knows that you need them all."[50] This fundamental acceptance of God's gifts—to "be content with what you have," in the words the Epistle to the Hebrews[51]—helps Christians ward off the "love of money," which is "the root of all evils."[52] If they trust God in this life, they may virtuously use their talents for worldly gain, but it is far more important that they strive to gain the "treasure in the heavens that does not fail."[53]

The early Christians brought a fourth economic theme to the fore—the centrality of community. Of course, the Christian community was not primarily economic; the Church was and is the body of Christ. However, the economic implications of this spiritual and liturgical communion are presented in the Acts of the Apostles as almost self-evident. In the protochurch of Jerusalem, "the company of those who believed were of one heart and soul, and no one said that any of the things he possessed was his own, but they had everything in common."[54] This communion was expected to be total. Ananias and his wife, Sapphira, were struck dead when they kept back some of the proceeds from the sale of a property.[55] Paul, who worked outside of Jerusalem, also demanded economic communion, although in the less extreme forms of almsgiving and hospitality.

Finally, the Bible basically endorses the spiritual dignity of all types of labor. There is little of this in the Old Testament, although King David's background as a shepherd can be interpreted as a protosocialist text. I have already discussed examples in the New Testament of the apparently friendly familiarity of Jesus with all sorts of labor, as well as the relatively recent development of the theological theme

---

49.   Lk 19:11–27.

50.   Mt 6:31–32.

51.   Heb 13:5.

52.   1 Tm 6:10.

53.   Lk 12:33.

54.   Acts 4:32.

55.   Acts 5:1–11. Exegetes dispute the exact reason for the death. I follow Ben Witherington III, *The Acts of the Apostles: A Socio-Rhetorical Commentary* (Grand Rapids, Mich.: William B. Eerdmans, 1998), 213–20.

of Joseph and Jesus as workers. Paul, like Jesus, is described as both a preacher and a professional craftsman. He works with fellow "tent-makers" and says that "these hands ministered to my necessities,"[56] although his main source of income seems to have been the contributions of believers.[57] In any case, what is perhaps most noticeable is something that Jesus and the Church described in the New Testament do not teach. Unlike the pagan philosophers of the time, they show no prejudice against the nonlearned and no preference for members of nobility or any sort of socially elevated economic activity. The early Christian social universalizing offers a particularly valuable challenge to the modern age because, as I explained at the beginning of this chapter, it was rapidly lost in Christian practice and is easily forgotten in Christian thinking.

In sum, the Bible teaches that we should be attentive to the world, grateful for and distrustful of wealth, humble before God, sympathetic to the poor, unreservedly generous to all, especially to members of our community, and eager to participate as best suits each of us in God's work in the world. Also, we should not be afraid to use our God-given skills and ingenuity to dominate the created world, but we should fear that excessive attention to domination leads to inattention to God. That list of injunctions is impressive and, I think, inspirational, but it is probably too long and complicated to be much practical use for understanding the Catholic Social Teaching. I would simplify the list into two basic and easier to apply principles. First, the economy should show and serve the glory of God. Second, there is no room for complacency about economic injustice, inadequate effort, or a mean-spirited approach to the poor. Each Christian in every generation and every society must try to put these teachings into practice. Philosophical analysis can help.

The Philosophical Base

The official documents of the Catholic Social Teaching do not provide an organized summary of the philosophy of economics. There are some wise indications throughout and a brilliant analysis of work, probably the most theologically and psychologically important economic activity, in Pope John Paul II's *Laborem Exercens*. In

---

56. Acts 18:3, Acts 20:34.

57. e.g., 2 Cor 11:9.

it, he explains the human value of work. "[T]he primary basis of the value of work is man himself, who is its subject. This leads immediately to a very important conclusion of an ethical nature: however true it may be that man is destined for work and called to it, in the first place work is 'for man' and not man 'for work.'"[58] The Polish pope's profound humanism has not only influenced this discussion in the two economic chapters of this book. It also provided the initial urge for my own somewhat presumptuous attempt to provide a philosophical description of this part of human nature in a way that accords with the Church's Social Teaching.[59] Here is an abbreviated summary of my analysis.

Humans, in their created nature, need and want to labor (or work)—to engage in purposeful activity in the world. Labor aims to humanize the world, sometimes through the production of things to be consumed, sometimes through the love and service of other humans, sometimes in the effort to imbue the world with some divine or transcendental glory. Labor is not only directed toward the world; it is also directed toward the good of the laborer. Indeed, it is universally an expression of the nature and dignity of each person. Labor, the human giving out to the world, is one side of economic activity.

Humans, in their created nature, need and want to consume. They need food and warmth to stay alive, but they want much more than these mere necessities to live the worldly life to the fullest— in worship, beauty, elegance, knowledge, friendship, pleasure, and comfort. Consumption, the taking in of fruits of labor in the humanized world, is the other side of economic activity. Men and women express important aspects of their personalities in both labor and consumption. Both can be spiritually valuable.

Humans, in their created nature, are primarily neither laborers nor consumers. Labor and consumption can never be fully separated from this world, whose form is "passing away,"[60] while people have an eternal calling to life with God. However much time and effort are dedicated to economic activities, they cannot take the place of the great commandments to love God and neighbor. Indeed, economic activities can only help people live out their divine vocation when they express this unconditional and total love. A misguided

---

58.   John Paul II, *Laborem Exercens*, 6.

59.   Edward Hadas, *Human Goods, Economic Evils: A Moral Look at the Dismal Science*, (Wilmington, Del.: ISI Books, 2007).

60.   1 Cor 7:31.

approach to labor and consumption can easily distract people from their divine calling, generally by inducing an excessive and excessively worldly concern for prosperity and by substituting Mammon, the demon of wealth and avarice, for the one true God of love.

Humans, in their created nature, are social. They live in communities. They make common cause in the pursuit of every good, including economic goods: good labor and good consumption, along with the goods that labor and consumption help make possible (life, health, and knowledge, for example). They work together and consume together. They organize economic activity socially, dividing and allocating responsibilities and fruits.

Humans, in their created nature, crave justice—to "render to each one his right," as Saint Thomas Aquinas defines the virtue, following the Aristotelian tradition.[61] Economic justice, one aspect of justice, is served when people are rewarded fairly for their labor, when they consume appropriately, and when the social arrangements of labor and consumption support the unity and good of society.

Humans, in their fallen nature, do not always follow their created nature as they should in economic matters. They shirk labor, they expect too much good to flow from labor, or they use their labor to exploit other people. They worry too much or too little about what they consume. They scorn the transcendental and wallow in the worldliness of economic matters. They use economic arrangements to divide rather than unify society. They are unjust in their economic dealings. Their interpretations of what is fair, appropriate, and beneficial to the common good are stained by greed and selfishness. When they do think beyond their individual desires, the community they think of often does not extend as far as all-encompassing Christian love demands.

This Christian description of the economic life—labor, consumption, secondary, social, just, fallen—cannot by itself resolve disputes about particular policies and priorities. It can, however, provide a sound framework for analyzing, praising, and criticizing the real workings of the economy. Catholic economics starts from firm understanding of what is at stake—an important aspect of both the dignity of every person and the common good of each society and of the entire world. Catholic economics works with a clear view of the possible good that economic activity can do—for the common good,

---

61. *Summa theologica*, II.II,58.1.

for the fullness of each life, and always subservient to the fullest good of salvation. Catholic economics is acutely aware that what may appear to be economic success, the bounty of the modern economy, can actually be suffused with sin, whether the greed of consumerism (discussed in the next chapter) or the bitterness of the struggle to get ahead in wealth or labor. Catholic economics provides a spiritually uplifting model of natural (prefallen) economic motivations—the fulfilment of God's command to master the earth and the desire to work with and care for our neighbors.

All the virtues of Catholic economics stand in sharp contrast with the anthropologically thin, sin-tolerant, and strangely gloomy model relied on for at least the past century by most professional economists. I discuss some aspects of that model in the next chapter.

For now, I turn to the moral-economic principles that follow from the Catholic understanding of the economy. These principles have been developed over 130 years of the modern Catholic Social Teaching, which starts with *Rerum Novarum*.

Five Principles

The lists of basic principles vary somewhat. I have chosen five to describe in this chapter. In chapter 3 I offer two general observations that might eventually lead to additional principles.

Principle 1: The Universal Destination of Goods

The belief that "private property" plays a crucial role in the organization of society is one of the new ideas that I alluded to in the introduction to the chapter. Thomas Aquinas, for example, treated the division of things among people as a generally helpful but not terribly important concession to fallen human nature. He divided what more modern thinkers would consider the single concept of property into three different activities: to procure a thing, to dispose of it, and to use it. He said that the first two could be done by individuals but declared that use was essentially communal: "man ought to possess external things, not as his own, but as common, so that, namely, he is ready to communicate them to others in their need."[62]

---

62. *Summa theologica*, II.II,66.1–2, quotation from 66.2 corpus. There is a good summary in Jan Hallebeek, "Thomas Aquinas' Theory of Property," *Irish Jurist* New Series 22, no. 1 (1987): 99–111.

ECONOMIC ISSUES IN AN INDUSTRIAL AGE 59

Thomas Aquinas wrote long before there was a clear distinction between the goods assigned to the government, state, or nation and those assigned to the monarch, so he could not have commented on the distinction, so crucial in the modern debate, between public property (owned by governments) and private property (owned by individuals or by legal "persons," including monarchs and the confusingly named publicly owned corporations).

Thomas Aqunias's subtle and essentially moral analysis of property had fallen from favor in de-Christianizing nineteenth-century Europe. By the time Leo XIII wrote, the fundamental rights and wrongs of "private property," which was always opposed to the property of the state, had become a hotly contested political issue. On one side were the capitalists, bourgeois liberals, and other adherents of the individualistic political philosophy, first articulated in the seventeenth century by John Locke, that considered private property rights to be inviolable. They believed that the nearly unfettered ability to acquire, use, and dispose of property—whether land, houses, comforts, luxuries or factories—was inherently just and also a crucial support for individual freedom.[63] On the other side, Marxists and other socialists argued that individual ownership was inherently unjust, socially divisive, and destructive of human freedom. They considered the private ownership of factories and other sorts of industrial capital especially pernicious. Socialists typically called either for the abolition of some types of private property or, something that amounted to the same thing in practice, for state control of all property.[64]

Both the positive and negative secular cases rely on an absurdly simplistic idea of ownership and express essentially godless approaches to society. It has not been easy for Leo and his successors to express the Christian theocentric understanding of what people can and should call "mine" in terms that secular philosophers and politicians could accept.[65] The concepts of both personal and government property will

---

63. John Locke, *The Works of John Locke. A New Edition, Corrected, In Ten Volumes*, vol. 5, *Second Treatise on Government* (London: Printed for Thomas Tegg, 1823 [1690]). For a rousing and influential Victorian defense of private property, see Herbert Spencer, *Social Statics* (London: John Chapman, 1851), chap. 10.

64. A quick and clear introduction to a rich debate in George G. Brenkert, "Freedom and Private Property in Marx," *Philosophy & Public Affairs* 8, no. 2 (1979): 122–47.

65. Some background on the lively debate on the nature of property is presented in Carol M. Rose, *Property and Persuasion: Essays on the History, Theory, and Rhetoric of Ownership* (Boulder, Colo.: Westview Press, 1994); Carol M. Rose, "Canons of Property Talk, or, Blackstone's Anxiety," *The Yale Law Journal* 108, no. 3 (1998): 601–32; and Jane B. Baron, "Rescuing

have one appearance when they are taken to be nothing more than useful, flexible, and potentially temporary tools that should never override the unity of all Creation which springs from its ultimate and always present divine origin, Thomas Aquinas's "sovereign dominion over all things."[66] These notions of property will seem quite different when they are looked at as rigid and crucial tools for either individual self-expression or social oppression. Considering this conceptual mismatch, it is not surprising that in a secular account the Church's Social Teaching on private property appears to have changed.

In *Rerum Novarum*, Leo XIII defended the concept. He explains that, without personal ownership of particular things, people cannot be justly rewarded for their labor, safe in their consumption, or able to nurture the primordial society of the family. Leo does point out that property owners have a responsibility to be generous with their possessions, because (quoting Thomas Aquinas), "[m]an should not consider his material possessions as his own, but as common to all, so as to share them without hesitation when others are in need."[67] However, he dedicates ten sections of the primordial modern social teaching encyclical to the vindication of property against the socialist claims, giving only one paragraph to the common nature of material possessions.

A century later, in John Paul II's discussion of property in *Centesimus Annus*,[68] the ratio is eight to one but in the opposite direction. The pope praises private property briefly but explains in careful detail the communal responsibilities that follow from the divine origin of all property. Human beings have a common origin and a shared vocation to serve God in the world. We are each our "brother's keeper,"[69] in all matters, including our economic lives, and with God as our common Father, we are all brothers and sisters. The multifaceted universality leads to what John Paul II had earlier identified as the "universal destination of goods and the right to common use of them."[70] The communal nature of property is particularly clear in

---

the Bundle-of-Rights Metaphor in Property Law," *University of Cincinnati Law Review* 82, no. 1 (2014): 57–101.

66. *Summa theologica*, II.II,66.1 ad 1. Locke also starts his discussion of property with divine sovereignty, but God is rapidly eclipsed by humanity.

67. Leo XIII, *Rerum Novarum*, 22.

68. John Paul II, Encyclical Letter *Centesimus Annus* (September 1, 1991), 30–32.

69. Gn 4:9.

70. John Paul II, *Laborem Exercens*, 14.

what the pope called the modern "business economy"—he generally avoided speaking of capitalism or the market economy. In sophisticated contemporary economic systems, the most important type of property is the shared effort and intelligence of humanity. "[T]he decisive factor is increasingly man himself, that is, knowledge, especially his scientific knowledge, his capacity for interrelated and compact organization, as well as his ability to perceive the needs of others and to satisfy them."[71] In such an economy, it is inappropriate to identify this or that thing as belonging solely to any one particular person, since the putative owner would have nothing without the efforts of many others.

Expressed negatively, this teaching holds that owners should not use their property merely to satisfy themselves, because any individual's property is entailed with a "social mortgage,"[72] an obligation to the use the property for the good of the community. Expressed more positively, all the goods of God's creation—whether in their raw form or after having been processed by human toil and intelligence—should be used for the good of all God's creatures.

Even leaving God out of the argument, the teaching is just. I may buy a piece of farmland or a telephone, but I cannot make good use of either without the cooperation, indeed the active aid, of thousands of people. All farmers, no matter how self-sufficient, use skills that have been built up over generations. The farm can be called mine, but it better understood as the shared heritage of my people and of all humanity and as carrying an unshirkable responsibility to future generations of farmers and of all humanity. The telephone would be no more than a piece of useless plastics and metals without networks of switches, computers, and servers; an organization of people who keep the networks working; and the rule of law that allows this organization to function. The networks, the organization, and the law serve the whole community. The telephone is mine, but it is also everyone's.

The teaching of the universal destination of goods is beautiful as well as just. It allows us to see creation, both nonhuman and human, as it should be seen—a common patrimony of humanity. It translates the tight spiritual-economic union of the first handful of Christians in Jerusalem into a spiritual-economic approach that is applicable everywhere. It ties private and common property together in a

---

71.   John Paul II, *Centesimus Annus*, 32.

72.   John Paul II, Encyclical Letter *Sollicitudo Rei Socialis* (December 30, 1987), 42.

way that is worthy of both personal and common human dignity. My property is, as Leo pointed out in an almost Lockean way, a just reward for my labor, a source of personal satisfaction, and a bulwark against governmental tyranny. Without this economic "mine," there can be no true "ours." Conversely, though, without a universal "ours," there is no all in which "mine" can be demarcated.

In modern business economies, much wealth is in fact treated as common property, as the teaching recommends. Governments take taxes from everyone and distribute benefits to everyone within a particular polity. Crucial services—roads, schools, health care, electricity, water, and telecommunications—are provided universally, again within national or some other political borders. In most jurisdictions, the law demands that corporations serve society as a whole, although the law is often in conflict with both the ideology of profits-before-all that flourishes in many companies and with the fact that many companies do business across political borders, so the society to be served is often unclear. The question asked of Jesus— "[a]nd who is my neighbor?"[73]—is as pertinent as ever.

The papal answer to that question is appropriately expansive. From Paul VI to Francis, the Magisterium has emphasized that in an increasingly globalized and interconnected economy the only truly appropriate scale for the common economic good is global. The whole world, not the people inside any political border, is the relevant universe for the universal destination of goods. This large perspective is easily lost—people find it much easier to share with neighbors they see than with people who still seem distant. However, the true Christian understanding must be truly catholic in the word's lowercase sense; it includes the whole world, both as it is now and as we are making it for the future.

How should the historical shift in emphasis from the defense of private property to the universal destination of goods be understood? A critic can easily create a narrative of cowardice: the blind fear of expropriating socialists gives way to an ill-considered endorsement of the welfare state, followed by naïve call for the rich to engage in some sort of extensive do-goodism toward the distant poor. That analysis is far too harsh. Some Catholics certainly had and have these sorts of intellectual weaknesses, but a more cogent explanation for the change is provided by the shift in the predominant socioeconomic flaws.

---

73. Lk 10:29.

ECONOMIC ISSUES IN AN INDUSTRIAL AGE   63

In Leo XIII's time, socialists argued that a small group of capitalists had so much economic and political power that, unless something was done, this elite would end up with virtually all the available property, while the proletariat majority would be reduced to penury and dependence. Many socialists believed that the abolition of private property was the best, perhaps the only, "something" that could change the otherwise inevitable course of history. Leo saw with great clarity that the supposed remedy could not cure the disease, because some private property is necessary for the promotion of human dignity. The communist experiments of the twentieth century verified Leo's judgment.

By now, however, private property is in ample supply in rich societies; its justice and usefulness are almost never questioned. The more pressing moral challenges come from the misuse of this property. The rich are often reluctant to share their abundant wealth with the poor, governments of all countries show only occasional and limited concern for the global common good, and some governments are reluctant to take responsibility, even within their jurisdictions, for such common concerns such as environmental depredation and the relief of misery. Under such pressures as these, the universal destination of goods is a more relevant teaching than the good of private property.

Christians should feel more comfortable with the current emphasis. The defense of private property too easily degenerates into a rejection, or at least a significant softening, of the Christian obligation to treat all neighbors with practical love. Leo XIII argued against any such softening, stressing the spiritual value of charity. Still, the promotion of the universal destination of goods brings the Social Teaching more obviously in line with the apparently impractically radical teaching of Jesus. Total communion of things as well as of hearts and souls is a goal toward which Christians should strive.

Principle 2: Preferential Option for the Poor

The teaching of the universal destination of material goods is radical, but it is not radical enough to reflect fully the extremism of Jesus. Christians should not merely share what they have in prudent measure. Their practical love for everyone should be overflowing, with the excess directed especially toward the people who most lack the good things of this world. Christians, in other words, should consider aid to the poor more important than any help to those who have more. (See "Those who are well have no need of a physician, but those who are *sick*."[74]) The rich are in the opposite position of the poor. Their worldly rewards are likely to distract them from the kingdom of heaven,[75] so they should be not be shown any preference They need lessons in humility rather than economic transfers and social honors.

The phrase "preferential option for the poor" and its broad social application are quite modern (I come to that development shortly), but as practical theology, the Christian pro-poor obligation is evident from the very beginning of the religion. As mentioned, in the first church in Jerusalem deacons were appointed solely to serve those in need.[76] The theological distrust of the rich was also there from the start. Also as mentioned, the epistle of James vehemently condemned Christian communities for their hypocritical preference for the affluent.[77] Both the preference of one and the distrust of the other have continued through the whole of Christian history. On the preference side, many saints have shown tremendous generosity to all types of poor people—destitute, neglected, ill, insane, and imprisoned. Religious communities were set up solely to provide relief. On the lack of preference side, the horror of allowing the rich to become richer at the expense of the poor was a leading motivation for the strict condemnation of usury (lending money with the hope of gain). As I mentioned, Saint Francis of Assisi showed his distaste for wealth by abandoning his merchant father's property and by instead embracing Lady Poverty.[78] He articulated the theology with particular eloquence but both before and especially after him a fair number of rich men and women followed the Lord's advice to sell all they have and give the proceeds to the poor.[79] Less extreme were the many rich men and women who remained rich but still provided generously for the needy, not to mention the countless unremembered acts of sacrificial charity for the poor from the spiritual heirs of the superabundantly generous widow in the Temple.[80]

---

74. Mk 2:17.

75. cf. Mt 13:22.

76. Acts 6:1.

77. Jas 5:1–6.

78. See Wolf, *The Poverty of Riches*.

79. cf. Mt 19:21.

80. Lk 21:1–4.

Although generosity is not rare, the saints of poverty will always be exceptional, almost by definition. In almost all societies, far more of the goods of this world are taken by those at the top of the hierarchy than by those at the bottom. Christendom was no exception and neither are post-Christian societies. Individuals will presumably have to deal with the tension between the preferential love of the poor and the maintenance of the social order until the Second Coming.

For societies, however, the meaning of the preferential option has changed significantly. More accurately, one of the new things of the modern era is the expansion of this option from individuals to whole societies. Until sometime in the nineteenth century, a broad social option was basically impossible, because neither the available ideas nor the possible economic actions really permitted coherent efforts to relieve the misery of all the poor all at once and forever. On the intellectual side, there were few protoeconomists to work on increasing production, few protosociologists to chronicle the dire effects of persistent poverty, and few protosocialists to condemn the structural injustice of the exploitation of the poor by the rich. The first writings that proposed that the eradication of poverty could be realistic appeared around 1800.[81] At first such ideas were rejected as foolish utopianism. That dismissive attitude was completely realistic. In narrowly economic terms, the history of production in every society gave no reason to falsify God's word to the Hebrews, "For the poor will never cease out of the land."[82] When Jesus told his disciples "[f]or you always the poor with you,"[83] he was merely stating the obvious.

Now, there are both new ideas about poverty and new economic practices. There are numerous economists, sociologists, and socialists to organize charity, and the new industrial prosperity has led to the near disappearance of material misery in developed economies. The United States, Japan (twice, both before and after the Second World War), and most European nations have done exactly what had long been assumed to be impossible: eliminate hunger, cold, filth, and nearly universal ignorance. Enough poorer countries are

---

81. The first chapters of Harry W. Laidler, *Social-Economic Movement: An Historical and Comparative Survey of Socialism, Communism, Co-operation, Utopianism, and Other Systems of Reform and Reconstruction* (London: Routledge & Kegan Paul, 1948) amount to a heroic, often mendacious, and ultimately unsuccessful effort to find genuine precursors to socialism.

82. Dt 15:11.

83. Mt 26:11.

66 CHAPTER 2

following these global leaders to demonstrate that absolute poverty can be eliminated fairly quickly in any society.[84]

Under the new circumstances, the traditional sporadic almsgiving of the rich, leavened by the voluntary poverty and communal property of some religious groups, is no longer an adequate social expression of the Christian obligation to bless the poor.[85] Since relatively straightforward social and economic changes *can* now eliminate extreme material poverty anywhere at any time, the persistence of this poverty *must* indicate a social structure of sin. The old piecemeal approach now looks like disorganized unchristian indifference to the least of Jesus' brothers.[86]

John Paul II made the moral change clear. The "option for the poor or the preferential love for them" now not only "affects the life of each Christian inasmuch as he or she seeks to imitate the life of Christ, but . . . applies equally to our social responsibilities and hence to our manner of living, and to the logical decisions to be made concerning the ownership and use of goods." In other words, the appropriate answer to the cry of the poor includes the creation and active support of social policies and practices that lead to the eradication of extreme poverty. To do less is to become "like the 'rich man' who pretended not to know the beggar Lazarus lying at his gate."[87]

This social standard has political implications. In any society where poverty is allowed to persist, the Christian preferential option inevitably involves a commitment to socioeconomic change. The greater the extent of the poverty, the more significant the needed change is likely to be. That statement is fully Christian, but it has a Marxist ring to it, so it not surprising that the Christians most involved in putting the preferential option for the poor into action have been influenced by Marxist economic and social thinking. For example, the French "worker-priests" who flourished in the years after the Second World War sometimes campaigned along with communist agitators for better pay and conditions.[88]

---

84. The first part of Martin Ravallion, *The Economics of Poverty: History, Measurement, and Policy* (Oxford: Oxford University Press, 2016) provides a useful historical and conceptual summary. His incomprehension of premodern thinking leads to some strained interpretations but is indicative of how much thinking has changed. The Oxford University Martin School's website (https://ourworldindata.org) provides fascinating graphs that show the development of many indices of prosperity.

85. cf. Lk 6:20.

86. cf. Mt 25:31–46.

87. John Paul II, *Sollicitudo Rei Socialis*, 42, translation altered, citing Lk 16:19–31.

88. See Michael Kelly, "Catholicism and the Left in Twentieth Century France," in *Catholicism,*

In Latin America, the gap between the few rich and very many poor was especially wide and was probably widening in the early 1960s. The situation did not seem to cause much distress to either the governments or their close allies in the economic, social, and Catholic episcopal elite. In response to that complacency, some Catholics developed a "theology of liberation."[89] Liberation theologians called the continued oppression of the poor the preeminent sin in their societies and declared that their liberation from material misery was the preeminent Christian responsibility. The agendas included far more than social justice and economic reform, but their first priority was usually to work for radical change in the economic and social orders.

The economic radicalism was controversial in many Catholic circles, not least because some of the theologians were, or at least wrote as if they were, adherents of the socialism that previous popes had so firmly condemned. However, the Vatican's judgment was essentially favorable. It recognized the new theology's calls for social and political change as truly Christian responses to the current sins of the world. A 1977 report by the advisory but authoritative International Theological Commission declared that the mixing of Christianity with social action provided "a richer understanding of the total unity that their calling to salvation involves." It noted the problems that came from "the cunning stratagems that characterize politics" but declared that they were not a valid excuse for inaction. On the contrary, the Church "can share in the blame *when it does not denounce the situation of the poor and the oppressed*, of those who suffer injustice—much more if it covers such a situation over and leaves it unchanged."[90] The ITC report was not purely laudatory. It recognized and rejected the theology's unchristian tendency to reduce "faith's praxis. . . . to changing the conditions of human society," because "besides laying injustice bare, faith's praxis includes such things as conscience formation,

---

Politics and Society in Twentieth Century France, ed. Kay Chadwick, (Liverpool: Liverpool University Press, 2000), 142–69, especially 156–59.

89.　For a brief but clear introduction to liberation theology, its sources, and the Vatican response, see Rosino Gibellini, *The Liberation Theology Debate,* trans. John Bowden (London: SCM Press 1987 [1986]). Very helpful is Gustavo Gutiérerrez, *A Theology of Liberation* (London: SCM Press 1988 [1974]), xvii–xlvi.

90.　International Theological Commission, *Human Development and Christian Salvation* (September 1977, summary of meetings held October 4–9, 1976), emphasis added.

change in mental attitude, adoration of the true God and of our Savior Jesus Christ."[91]

John Paul II followed the commission's largely positive line. He endorsed the liberation theologians' focus on desperate and avoidable material poverty. He agreed that the liberation from sin in a structurally oppressive society was incomplete unless economic injustice was overcome. He adopted several of the new theologians' terms, including "preferential option." He also firmly rejected Marxist revolutionary economics and the related reductive materialist social analysis. However, he was by no means an economic conservative. The first foreign visit of his papacy was to Latin America, where he called on the rich to "organize socio-economic life so that it promotes equality among men and not an abyss between them."[92] The evangelical and resolutely practical callings were inseparable: "It is not just, it is not human, it is not Christian to continue with certain situations that are clearly unjust. It is necessary to carry out real, effective measures."[93]

The Marxist materialism of some liberation theologians was partly a confused response to injustice. However, the ease with which they adopted such unchristian ideas suggests a deeper error. It is wrong to interpret the preferential option for the poor as if "the possession of more and more goods [were] the ultimate objective" of development, as Paul VI explained.[94] The basic error is to forget that the Christian Good News of human liberation from sin is not a "purely earthly gospel," as the Congregation for the Doctrine of the Faith explained to liberation theologians.[95] A single-minded effort to increase wealth is particularly dangerous in today's post-Christian societies, even the poor ones. In Benedict XVI's philosophical terms, the secular values that seem always to come with increased material prosperity can bring a "reductive vision of the person and his destiny to poor countries."[96]

The right goal of the preferential option for the poor is what Paul VI called both "authentic development" and "integral human

---

91. International Theological Commission, *Human Development and Christian Salvation.*

92. John Paul II, Speech in Rio de Janeiro *Visit to the "Favela Vidigal"* (July 2, 1980), 4.

93. John Paul II, Speech in Cuilapan, Mexico *Meeting with Mexican Indios* (January 29, 1979).

94. Paul VI, Encyclical Letter *Populorum Progressio* (March 26, 1967), 19.

95. Congregation for the Doctrine of the Faith, *Instruction on Certain Aspects of the "Theology of Liberation,"* (August 6, 1984), 4.

96. Benedict XVI, Encyclical Letter *Caritas in Veritate*, 29.

development."[97] This sort of all-around enrichment requires a "new humanism, one that will enable our contemporaries to enjoy the higher values of love and friendship, of prayer and contemplation, and thus find themselves."[98] The higher fulfilment is undoubtedly eased by the elimination of abject material poverty, so the goal of authentic development deepens, rather than weakens, the preferential option. (Authentic development also includes respect for the environment, which I discuss in chapter 7.) In any case, caution about materialism is not an excuse for inaction. The persistence of material poverty in a world capable of eliminating it amounts to a scandalous global preferential option for the rich.

The scandal is made more outrageous by the behavior of the rich. As a group, they are reluctant to make significant material sacrifices. On the contrary, they are anxious to better their already wasteful lifestyles. Even when their consumption practices and cravings do no direct harm to the poor, their attitude of effective indifference to those in need amounts to a sin of omission. In *Evangelii Gaudium*, Francis gave a dramatic description of the damage done. "To sustain a lifestyle that excludes others, or to sustain enthusiasm for that selfish ideal, a globalization of indifference has developed. Almost without being aware of it, we end up being incapable of feeling compassion at the outcry of the poor, weeping for other people's pain, and feeling a need to help them, as though all this were someone else's responsibility and not our own. The culture of prosperity deadens us."[99]

It must be admitted that some of Francis's descriptions of the global economy are more emphatic than accurate. A prominent example is his fulmination on widening inequality in the same document. "While the earnings of a minority are growing exponentially, so too is the gap separating the majority from the prosperity enjoyed by those happy few."[100] The statement is at best misleading. Comparing actual standards of living, the real material gap between the world's rich and poor has narrowed year by year, solely because the poor of the world have overall become steadily richer in ways that significantly improve their material quality of life. Each year, a higher

---

97. Paul VI, *Populorum Progressio*, 20, 7.

98. Paul VI, *Populorum Progressio*, 20.

99. Francis, Apostolic Exhortation *Evangelii Gaudium* (November 24, 2013), 54.

100. Francis, *Evangelii Gaudium*, 56.

proportion of the global population enjoy the benefits of clean water, adequate food, basic health care, electricity, and all levels of education. The proportion of the global population living in poverty, both abject and mild, is the smallest ever.[101] Meanwhile, while the rich continue to get richer in monetary terms, their additional income overall buys little substantial gain in living standards.

From a Christian perspective, however, Francis's indignation is completely justified. The world may be less cruel to the poor than it was fifty years ago, but it *could* be—and thus *should* be—much kinder. Too much of the economic effort in rich countries is undoubtedly dedicated to trivial goals or even to the promotion of economic evils such as greed (for example in much of finance) and gluttony (for example in the marketing of food). Too little attention is paid in both rich and poor countries to creating and justly sharing true wealth. There is no justification for such complacency, especially among those who already have so much.

How should the preferential option be put into practice? Paul VI emphasized a global approach. "[I]t is only fitting that a prosperous nation set aside some of the goods it has produced in order to alleviate their [poor people's] needs; and that it train educators, engineers, technicians, and scholars who will contribute their knowledge and their skill to these less fortunate countries."[102] The call for global solidarity is truly Catholic (as I explain a little later), but the just-mentioned economic improvements have changed the most appropriate forms of sharing.

Both as a cause and as a result of these gains, the global economy and financial system have become less hostile to what are now optimistically but generally accurately known as developing economies. Cross-border trade terms for poor countries have become less harsh. Both remittances, the payments received in poor countries from family members who have migrated to richer lands, and the skills of returning emigrants have become significant sources of money and

---

101.   For a clear and up-to-date overview of the scale of progress in such key aspects of human flourishing as health, life expectancy, literacy, tourism (a proxy for abundant leisure time) and energy use (a proxy for material security), see the ourworldindata website. Julian Simon, *The Ultimate Resource* (Princeton, N.J.: Princeton University Press, 1996, rev. ed.) is sometimes irritatingly simplistic but provides a longer-term perspective and a historical model that for the most part supports the Catholic understanding of the relationship of humanity to the rest of creation.

102.   Paul VI, *Populorum Progressio*, 48.

expertise.[103] However, many significant improvements are still possible. Recent campaigns to encourage global companies to spread higher wages through their supply chains are worthy heirs of Paul VI's way of thinking. Also, while there are far more skilled professionals from developing countries than Paul might have expected, there is still more than enough poverty to provide ample opportunities for aid workers from rich countries. Modern popes have also argued strongly in favor of allowing people to move to wherever they think they can escape from poverty. The suggested permission to migrate comes with qualifications, which I discuss in chapter 6.

Christians living in rich countries face two moral challenges in living out the preferential option for the poor. First, they must simultaneously prefer two quite different groups of poor people—the one or two billion of the world's seven billion people who lack basic goods and the much smaller but physically much closer group of materially and spiritually poor people in their own neighborhoods and nations.[104] Since there are finite quantities of time and resources, choices have to be made. In making them, there are several relevant considerations, which point in different directions. To start, the poorest people in rich countries are almost all quite well off materially by global standards, thanks both to rich countries' high overall level of prosperity and to state welfare programs that already spread some of that prosperity to relatively poor residents. However, the poor-among-the-rich are sometimes relatively very poor relative to the local material standard of living, and such local standards are relevant to the administration of social justice. Another issue is that the needs of these relatively poor people are often primarily spiritual or psychological rather than strictly economic. Finally, Christians must remember that an impoverished fellow American or fellow resident of North London is a neighbor in need. It is inappropriate to see walk past an injured person on the other side of the road, even when hurrying to send aid to a much needier person in a distant land.[105]

Second, Christians must not let charity get in the way of the efforts of poor people and poor nations to help themselves. As Paul

---

103. http://www.worldbank.org/en/news/infographic/2017/04/21/trends-in-migration-and -remittances-2017.

104. The ourworldindata website estimates that 730 million people lived in "extreme poverty" in 2015, and another 1.2 billion in poverty. See https://ourworldindata.org/extreme-poverty and https://ourworldindata.org/poverty-at-higher-poverty-lines.

105. cf. Lk 10:31–32.

VI put it, the poor must be "the artisans of their destiny."[106] That practical necessity is also a spiritual warning to wealthy do-gooders. They should not bask in self-satisfaction at saving the poor from their own incapacity. Of course, it is not always easy to integrate the teaching that the poor have to do their own work for development with the teaching of the preferential option, which is aimed primarily at shaming the rich into action.

However, rich people and countries should certainly not use either the complexity of balancing local with global charity or the tension between help and self-help as excuses for inaction. Rather, they should search for imaginative ways to help all the poor, everywhere and over time, as effectively and generously as possible.

Principle 3: The Priority of Labor over Capital

For Christians, "the primacy of the person over things" is a fundamental truth of creation.[107] Humans, made in the image and likeness of God, have been given the rest of creation to dominate, cultivate, and appreciate. It makes no difference whether the "things" in question are animals, inanimate objects in the natural world, physical idols constructed by human hands, or inhumane concepts dreamed up by fallen human intellects. All of things of the created world are less important than is each human person, for only humanity is made in God's image and redeemed into the fullness of the divine life of love.

In economic activity, human primacy should hardly come into question. Both of the two sides of economic activity, labor and consumption, are primarily and essentially concerned with people, for it is the labor and consumption of people that make, shape, use, and use up the various things of economic life. People, not their tools or any or nonhuman entities, have full dominion in the economic world. They bear the moral responsibility for how that authority is exercised. It is people, not companies, industries, or concepts, such as capital or technology, who are responsible to dealing the environmental issues that I discuss in chapter 7.

Unfortunately, this primacy is not fully recognized in standard economic theory. Instead, people are often portrayed as impotent victims

---

106.   Paul VI, *Populorum Progressio*, 65.

107.   John Paul II, *Laborem Exercens*, 13.

ECONOMIC ISSUES IN AN INDUSTRIAL AGE 73

of some nonhuman thing, force, or forces. In economic practice, they are sometimes treated as if the true human good either cannot or should not be given precedence over the needs or operating logic of some nonhuman entities. In particular, "capital" is often presented as something structurally opposed to, even at war with, workers, who are themselves subsumed into another almost inhuman abstraction, "labor." Marxist economists were mostly responsible for creating the sharp opposition between capital and labor, but the split is now basically accepted by anti-Marxist defenders of the "capitalist" system.

The exact constituents of capital are subject to debate. Some economists separate natural capital of earth, water, air, and all that is in them from what can be called man-made, physical, or fixed capital— the mines, factories, machines, and tools used to make the things that people consume. This fixed capital is sometimes distinguished from working or circulating capital, which is made up of the unfinished components of those consumable things, completed things that have not been sold, and the money needed for trading. More recently, several new and rather nebulous sorts of capital have been postulated. The most notable is human capital, which is supposed to be a measure or an appreciation of the economic value of education and skills. There is also social capital, which is defined either as the organizations that operate the economy or as the quality of trust needed to run these organizations. Then there is intellectual capital, which refers either to the value of specific inventions and other works of human intelligence or to the shared knowledge required to build and operate machines, factories, and such complex organizations as schools, police departments, and hospitals. There may also be cultural capital, a concept used to explain why some countries and some companies lead and other lag. From a different perspective, many economists focus on financial capital, which is a monetary measure of various sorts of capital. All of these types of capital can be associated with the economic system known as capitalism, all of them can be attributed either to entities or to whole societies, and all of them, except perhaps cultural capital, are generally associated with some sort of owners, who are often called capitalists.[108]

---

108. My list of types of capital is not meant to be exhaustive. A similar list is found in Neva R. Goodwin, "Five Kinds of Capital: Useful Concepts for Sustainable Development." Global Development and Environment Institute Working Paper Number 03–07, Tufts University, Medford, Mass., 2003. The idea that capital can be intangible is quite recent—for example, the idea of "intellectual capital" was only articulated in the 1980s. The term was first popularized in the

Some of these types of capital are assumed to need profits in much the same way that mythical monsters needed maidens to devour, or, in economic theory, in the same way that labor requires wages and that land earns rent. These profits, also known as the return on capital, are treated by some economists as cultic objects of worship. The search for profit, sometimes called the profit motive, is often taken as an impersonal and implacable economic drive that can only be thwarted at the expense of the overall economic good. The profit motive is not relevant for some of the more inclusive and economically relevant types of capital I just listed, but economists often gloss over that complication. The notion of an ineluctable, rapacious, and amoral force of capital continues to damage the discourse of economics and to harm the actual economy.

In fact, it is unrealistic to assume an inherent antagonism between a totally inhuman and inhumane capital and some abstract force of labor. The division ignores the obvious reality that capital cannot be an autonomous thing. The constituents of capital, however it is defined, are always human. They may be the authority, habits, and knowledge of actual people or they may be things, either concrete or conceptual, that are ultimately under the control of people. In actual practice, the working of machines and factories may indeed have bad effects on the people working with and in them. As John Paul II explained, technology can take away "all personal satisfaction and the incentive to creativity and responsibility, when it deprives many workers of their previous employment, or when, through exalting the machine, it reduces man to the status of its slave."[109] However, it is also true that the machines are made by and for people and are ultimately under people's control. Those owners or controllers of capital may be the rich and powerful in the economy. Alternatively, the capital controllers may be the skilled participants in the bureaucracies of economic arbiters and regulators or they may be almost everyone in the economy. In any case, these capital-concerned men and women are just as much part of the social hierarchy, just as subject to sin, and just as capable of virtue as the people whom economists lump together as labor.

1990s, as Jay Chatzkel points out in the first chapter of *Intellectual Capital* (Oxford: Wiley, 2002). The business and economic writers on the topic almost never mention John Paul II, to their detriment. For Catholic perspectives on the human center of capital, in all its varieties, see the papers in Edmond Malinvaud, ed., *Forum on the Meaning of the Priority of Labour, 5 May 2003, Miscellanea 4* (Vatican City: The Pontifical Academy of Social Sciences, 2004).

109. John Paul II, *Laborem Exercens*, 5.

ECONOMIC ISSUES IN AN INDUSTRIAL AGE   75

Any crude capital-labor division also passes over the subtler fact that the original insight that defined capital as distinct from people is simply invalid in a complex modern economy. The list of nebulous types of capital demonstrates that an impersonal capital that can be abstracted from the people who make, maintain, and use it does not exist. Economic reality also invalidates the conventional treatment of labor and capital as exchangeable "factors of production." There is little evidence for the economists' assumption that labor can and will be substituted for capital, or vice versa, depending on relationship of profits and wages. The characterizations and calculations of such capitalist economics are deeply inhumane because they obscure the noble truth of labor as a human activity. Labor is not fundamentally an alternative to machines. It is the dignified action of men and women, each one made in the image of God.

From the beginning, the Catholic Social Teaching has rejected all theories that dehumanize economic relations and activity. In particular, the treatment of capital in what John Paul II called "economism and materialism"[110] is incompatible with Catholic anthropology. The Magisterium has provided two reasons for rejecting the standard, rigid, and deterministic capital-labor split. First, capital and labor are equally human. Second, labor should be treated as more important than capital, but capitalist economics always gives capital priority. The two objections are not quite consistent, but the logical gap can be forgiven. Both arguments point toward a single central concern: too many economic actors—not only economists but politicians, financiers, and some regular workers—endorse an erroneous hierarchy of economic goods. They fail to undertake the needed serious moral analysis of the diverse goods of consumers, laborers, and the overall society. Instead, they let their thoughts and deeds be guided by the allure of some simple and impersonal pseudogood.

Capital is the most traditional of these pseudogoods. The dangers of idolizing it are real enough. A morally blind search for maximal profits demeans people. The fixation on profits can lead to unjustly low monetary rewards for labor, because to some extent higher profits go with lower wages. In addition, the common good is badly served when the search for profit is not kept under conscious moral control. Without these controls, profitable evils such as pornography and wasteful consumerism will undoubtedly flourish.

---

110.   John Paul II, *Laborem Exercens*, 13.

However, capital is not the only abstract economic thing that is idolized in the contemporary economy. Indeed, in the past half century economists have increasingly added other "deities" to their pantheon. A relatively new and extremely popular creed is maximizing the gross domestic product, a number that is purports to quantify the total production of paid-for goods and services in a country. This GDP is a useful measure in some contexts but an incomplete and misleading index of actual economic activity, let alone of the economic good.[111] The goal is pursued with no reflection on how well this abstruse measure expresses the common good. Then there is the "market," a more traditional divinity for the profession, whose popularity has probably increased in the past few decades. I discuss this idea in the next chapter. Even noneconomists are well aware of another tempting force, the simple and ultratraditional passion that Pope Francis called "greed for money." In his dramatic words, when the desire for this morally dangerous token of material wealth "presides over the entire socioeconomic system—it ruins society, it condemns and enslaves men and women, it destroys human fraternity."[112]

Capital is a force, GDP is a goal, markets are a process, and money is an abstract thing. These elements of the economy are quite different, but they have two common features. First, none of them have any inherent moral content. This lack makes them unsuitable guides for economic analysis, which should be oriented to the common good. Second, none of them have any transcendental value, so they make unworthy idols. The Church's warnings against craving such things are more relevant than they should be to professional economists, whose training often leads them to a narrow approach to their discipline , and to legislators and policy makers, who rarely consider carefully the appropriate goals for their labor in economic matters.

Still, while a truly person-based economy is still a long way off, recent history provides at least one encouraging sign. The sacrifices of labour to the idol of capital have become less significant. Thanks to the development of new attitudes, extensive laws, and deeply embedded organizational practices, workers in developed

---

111.   Diane Coyle, *GDP: A Brief but Affectionate History* (Princeton, NJ: Princeton University Press, 2015) provides some helpful background on the history and limits of the measure. For a more conceptual approach, see David Pilling, *The Growth Delusion: The Wealth and Well-being of Nations* (London: Bloomsbury, 2018).

112.   Francis, *Address at the Second World Meeting of Popular Movements,* Santa Cruz de la Sierra, Bolivia (July 9, 2015).

economies are now mostly paid and treated in reasonably fair ways. Of course, sin is always present, so the powerful still take advantage of the weak, and in the last few decades the balance has probably shifted in favor of the powerful.

In labor relations, the power tends to be in the hands of the employers. The popes have both called for the responsible use of that power and endorsed organizations of employees that could both work with employers when possible and resist them when necessary. From the beginning of the modern Catholic Social Teaching, popes have portrayed such unions of workers as organizations having the positive mission of promoting the dignity of laborers and a more negative task of defending workers from any rapacious designs of their employers. Leo XIII wanted Catholic-inspired unions that would promote community and piety among workers as well as infusing "a spirit of equity into the mutual relations of employers and employed."[113] Eight decades later, Paul VI recognized and praised the primarily secular agenda of these unions. "The important role of union organizations must be admitted: their object is the representation of the various categories of workers, their lawful collaboration in the economic advance of society, and the development of the sense of their responsibility for the realization of the common good."[114]

When Paul wrote that in 1971, the labor organizations that had been founded as explicitly Catholic, for example, the French Confédération Française des Travailleurs Chrétiens (French Confederation of Christian Workers or CFTC), had lost almost all their religious identity. Most of the CFTC had migrated into the secular Confédération française démocratique du travail (French Democratic Confederation of Labour or CFDT) in 1964. However, unions themselves were still an important social force. Paul took their power for granted, warning against unmerited strikes that crossed "limit beyond which the harm caused to society become inadmissible."[115] The world then changed. Union membership declined significantly in subsequent decades. In the OECD, a group of mostly rich countries, the proportion of workers who are members of unions has fallen to 3 percent from 16 percent since 1978.[116] The explanation

---

113. Leo XIII, *Rerum Novarum*, 55.

114. Paul VI, Apostolic Letter *Octogesima Adveniens* (May 14, 1971), 14.

115. Paul VI, *Octogesima Adveniens*, 14.

116. From "Trade Union Density" at https://www.oecd.org/employment/collective-bargaining .htm.

78   CHAPTER 2

for the drop is disputed. In my view, it is both a sign of the spread of alienation, the fundamental loneliness of modern society that is discussed several times in the course of this book, and a tribute to the increasingly fair treatment of workers.

Whatever the reasons for the unions' troubles, however, their diminution challenges the traditional prounion slant of the Catholic Social Teaching. The challenge is increased by the narrowing of the perspective of many leaders and members of surviving labor unions. Too often unions have become little more than self-interested lobby groups that vigorously defend their members' narrow interests while showing depressingly little interest in national or international solidarity or justice. Benedict XVI took note of the problem, challenging the policy of "defending the interests of their registered members." He argued that unions can "demonstrate authentic ethical and cultural motivations" through the preferential option for the poor, by helping "workers in developing countries where social rights are often violated."[117] That call has received almost no response from unions, a silence that suggests that this part of the teaching is due for a substantial refinement.

The next two principles are not exclusively, or even primarily, economic, but they fit in this chapter because they emerged largely in the economic discussions in the early decades of the development of the teaching.

Principle 4: Subsidiarity

To understand subsidiarity (as well as solidarity, which follows), I think it is helpful to start with the line of thinking that best articulates the opposition to this doctrine—the political-historical synthesis of G. W. F. Hegel.[118] I should say at the beginning that this

---

117. Benedict XVI, *Caritas in Veritate*, 64.

118. The key text is G. W. F. Hegel, *Philosophy of Right*, trans. T. M. Knox (Oxford: Oxford University Press, 1942 [1821]). The range of interpretation of Hegel's ideas is vast, in part because his ideas are wide-ranging and have been so influential and in part because his writing is so obscure. Paul Franco, *Hegel's Philosophy of Freedom* (New Haven, Conn.: Yale University Press, 1999) expounds the political philosophy much as I understand it, although I think he underestimates Hegel's fundamental hostility to the typical "liberal," noninterventionist, and self-expressive ideals of political and personal freedom. Rose, *Property and Persuasion*, chap. 2, somewhat unwittingly sketches out one of the Hegelian developments of the early modern period—the replacement of particular and irrational "ancient constitutions" with the modern style of centralizing and rationalizing written constitution, most notably the American version.

ECONOMIC ISSUES IN AN INDUSTRIAL AGE 79

approach is idiosyncratic. To my knowledge, few writers have placed crucial elements of the Social Teaching in a dialogue with this particular intellectual counterparty.[119] It is far more common to present subsidiarity as a response to some directly political ideas and to see socialism, classical liberalism, or some post-Christian cultural-political amalgam as the leading foil of the Catholic Social Teaching as a whole. This is not the place for a robust defense of my use of Hegel, but I hope the following discussion will at least provide some insight into the central Catholic claims about freedom and virtue in modern societies.

I admit that Hegel's name does not appear in any magisterial document (to my knowledge). However, I think that his visions of the right and inevitable direction of history and society and of the nature of human fulfilment present something like an antithesis of the Catholic understanding. In my view, his ideas and the ways in which they have been deployed express much of what is both best and worst about the modern world.

There is little question about the influence of Hegel's ideas on modern society. It has been tremendous, if often indirect. He and his intellectual followers helped frame all forms of socialism, totalitarianism, and big government liberalism. I would argue Hegelian considerations have also helped shape the bureaucratic administrations that are common to social democracy and its politically more authoritarian rivals. The interwoven political-technical-social arrangements of bureaucracy come in many varieties, but, taken together, they can be considered the preeminent contemporary system for organizing, separating, and integrating the government and the economy. They all share a Hegelian commitment to uniting the whole population under and into a spiritual-administrative organization.

What is this Hegelian vision? The Prussian thinker argued that human history is guided by a Spirit that has led humanity along a crooked but positive historical path. The narrative started with slavery—to human masters, to the physically hostile world, and to individual passions. It will end in the fullness of freedom, a freedom

---

119. One who has, at least briefly, is Archbishop Roland Minnerath. See his "The Fundamental Principles of Social Doctrine. The Issue of Their Interpretation" in *Pursuing the Common Good: How Solidarity and Subsidiarity Can Work Together*, ed. Margaret S. Archer and Pierpaolo Donati (Vatican City: The Pontifical Academy of Social Sciences, 2008), 45–56, reference to Hegel on p. 53.

that has much more in common with the Christian notion of freedom as living in truth than with the mere lack of restraint so often praised by modern, non-Hegelian philosophers. Between the beginning and the end, the Hegelian Spirit develops through a long series of conflicts, each one ending with societies dominated by larger and more abstract—*rational* is Hegel's word—organizations than those that came before. These organizations work more closely with governments that unevenly but steadily become less tyrannical and arbitrary, more constrained by law and written rule, more reliant on reasonably impartial bureaucrats, more centralized and uniform in their practices, and less buttressed by their own traditions and by the authority of organized religions.

As history advances along this inescapable path, small and personal organizations are gradually replaced by larger and more impersonal ones. Propriety and mutual obligations are reduced to property and rights, sentiment yields to more rational considerations, and rituals and customs to more calculated contracts. The religions, sciences, arts, and philosophies advance as part of the Spirit, all expressed in accord with the unifying and elevating will of the Hegelian State.

The terminus of this Hegelian history, which will come in the indefinite future, is the formation of the totally abstract and rational society, to be embodied in a single Spirit-guided State. By then, all nonstate organizations—whether based on family, business, culture, religion, or leisure interests—will either have withered away completely or have become totally aligned with, and totally subservient to, the State. This may sound totalitarian, but in Hegel's mind it is the fulfilment of freedom, because this State perfectly expresses both the universal Spirit of the Idea of Reason and each individual person's spiritual and rational will. In Hegel's words, "a State is then well constituted and internally powerful when the private interest of its citizens is one with the common interest of the State; when the one finds its gratification and realization in the other."[120] The initiative and genius of individuals and societies helps shape the crooked path of history, but all the jagged and apparently random twists and turns lead to a single end. Societies are destined to be superseded by or subsumed into the total good, which is identified exclusively with and by the State.

---

120.   G. W. F. Hegel, *The Philosophy of History* (Kitchener, ON: Batoche Books, 2001[1840]), 37.

A Catholic might think of Hegel's State as an inferior and excessively worldly imitation of the Church that is the body of Christ. In the Church, after all, each person's private interest in salvation is identical to the body's common interest in joining with its head, who is the Christ. In Hegel's understanding, it is the Church that is inferior. While Christianity first fully revealed the nature of God to humanity, history moves forward. Even Protestant Christianity, which Hegel saw as the most advanced religion, can only offer a limited dimension of the Spirit's freedom and truth. At the end of history, there will be no place for any independent Church because the completed State will be "the way of God in the world,"[121] expressing and embodying the fullness of the Spirit. History is getting closer to those end times, when the State is everything, when families will have no reason to emulate the Holy Family, and when supposedly there will be no Holy Spirit who will be able to blow where it wills.[122]

Hegel was especially scornful of what he saw as the retrogressive anachronism that was the Catholic Church, clinging to its arcane doctrines and arbitrary hierarchy. Indeed, he saw Catholicism, with its sensuality, its priests, and its claim to a higher loyalty than the State, as almost the antithesis of his notion of a true religious manifestation of the Spirit. His deep and lifelong antagonism to Catholicism was not merely an accident of his Protestant education or an emotional reaction to the rigidity of too many Catholic thinkers of his time. It was entirely in accord with his entire philosophy of history and with his understanding of true religion as both essentially private, a common theme in the modern thinking I described in chapter 1 and practically, if only eventually, subservient to the full political, cultural, and social control of the State.[123]

The Church's call for "subsidiarity" was and is one Catholic way of saying that the post-Catholic phases of the Hegelian progression is to be feared rather than welcomed. True, Pius XI did not mention Hegel when he introduced subsidiarity as a "most weighty principle, which cannot be set aside or changed." He explained that "it is an

---

121.   Hegel, *Philosophy of Right*, addition to sec. 258.

122.   cf. Jn 3:8.

123.   For Hegel on Catholicism, see Lawrence S. Stepelevich, "Hegel and Roman Catholicism," *Journal of the American Academy of Religion* 60, no. 4 (1992): 673–91; Peter Jonkers, "Hegel on Catholic Religion," in *Hegel's Philosophy of the Historical Religions*, ed. Bart Labuschagne and Timo Slootweg (Leiden: Brill, 2012), 177–206; Henri de Lubac, *La postérité spiritualle de Joachim de Flore* (Paris: Editions Lethielleux, 1979), vol. 1, 360–77.

injustice and at the same time a grave evil and disturbance of right order to assign to a greater and higher association what lesser and subordinate organizations can do. . . . The supreme authority of the State ought, therefore, to let subordinate groups handle matters and concerns of lesser importance . . . those in power should be sure that the more perfectly a graduated order is kept among the various associations, in observance of the principle of 'subsidiary function.'"[124] However, in less august words, he is saying that Hegel is wrong to think that "civil society," his term for every community outside of the State, becomes freer when it is guided by and fully aligned with the will and good of the State. On the contrary, according to Pius, governments and all the organs of civil society ("associations") have their own appropriate scope of action. Governments are at the top of hierarchy of authority, so they should limit their direct action to issues with the broadest scope. The central state is at the top of all governments and its direct action should be especially limited.[125]

Subsidiarity expresses the richness of the Catholic understanding of how organizations should tie together three disparate elements of the human condition: created humanity's need for community, sinful humanity's need for direction, and potentially redeemed humanity's ambition for higher things. In particular, the hierarchical organization of the Church was described in one of the documents of the Second Vatican Council as an organization built on what amounts to subsidiarity. The bishops' power "is not eliminated by the supreme, universal power [of the Pope]; on the contrary, it receives from it assertion, strength and vindication."[126]

In the same spirit but more politically, Benedict XVI articulated the principle of subsidiarity in a splendidly positive way. "Subsidiarity respects personal dignity by recognizing in the person a subject who is always capable of giving something to others. By considering reciprocity as the heart of what it is to be a human being, subsidiarity is the most effective antidote against any form of all-encompassing welfare state."[127] This welfare state, a powerful manifestation of Hege-

---

124. Pius XI, Encyclical Letter *Quadragesimo Anno* (May 15, 1931), 79–80.

125. For helpful historical background on the concept of subsidiarity in the context of Church, legal, and social history, see Russell Hittinger, "The Coherence of the Four Basic Principles of Catholic Social Doctrine—An Interpretation," in *Pursuing the Common Good*, ed. Archer and Donati, 75–123.

126. Vatican Council II, *Lumen Gentium*, (November 21, 1964), 27.

127. Benedict XVI, *Caritas in Veritate*, 57.

lian development, is discussed in more detail in chapter 6. Here my interest is in what might be considered its antithesis, subsidiarity. The subsidaristic approach to social organization upholds human dignity, reflects the multiplicity of human social arrangements, and emphasizes that the government is there to serve the common good of the governed, rather than to compel the people to idolize the state and to live by state-endorsed moral standards, standards in post-Christian countries are moving away from their Christian roots.

The idea of subsidiarity is often present when the word is not used. Any understanding of society as a community that is made up of many smaller communities is an endorsement of subsidiarity. Any argument in favor of local control of local decisions, reliance on nongovernmental organizations, spontaneous local organizing, locally owned businesses, and direct community involvement is a call for subsidiarity. Any argument against overbearing, impersonal, and culturally distant bureaucracies, against intrusive governments, against the standardization of mass production, or against the centralization of authority ultimately rests on the value of something like subsidiarity.

In practice, subsidiarity is found wherever the smaller is supported by the larger. It is found when the enveloping communities help families fulfill their responsibility to raise children in love, truth, and faith. It is not found when the domineering state takes over this responsibility, often defining its own truth and denying any religious faith. Subsidiarity is found in businesses that set their own course, aided by regulations and by helpful financial systems. It is not found in government-industrial, government-commercial, and megafinancial complexes that are dominated by gigantic corporations. Subsidiarity is found in charitable organizations that are inspired by love of neighbor and in educational institutions that are inspired by the love of truth. It is not found when those organizations and institutions are treated as tools of the proto-Hegelian State. Subsidiarity is found is leisure activities in which the participants set the pace and define the goals. It is not found in industries of commercial leisure activities that aim to entrance and sedate the masses. Subsidiarity is found in local governments that address local problems with due attention to the wider implications of policies. It is not found in centralized administrations that impose standardized solutions. Subsidiarity is found in artistic and spiritual endeavors, both individual and shared,

84   CHAPTER 2

that are supported by communities. It is not found when art and worship are under the control of official or quasi-official Ministries of Taste.

Although praise of "localism" and complaints about centralizing Hegelian tendencies are fairly common, the word *subsidiarity* is rarely used outside of Catholic circles and not all that often within them. Aficionados of the European Union know of an exception, since subsidiarity has been a legally binding principle governing this supernational venture since 1992.[128] The affirmation, contained in the Maastricht treaty, was almost ironic. It accompanied an expansion of the EU's centralized and bureaucratic authorities.

The European development is typical. Subsidiarity has been on the losing end of history for centuries. Hegel himself took note of one of the turning points. When he described Napoleon as "this world-soul [i.e., representative of the Spirit of history] . . . who . . . astride a horse, reaches out over the world and masters it,"[129] he intuited something more than the French leader's military prowess. Napoleon brought to his empire the latest and most rationalized French version of centralized and competent bureaucracies, standardizing everything from educational systems to house numbers and weights and measures. The antisubsidiarity mindset and methods took root, eventually flourishing in all of Europe and around the world. One nadir was reached with the secular dictatorships of the twentieth century. The common goal of all these authoritarians was this: "Everything in the State, nothing outside the State, nothing against the State,"[130] in the succinct formula of Italian dictator Benito Mussolini. The omnipresence, omnipotence, and exclusivity of a single guiding national force, whether a party, a semidivine ruler or a people (represented by a government), was the antithesis of subsidiarity.

Some observers thought that this mind-dominating state was destined to disappear after the Soviet Union collapsed in 1991. As

---

128. Council of the European Communities, *Treaty on European Union* (Maastricht 1992), Preamble and II (4). 2018. See also EUR-lex. "The Principle of Subsidiarity". European Union, 2015.

129. From G. W. F. Hegel, "Hegel to Niethammer, October 13, 1806," in *Hegel: The Letters*, trans. Clark Butler and Christine Seiler (Bloomington, Ind.: Indiana University Press 1984). On the spread of French ideas through Europe, see Michael Broers, "'Les Enfants du Siècle': An Empire of Young Professionals and the Creation of a Bureaucratic, Imperial Ethos in Napoleonic Europe," in Crooks and Parsons, *Empires and Bureaucracy*, 344–63.

130. Benito Mussolini, "Discorso del 28 Ottobere 1925 ai cittadini milanese." Accessed at http://www.mussolinibenito.it/discorsodel28_10_1925.htm (my translation.).

I write, though, reports of this death look vastly exaggerated. The current authoritarians in Russia, Turkey, and the Philippines share the grimly familiar ideology of state-before-all, state-defines-truth, state-above-law. Less grim, at least superficially, is the progress of the centralizing Hegelian Spirit in democratically governed countries. Although this type of political system may well offer the least toxic realistic political alternative to oppressive dictatorships, democratically elected governments have certainly not supported subsidiarity. On the contrary, the organs of these extensive states have gradually woven themselves ever more intricately, and with ever more domination, into the overall social fabric. They have undermined or co-opted the authority of families and an increasing number of nongovernmental bodies. The result is that social democratic societies have ever fewer truly independent organizations and institutions to stand between individuals and their welfare-providing, school-operating, economy-regulating, and wealth-redistributing governments. Whenever a democratic government takes over the tasks or funding of a nonstate charity or whenever such a government mandates the goals and rules for any aspect of social life, something is either actually or potentially being "absorbed"[131] into a proto-Hegelian State.

Any reduction of subsidiarity always can be justified as promoting something good—social improvements, economic efficiency, or even, as I explain shortly, the recognized Catholic virtue of solidarity. Still, Catholics should be uncomfortable about the trend. Institutionally, the decline of subsidiarity is a threat to the Church, which is itself a subsidiary institution of civil society. Culturally, Pius XI and his successors have been quite right to identify the loss of subsidiary as a loss of personal freedom and mutual enrichment.

Discomfort is different from surprise. Catholics should understand that the expansion of the state reflects the great internal weakness of the individualistic approach to freedom expounded by some philosophers of popular democracy. These heirs to the tradition of John Locke and John Stuart Mill, sometimes called classical liberals and sometimes libertarians, genuinely believe that modern governments can and should be small. They are mistaken for at least two reasons.

First, social structures that fully support the amoral liberties of individuals without promoting any transcendental orientation are

---

131. Pius XI, *Quadragesimo Anno*, 79.

unnatural and unsustainable. As I explained in chapter 1, people want and need communities, transcendence, and authoritative guidance. If a society that embodied totally the values of Lockean liberalism could ever be created, it would not last. Social authorities cannot merely protect property rights and prevent violent conflicts, because people need more than that to thrive in their created, fallen, and redeemed nature, as members of ordered and purposeful communities. The citizens of a putative minimal Lockean state would quickly and inevitably ask for help in satisfying their fundamental social needs and desires. The political authorities would be one of the first places they would turn. The popes have understood this well. Pius XI looked back at the budding nineteenth-century culture of "liberalistic individualism, which subordinates society to the selfish use of the individual"[132] and saw that it was fatally flawed. Its godlessness left people open to the lure of the "autocratic abuse of State power,"[133] first in "atheistic communism"[134] and subsequently in what one of his successors would call the liberal societies' "burdensome system of bureaucratic control which dries up the wellsprings of initiative and creativity."[135]

Second, classical liberals believe that only truly autonomous individuals can make truly free decisions. In a sense, Catholics agree. The Second Vatican Council noted approvingly that "everywhere there is growing steadily a sense of autonomy and responsibility [that is] extremely important for the spiritual and moral maturity of men."[136] However, even without considering how modern autonomy can lead modern man into the false belief that "he is self-sufficient,"[137] minimal governments cannot protect and promote true autonomy.

Autonomy requires freedom, and freedom is incomplete when it is limited by ignorance, poverty, illness, or oppressive obligations to other people. In addition, people are not free when they are enthralled to any creed or organization that falsely claims to provide binding rules or divine guidance. The governors of any self-declared liberal society must overcome every item on this daunting list of obstacles. The responsibilities are awesome. For example, rulers must decide

---

132.   Pius XI, Encyclical Letter *Divini Redemptoris* (March 19, 1937), 29.

133.   Pius XI, *Divini Redemptoris*, 29.

134.   Pius XI, *Divini Redemptoris*, 3.

135.   John Paul II, *Centesimus Annus*, 25. Jacques Maritain, *La personne et le bien commun* (Paris: Desclée de Brouwer, 1947); chap. 5 presents this argument in more philosophical detail.

136.   Vatican Council II, *Gaudium et Spes*, 55.

137.   Vatican Council II, *Gaudium et Spes*, 57.

ECONOMIC ISSUES IN AN INDUSTRIAL AGE 87

what ignorance is and how to combat it, how to eliminate poverty and control illness, what obligations are oppressive and how to lift them, and which creeds and organizations are deceptive and how to limit them. In short, for a liberal society to protect freedom, it must become ever more like the Hegelian State, for better and for worse.

The historical shift in the use of the word *liberal* demonstrates the paradox.[138] The classical liberalism of the nineteenth century, supposedly revived in recent decades as neoliberalism, promoted a small state, while twentieth-century American liberalism endorsed big government. This verbal shift echoes the French Revolution's much quicker transition in policies, from the National Assembly's proclamations of individual liberties to the Terror's democratic tyranny.[139] In recent decades, it has become clearer than some of the claimed freedoms offered by the liberal Me Society are strikingly similar to those promoted by the authoritarian Big State. In particular, Catholics are increasingly aware that both promote an oppressive liberty from claims to unconditional obedience by any organization other than the state and from any organization that proclaims an absolute or God-given truth.[140]

However, any proto-Hegelian governments operates, whether it is democratic or authoritarian, dutifully and fairly elected or held in power through fear and force, subsidiarity is always an impediment to its goals. Any organization or institution that opposes the agenda of the ruler or the ruling ideology will be considered an obstacle to progress or the forces of history. Catholics should recognize that under such a government the Church can only be tolerated as long as it is ineffective. At worst, the historical legacy of liberal anticlericalism leads to total religious intolerance. At best, any strong evangelical Christian movement will face significant hostility from any government with even modest Hegelian ambitions or in any society in which the Spirit has moved past the age of religious organizations. (I discuss church-state relations in chapter 4.)

138. See the sources cited in note 49 for background information.

139. My approach to the French Revolution and its role in history is strongly influenced by François Furet, both his *Penser la révolution française* (Paris: Gallimard, 1978) and, with Denis Richet, *La révolution française* (Paris: Hachette, Nouvelle édition 2001).

140. Personally, I agree with the argument that the entire Lockean ideas of freedom is "ultimately inimical" to the true freedom and freely proposed truth of the Catholic Church. However, I have not made this radical claim in this book, because the Magisterium has come nowhere near endorsing it. The quote is from Michael Hanby, "Absolute Pluralism: How the Dictatorship of Relativism Dictates," *Communio International Catholic Review* 40 (2013): 556.

Christians must reject Hegel's historical determinism, but their rejection has to be tempered with realism. They should admit that modern governments have done just what the philosopher said they would do, just what Pius XI said they should not do. States have increasingly absorbed the functions or shaped the purpose of many smaller organizations, including charitable and economic ones. In the economic realm, the main concern of this chapter, government are now by far the largest single force. There are still many non-state economic organizations, some of which are fiercely or mildly independent, but the trend is clearly away from subsidiarity. Private enterprises must follow every more extensive and detailed government rules (even in the United States in the time of President Donald Trump), big companies steadily take market share from small, distant industrial production replaces local craftsmen, and decisions on matters as diverse as technological standards and indications for surgery are made at the highest, rather than the lowest, possible level.

Realism about the practical weakness of subsidiarity and the effectiveness of antisubsidiarity governments leads to an intellectual quandary, a problem or paradox that is one of the central themes of this book. The modern world is neither simply bad nor good, so the right Christian judgments on that world and its motivating principles must be nuanced and mixed. Catholic thinkers are often tempted to reject such complex judgments. Their resistance is certainly understandable. In this case, for example, it would be easier for anyone writing about the Catholic Social Teaching if all the effects of every move against subsidiarity were dreadful. Then a straightforward condemnation would be possible. The truth, though, is far too complicated for such a simple judgment. Some denials of subsidiarity, for example those enforced by totalitarian governments, have certainly been purely awful, but mixed judgments are needed for such systems as industrial mass production and welfare states. As I discuss in chapter 5, both certainly violate the principle of subsidiarity; they always and everywhere supplant the initiative of individuals, small organizations, and even whole communities. However, mass production has helped feed, house, and care for the poor and has made labor less onerous and life safer and more comfortable. Welfare states, discussed in chapter 6, have not only restrained some sorts of cruelty that were widespread in the early years of the industrial economy. They have also spread many of the gains of industrial prosperity throughout society.

The undeniable benefits from the decline in subsidiarity, along with the concomitant rise of ever more comprehensive and bureaucratic organizations, have inevitably shaped the development of the Catholic Social Teaching. An original hostility to modern governments with their secular agendas gradually gave way to a sometimes-grudging endorsement of particular programs, both established and desired. For the past century, principled papal and episcopal attacks on the modern reduction of social life to the dangerous polarity of state and individual have frequently been accompanied by practical calls for additional government action: to protect the environment, redistribute wealth, control incomes, create jobs, and respond to various other pressing social problems.

This particular historical trend toward greater magisterial enthusiasm for secular government may be coming to an end. Although bishops in many countries often still demand more from governments, John Paul II, Benedict XVI, and Francis have all expressed grave doubts about the moral direction of what the first of them called the "Social Assistance State."[141] Indeed, the Church may be in the process of breaking the uneasy unofficial concordat between it and increasingly Hegelian States. The disputed issues are primary moral (the promotion of same-sex marriage, for example), rather than economic, but Catholics who reject or resist some of the demands of the state in favor of subsidiarity should also expect to make some significant economic changes.

Principle 5: Solidarity

In Hegel's vision, all merely individual bonds become less meaningful as history advances. At the end, only the State will matter. During the increasingly large-scale conflicts that inevitably precede the formation of that State, individuals become ever more subservient to ever-larger and ever more impersonal warring groups. Marx put an economic spin on the Hegelian vision, arguing that the predominant struggle in industrial economies will ultimately be between the almost totally impersonal forces—the bourgeoisie with their "capital" and the proletariat lump of "labor."[142]

---

141.   John Paul II, *Centesimus Annus*, 48.

142.   Karl Marx and Friedrich Engels, *Marx/Engels Selected Works*, trans. Samuel Moore, vol. 1, *The Communist Manifesto* (Moscow: Progress Publishers, 1969 [1848]), 98–137. "Society as a whole is more and more splitting up into two great hostile camps, into two great classes directly facing each other—Bourgeoisie and Proletariat" (15) and "In proportion as the bourgeoisie, i.e.,

90 CHAPTER 2

To its proponents, liberal (or methodological) individualism is at the opposite theoretical pole from Hegel's dialectic of history, but, as I just suggested, in many ways it also fits into the Hegelian model. For example, it is almost as dismissive of the inherent value of received social institutions and bonds. Influential thinkers such as Locke, Mill, and John Rawls gave priority to the individual: his or her safety, desires, and judgment. For these philosophers, all social groups—whether families, clubs, churches, or nations—are secondary. They are only formed and maintained because the individual members found and continue to find them useful.

In contrast, the Christian understanding of human nature and society is truly anti-Hegelian. As I noted in chapter 1, Christians consider social bonds, the ties of love, to be primary. People do not and should not strive above all to promote their own survival and flourishing, as the individualists say, or to promote the Spirit of History, as the various types of Hegelian statists claim. Rather, God creates all people with a mission, namely, to love God and each other. That mission, that fullness of humanity, can only take place within and through the various familial, vocational, political, and spiritual groups to which all people belong. This multifaceted socialization is essential and unchanging, not a historical phase to be transcended.

All of these communities are always ultimately based on love, because love is at the center of created and redeemed human nature. For fallen humanity, however, the obligation of love can look like grim duty. The Christian duty to love extends even, or indeed especially, to those who do not seem loveable. The duty is often unbearable without divine grace and unlikely to be fulfilled without worldly discipline. Because this joyful-dutiful love is so difficult, it is often forgotten or distorted. Communities fall into discord. They divide into warring factions and fight against each other. People, organizations, and societies can only live in love when they consciously strive to resist the temptation to replace love with hostility.

In the language of the Social Teaching, the striving for Christian love throughout society is called solidarity, the "commitment to the good of one's neighbor with the readiness, in the gospel sense, to 'lose oneself' for the sake of the other instead of exploiting him."[143] In

---

capital, is developed, in the same proportion is the proletariat, the modern working class, developed—a class of laborers, who live only so long as they find work, and who find work only so long as their labor increases capital" (18).

143. John Paul II, *Sollicitudo Rei Socialis*, 38.

ECONOMIC ISSUES IN AN INDUSTRIAL AGE 91

other words, the Christian love of each individual neighbor requires social relations that are generous to the point of sacrifice. If this practical love is spread throughout a society, it will be possible to build a civilization of love. If this love is missing, though, not only society but each member is in danger of living in isolation, which is "[o]ne of the deepest forms of poverty."[144]

As a practical matter, solidarity is the "virtue" that corresponds to and inspires every organization that reinforces the "interdependence, sensed as a system determining relationships in the contemporary world, in its economic, cultural, political, and religious elements, and accepted as a moral category."[145] Solidarity is needed for any aspect of social life to be lived in a Christian way. For example, solidarity of the healthy with those who suffer in body and mind is the best inspiration for devoted medical care. Without solidarity in spiritual matters, dialogue among religions will be sterile. Solidarity between peoples is the prerequisite for true and lasting peace (Paul VI's original phrase was a "civilization of love and peace.")[146] Solidarity on a global scale supports many cross-border commitments to the common good, seen in, for example, the globalization of air transport, sports events, environmental standards, and disaster relief. At the highest political level, global solidarity in a sinful world is enhanced by organizations that have the authority to guide and chastise nations, a theological-historical reality that has led the popes to expect much of the United Nations, perhaps too much.

I return to the larger implications of the virtue of solidarity in a little while. First, I want to follow the Catholic Social Teaching's historic interest in economic solidarity, more specifically its condemnations of the appalling lack of this form of commitment to the common good. In the modern world, the most obvious sign of this deficiency is the wide economic gap between rich and poor, which I mentioned in the discussion of the preferential option for the poor. The inequality, as it is often called, shines out in the quantity and quality of consumption, the lives of labor, and the large disparities of economic power, security, and opportunity. The gap is found within countries, both poor and rich, but most notably between the relatively few people who live in rich lands and many more inhabitants of poorer countries.

---

144. Benedict XVI, *Caritas in Veritate*, 53.

145. John Paul II, *Sollicitudo Rei Socialis*, 38.

146. Paul VI, Angeles Message *Regina Caeli* (May 17, 1970).

Pope Francis has provided a firm contemporary statement of the Social Teaching's long-standing response to this inequality: "In the present condition of global society, where injustices abound and growing numbers of people are deprived of basic human rights and considered expendable, the principle of the common good immediately becomes, logically and inevitably, a summons to solidarity."[147] In effect, the continuing injustice of global inequality is a failure of solidarity, even if the inaction comes from someone who did not personally cause the injustice and is not knowingly doing anything to continue it.

John Paul II provided a more practical agenda: the "influential" should feel "responsible for the weaker and be ready to share with them all they possess," while the weak "should do what they can for the good of all." Members of intermediate groups should "respect the interests of others."[148] What this means for particular policies is of course open for debate. The case is fairly clear for what might be called sins of commission, any practices and policies that are clearly contrary to this social virtue. Exploitative contracts, unfair trade rules, unneeded restrictions on economically motivated migration, and other injustices should simply be eliminated. However, the sins of omission are probably more significant and are much harder to identify. "What should I do?" is a haunting question.

Beyond these excellent economic teachings, solidarity has much broader implications. In particular, it guides the Christian responses to two ideas that are fundamental to some modern worldviews. One of these ideas is totally rejected and the other is warmly endorsed.

The negative response is to the idea that conflict is more natural than is concord. That presupposition is common to apparently unrelated or even antagonistic modern thinkers. For Hegel, the Spirit of freedom progresses through history by causing and then resolving often violent battles of ideas and social groups. (As I discuss in chapter 5, Hegel was persuaded that wars played a necessary and important role in the advance of the Spirit.) A similar reliance on discord can be seen in the political liberals' dislike of royalty, which presupposes or claims a fundamental, hierarchical unity, in which, in its ideal form, the divinely sustained king or queen is supported and supports his or her loyal subjects. Liberals prefer elected representative governments, which are formed from sparring political

---

147. Francis, *Laudato Si'*, 158.

148. John Paul II, *Sollicitudo Rei Socialis*, 39.

parties and which are limited by a collection of essentially hostile "checks and balances." Modern critics of political liberalism, such as Max Weber and Carl Schmitt, are no more inspired by a vision of unity. They have generally identified government as the body that can legitimately exercise violence in a society, often seeing the always-present potential to lift any self-imposed restraints on violence as the center of all power. In psychology, Sigmund Freud postulated an endless social struggle between the forces of civilization and the temptation to violence, a struggle that socialized the lifelong psychic war within each individual between responsibility and desire. In economics, there are far fewer believers in a model based on any sort of concord, for example a bureaucratic hierarchy, than devotees of a "free market" war of all against all (discussed in the next chapter), or of some sort of Marxist historical vision based on continuing Hegelian conflicts between classes or interest groups.

In the quite different Christian vision, conflict is in accord with fallen human nature, but society becomes more in accord with original and redeemed human nature whenever solidarity triumphs over discord. Peace is always better than war, agreement is always more beneficial than bitterness, sharing and cooperation are always preferable to division and strife. Any "we" is truest to our unfallen nature when we offer a unified loving response to God and neighbor. The truly human society is a civilization of love, not of repression. Sin creates divisions; solidarity heals them. Of course, nature is corrupt, so sin is unavoidable, but with grace and hard work it can be held in check.

The positive response is to universalism, the modern desire to look at the world as much as possible as a single whole. The enthusiasm should not be surprising. The modern Christian praise of social solidarity is basically a spiritual deepening of the French Revolution's virtue of *fraternité*, but that secular virtue, the brotherhood of humanity that transcends governments and all the intermediate organizations of civil society, was itself a secularization of the original Catholic Social Teaching about the ultimate divine-human community of the Christian Church. From the Acts of the Apostles onward, it was an article of faith that baptism creates a community of mutually committed Christians, a community that crosses every sort of traditional boundary: geography, language, culture, and social position.[149] The more modern Catholic emphasis on the universal scope of God's saving will, even beyond the boundaries of the visible Catholic Church, creates a solidarity that crosses the borders of professed religions. Indeed, before John XXIII introduced the word *solidarity* into the papal vocabulary,[150] it was mostly used to describe a distinctly nonreligious and purely worldly sharing.[151]

The alignment of solidarity with universalism ensures that the Church is basically pleased with the modern trends to set global standards for human rights and to share what is best about all cultures. John Paul II explicitly praised the communications technologies that allow "men and women in various parts of the world [to] feel personally affected by the injustices and violations of human rights committed in distant countries, countries which perhaps they will never visit."[152] Francis, who worries about global threats, calls for states to recognize their universal responsibility "to participate in the edification of the common good of humanity, a necessary and essential element for global balance."[153]

Conversely, Catholics should be wary of the ideology of nation-states, which often moves from a healthy solidarity of people who share a geographical, political, or cultural identity to hostile policies against foreigners and even domestic nonmembers of the "genuine" national group. John Paul II, who always considered himself a Polish patriot, said that "true patriotism never seeks to advance the well-being of one's own nation at the expense of others. . . . Nationalism, particularly in its most radical forms, is thus the antithesis of true patriotism."[154] The thought is pleasing, but it is often hard to decide whether a particular sentiment or policy actually expresses good patriotism or is really a manifestation of bad nationalism. Francis has attempted to draw a clearer line. "The Church has always encouraged love of one's people, of country; respect for the value of various cultural expressions, uses, and customs and for the just ways of living rooted in peoples. At the

---

149.   e.g., Gal 3:28.

150.   John XXIII, Encyclical Letter *Mater et Magistra* (May 15, 1961), 23.

151.   For a clear and profound discussion of the word's use and the spiritual understanding of solidarity, see Joseph Ratzinger, "Eucharist, Communion, and Solidarity," Lecture given at the Bishops' Conference of the Region of Campania in Benevento, Italy (June 2, 2002).

152.   John Paul II, *Sollicitudo Rei Socialis*, 38.

153.   Francis, *Address to the Pontifical Academy of Sciences* (May 2, 2019).

154.   John Paul II, *Address to the Fiftieth General Assembly of the United Nations* (October 5, 1995), 11.

same time, the Church has admonished individuals, peoples and governments regarding deviations from this attachment when focused on exclusion and hatred of others, when it becomes hostile, wall-building nationalism, or even racism or anti-Semitism."[155]

Solidarity is a beautiful expression of the Christian understanding of the true community of all people, but in the discussion of policies there can be a tension between this universalist solidarity and the principle of subsidiarity, which expresses a preference for entrusting decisions to the smallest effective organization of civil society. In practice, the more the world is standardized and unified—the less it is divided into small units of civil society—the easier it is to see a distant neighbor as worthy of love. However, the more the world is standardized and unified, the more cultures will tend to be blended, homogenized, and detached from particular communities. The two virtues, subsidiarity and solidarity, certainly can coexist and even reinforce each other, most wonderfully in the ideal of an intensely local and still completely unified terrestrial Catholic Church, but one or the other may be more urgently needed in particular times and places.[156]

Over the past five decades, the Magisterium has praised both virtues, but in practice has more often called for solidarity than for subsidiarity. That was the appropriate response to a world in which expanding welfare states and economic globalization, both signs of solidarity, primarily promoted virtue, while the gap between rich and poor in the world, a sign of the absence of solidarity, was widening. It may be time to reconsider the balance, now that welfare states are less supportive of the Christian understanding of the good life, as I discuss in chapter 6, and global material poverty is receding.

To suggest that subsidiarity may be due for a revival is almost to predict an apparent reversal of some of the advice of the Catholic Social Teaching. It is, of course, not a prediction that the truth will change, for truth is unchanging. However, the changes in the world might bring different aspects of the constant truth into greater prominence. The changes in the economic world are certainly significant. I begin the next chapter with a discussion of two such changes, both of which—I predict—will have a significant influence on the Catholic Social Teaching of the future.

---

155.   Francis, *Address to the Pontifical Academy of Sciences.*

156.   For a collection of essays exploring the tensions, many of which claim that they either do not really exist or can easily be reconciled, see Archer and Donati, eds., *Pursuing the Common Good.*

CHAPTER 3

Economics Ideas, New and Old

AT THE END OF THE LAST CHAPTER, I promised to discuss two changes in the economic world. They are closely related. The first, the increasing confidence in the ability of people to shape the world according to their will, raises questions of judgment—whether or when this trust is merited and whether the human technological will is actually good—and of religion—whether technology itself has become an idol. The second change, the tremendous increase in affluence that this world-shaping ability has generated, changes the balance of moral challenges related to economics, because greed takes new forms in the more prosperous world.

I have to admit that the Magisterium has not fully shared my interest in any of these questions. I certainly wish it were otherwise, since I believe that the Catholic intellectual tradition is particularly well equipped to offer helpful and wise counsels of imperfection on both of them. Some of my comments are basically expansions of the hints provided in magisterial documents, but much of what I say takes the form of questions, suggestions, or speculation.

The Virtues and Vices of Technical Ingenuity

Rerum Novarum was prescient in some ways, but Leo XIII was clearly not thinking about some important components of economic change. In particular, he did not mention any of the significant technical developments of the preceding century: the railroad, steamship, and telegraph; the massive increase in agricultural productivity; or the discovery of antisepsis and anesthesia. In common with all the leading economists of his day, he seemed hardly to notice the crucial contribution the new machines and new sources of energy were making to everyday life and to social relations. If anything, Leo's economic ideas seemed to be set in the predominantly agrarian economy that was waning rapidly in much of Europe by 1891. By then, his encouragement of frugal living to allow the purchase of the "working man's little estate" was already old-fashioned.[1]

Since Leo's time, the Magisterium has caught up with industrialization. In 1963, the Second Vatican Council praised "wonderful technological discoveries."[2] John Paul II wrote in 1987 about "the many real benefits provided in recent times by science and technology, [which] bring freedom from every form of slavery" and about the "created goods and the products of industry . . . constantly being enriched by scientific and technological progress."[3] The mention of slavery is especially significant. John Paul understood that as labor became more productive, the grip of necessity's grim hand was lightened. The drudgery of labor was lessoned, and there could no longer be an economic justification for actual legal slavery or other socially oppressive work arrangements.

Technological ingenuity deserves the magisterial respect it has already received. I believe it probably deserves still more. The commendation that Jesus gives to the merchant who multiplies the king's talents is now due to the whole modern economic community,[4] which has spread so much good through new tools, techniques, and organizations. There are many ways in which all people today, especially but not only those who reside in rich countries, can now live more in accord with their created and redeemed nature than ever in the past. The earth can support more people who can love each other and worship God; more of those people can be expected to live their full span of years; more people have the time and material things needed to develop and take advantage of their God-given intellectual, artistic, and emotional gifts; distance hardly restricts the spread knowledge or limits the gifts of friendship.

The various aspects of modern economy that have allowed this technological ingenuity to flourish and spread its valuable fruits

---

1. Leo XIII, *Rerum Novarum*, 5.

2. Vatican Council II, Decree on the Media of Social Communications *Inter Mirifica* (December 4, 1963), 1.

3. John Paul II, *Sollicitudo Rei Socialis*, 28, 29.

4. Mt 25:14–30.

around the world also deserve praise. Quite rightly, Paul VI and John Paul II commended businesspeople for their spirit of enterprise. This spirit creates economic organizations that are effective, imaginative, careful, ambitious, and ethical. It builds or supports administrative skills, dynamic leadership, professional integrity, careful training, responsive communities, strong consciences, disciplined obedience, organized creativity, and social flexibility. These characteristics are all in accord with original and redeemed human nature and all have flourished in prosperous industrial economies.

Christians should appreciate the worldly improvements wrought by technology and the best of the modern business spirit, but they must also be wary of the lures that this worldly ingenuity has brought. Technology is easily turned to destruction; Christians must, for example, fight against the destructive consequences of the arms industry's all-too-modern efficiency. The attention paid to technology and innovation can distract people from the kingdom of heaven, which is far greater good than anything earthly; Christians must keep their spiritual bearings. The pursuit of worldly improvement for consumers can lead to the mistreatment of the people who labor at production; Christians need to recall the priority of all people, workers and customers, over things. In rich countries, many people seem to suffer from consumerism, the unhealthy desire for ever more stuff; Christians should remember that they are called to desire love in excess, which should lead to a diminishment of selfish desires for things (I discuss consumerism later in the chapter).

Pope Benedict XVI was particularly concerned with the dangers of a narrowly technical understanding of development. He feared a this-worldliness and an exaggerated reliance on human ability, which both emerged out of and led people further into a spiritual wasteland where God could have no real role. People would be so enthralled with the things of this world that they would lose their appreciation for the underlying and ultimate goods of being and truth. They would be tempted to treat technology as "an ideological power."[5] Purely human ideologies that mimic the truth of faith are tremendously powerful in the modern age. Benedict feared that technology was becoming one of these false gods of the era, and a particularly dangerous one.

More generally, Benedict worried that the treatment of social

---

5.   Benedict XVI, *Caritas in Veritate*, 70.

problems as solely "technical," rather than as fundamentally moral, both springs from and encourages the "confusion between ends and means."[6] Ever more ingenious manipulations of the material world can stall the true development of solidarity and other virtues. The confusion easily leads to a blind acceptance of all technical advances as basically good and to the unthinking assumption that all human problems have technical solutions. Francis expresses the same idea in his usual trenchant terms: "Technology tends to absorb everything into its ironclad logic."[7] There can be, however, no merely technical answer to sin, whether personal or social. I discuss the context and wider implications of the papal discussion of technology and the "technocratic paradigm"[8] in chapter 8.

The Fading Challenge of Poverty and the New Challenges of Affluence

In the history of the Catholic Social Teaching, and indeed in the history of humankind, poverty—widespread, persistent, and apparently inevitable—has long been a central problem. Pope Leo XIII looked with dismay at a new sort of poverty, the swelling masses of the urban proletariat. As I mentioned in the last chapter, his gloom was premature. Thanks in part to the adoption of the sort of policies encouraged by the Magisterium, the descendants of the wretched poor of Europe and America have become today's prosperous working and middle classes. Material desperation, which seemed to be on the rise through most of the nineteenth century, has all but disappeared in Italy and many other traditionally Catholic and Christian countries.

The improvements in industrialized countries were welcome, but John XXIII and Paul VI were shocked by the widespread poverty in the rest of the world. In particular, they were appalled at the enormous gap in lifestyles between the world's relatively few rich people and the poor masses. Even worse was the difference in the pace of development: "the rich nations are progressing with rapid strides while the poor nations move forward at a slow pace."[9] That reading of relative economic gains was common and defensible at the time,

---

6. Benedict XVI, *Caritas in Veritate*, 70, 71.

7. Francis, *Laudato Si'*, 108.

8. Francis, *Laudato Si'*, 101–14.

9. Paul VI, *Populorum Progressio*, 8.

but it has been proven wrong. The gap between the world's rich and poor has narrowed. While the billion or two people who still live in terrible poverty are a billion or two too many, both the number of people and the proportion of the world's population in this tragic position has been shrinking steadily. Barring cataclysm, both number and ratio should continue to shrink—far too slowly, to be sure— as education spreads and the proven habits of prosperity take firmer hold in more economically backward places.

The progress has been slow enough that Francis is quite justified in railing against complacency over the remaining huge wealth gap. From a global perspective, rich countries and the rich class in poor countries remain relatively small wealthy islands surrounded by large seas of poverty. However, if the recent trends continue, the moral economic balance will change. Not only will crude physical want become ever less of a global scandal, but wealth will increase enough everywhere for the moral challenges of widespread affluence to become a significant part of the Catholic agenda. From a worldly perspective, these challenges may seem minor in comparison to starvation, but, in the light of eternity—the only light that should be used to illuminate Christian judgments—they can be even more daunting. Jesus, after all, worried more about the moral difficulties of the rich than about those of the poor.

Here is a preliminary list of the issues.

Consumerism

The desire to accumulate stuff for unworthy reasons—whether for trivial pleasures or to demonstrate power and social position—is literally as old as sin. Eve presumably felt a bit of this "lust of the eyes" when she saw that "the fruit of the tree was good for food and pleasing to the eye."[10] Whether the advent of widespread prosperity has increased the temptation to waste spiritual and practical effort on acquiring possessions is a question for philosophers and for theologians of history. It may well be that the causality was primarily in the other direction; the desire for more stuff motivated people to put additional effort into improving technology and adding to material prosperity. In either case, industrial wealth certainly provides many new opportunities for the excessive love of things, and those things

---

10. 1 Jn 2:16; Gn 3:6.

ECONOMICS IDEAS, NEW AND OLD

are much desired in a culture that favors "having" over "being," as John Paul II liked to say,[11] and that has "too many means and only a few insubstantial ends,"[12] as Francis put it.

The desires for extravagances and status symbols are long-standing targets for Christian moralists. In a sense, today's more affluent people and societies have merely added a new kind of materialist desire to be condemned. Thanks to the wonders of mass production, the masses can engage in an endless search for the new and better, the more comfortable and the slightly different. The combination of industrial prosperity and material ambition can turn shopping into an intoxicating activity, in which the rituals of choosing and buying become a sort of fixation.

The popes have long been aware of this modern variation on a universal theme of fallen human nature. John Paul II helpfully introduced an already established sociological term, consumerism, to describe and condemn this denigration of human dignity. He identified it as a sort of false progress, a "super-development, which consists in an excessive availability of every kind of material goods." It "easily makes people slaves of 'possession' and of immediate gratification, with no other horizon than the multiplication or continual replacement of the things already owned with others still better." The "crass materialism" is "at the same time a radical dissatisfaction, because one quickly learns . . . that the more one possesses the more one wants, while deeper aspirations remain unsatisfied and perhaps even stifled."[13]

Like all kinds of greed, consumerism is rarely perceived by its practitioners as a vice. Rather, it takes the form of an unobserved or denied excess of a genuine virtue. The new coat, house, tourist voyage, or gadget is not consciously desired for the mere sake of having more, but because there is a need for, a benefit from, or just a harmless pleasure in this or that additional bit of consumption. Similarly, the excesses of consumerism undermine the genuine communities that can be created and fortified by consumption. A frantic craving for the latest fashion item or a table at the coolest new restaurant is a consumerist exaggeration of the virtuous desire to build up solidarity and community though buying similar clothes or eating together.

---

11.   cf. John Paul II, *Sollicitudo Rei Socialis*, 28.

12.   Francis, *Laudato Si'*, 203.

13.   John Paul II, *Sollicitudo Rei Socialis*, 28.

The popes since John Paul II have regularly condemned consumerism. Francis began his first major papal writing, *Evangelii Gaudium*, by associating it with "the desolation and anguish born of a complacent yet covetous heart, the feverish pursuit of frivolous pleasures, and a blunted conscience,"[14] and later in the apostolic exhortation says that "[t]oday's economic mechanisms promote inordinate consumption, yet it is evident that unbridled consumerism combined with inequality proves doubly damaging to the social fabric."[15] However, he has joined his predecessors in not providing anything like a clear definition of what consumption is in fact "inordinate." The omission is particularly regrettable, because consumerism is a form of greed, and greed is particularly easy to identify in others and especially hard to recognize in oneself.

Christians must try to tell the wheat from the tares,[16] to distinguish humanly fulfilling consumption from soul-damaging consumerism. They should look for the virtuous mean of moderation in consumption, recognizing that this mean is not easily defined in industrial economies. Should moderation be understood relative to objective needs, so excess desire for consumption begins as soon as we want much more than we need to survive or more than society assigns us as members of a certain social class or community? Or is the excess only found in our "unbridled" subjective desires? Or perhaps we should set some objective standard of moderation, based on an analysis of the human good, social justice, and the current potential production of the economy. If so, is the relevant economy global or local? Again, I would love some more papal guidance.

Jealousy and Exclusion

At the beginning of the industrial age, some morally naïve observers predicted that the advent of universal riches would keep anyone from feeling poor. It has turned out quite differently. Many residents of rich countries seem to feel poorer than ever. Rather than glory in the panoply of things that they have, they are anxious to have more things, envious of others who have more things, bitter when anything has to be given up, and covetous of the relatively few things they lack.

---

14.   Francis, *Evangelii Gaudium*, 2.

15.   Francis, *Evangelii Gaudium*, 60.

16.   cf. Mt 13:24–30.

Social structures can provide one justification for this jealousy. The relatively poor are sometimes excluded from rich societies' genuine goods. For example, the best university educations are often reserved almost entirely, in practice if not in theory, for the children of the affluent. More usually, social structures provide an explanation for jealousy that is far from a justification. As social borders have become both more frequently defined by material possessions (e.g., owning this sort of house in that sort of neighborhood) and easier to cross, individuals are likely to feel less content with their current consumption and more resentful of other people's superior consumption experiences.

Christians can campaign for social justice, for example, for fairer access to elite education. However, they should firmly reject all materialist anxiety. The unchanging basic moral analysis of wealth and poverty condemns the bitterness of the rich at least as much as the misery of the poor. I expect the identification and moral analysis of consumption justice and jealousy will move closer to the center of the Catholic Social Teaching.

The Indolence of Affluence

Rich economies produce their consumption abundance with remarkably little effort, leaving most people much time for other tasks. What should be done with this excess? Should people have larger families? Spend more time with their children? More time studying? In prayer? Developing creative talents? In leisure activities? Shopping? Caring? Traveling? Should they be kept busy with economically pointless but time-consuming jobs? These are hard questions, which as yet do not seem to have been answered well, by either secular or religious thinkers.

I believe that too much of the time freed from necessary labor is actually spent in trivial activities. However, this indolence of industrial affluence has been poorly studied, in large part because most economists barely admit the possibility of its existence. I do not have any definitive answers, although more shopping is unlikely to feature on the list of Christian recommendations for things to do in retirement and days off. However, I am persuaded that this surplus of labor time presents a great social-moral challenge, one that will only become greater as machines and organizations become more efficient. I discuss one aspect of the problem, the faulty integral ecology of leisure, at somewhat greater length in chapter 8.

Dehumanization of Labor

Even when indolence is not a problem, work in highly efficient industrial economies tends to be boring. Much of it is repetitive, turning people into cogs in the machine of production. The advent of more powerful manufacturing machines and computers has decreased some sorts of tedious work but has increased the quantity of another type of labor that is often almost as tedious, the toil at what used to be called paperwork. In addition, many jobs are impersonal or offer only brief, formulaic, or artificial personal interactions. Worse, many jobs, indeed many whole industries, contribute nothing or next to nothing to the common good, so that thoughtful workers in them justly conclude that they are paid for wasting their time and skills. Some women seem to find the life of paid labor particularly unappealing, especially when they perceive a conflict with their distinctive feminine role of mothers and caregivers. In the modern economy, the wages for paid caring labors are generally low, as is the social status of unpaid caring labor.

All in all, the contemporary life of labor increasingly leads to social alienation (to use a Marxist word). In a generation or two, the spiritual poverty of labor could replace the material poverty of consumption as a central theme for the Catholic Social Teaching.

That is a challenge for the future. I now turn to the lingering influence of a pernicious idea of the past.

Free Markets

Some loyal Catholics seem almost to revere the economic arrangement known as the free market, free enterprise, or capitalism. The Magisterium is less keen. While the Church has many positive things to say about the modern business economy, the papal judgment of market competition has been and remains far more critical than enthusiastic.[17]

---

17. The promarket Catholic writing is extensive. Michael Novak's *Spirit of Democratic Capitalism* (New York: Simon & Schuster, 1982) is representative and popular. The voluminous publications of the Action Institute (https://acton.org/) offer the most cogent promarket Catholic thinking. The debate among Catholics is well encapsulated in Doug Bandow and David

The economists' free markets are places, sometimes literal but more often metaphorical, where individuals and entities compete freely and perhaps greedily for business, in particular for contracts to perform some economic act—labor, production, or distribution. In this model, the competition to sign such contracts leads to a continuing series of mutually agreed-upon and mutually beneficial arrangements. The most extreme enthusiasts for such markets claim that a system that relies on nothing other than self-interested competition and temporary contracts naturally produces a better economy than does any alternative, including systems that rely primarily or in part on divine law (necessarily interpreted by people), beneficent human authority, cooperative endeavors, the protection of tradition, the promotion of virtue, the pursuit of justice, and analytically guided bureaucratic management.

The moral history of this market thinking is relevant for Catholics who wish to evaluate it. The first popular work to promote what came to be called the competitive market economy was Bernard Mandeville's 1714 tale, *The Fable of the Bees*. In it, the English writer not only admitted the truth of the most prominent objection to relying on self-interested competition to guide society: that it encourages greed and frivolous consumption. He extolled the free pursuit of these "private vices" as the best way to achieve the great "public benefit" of busy workers and national wealth. Mandeville, who claimed to be a believing Christian, was popularizing a paradoxical idea that had been propounded over the previous century by a few theologians—in a society with unconstrained economic activity, the invisible hand of divine providence would somehow cancel out the conflicting desires of human depravity.[18]

This market idea percolated through the European intellectual community over the course of the eighteenth century. For example, the "invisible hand," now social rather than divine, was mentioned briefly in Adam Smith's 1776 *Wealth of Nations*. The founder of

---

Schindler, eds, *Wealth, Poverty and Human Destiny* (Wilmington, Del.: ISI Books, 2003).

18.   Bernard Mandeville, *The Fable of the Bees or Private Vices Publick Benefits*, Irwin Primer, ed. (New York: Capricorn Books, 1962 [1714]). For an analysis of the early history of this idea, see David Singh Grewel, "The Political Theology of Laissez-Faire: From *Philia* to Self-Love in Commercial Society," *Political Theology* 17 (2016): 417–33. Also helpful is Albert O. Hirschman, *The Passions and the Interests: Political Arguments for Capitalism Before its Triumph.* (Princeton, N.J.: Princeton University Press, 1997 [1977]). Emma Rothschild, *Economic Sentiments: Adam Smith, Condorcet, and the Enlightenment* (Cambridge, Mass.: Harvard University Press, 2001); chap. 5 includes a fascinating discussion of the history of the phrase "invisible hand."

modern economics is often associated with the praise of self-interest and unconstrained competition, but that is a serious misrepresentation of his views. Like other thinkers of his era who were finding their way toward a secular moral code, Smith put great emphasis on the human capacity for individual sympathy and on the value and difficulty of civic virtue. However, the economic liberals who claimed to be his intellectual followers found it useful to credit Smith with their own ideas about the ideal economic relations between individuals—competition among self-interested persons modulated only by freely agreed-upon contracts—and the ideal economic position of governments—minimal.[19]

As might be expected from a tradition that aimed, among other things, at reducing the social and political role of religious authorities, Enlightenment and rationalist enthusiasm for economic competition was generally associated with religious skepticism. For example, the Marquis de Condorcet—who was an intellectual father of the French Revolution, one of its early leaders, and eventually one of its victims—praised economic liberty. He considered commercial freedom to be part of what might be called an intellectual package that included political liberty and freedom from religious oppression.[20] Thomas Malthus, an Anglican minister who objected to Condorcet's optimism, provided a religious argument in favor of competition in his 1798 *Essay on the Principle of Population*, although he took his praise to what many people, both then and later, thought was an impious extreme. The young Malthus claimed that divine providence had ordained a permanent surplus of population over the supply of food. The perpetual shortage created a sort of market for life itself, a brutal and continual struggle to avoid starvation. Malthus believed that God's goal in creating this arrangement was to better the human race by allowing what some of his followers would later call the survival of the fittest.[21]

---

19. Adam Smith, *An Inquiry into the Nature and Causes of the Wealth of Nations* (Sao Paolo: Metalibri, 2007 [1776]). The only reference to the "invisible hand" itself is on p. 349, although, as discussed in the works cited in the previous note, the concept comes up in several other places.

20. See the excellent Editors' Introduction to Condorcet, *Des progrès de l'esprit humain*, eds. Monique and François Hinker (Paris: Éditions Sociales, 1971 [1795]).

21. Thomas Malthus, *An Essay on the Principle of Population* (Electronic Scholarly Publishing Project, 1998 [1798]), chap. 18. As always, the intellectual history is complicated. The Malthus of the history of economics is largely based on the first edition of this work, which strongly influenced his friend David Ricardo, while the actual Malthus went on to become a fairly tame social reformer. Donald Winch provides a clear summary, including the thought of Malthus's other named opponent, William Godwin, in "Secret Concatenations: Mandeville to Malthus.

Subsequent economists were greatly influenced by the thinking of Mandeville and especially the early Malthus. By the end of the nineteenth century, it was conventional wisdom, outside of the sphere of socialist thinking (I will come to that in a moment), that competitive markets, unhindered by governments, higher moral purposes, or traditional social standards, were almost definitionally the best process for making individual and social decisions about production, prices, wages, investments, and allocation. By then, market economists had almost entirely jettisoned the always tattered religious wrappings with which some pioneers had decorated the competitive struggle. On the contrary, as with Condorcet, the enthusiasm for free markets and competition was more often than not part of a worldview that was resolutely anticlerical, if not necessarily totally antireligious or antispiritual. Knut Wicksell provides an extreme example. The late nineteenth-century Swedish economist was a pioneer of neoclassical economics, which has become the standard theoretical model. It assumes the near ubiquity of highly efficient markets. Wicksell was also a committed atheist and a devoted early advocate of birth control (as a remedy to the Malthusian curse). He even spent two months in prison for mocking the virgin birth of Jesus.[22]

The connection of markets to religious freethinking was not accidental. Condorcet's intellectual combination was coherent. People who liked the economic freedom of markets—including freedom of contracts, market entry, and international trade—also tended to like political freedoms, most notably from the restraints of royal rule, and individual freedoms, particularly from all sorts of religious interference and social thought control. The unified antiestablishment cult of freedom is one of the incarnations of liberalism, a word that has come up several times already, almost always as something hostile to the Catholic understanding of the world and to the practical teachings of the Church. Even the most religiously inclined of early economic liberals generally abhorred what they saw as the inherent repression of the human spirit in the traditionalist Catholicism of the popes of the nineteenth and early twentieth centuries.[23]

The Carlyle Lectures: Oxford, 1995." Also, William Petersen, "The Malthus-Godwin Debate, Then and Now," *Demography*. 8 no. 1 (1971): 13–26.

22. See Torsten Gårdlund, *The Life of Knut Wicksell*, trans. Nancy Adler (Cheltenham, UK: Edward Elgar, 1996 [1958]), especially 249–255.

23. See footnote 43 in chap. 1 for references to the history or histories of liberalism. Jeremy Jennings, "Liberalism and the Morality of Commercial Society" in Wall, *The Cambridge*

108   CHAPTER 3

As I just mentioned, in economic matters, the liberals were not the only group of modernizers and revolutionaries. Their principal opponents were the various families of socialists. Many socialists had liberal views on questions of political and individual freedom, although some, including the communists who eventually took over Russia, thought a domineering state was needed to protect all sorts of personal freedoms from backward ideas. On economic freedom, socialists were united in their opposition to the liberal creed. They believed that free markets were not so much undesirable as illusory, a trick to hide the real locus of power. True economic freedom required, first, the extirpation of capitalist oppression and, then, extensive government control of the economy. As discussed in chapter 2, the arguments between state-loving socialists and market-loving liberals were bitter. However, the two sides had much in common. Both protagonists believed they were answering the Enlightenment call for people to take control of their destiny, both believed that education and sensible public policy could overcome sin, and both rejected the oppressive illusions of irrational and hierarchical religion.

Unsurprisingly, the nineteenth-century popes condemned all these radical ideas—economic and social liberalism as well as all varieties of socialism. Leo XIII dedicated an entire encyclical, *Libertas*, to what he saw as the errors of intellectual, religious, and political liberalism. It did not mention economic liberalism, but that branch of the doctrine is subject to the document's fundamental criticism of the liberal "ethical system which . . . under the guise of liberty, exonerates man from any obedience to the commands of God, and substitutes a boundless license . . . [It leads to] the doctrine of the supremacy of the greater number. . . [and] is in contradiction to reason."[24] The encyclical included "socialists and members of other seditious societies" among the quasi-liberals who repudiate "the empire of God over man and civil society."[25]

In *Rerum Novarum*, a primarily economic document, Leo was mainly concerned with the danger of socialism, but in passing he mocked those who praise freely agreed-upon contracts, a key element in liberal market economics. "Wages, as we are told, are regulated by

---

Companion, 42–56, provides a broad introduction to the religious views of liberal thinkers, although he is perhaps too willing to accept vague religious references as evidence of sincere belief.

24.   Leo XIII, Encyclical letter *Libertas Praetantissimum* (June 20, 1888), 15.

25.   Leo XIII, *Libertas Praetantissimum*, 16.

free consent, and therefore the employer, when he pays what was agreed upon, has done his part."[26] Sounding like a cross between a Marxist and a Thomist, he dismissed the idea that an agreement was just as long as both sides had agreed to it—"there underlies a dictate of natural justice more imperious and ancient than any bargain between man and man, namely, that wages ought not to be insufficient to support a frugal and well-behaved wage-earner."[27]

When Pius XI went over the some of the same economic ground in *Quadragesimo Anno*, in 1931, the negative papal judgment on the liberal idea of markets was harsher and more explicit. By then, both socialism and liberalism had developed; both had become more toxic. Socialism had brought the Soviet Union, with its religious persecutions and government of terror, but the society of capitalism and markets had hardly done better. Europe had been devastated by the greatest war it had ever seen, and the subsequent peace was notable for cultural despair and grave economic difficulties.

In response, Pius explicitly rejected the "false ideas" and "erroneous suppositions" of the "so-called Manchesterian Liberals." (Several of the most prominent early defenders of free-market, antitariff, anti-imperialistic, prosperity-based policies were based in the leading English industrial city of Manchester.) Saying that liberals expected all the gains of industrial prosperity to accrue to the rich owners of capital,[28] he condemned "individualist economic teaching" that "held that economic life must be considered and treated as altogether free from and independent of public authority, because in the market, i.e., in the free struggle of competitors, it would have a principle of self-direction which governs it much more perfectly than would the intervention of any created intellect." The dismissal was softened only by a lukewarm admission that "free competition" is "justified and certainly useful provided it is kept within certain limits."[29]

For Pius XI, market competition ultimately undermined the common good, because in the "unlimited freedom of struggle among competitors . . . only the strongest survive; and this is often the same as saying, those who fight the most violently, those who give least

---

26. Leo XIII, *Rerum Novarum*, 43.

27. Leo XIII, *Rerum Novarum*, 45.

28. Pius XI, *Quadragesimo Anno*, 54.

29. Pius XI, *Quadragesimo Anno*, 88.

heed to their conscience."[30] The eventual result was some variety of political-economic authoritarianism, a dictatorship of the strong, the rich, and the powerful, whether "[o]n the one hand, economic nationalism or even economic imperialism; [or] on the other, a no less deadly and accursed internationalism of finance or international imperialism whose country is wherever profit is."[31] A doctrinaire Leninist could hardly have been harsher.

By 1967, all the most prosperous nations were commonly thought to have "market economies," but a sociologist would have found that description inaccurate. She would have preferred adjectives such as law-bound, regulated, technocratic, or bureaucratic. Paul VI, however, continued to think in the terms of economists. He was no more enthusiastic about them than his predecessors were, condemning the "pernicious economics concepts" of "unbridled liberalism": "profit as the chief spur to economic progress, free competition as the guiding norm of economics, and private ownership of the means of production as an absolute right, having no limits nor concomitant social obligations." He carefully separated these "improper manipulations of economic forces" from the nonmarket "labor systemization and industrial organization," which have played a "vital role in the task of development."[32]

Francis has continued this long-standing antiliberal, antimarket papal thinking. His condemnation of the market economy is almost as unconditional as that of Pius XI. "Today everything comes under the laws of competition and the survival of the fittest, where the powerful feed upon the powerless. As a consequence, masses of people find themselves excluded and marginalized: without work, without possibilities, without any means of escape."[33]

The "everything" of Francis is an exaggeration. The sociological phenomena that Paul VI did not pay much attention to have only been amplified in succeeding decades. In both rich and poor countries, any potential Darwinian competitive struggles are significantly softened by the intrusive regulatory apparatus of proto-Hegelian governments, generally supported by popular pressure and the consciences of businesspeople. In addition, the governments themselves

---

30. Pius XI, *Quadragesimo Anno*, 107.

31. Pius XI, *Quadragesimo Anno*, 109.

32. Paul VI, *Populorum Progressio*, 27.

33. Francis, *Evangelii Gaudium*, 53.

are very large employers, as are a variety of not-for-profit enterprises. Francis's claim that the rich exploit the poor more than ever is doubtful, since there is far less absolutely poverty than ever before. Still, Francis's goal was not to provide a measured and dispassionate economic survey. He wanted to inspire indignation, since there are certainly enough serious injustices associated with "capitalist" economies to merit fury and action.

Francis's fierce and exaggerated condemnation of the market mechanism should be balanced by the more balanced papal view of markets and economic practice in the modern world presented in *Centesimus Annus*, John Paul II's 1991 encyclical. The Polish pontiff, who knew communism from firsthand experience, responded cautiously to then recent fall of this extreme version of atheistic materialism. Unlike many Catholics in countries with supposedly capitalist economies, John Paul II did not see the end of communism as the triumph of a Christian culture, admittedly a diluted one, over an atheistic anticulture, or even as the triumph of a distinctly different and clearly superior free enterprise economic system over the defective communist system, with its reliance on state monopolies and central planning. Rather, he saw something like a victory by default. The survivor was a deeply flawed political-social-economic system that tended to "an excessive promotion of purely utilitarian values, with an appeal to the appetites and inclinations toward immediate gratification, making it difficult to recognize and respect the hierarchy of the true values of human existence."[34]

John Paul had much good to say about what he called the "modern business economy." He praised its ingenuity and accomplishments. He admired the genuine freedom permitted by the development and spread of new technologies. More profoundly, the pope appreciated how increased prosperity and more powerful technologies had shifted the emphasis in economic activity from the crude overpowering of the material world to something higher, to "man himself, that is, his knowledge, especially his scientific knowledge, his capacity for interrelated and compact organization, as well as his ability to perceive the needs of others and to satisfy them."[35] However, the praise was balanced with sharp criticisms. John Paul lamented the persistence of material poverty, the spread of ecological damage, the

---

34. John Paul II, *Centesimus Annus*, 29.
35. John Paul II, *Centesimus Annus*, 32.

rise of spiritually destructive consumerism, and the social and spiritual alienation created by excessive desires for profits and for ever-higher quantities of production.

As for markets, John Paul noted that they contribute to what is good about this economy. "It would appear that, on the level of individual nations and of international relations, the free market is the most efficient instrument for utilizing resources and effectively responding to needs."[36] He expanded that thought a little later in the document: "[T]he mechanisms of the market offer secure advantages: . . . they promote the exchange of products; above all they give central place to the person's desires and preferences, which, in a contract, meet the desires and preferences of another person."[37] Such statements amount to an acknowledgment that the dominant Western economic model, which relies to some extent on free markets, had addressed some of the worst abuses identified by his predecessors.

However, the endorsement of markets was unenthusiastic and limited. Praise was paired with a critical psychological observation—the focus on the competition to buy and sell is likely to have a deleterious effect on people's moral ambitions. "[T]hese mechanisms carry the risk of an 'idolatry' of the market, an idolatry which ignores the existence of goods which by their nature are not and cannot be mere commodities."[38] In particular, the market treatment of labor as a commodity to be traded in a market was, John Paul had said in an earlier encyclical, an "error of early capitalism"[39] that should be overcome completely. More generally, the economy, like everything in society, should not rely on any mechanical or debased view of human motivations and interactions but rather on the great dignity of human nature. All people share the vocations to rule the earth, build communities, and search for heaven. These universal vocations are best served in a "society of free work, of enterprise, and of participation."[40] Competition is not on his list of crucial attributes.

In sum, John Paul saw the contracts and exchanges of markets as sometimes very useful tools. However, he understood that the tools can serve the good if they are kept in their right, subservient

---

36. John Paul II, *Centesimus Annus*, 32.

37. John Paul II, *Centesimus Annus*, 40.

38. John Paul II, *Centesimus Annus*, 32.

39. John Paul II, Encyclical Letter *Laborem Exercens* (September 14, 1981), 7.

40. John Paul II, *Laborem Exercens*, 35.

place. "Such a [good] society is not directed against the market, but demands that the market be appropriately controlled by the forces of society and by the State."[41]

I pointed at the beginning of this book that some of the counsels of the Catholic Social Teaching have changed over the years. For example, as I discussed in the previous chapter, the emphasis on the virtues of private property has yielded to an emphasis on the social mortgage that always comes with such property. The magisterial judgment of the modern business economy has also shifted, although more modestly. The almost total hostility of Pius XI has undoubtedly been moderated by his successors. For the most part, the view has changed because this economy has itself changed to become more supportive of justice for workers, more willing to take up social responsibilities, more responsive to calls for improvement from civil society, and less wedded to a doctrine of socially ruinous competition. The popes have also taken appropriately approving note of the many benefits the modern economy has brought to the human material condition and of the flexibility of its operations. There has been, however, no softening of the criticism of the material, social, and spiritual damage that the modern business economy has caused or allowed. There has been no change whatsoever in the negative judgment of the ideology of free markets.

These judgments are not confused or mistaken, as some market-loving Catholics claim. It is not really possible to reconcile the tenets of free market economics with the Catholic understanding of society, human nature, and the common good.

The most basic difficulty is with the fundamental market principle that open and fair competition is a good thing in itself that inevitably or generally does good things for society. According to this model of reality, victory in the endless striving for self-interested advantage naturally goes to the individual or entity that best serves other individuals and entities. Furthermore, this struggle naturally serves the whole community.

To be fair, few contemporary economists adopt the purest case, because they have learned not to trust markets unconditionally. Only the keenest enthusiasts, sometimes called libertarians, believe that fair competition almost always produces fair prices and wages, useful innovations, high quality products and services, and social justice

---

41. John Paul II, *Laborem Exercens*, 35.

to boot. More cautious promarket economists grant that fair competition is not always possible, so they recognize that markets do not work well for some important economic activities. They expect governments to correct the market when it leads to unjust allocations of income or economic opportunity. Even such market moderates, though, generally believe that economic organization should rely as much as possible on the basic market process, the mix of open rivalry among suppliers and informed choice among customers. The moderates usually describe noncompetitive economic arrangements as unfortunate but necessary responses to what they consider to be "market failures."

For Christians, the idea that *any* important part of society could work best by relying primarily on conflict and rivalry is diametrically opposed to the truth of human nature, which is created in the image and likeness of the God who is love. There is nothing that resembles rivalry in the trinitarian life of God, so there should be as little rivalry as possible in the life of human communities. There is room for a competitive struggle for excellence—Saint Paul praises athletic training[42]—but societies should be fundamentally oriented to love and generosity. Excessive philosophical praise of economic competition also ignores the grim reality pointed out by Pius XI. Without some moral guidance, the winners in such fights will not necessarily be good. On the contrary, in our fallen world sinful greed and the sinful lust for power often help lead the wicked to victory. Also, the praise of markets is often blind to what the wicked can do with their position of strength. Even a slight economic advantage can permit severe social injustices.

An economic model worthy of humankind, in both its greatness and its baseness, must encourage a manifest concern for neighbor and community, must recognize the moral ambiguities of desires, and must consciously strive to counter the disorders of the world and the human heart. The market model, based on amoral, mechanical, and individualistic competition, falls far short.

Then there is the market enthusiasts' praise of freedom. In a free market, each individual customer can choose what to buy and every supplier can choose what to sell. The capitalist system also offers the freedom to set up businesses, to design new products and services, and to find new ways to compete. Supporters of this capitalism,

---

42.   1 Cor 9:24–25.

including some Christians, often praise these freedoms as good in themselves, because autonomy and choice are inherently desirable.

Such support needs to be carefully qualified. In the Christian understanding of the hierarchy of goods, the freedom of free markets is certainly not bad, but that it is fundamentally different from, and essentially less valuable than, the freedom of the good life. The economists' market offers freedoms of choice, while Christians know that "[o]nly the freedom which submits to the Truth leads the human person to his true good. The good of the person is to be in the Truth and to do the Truth."[43] At best, the ability to choose among alternative worldly goods provides a modest degree of this true freedom. Today's economies often provide many similar products and little genuine choice, so even this freedom is somewhat curtailed by the way markets actually work. At worst, for example in the freedom to create lively markets for dangerous drugs and pornography, the competitive market provides only the false freedom to choose whether or how to accept the slavery of sin. Overall, the pursuit of mere freedom of choice is often less an expression of the human vocation to find the liberating truth than it is a distraction from this great human task.

Finally, the psychological motivations required for markets to be successful raise doubts for Christians. Market economists disagree among themselves about the appropriate orientation, but the traditional idea that calculating self-interest is the sole guiding principle for all participants remains widespread. This moral-psychological claim does not exclude other motivations in other domains, for example in religion, romance, or politics. It claims only to describe economic desires. In the market, each person is assumed to be what is called an economic man (*homo economicus*), an isolated individual who follows a strictly utilitarian agenda of maximizing his or her pleasure and minimizing his or her pain.

This psychological agenda is a reasonable restatement of Mandeville's approach, but it is far more radical than the classical liberal idea of benign individualism. For economic men, the market can be little more than a mechanistic conflict among isolated monsters of selfishness. Such a reductive and virtue-free psychology appalls Christian enthusiasts for markets, as well as ringing false to anyone who has studied human psychology at any depth. The critics of *homo*

---

43. John Paul II, *Discorso ai partecipanti al congresso internazionale di teologia morale* (April 10, 1986), 1, quoted in John Paul II, Encyclical Letter *Veritatis Splendor* (August 6, 1993), 84.

economicus offer various alternative models, often postulating the presence of what Adam Smith, an exponent of the classical liberal psychology, called "moral sentiments" to guide market behavior.[44] These sentiments are similar to what Christians and other traditional philosophers called virtues. There is a lively debate about how many and what sorts of sentiments or virtues are required for markets to work well. Some claim that all that is needed is the almost universal willingness to obey the laws. Others think markets can only work well when there is a widespread desire to be admired for making society wealthier or better or when businesspeople can rely on a shared general concern for future generations. A few economists even mandate a shared commitment to the common good, almost the opposite of Mandeville's initial vision.

Pierre de Lauzun, a thoughtful French Catholic economist, provides a helpful historical and psychological perspective. He notes that premodern markets in Christian societies were typically at least as much collaborative as competitive. He claims that a healthy market psychology values moderation and cooperation more than it does self-interest.[45] John Paul II might have liked this analysis, but unfortunately it is far from the mainstream of market thinking, even among Catholic capitalists.

Since, like Pope Francis, I am deeply suspicious of what sounds too much like "a magical conception of the market,"[46] I struggle to understand the enthusiasm of many intelligent and well educated Catholics for any markets other than those described by de Lauzun. I do try. I think that their strongest argument is an updated version of the classical liberal (now known as neoliberal) criticism of intrusive government. Calls for more market mechanisms can fairly be presented as calls for less state control of our lives. The logic is simple. Competitive markets are supposed to work by themselves, so they require little government activity and promote individual freedom. The classical liberal proponents of markets in the nineteenth century took this principle past the point where it could serve the common good. They not only opposed such government "interventions" as

---

44. Adam Smith, *The Theory of Moral Sentiments* (London: Henry G. Bohn, 1853 [1759]).

45. Pierre de Lauzun, *Finance, un regard chrétien* (Paris: Éditions Embrasure, 2013). Stefano Zamagni presents a similar argument in "Catholic Social Thought, Civil Economy, and the Spirit of Capitalism," in *The True Wealth of Nations: Catholic Social Thought and Economic Life*, ed. Daniel K. Finn (New York: Oxford University Press, 2010), 63–95.

46. Francis, *Laudato Si'*, 191.

tariffs and duties but also the legal regulation of working conditions and manufacturing processes. Since the mid-twentieth century, market enthusiasts have had much more economic government to dislike, especially in developed economies, where prosperity and the sway of government activity have largely increased together.

Like market enthusiasts, the Magisterium asks for the reversal of some governmental accretions and the reconsideration of the appropriate role for the state. I mentioned the rule-based bureaucracies that increasingly guide modern societies in the discussion of subsidiarity in chapter 2. In chapter 6 I discuss how the welfare state has undermined or co-opted many social structures. The genuine damage done by oppressive governments does not, however, validate the case for free markets. On the contrary, as the popes have consistently taught, the ideas behind free markets are largely drawn from the same well of essentially atheistic thinking as the contemporaneous ideas about amoral bureaucracy and the all-encompassing state. Christians reject these ideas, because they believe that human communities are best when they are bound by love, mutual respect, and noble, or really transcendental, aspirations. For all their problems, families and churches are generally good examples of such solidarity. Universities, hospitals, and commercial enterprises can also fundamentally be oriented toward virtue. Neither the Hegelian State nor the liberal market can be.

A Better Way

I regret the vast amount of Catholic intellectual energy that has been dedicated to a basically sterile debate over how the Social Teaching should respond to the largely anti-Christian economic ideal of free markets. Since the promarket view is almost exclusively found in English-speaking countries, the debate has created an unhelpful geographical division within the Church. I strongly counsel ignoring the whole topic. Instead, Catholics interested in economics should focus on a genuinely helpful schema for economic analysis, the tripartite division sketched out by Pope Benedict in sections 36–39 of *Caritas in Veritate*.

Benedict's text is brief and not especially clear, so my interpretation is necessarily conjectural rather than dogmatic. He does not claim to have found a universal key to how economies do or should work, so his three types of economic relationships are not meant to be exhaustive. Also, a warning is needed. My exposition goes well beyond his precise text. I believe, though, that my thinking is in accord with the logic, anthropology, and theology of the Magisterium.

The explicit goal of Benedict's description is to provide a profoundly Christian analysis of the nature and varieties of justice in economic activity. The goal is worthy, because Christians urgently need to find their own ways to discuss economic justice. All the conventional economic types of analysis are totally unsatisfactory. The dominant market theory, as I have just said, is morally dangerous and practically unhelpful. A related approach is based on the philosophical concept of utility, which is both even more anti-Christian than are markets and even less helpful in practical analysis. Sociologists are somewhat more helpful. They can describe arrangements reasonably well, but they lack the philosophical tools needed for ethical judgments.

Christians have those tools, should they choose to use them. Revelation, tradition, and two millennia of philosophy provide a clear understanding of human nature in its grandeur and baseness, along with the recognition that the City of Man will always reflect both the good and bad in fallen nature, so its residents and leaders can only strive for a less imperfect reflection of the sinless City of God. In his economic discussion, Benedict draws on this rich heritage.

Indeed, he turns to a part of the heritage that he usually passes over, the Aristotelian style of division that was developed and Christianized by Saint Thomas Aquinas. The reliance makes good sense, as the tradition offers a sophisticated typology of justice. Each of the three economic categories Benedict proposed is based on a kind of justice: the most basic commutative justice of equivalence, which ensures the equivalence of what is given and what is received; a broader distributive justice, which provides what is merited or needed, and the highest justice of supernatural self-giving, which is motivated by the overflow of charity. For all three types, the moral purpose shapes the practical arrangements. Of course, morality is easily deformed by sin. Benedict explains how "man's darkened reason" can create injustice in any economic arrangement by separating economic thinking and action from the "authentically human social relationships of friendship, solidarity, and reciprocity" that are always needed to ensure justice.[47]

---

47.   Benedict XVI, *Caritas in Veritate*, 36.

At the lowest level of the three-step hierarchy is "giving in order to acquire." This is something like a market, which consists of innumerable exchanges of things that are held to be of equal value by the two sides. However, the Christian understanding of "giving for having" (a closer translation of Benedict's Latin phrase) differs from the conventional market approach in two significant ways.

First, the market model is based on conflict. Both sides are assumed to be purely self-interested, so the buyer always wants to provide less and the seller always wants to receive more. With such motivations, actual transactions will always be somewhat unsatisfactory compromises. The market model has no room for a joint commitment to moderation or for any effort to find a price that is objectively just. Believers in the reality of markets assume that any talk of fair deals or justice must be a bargaining tool, like the "savings" advertised by producers in search of buyers. The claim of fairness is seen as a lure to lull the unwary.

The Christian logic of exchange is quite different, although Benedict does not discuss this background in *Caritas in Veritate*. From the Middle Ages onward, the starting point has been a shared desire for justice. While people do in fact often try to get an edge, that desire is viewed as likely to be sinful and socially disruptive. The negotiations over any exchange are only successful if the result promotes the genuine good of both sides.

Before the modern social teaching, some Catholic economic thinkers argued for a "just price." For the most part, this would be the price set by fair negotiations of buyer and seller, what a modern economist would call the market price. However, unjust collusion of both buyers and sellers was almost always condemned, as were deceit and the exploitation of gullible and desperate buyers.[48] The modern teaching focuses more on wages. The change is a clear improvement over the previous discussions, as the dignity of workers is more important than the pricing of products. Besides, the justice of wages is easier to identify than is the fairness of prices. I already mentioned Leo XIII's declaration that pay "ought not to be insufficient to support a frugal and well-behaved wage-earner."[49] The terms may sound quaint, but the principle is sound. He and his successors have consistently stated that wages and prices that are

---

48. See note 5 in chapter 2 for references.

49. Leo XIII, *Rerum Novarum*, 45.

agreed in a competitive market, even one without blatantly unfair practices, are not automatically just. The civil authorities have the duty of overruling unjust markets.

That relying on a maximizing market approach to transactions can be bad for society is not merely a theoretical claim. Stronger buyers or sellers often force counterparties to agree to unfair deals, whether too high prices from monopolistic producers or too low wages to workers in a time of high unemployment or in a place with few potential employers. The injustice is evil in itself, and the bitter feelings of the mistreated party can be socially disruptive. In sharp contrast, economic exchanges that aim to be just strengthen social ties. Fortunately, the Christian understanding of exchange as a fair transaction is actually common in successful economies, especially outside of university economics departments. Unjust wages and prices are sometimes illegal. Even when they are not, the goal of justice is commonly accepted by employers and producers—not merely endorsed as a negotiating or marketing ploy. In contrast, the negotiated exchanges between rich and poor countries still often seem to favor the rich, the side that has the greater economic and political strength.

The second significant difference between fair and market exchanges concerns what is exchanged. In the market model, the good or service in question is always precisely defined. I promise to provide precisely this amount of labor or this amount of money while you promise to provide precisely this amount of money or exactly this good or service. Without such exactness, it would be impossible for self-interested individuals to decide how much they are willing to offer or accept. It is quite different in the fair exchange model. Transactions are never discrete or precise. They are always embedded in the history and broader context of a society. Any particular deal is made with an eye to past and future deals and to the many obligations and ties that bind the two sides into a common life. The transactions must not merely be just for both sides. They must not subvert a wider community that started in the forgotten past and that is expected to last well past the deaths of both parties.

In this broad understanding of just exchange, it is better to think mutual giving than of selling and buying. Gift, after all, is essential to Christianity—the religion is founded on God's free gift of grace and salvation. Transactions are not a way for grasping, selfish people to take advantage of each other. They are open-ended exchanges of gifts, not too distant from what anthropologists call a gift economy.[50] The term refers to premodern societies in which the giving of gifts plays a major role in demonstrating social relations and in protecting social unity. All gifts are made as returns for previous gifts received and with the expectation of future gifts in return. The series is endless, because one gift always merits another.

Perhaps I am getting carried away, but I think the fullest embodiment of this lowest moral level of economic justice might be a vision of the entire economic world as a sort of universal gift exchange. God gives to each person life, talents, a community, and the created world. Thanks be to God, the world is designed so that with labor people can transform those gifts from God into things that can be given back to God as worshipful offerings and, with divine blessing and instruction, to themselves and their neighbors. In this universal vision, the equivalence of individual transactions is actually an illusion. Just as God always gives us more than we can return, there is no need for precise equivalence between one person's gift to the world in the form of labor and the world's gifts in return, in the form of economic goods.

Leaving that extravagant vision aside, I note that in fact Benedict does not discuss in any detail the internal weaknesses of exchanges that are supposed to be fair. However, sin cannot ever be avoided completely, even when there is no conscious pursuit of self-interest. It is all too likely that my idea of what is fair in an exchange will actually favor my interests. Such an unconscious distortion of judgment is less morally repellent than a statement that I will intentionally charge an unfair price merely because I have the power to do so. However, sins that hide behind the shield of logical judgment are still sins, and they are often more difficult to root out than the more blatant variety.

An economy that relied only on even the most generous sort of fair exchanges could not be fully just. Benedict XVI expressed this idea in reference to the global economy: "Without fully internalized forms of solidarity and mutual trust, the market cannot completely fulfil its proper economic function."[51] Benedict called for all economic actors to live up to their moral responsibility, because "every

---

50. The raging anthropological debates on the meaning or meanings of gifts in different cultures are summarized in Jonathan Parry, "The Gift, the Indian Gift and the 'Indian Gift,'" *Man* New Series 21, no. 3 (1986): 453–73.

51. Benedict XVI, *Caritas in Veritate*, 35, translation altered.

economic decision has a moral consequence."[52] Full justice requires both contracts and "forms of redistribution governed by politics," so that "political logic" can serve "fraternal reciprocity."[53] Benedict speaks of "giving through duty."[54] All members of an economic community are obliged to give so that all people can receive what they deserve. That allocation can be personal, to this or that individual or family. It can also be social through the creation or maintenance of shared goods and services from medical care to bridges. Benedict echoed and updated Pius XI, who pointed out that "the riches that economic-social developments constantly increase ought to be so distributed among individual persons and classes that the common advantage of all . . . will be safeguarded . . . By this law of social justice, one class is forbidden to exclude the other from sharing in the benefits."[55]

The most obvious economic example of this sort of distributive justice, which Benedict also calls the "logic of public obligation,"[56] is the tax system. The government requires people and organizations to share with each other. It sets rules to determine how much each must give and how much each will receive. The individual taxpayer, the giver, is also often a recipient of direct and indirect government support.

The government's contribution to this distributive justice is not limited to taxes and expenditures. Various parts of the legal system can be used to prevent the privileged from taking unjust advantage of their wealth and power, as well as to enforce or encourage respect for human dignity and environmental integrity. Also, as Benedict points out, individual governments are not the only administrators of this sort of justice. Above them are groups of nations. Most notably, the preferential option for the poor has a global dimension. At the smallest scale, justice according to duty and need is almost always the guiding principle of allocations and arrangements in families. Healthy adults contribute more in material terms than they take out, while children and people who are feeble take out far more than

---

52. Benedict XVI, *Caritas in Veritate*, 37.

53. Benedict XVI, *Caritas in Veritate*, 37, 38.

54. Benedict XVI, *Caritas in Veritate*, 39.

55. Pius XI, *Quadragesimo Anno*, 57. This is first use in an encyclical of the term "social justice." In the next section of the encyclical Pius XI identifies it as synonymous with at least some aspect of the "common good." For a critical discussion of excessively political uses of the phrase in some Catholic writing, see J. Brian Benestad, *Church, State, and Society: An Introduction to Catholic Social Doctrine* (Washington, D.C.: Catholic University of America Press, 2010), 150–64.

56. Benedict XVI, *Caritas in Veritate*, 39.

they currently put in. Between these extremes of scale, insurance pools are more businesslike examples of the logic of public obligation at work. Many people buy policies from an insurer that provides money to the few who merit payments. Also, churches, universities, and hospitals often strive to distribute economic goods and services in accordance with need.

Once again, Christians should consider the taxes they pay and all their other contributions to this "distributive justice and social justice" as a sort of gift.[57] That thought might sound confused, since the defining feature of a gift is that it is voluntary while compulsion is a defining feature of any tax. At a more spiritual level, though, the rethinking is completely right. Taxes and similar payments from duty are gifts that sin makes us reluctant to offer. We can, though, recognize our shared responsibilities for all the members of our community. We can also remember that we would have nothing without the gratuitous (free) gifts of God and the shared labor of our community, so we can, with this spiritual-intellectual effort, see our offerings as repayments of obligations. Sin has reduced but not eliminated our generosity and awareness of the common wealth, so we are willing to be forced into virtue, although we may grumble about the obligation to live up to our best nature.

Justice is at least as central to the logic of public obligation as to the logic of exchange. An old socialist slogan expresses the principle clearly if a bit simply: From each according to his ability, to each according to his need. A Christian might speak of merits rather than bare needs, but that substitution only increases the difficulty of deciding what distributive arrangements are just. It is never obvious what any person is able to offer or what any person really merits. The Church can only offer a few basic principles. In considering ability to give, the universal destination of goods (discussed in chapter 2) should never be forgotten. In considering the merit of receiving, the equal dignity of all people and the preferential option for the poor should be respected. A hierarchical social order can be just, but any distinctions of opportunity and outcomes need to be justified.

Benedict's third and highest level of justice is found in what he calls "actions of gratuitousness." He only hints at the form these free gifts might take in the economy, but he emphasizes their importance—"economic, social, and political development, if it is to be

---

57. Benedict XVI, *Caritas in Veritate*, 35.

124   CHAPTER 3

authentically human, needs to make room for the *principle of gra-tuitousness* as an expression of fraternity."[58] This third level of justice is the last term in a short sequence. First, there are gifts that come with roughly equal returns and then gifts with unequal although just returns. The next natural, or perhaps supernatural, step in the progression is gifts with no expected return at all, at least no returns in this life. Understood in this way, Jesus both counsels the paradigmatic gratuitous action and embodies it. In worldly terms, there is his suggestion that the fullness of virtue comes with the donation of all earthly treasure. In what theologians traditionally called the economy of salvation, the Savior makes the greatest of gifts, his life. What is now called economic activity can shadow that divine economy.

Both the advice and the example of Jesus present counsels of perfection. These are calls for heroic virtue that only a few people will ever come close to answering. However, imperfect virtue is far better than vice. Benedict clearly believes there are many ways to imitate the generosity of Jesus in the economy. He gives the example of not-for-profit organizations, but gratuitous good goes well beyond any corporate form. Uncalculated generosity should permeate labor, consumption, and distribution.

The theological virtue of charity involves far more than simply giving away money and resources, but those donations are good starting place for the gratuitous economy. We should give as freely as we have received from God.[59] Paul's frequent praise of hospitality brings this charity into the home.[60] In business, the spirit of gratuitousness also includes both a commitment to do good, cost what it may, and an unceasing desire always to do a little bit more for customers, suppliers, employers, rivals, governments, and everyone in the community, simply to be sure that we are not holding anything back out of a falsely narrow sense of justice.

Obviously, this call to give more than we get is directly opposed to the logic of free markets. Unsurprisingly, many defenders of that ideology responded to Benedict's suggestion with outrage and incredulity.[61] They were both wrong and blind. Many of the greatest accomplishments of the business economy rely on exactly the spirit

---

58.   Benedict XVI, *Caritas in Veritate*, 34.

59.   Mt 10:8.

60.   e.g., Rom 12:13.

61.   A leading example is George Weigel, "*Caritas in Veritate* in Gold and Red," *National Review*, July 7, 2009.

that Benedict identifies. The "green revolution" of the 1960s, which introduced more effective seeds and fertilizers to countries that did not themselves have the resources needed to develop them, is an obvious example. Most of the hardest work was done without any expectation of personal gain. The voluntary offers of economic aid from rich to poor countries also fit, as does the now sadly dwindling willingness of rich countries to accept impoverished immigrants. The arts, education, and scientific research have all benefited from the donations of rich people, usually made primarily from a generosity of spirit.

I would go further still. I do not think this spirit of gratuitousness is found only in the just listed activities, which can all be described as not-for-profit. In my opinion, gratuitousness also helps form much activity that superficially seems to be aimed largely toward individual gain. Businesspeople are often far more generous than the law or any analysis of fair exchange requires because they want to help out. Inventors and entrepreneurs may hope to become rich, but they know that, if they are successful, the gains that they give away to the users of their products and services—in convenience, comfort, health, safety, beauty, or whatever—will far outweigh their personal fortunes. If they did not want to share, they would not be inspired to put the needed effort and take the unavoidable risks that come with innovation.

I do not mean to say that this spirit of gratuitousness is so prevalent that all is right with the economic world. On the contrary, as Benedict complained and as Francis has reiterated even more strongly, that there is a shocking shortage of gratuity relative to the great needs of the world's poor and to the great resources of the world's rich. In the logic of gratuity, the current response to the generosity of God can be described as miserly.

The beyond-market analysis of the types of economic justice has received little attention from either secular economists or from students of the Catholic Social Teaching.[62] I think this is a great omission. In my judgment, the willingness to go beyond narrow conceptions of justice to integrate the Christian idea of free gift is a significant intellectual breakthrough in economic thinking, not to mention a gratuitous offering from the Church to the world of ideas.

---

62. A pleasant exception is "Building the Common Good," an essay by Justin Welby, the Anglican archbishop of Canterbury, in *On Rock or Sand? Firm Foundations for Britain's Future*, ed. John Sentamu London: SPCK, 2015, 27–52.

Despite that last piece of concrete advice, readers can justly complain that the discussions in this chapter and the previous one are far too vague. I have given almost no suggestion of how individuals, agencies, or governments can promote gratuitousness, economic justice, or any other aspect of the economic good. I have glossed over most of the actual workings of the business economy. I have hardly discussed any detailed policies and initiatives. I only glanced at trade rules and had no time to deal with such important topics as corporate purpose, debt forgiveness, financial markets, or the mostly unpaid labors of love. I also largely avoided the highly relevant debate on the extent of the Church's expertise in detailed matters of policy. Personally, I am especially frustrated to have only touched on the questions of how widespread affluence may have changed the meaning of economic moderation and how the spiritual value of poverty, so firmly praised by Jesus, can remain central to the Christian life in an age of affluence.

The desire for brevity is my only excuse for such vagueness. To do justice to these topics would require many more words, testing the patience of readers and perhaps distracting them from the many other parts of the Social Teaching. Still, I do hope that the theological, philosophical, and historical background provided in these two chapters will enrich discussions of all economic questions. Now onto government.

CHAPTER 4

Government—Church and State

THE RELATIONS OF THE Roman Catholic Church with governments were far from a "new thing" when *Rerum Novarum* appeared in 1891. On the contrary, Christians, both individually and as churches, had consistently struggled to find the right way to deal with any number of secular authorities ever since the legitimate Roman authorities crucified Jesus. Many relationships were tried over the centuries, but none was ever completely satisfactory. My principal argument in this chapter is that none ever will be, because it is impossible to serve both God and Caesar in the way that each master desires.

Still, while the political authorities' challenges to Christian life and to the Church may be sempiternal, in some ways the questions posed by the typical modern government are as unprecedented as the blessings and threats of the modern economy. In particular, the separation of many governments from all sorts of religious engagement and support has raised new issues for both the Catholic Church and for societies.

My discussion of the issues raised by modern political life and the various Catholic responses to them stretches through the next two chapters. The topic of this one of these is the most fundamental issue, the relations between what are now called church and state but that is better understood more broadly as the interaction of society's spiritual and worldly organizations and orientations. My goal, as always, is to cover too much too fast: a mix of biblical, philosophical, and historical analysis with some suggestions about the current tensions within the Catholic Social Teaching.

128 CHAPTER 4

Before getting into the detailed arguments, three general comments are in order.

First, I put economics before politics in the order of this book only out of respect for the history of the Catholic Social Teaching. Objectively, politics is more important, because evil in the economic life of labor and consumption can only kill the body, but evil in the political life, the organization of human relations in communities, can kill both body and soul.[1] More positively, economic activity is much less uniquely human than is the political life, profiting much less from the unique human gifts of reason and love. Animals labor and consume, but no animal community can promote or fail to promote justice, true freedom, glory, love of neighbor, and social virtue. Conversely, the sins of economic life are always more basic and often more brutal than are those of political organizations. Economic sin clearly turns labor into toil and fairly evidently perverts consumption into want, greedy excess, or exploitation. In politics, sin often insinuates itself, leading would-be virtuous rulers into painful moral compromises and undermining the moral foundations of even the most well-intentioned political constructions.

Second, the study of politics requires humility, because so much is not understood. For almost three millennia, some of the world's best minds have given serious thought to the essence, universal features, and common excellences of political organization, but to little avail. From Aristotle through Saint Thomas Aquinas to John Locke and John Rawls, political philosophers have rarely been able see far past the debates on the governmental structures and social arrangements of the day. All of the more recent methodologies—the studies of the sociology of government, the anthropology of authority, and the psychology of social hierarchy—seem to face similar limits.

Finally, serious political questions never have simple answers. Social life is too full of practical and moral ambiguities to allow any political equivalent to the preferential option for the poor or the priority of labor over capital. Proposed grand philosophical judgments about the right political order should be treated with great suspicion. All suggestions of clear paths to political perfection should be rejected out of hand. The best that can be hoped for is suggestions of how to improve on the current situation, which is always more or less of a mess.

---

1.   cf. Mt 10:28.

The Biblical Base

The Bible's political teachings, like its economic discussions, offer something more like a set of challenges than a model for individual behavior or social organization. The political lessons that can be drawn from the history of the Jews, the exhortations of the prophets, the sayings of Jesus, and the description of the experience of the earliest Christian communities are not easily reconciled with each other, let alone converted into anything like universally relevant practical instructions. Still, the Scriptures do sketch out the basic and inevitable moral struggles in the relations between, one on side, the believers and leaders of revealed religion and, on the other, the political authorities, both those of co-religionists and those of religious outsiders. I find four basic themes in the Old and New Testaments.

Terrestrial Governing Is Not the Chief Concern of a Priestly People

In their long history, the Israelites, the people of the Lord, sometimes had kings. They were even very briefly something of a regional power. Conventional royal rule, though, is not at the center of the biblical account of the people's theological-political development. Throughout the recitation of, and prophetic commentaries on, the scattered successes and frequent failures of the various authorities in Judah and Israel, the Scriptures emphasize that the keys to understanding this divinely chosen people's history are not the decisions or strategies of either Jewish or gentile rulers. The central theme of the history is, rather, the dialogue between, on one side, the liberating and punishing actions of the Lord and, on the other, the people's response, too often ungrateful and inadequate, to divine invitations and injunctions.

The Israelites found the fundamental teaching—that history is in God's hands—hard to absorb. Indeed, it never was fully absorbed in the course of the biblical narrative. This obtuseness is hardly surprising, as the teaching makes little worldly sense. Reasonable people using conventional standards of judgment cannot easily accept that military defeat, political collapse, and physical exile—a brief summary of the Israelite experience—are actually signs of God's loving will.

However, the Israelites were supposed to understand that their position was unconventional. They were not to be "like the other nations."[2] Instead, they were to be a priestly people whose holiness and obedience of the Law would show God's ways to "the nations," the whole non-Jewish world. The troubled history of the Jews in biblical times shows how difficult it was to fulfil this role. For example, the Maccabees, self-consciously pious Jewish warriors, tried refusing to fight on the Sabbath, in line with the fourth commandment. After a crushing slaughter, they accepted the realpolitik solution of armed defense on the Lord's day.[3] That unpriestly preference for military success over piety may not have pleased later Jews, who had no armies of their own. Disdain might explain why the account of the Maccabees' revolt was not included in the canonical Hebrew Scriptures (it is in the Greek version).

Christians, who claim to be the new Israel, must also wrestle with the challenge of being a priestly people, under the leadership of the one High Priest and great King, Jesus Christ. This set-apart status might tempt them to argue that conventional government is not their affair. They could try to justify political abstinence with their founder's injunction to pay "Caesar the things that are Caesar's."[4] Alternatively, their status as vicars of the messianic ruler might tempt them to claim a place as guide to the nations, whether predominantly Christian or not, in politics as well as in piety. Neither total isolation nor total control, however, is realistic. Besides, neither is right. Total isolation looks like a shirking of the duty to be the "light of the world"[5] while organized Christian domination easily slips into a repression of each person's freedom of conscience. It is actually impossible to be a priestly people in the sinful world without either accepting great suffering or adopting some morally unattractive positions. That is a hard but necessary biblical truth.

Earthly Rulers Should Be Just and Pious

From a worldly perspective, the reigns of Kings David and Solomon were the high point in the history of the Hebrew people. They ruled with the conventional splendor of the period in the region. But God held them to a much higher moral standard than he did their Middle

---

2. 1 Sm 8:5.
3. 1 Mc 2:34–41.
4. Mt 22:21.
5. Mt 5:14.

Eastern peers. They were expected to be just, especially to the weak. The newly anointed King David was strongly rebuked by the Lord (though the prophet Nathan) for taking advantage of his royal authority to have sexual relations with another man's wife.[6] Rulers were also expected to be pious. When Solomon failed to obey the highest commandment, which is to worship only the one God, the Lord, his apostasy far outweighed his wisdom in the Lord's judgment.[7]

In the New Testament, there is no discussion on how Christians should govern. It was not a relevant question for the tiny and at best barely tolerated early church. Still, it is reasonable to believe that Christian rulers who represent the new Israel should be at least as just and pious as the rulers of the old Israel were expected to be.

Political Authority Should Generally Be Respected

In the course of the history recounted in the Old Testament, the Israelites are much more often than not ruled by foreign powers. There is little discussion of whether these rulers should be obeyed, perhaps because obedience rarely had any implications for the people's relations to their God or perhaps because it was assumed that rulers had to obeyed, except when they commanded apostasy. The earliest Christians continued the tradition of obedience. Paul explained the reasoning: "Everyone is to obey the governing authorities, because there is no authority except from God, and those that exist have been instituted by God. . . . Therefore one must be subject, not only to avoid God's wrath, but also for the sake of conscience."[8] If such respect is demanded for non-Christian rulers, Paul might be expected to be even keener on respect for Christian kings and parliaments, but he does not actually address that then purely hypothetical question.

Unjust Authority Should Be Resisted

Apostasy is the issue for the Maccabees. The two biblical books that bear their names laud the refusal to obey the orders of what would seem to be legitimate political authorities. Using a more modern vocabulary, we might say that in the rebels' judgment, the command

---

6.   2 Sm 11–12.

7.   1 Kgs 10–11.

8.   Rom 13:1, 5.

132 CHAPTER 4

to worship other gods deprived the government of its legitimacy. Catholics, unlike Jews and many Protestants, accept the canonical status of two books of Maccabees, so they can be inspired by the heroic Jews' fight to cleanse the temple from defilement and to protect key religious rituals. All Christians can also take a broader political inspiration from the promise of God to shatter his enemies and break "the bow of the mighty,"[9] a prophetic promise echoed by Mary in her praise of God's generosity in history.[10] A Christian who tries to "pull down princes from their thrones,"[11] whether violently or through more gentle means can claim to be doing what Mary's "Magnificat" says is God's intention. Christian political resistance is also justified by Peter's statement of resistance to the Jewish leaders. The first leader of the Church explained: "We must obey God rather than men."[12]

Obviously, the injunctions to respect authority and to resist unjust authority can come into direct conflict. Since no political authority in this fallen world will be perfectly just, there will always be a biblical argument for resistance. Since no authority in this God-loved world will be perfectly evil in every respect, there will always be a biblical argument for obedience, at least in matters that are not essential to the holy life. Wisdom is required to discern which of these arguments is more relevant in any given situation. Human wisdom always being inadequate, disagreement is inevitable.

In short, the Bible teaches obedience and justice for those who are ruled and priestly purity for rulers. It is hard to turn this combination of injunctions as a practical guide. Still, I see three implications.

The first has already been mentioned, but it is worth repeating. Since neither rulers nor religious authorities can always live up to their moral obligations, their relations are generally troubled. The failures are clear in the Scriptures. Moses, the primordial lawgiver (or law transmitter) discovers that his priestly brother, Aaron, has endorsed the worship of the golden calf.[13] Conversely, as mentioned, the prophet Nathan discovers King David has abused his royal authority.[14] Later, God punishes King Uzziah for trying to usurp the

---

9.   1 Sm 2:4.
10.   Lk 1:46–55.
11.   Lk 1:52.
12.   Acts 5:29.
13.   Ex 32.
14.   2 Sam 11–12.

priestly authority to offer sacrifice by making him leprous.[15] Uzziah is actually only a mild offender. The history books and some of the prophets consistently accuse rulers of "doing what is evil in the sight of the Lord." Unlike David, whose repentance under prophetic guidance is a moral highpoint in the history of Jewish governance, later kings often ignore or persecute the prophets.

Second, government is part of the virtuous life. There is virtue both in the governors' obedience to the commands of God and in the willing obedience and just resistance of the governed to those who govern. The demand that rulers be good in God's eyes may be the more challenging one, since it is all too easy for people in exalted positions to believe they are exempt from the exhortation of Saint Paul, "Why not rather be wronged? Why not rather be cheated?"[16] The New Testament's focus on the heavenly kingdom implies that the way of virtue for both rulers and ruled in earthly kingdoms is one of humility. Rulers and ruled should all be willing to accept less in this world—less political freedom, less protection from the government, less justice, less authority, less grandeur and glory—for the sake of a place in the final, heavenly kingdom.

Third, Christians should have profoundly mixed feelings about taking up the responsibilities of government. One on side, it is appropriate to serve our neighbors in any way necessary, including through the exercise of political authority. On the other, it is not appropriate for anyone oriented to heaven to covet worldly glory. The responsibility also brings moral challenges, because the peace of this world is so different from the peace that Jesus offers.[17] Worldly authority is always tinged with actual or potential violence, and worldly power easily overpowers the social restraints that can restrain sinful desires. David was neither the first nor the last ruler to take simultaneous advantage of his power and a beautiful woman.

This three-part biblical guide to politics has rarely been followed, to judge by the historical record presented in the Scriptures, the history of governments in the Christian era (to be discussed later), and a more philosophical analysis (coming in a moment). Even leaders who sincerely wish to be good and holy can never fully align their positions in whatever sin-stained struggles currently threaten the

---

15.   2 Chr 26:1–21.

16.   1 Cor 6:7.

17.   Jn 14:27.

134 CHAPTER 4

earthly city with their striving for the eternal blessed life in all people's true homeland, the City of God.

Philosophical Tensions

"'My kingdom is not of this world.' . . . 'You are a king, then!'"[18] This dialogue of Jesus and Pontius Pilate contains the philosophical core of the Catholic Social Teaching about church and state. The relations between worldly and heavenly authority is an encounter of two kingdoms: on one side, the redeemed and sinless eternal kingdom of heaven and, on the other, the shifting and sin-stained power-structures of human societies. Human societies can neither avoid nor resolve the debate between the two authorities. As the Italian philosopher Giorgio Agamben noted, the meeting of Pilate and Jesus brings together two always-present standards of judgment, two sources of power, and two standards of victory.[19] For the more than two millennia of Christian history, philosophers, theologians, kings, politicians, soldiers, citizens, subjects, and believers have repeated innumerable variations of this enigmatic biblical dialogue, almost always marked by a mutual refusal to yield, an often-violent earthly finality, and an unending hope of eschatological peace.

Not Just a Christian Problem

The relations between Christians and their political authorities are only the purest form of an inevitable confrontation, one built into the human condition. The issue springs from what I described in chapter 1 as the ubiquitous natural desire for the supernatural. I repeat and extend that argument now, following the teaching of the Second Vatican Council and of the subsequent popes.[20] Human nature, both fallen and redeemed, exists at two levels. In each person, the transcendent and immortal life of supernatural grace is elevated above, and distinct from, the mortal and fallen life of worldly

---

18. Jn 18:36, 37.

19. Giorgio Agamben, *Pilate and Jesus*, trans. Adam Kotsko (Stanford, Cal.: Stanford University Press, 2015 [2013]).

20. I follow the line of Henri de Lubac, which I believe is expressed in *Gaudium et Spes*. See his late summary of his own thinking, *Le mystère du surnaturel* (Paris: Aubier, 1965) and, for example, Robert F. Gotcher, "Henri de Lubac and *Communio*: The Significance of His Theology of the Supernatural for an Interpretation of *Gaudium et Spes*" (PhD diss., Marquette University, 2002).

concerns. However, at the very center of this lower, worldly life there is an inherent incompleteness, a yearning or craving that only the higher, transcendent life can satisfy. Societies are like the individuals who constitute them. In them, too, heavenly and worldly living coexist, necessarily but uneasily. The higher life is the pole around which all organized religions turn, while the political system is primarily concerned with the ordering of the lower life.

The two spheres always interact throughout society. At least in the most theologically developed societies, there is typically a debate at the highest levels between the representatives some much-demanding church and the authorities of some extremely powerful state. However, everyone at every level in the social order always has multiple social roles in both spheres, particularly as members of various subsidiary organizations, each with its own relations of the religious and the civil. The relations can never be static. Over time, various religious rituals, understandings, and eventually creeds advance, alter, and decline, as do civil customs, rules, and social concerns. Through most of the history of most of the world's cultures, the religious and the civil (or secular) spheres have been thoroughly entwined, so much so that contemporary scholars often condemn all efforts to separate them as artificial and inappropriate impositions of modern Christian and post-Christian social orders on cultures in which these concepts do not fit. Christians, however, should view all history and every society as formed and more or less conformed to the great human-divine story of Incarnation and Redemption. They understand the reality of a universal religious or spiritual desire. As the human condition is inherently social, this human striving for the divine is inevitably manifested in the social order.[21]

The relations of the two spheres, heavenly and worldly, will always be both harmonious and hostile. The harmony comes from created human nature. Without sin, the two different but overlapping systems would pull organizations and individuals in exactly the same

---

21. For the past two centuries, the relations of the religious and political spheres of life have most often been studied from a distinctly antireligious perspective. A brief and reasonably sympathetic account of some key issues in Daniel H. Levine, "Religion and Politics in Comparative and Historical Perspective," *Comparative Politics* 19, no. 1 (1986): 95–122. The scholarship that denies the existence of religion as a meaningful social category is summarized in chap. 2 of William T. Cavanaugh, *The Myth of Religious Violence: Secular Ideology and the Roots of Modern Conflict* (Oxford: Oxford University Press, 2009). For a succinct modern summary of the Christian view, see Hans Urs von Balthasar, *Theologie der Geschichte: Ein Grundriss* (Einsiedeln: Johannes, 2004 [1959]).

136 CHAPTER 4

direction, toward the fullness of all aspects of human nature. The hostility comes from sinful, fallen nature. Sin distorts judgments and actions in every person and in all political and religious organizations. The result is that the two sides' ambitions, fears, and responsibilities both overlap and diverge, often engendering conflicts of goals and authorities.

These universal philosophical considerations have been played out throughout history. From the ancient Egyptian political-religious controversy over the monotheism of the pharaoh Akhenaten to the twenty-first-century persecution of non-Hindus in India and non-Buddhists in Myanmar, history is full of examples of conflict between spiritual and political forces. Chinese and Japanese emperors wrestled with Buddhist monks, Middle Eastern rulers with various Islamic authorities and various groups of Muslims, and Hindu and Muslim Indian leaders with various groups of Muslims and Hindus. The Middle Eastern rivalries demonstrate that bitter conflicts between the civil and religious spheres can be based on disagreements that can seem trivial to outsiders.

A Particularly Christian Struggle

The Christian struggles between the supernatural and natural lives certainly belong on the list. Indeed, the Christian understanding of the universal scope of the true religion almost inevitably creates a particularly sharp civil-religious conflict.

The inherent hostility is exemplified by the structure of what is usually considered a foundational text of Christian political philosophy, Saint Augustine's *City of God*. The early fifth-century bishop and theologian, who himself often exercised significant political authority in his region of North Africa, wanted to show that that the Christians were not responsible for the sacking of Rome in 410. To do so, he used the apologetic conceit of contrasting the City of God, the "surpassingly glorious" heavenly home of all true Christians, with the "earthly city, which, though it be mistress of the nations, is itself ruled by its lust of rule".[22] Rome was the archetypical example of the latter, while the former would only be constituted in a single place after the end of history, when "a new heaven and a new earth" will be seen "coming down

---

22. Augustine, *City of God*, trans. Marcus Dods (Edinburgh: T&T Clark, 1871 [426]), preface.

out of heaven from God."[23] Meanwhile, the heavenly city exists in some inchoate form in the earthly Christian diaspora.

Augustine's long parallel accounts of secular and salvation history include little concrete advice on how Christians should relate to earthly authorities, whether pagan or Christian. However, the whole structure of the argument makes it clear that members of the Church should treat their terrestrial home as temporary and secondary. Their life in the City of Man should be shaped entirely around the primary goal of human existence, entry into the City of God. The political implications of that single-minded dedication are potentially dangerous for established temporal authorities. Those earthly powers are not to be obeyed if and when obedience would violate Christian morality. Since the authorities in the sinful City of Man will always be corrupt, some of their commands are likely to be sufficiently immoral to merit disobedience. In any case, the principle is clear. All worldly commands are subject to veto by the Christians' true ruler, the king of heaven.

In normal times, the citizens of the City of God will lead normal worldly lives in their particular neighborhood of the fallen and sin-filled City of Man. However, they should not be unduly concerned by their success according to that city's worldly standards, because they will remain mere "sojourners" there, until the "day of the resurrection."[24] In effect, Christians will have something like dual nationality, heavenly and earthly, for as long as history lasts. The dual loyalty creates discomfort in both spheres. Earthly leaders fear Christian disloyalty and Christians are wary of worldly corruption.

The advent of Christian government did not eliminate the conflict. Already in Augustine's time, debates over religious orthodoxy had blighted the still newly Christian Roman empire. Subsequent Christian leaders have tended to believe that their chosen political arrangements are in accord with the dictates of religion, making them at least as likely as non-Christian rulers to see treason and rebellion when Christian subjects or citizens give religious reasons for balking at any rules. Conversely, enthusiastic believing Christians are less likely to be tolerant of the sins of their Christian leaders than they would be of similar behavior from people who could not be expected to know any better.

---

23.   Rv 21:2.

24.   *City of God.* 15.1.

A Very Particularly Catholic Issue

The tension between Christians and governments is intensified when the Christians in question are Catholic. Catholics owe allegiance to an earthly hierarchy that is a particularly thorough and authoritative countervailing force to any other human authority. The bishops and popes have often taken a broad view of their appropriate sphere of influence and a narrow view of the freedom of faithful Catholics to dissent from the counsels of the Magisterium. The most extreme claim was made by Pope Boniface VIII in 1302. "[W]e declare, we proclaim, we define that it is absolutely necessary for salvation that every human creature be subject to the Roman Pontiff."[25] In the modern era, Pope Leo XIII was less extreme, but still ambitious and unambiguous. "Whatever . . . in things human is of a sacred character, whatever belongs, either of its own nature or by reason of the end to which it is referred, to the salvation of souls or to the worship of God is subject to the power and judgment of the Church."[26] Since the entire worldly life "refers" to "the salvation of souls," Leo's second "whatever" potentially puts just everything under ecclesial "power and judgment." I provide some examples of the extent of the pontifical claims in the next section.

In practice, Catholics have usually managed their dual loyalty without actually undermining the local authorities of the human city they happened to inhabit, or at least without undermining them any more than dissident followers of some liberal or universalist ideology might do. Still, as a matter of philosophical principle, anti-Catholic complaints about the imperfect national loyalty of Catholics cannot be dismissed as totally baseless. In many domains, the authority of the Church really is supposed to take precedence over all worldly authorities.

Radical Unions Do Not Work

It might seem that the easiest way to resolve the tensions between religious and civil authorities is to combine the two into a single, all-powerful structure. The union might be led by either side. Civil leaders could take ultimate responsibility for all religious affairs, an arrangement sometimes known as caesaropapism. Alternatively,

---

25. Boniface VIII, Papal Bull *Unam sanctam* (November 18, 1302).

26. Leo XIII, Encyclical letter *Immortale Dei* (November 1, 1885), 14.

religious authorities could have full control over all civil matters, an arrangement long known as theocracy.

Were there no sin, such setups would make philosophical sense. The common good of a society is both natural and supernatural. While the two need not coincide completely, in a sin-free world they could not really be in contradiction. There is sin, though, and in the fallen world the orientation of the two parts of life are too different to be combined without doing great social damage. Religious leaders with too much civil authority will eventually either make impossible demands for holiness from their subjects or will be corrupted by the messy moral compromises that inevitably mark the political realm. Secular leaders with too much religious authority would lose the helpful external checks that even imperfect religious leaders can provide and will eventually use faith and religious structures for their own political purposes.

Muddled Sharing Does Not Work Well

The total union of religion and politics does not work in a fallen world, but some sharing of authority is appropriate for "two spheres [that] are distinct, yet always interrelated," as Benedict XVI put it.[27] A mix of union and separation—overlapping, shared and interlocking responsibilities—might be the best possible pragmatic arrangement. This was certainly the standard approach in the years of Christendom. From the conversion of Constantine (to be discussed soon) at least until the founding of the United States, almost every Christian society had a complex interweaving of ecclesial and civil power and responsibility. The existence of such titles as prince-abbots and prince-bishops provides an extreme example of the close relations of ecclesial and civil powers. Even when the actual offices were clearly divided, as they mostly were, the borders of authority were fuzzy and were easily and frequently contested. Many church dignitaries had significant political power, kings and other secular rules had some authority over religious appointments and lands (including imperial and regal vetoes of papal candidates), secular rulers were often given religious honors, and the Vatican long exercised full political authority in various parts of the Italian peninsula.

---

27.   Benedict XVI, Encyclical Letter *Deus Caritas Est* (December 25, 2005), 28.

140 CHAPTER 4

Although the two sides theoretically respected each other, few of these church-state arrangements were enduring successes. Disputes over precedence were frequent, long, and bitter. Each side presented theological, philosophical, and historical arguments for its own ecclesial and temporal superiority, arguments that usually included the claim that the legitimacy of the other side's necessarily limited authority depended entirely on the good side's revocable endorsement.[28] The battles of ideas were all too often connected to battles of arms. Also, all too often, the rivalry did not keep away the disadvantages of combining religious and secular power. The religious were sullied by their political and social machinations while the secular leaders often took an instrumental approach to religion.

Radical Separation Does Not Work

Because of sin, both the merging and the muddling of civil and religious authority work badly. Unfortunately, the only other alternative, a clean break between the two, is no better. A total separation of the two powers is neither possible nor desirable.

Such a separation is not really possible because the natural and supernatural worlds are too closely connected to be divided without doing violence to both of their natures. Jesus Christ, fully God and fully human, "fully reveals man to man himself and makes his supreme calling clear."[29] That calling, like the person of Jesus, is both fully human and fully divine. It somehow straddles heaven and earth. The personal connection is echoed in each society's religious and civil authorities. There will always be a relationship between "two powers [with] authority over the same subjects." Isolation is merely one kind of relationship, a bad one. Rather than establishing what Leo XIII, called "a certain orderly connection, which may be compared to the union of the soul and body in man,"[30] the legal separation of church and state is an attempt to detach the naturally superior social soul,

---

28. The literature on this topic, in detail and in general, is voluminous. For a succinct and only slightly dated brief summary, see David Knowles, "Church and State in Christian History," *Journal of Contemporary History* 2, no. 4 (1967): 3–15. Some particularly sensitive observations on the religious nature and implications of political authority in Christendom in Marc Bloch, *Les rois thaumaturges: Étude sur le caractère surnaturel attribué à la puissance royale particulièrement en France et en Angleterre, nouvelle* édition (Paris: Gallimard, 1982 [1924]).

29. Vatican Council II, *Gaudium et Spes*, 22.

30. Leo XIII, *Immortale Dei*, 13, 14.

the church, from its physical body, the state. For people, the separation of soul and body is a definition of death. For communities, the comparable division is a grave disorder.

The efforts to create a radical separation of religion and government are not desirable, because the closer they come to success, the worse the results will be for both religion and society. For religion, the exclusion from political and other socially powerful spheres reduces its grounding in members' lives and its ability to provide moral guidance and a public presence of the transcendental order. For societies, at best it is awkward for governments that take care of such social concerns as health care, education, and food safety to leave religion entirely to the consciences of individuals. At worst, this abdication allows the forces of moral disorder to flourish.

The Catholic Position in the Abstract

Since total union, total separation, and any mix of union and separation are all unsatisfactory, the only possible guiding principle of civil-religious relation is imperfection. Any actual arrangement will be more or less unsatisfactory.

It should be said that the following brief description of how Catholics ought to deal with the inherent tensions of this social imperfection is different from anything that loyal Catholics in the days of Leo XIII would have thought. At that time, the wake of the receding Christian tide still washed over many governments and social organizations, so it seemed natural to Christians that even secular governments would be in some basic way respectful of their religion. The advent of mass atheism has challenged and purified Catholic political philosophy.

In this new world of less religion and more doubt, Christians still have extensive responsibilities in the earthly city. Catholics, especially those in authority, are obliged to offer counsel to both the governed and those who govern on all political matters. Benedict XVI provided a good example when he reminded German legislators of their moral obligations. "To serve right and to fight against the dominion of wrong is and remains the fundamental task of the politician. At a moment in history when man has acquired previously inconceivable power, this task takes on a particular urgency."[31] If

---

31. Benedict XVI, Speech *Visit to the Bundestag* (September 22, 2011).

this duty of political participation is shirked, then the whole society, believers and nonbelievers alike, will lose out. The self-imposed near silence of many Catholic leaders about the harmful effects of sexual license and ready divorce on souls and society provides a searing and pertinent example of the loss.

On the other side, even the most secular authorities have serious religious responsibilities. As I mentioned in chapter 1, one of the basic duties of any government is to celebrate, encourage, and reinforce the respect for transcendental goods—God or the gods, beautiful monuments, cultural achievements, or perhaps even military glory (the moral ambiguities of war and conquest are discussed in the next chapter). Organized religion is naturally at the center of this responsibility, since it is the most profound manifestation of the human tie to the transcendental. Leo XIII expressed the government's obligation in strong words in 1888. "Justice therefore forbids, and reason itself forbids, the State to be godless."[32] He would only admit that the "false principle of separation" of church from state could sometimes be "worthy of toleration" because in practice other arrangements "might be worse."[33]

In general, though, the right principle is that a responsible government is a coworker in the truth.[34] The whole truth "subsists" in the Catholic Church, "the one Church of Christ,"[35] so it would of course be the ideal religious partner for all governments, but the world is far from ideal There are many imperfect ways for governments and the institutions of civil society to support the spiritual life of the governed, even though few Western politicians or constitutions are even willing to admit the existence of these responsibilities. The results are sad. The political authorities rarely help provide the young with a spiritually rich education. Religious establishments and organizations are more likely to be tolerated or undermined than protected and nurtured. Physical tokens of worship are more likely to be removed from than placed in public spaces. Governments increasingly avoid encouraging or sponsoring rituals and festivals that connect the cycles of life and of the seasons to a higher reality.

---

32.   Leo XIII, *Libertas Praetantissimum*, 21.

33.   Leo XIII, Encyclical Letter *Aux milieux des sollicitudes* (February 16, 1892), 28.

34.   3 Jn 8.

35.   Vatican Council II, *Lumen Gentium*, 8.

GOVERNMENT—CHURCH AND STATE   143

Leaving aside for now the practical difficulties of improving religious-worldly relations in today's hypersecular states, Catholic social teaching's logic of imperfection provides two helpful general principles for evaluating any current situation. First, there is no religious and civil structure that is always best. What is most desirable, or perhaps what is least problematic, varies with the society's history and current sociology. Second, any existing arrangement can and should be improved. Virtue can always diminish the power of sin, and sin will always become more powerful unless there are constant and ever new attempts to be virtuous.

Following the first principle, Christians can endorse a wide range of church-state arrangements, including deep mutual respect with few direct institutional ties, state-sponsored ("established") religion, and a religiously invested ("anointed") civil authority. However, the second principle teaches that all these arrangements will always have problems, so Christians should be expected to criticize them constantly and to strive for something better. Of course, it is never easy to apply either principle in any particular historical place and time. The determination of the best arrangement and the most helpful changes will always require what philosophers call discernment, prudence, or practical wisdom. A brief historical survey may be helpful for that.

Historical Perspective

I hope I have shown that both biblical and philosophical analysis demonstrate that religion and its authorities will always be troublesome for governments and that governments will always be troublesome for religion. The conclusion is universal, but the implications are particular. Each religion, each land, and each time has its own debate and tensions.

The debates will be especially fraught for Catholics, because the Church makes uniquely strong claims about the religion's truth, universality, rationality and, at least at some times, about the Church's own authority over its members. I already quoted Leo XIII's broad understanding of the scope of the Church's temporal sway and mentioned that the theological claim should not be taken as a description of the Church's actual role in political governing and social organizing at any particular time or place in Christian history. In practice, political reality has always limited the papal control of rulers and

144   CHAPTER 4

legislators. Similarly, ecclesial reality has always limited the subservience of Catholic bishops, religious orders, and all the baptized. Popes always recognized that Rome's concrete moral, spiritual, and political authority was more negotiated than imposed. The many counterparties were at least as likely to limit the power of the successor of Peter as the other way around.

Perhaps the closest Leo's 1885 claim came to reality in modern times was in the concordat the Vatican had signed with Austria three decades earlier, in 1855. The successor government to the Holy Roman Empire was exceptionally desirous to be identified as Christian (Holy) and Catholic (Roman), so the agreement, which was held to supersede existing laws, gave the Holy See final decisions on all relevant issues. In particular, the emperor promised to protect the Church, and his traditional right to nominate bishops was described as a privilege granted by the pope. The church was to control education and marriages, while the state agreed to suppress books deemed hostile to the church.[36]

That concordat was exceptional when it was signed, was immediately unpopular in Austria, and was largely repealed by 1869. Indeed, Leo's ultramontane agenda was probably a less realistic aspiration for governments when he wrote it than at any time during the preceding millennium. Since his time, the worldly "power" of the Church has continued to wane. The Vatican's influence in political matters is now insignificant in all of Europe and fading in every other traditionally Catholic country. Concordats with governments continue to be negotiated and some privileges have been retained, but the overall retreat has been dramatic. How could it not have been, when the Catholic view of the world was increasingly dismissed as irrelevant if not ridiculous?

There has been one papal victory, but it is more bitter than sweet. The once-great controversies over who should choose and who could veto the choice of bishops have faded away in most of the world, but only because these titles come with so little worldly power or influence that few governments care. The current reluctance of the political authorities in China and Vietnam to allow the Vatican to appoint bishops without government approval is much more a sign of irrational fears than a tribute to potential Roman influence.

---

36.   See Roger Aubert, et al, *The Church in the Age of Liberalism*, trans. Peter Becker, vol. 8, *History of the Church*, ed. Hubert Jedin and John Dolan (London: Burnes & Oates, 1981 [1971]), 108–9.

How did the Church find itself in such a weak position? Some historical background might help clarify the retreat. Of course, the history of Christian relations with governments deserves an entire library, not a summary of a few pages. Still, I think it is helpful to sketch out three themes, each belonging primarily to a single period. I am discussing specifically the history of the Christian and then Catholic heartland (and the European settlements around the world), but the themes are, I believe, relevant everywhere.

Pre-Constantinian

The first period is the pre-Constantinian, which lasted from the apostles' first reception of the Holy Spirit until roughly the conversion of Roman emperor Constantine in 318. The theme of the pre-Constantinian era is separation. All Christians lived under governments that were neither officially Christian nor dominated by Christians. The authorities of the era either ignored believers or disapproved of them.

When the disapproval took the form of active persecutions, then the only acceptable Christian way was clear, if hard: to proclaim the faith to the point of death. If it came to that extreme, martyrs had much to comfort them. By making the right choice between dishonor and death, they were guaranteed eternal life. The witness of blood (the word *martyr* comes from the Greek word for witness) was appealing enough that some early writers felt obliged to counsel against actively courting the death penalty.

More often, however, pre-Constantinian Christians did not face active persecution. Rather, they lived in an uneasy peace with a more or less hostile world.[37] The few descriptions that have come down to us suggest that they made many uneasy compromises. It was usually not difficult to avoid proscribed professions such as idol-making, pimping, and gladiatorial combat, but much harder for successful Christians to deal with the official paganism required of soldiers and magistrates or for Christian parents to avoid the paganism that permeated schooling. Christians tried to live as their neighbors did as

---

37. For discussions of what we know about early Christian life, see Wayne Meeks, "Social and Ecclesial Life of the Earliest Christians," in *The Cambridge History of Christianity*, eds. M. Mitchell and F. Young (Cambridge: Cambridge University Press 2006), 144–74; Henry Chadwick, *The Church in Ancient Society: From Galilee to Gregory the Great* (Oxford: Oxford University Press, 2001; and Jean Daniélou and Henri Marrou. *Nouvelle histoire de l'Église. Tome I : Des origines à saint Grégoire le Grand* (Paris: Éditions de Seuil, 1963).

much as religion permitted, but they were expected to demonstrate Christian virtues, especially fasting, almsgiving, and care of the poor, while avoiding such pagan vices as sacrifice to idols, abortion, and polygamy. The definition of truly Christian behavior was disputed. The second-century Montanists prohibited women's ornaments and the remarriage of widows, but they were condemned as heretical. Orthodox bishops considered such restrictions to be excessive. The canon of the early fourth century synod of Elvira, in modern Spain, banned intermarriage with Jews and set harsh ecclesial penalties for fornication and for "a woman in a fit of rage [who] whips her maid-servant so severely that she dies a horrible death within three days."[38]

Pre-Constantinian Christians are not a perfect model for today's Christians, whether they live inside or outside of the former lands of Christendom. The consecutive rises of Christianity and various post-Christian creeds and "isms," not to mention the latest intrusive proto-Hegelian governments and the vast global flow of people and ideas, have created a very different world from anything seen in the first through third centuries. Still, the old years of separation can perhaps offer some tentative lessons for the current period of Christian isolation.

When Christians are a minority group—whether respected, tolerated, or persecuted (or some combination or alteration among the three)—they band together. As much as possible, they try to establish their own political and communal authorities, setting and enforcing their own rules. The political separation can never be complete, as Christians must always live under higher secular or other-religion authorities. In dealing with these powers, the Christians' goals are necessarily limited and tactical. When Christians are relatively strong and respected, they can ask for more autonomy and greater respect for their distinctive practices and for their religious and charitable institutions. When the faith and its institutions are grudgingly tolerated, believers try to protect themselves by showing political loyalty, finding powerful allies, and providing services to nonbelievers. When Christians are weak or despised, they must do their best to deflect hostility.[39]

---

38. Synod of Elvira, *Canons* (c305), Canon 5.

39. For a good summary of contemporary strategies, see "In Response to Persecution," a report from the Under Caesar's Sword project of Notre Dame University, available at http://ucs .nd.edu/assets/233538/ucs_report_2017_web.pdf.

Constantinian

The second period is the Constantinian. Although the implications of the first globally significant official endorsement of Christianity unfolded over a few centuries, the Christianization of the Roman Empire and the imperialization of the Roman Catholic Church marked a fundamental change in the relations among believers, their churches, the leaders of the Church, and the political authorities. (Constantine's conversion followed that of King Tiridates III of Armenia in 301, but the latter's change of the state religion had no lasting influence outside of Armenia.) Like its establishment, the dissolution of the Constantinian relations of church and state was gradual, but there was not much left by the time Napoleon ended the Holy Roman Empire in 1806.

The theme in this period is integration. European society was so deeply Christian that the whole region was aptly called Christendom. Through its many centuries, most of the population could take it for granted that almost anyone whom they encountered— relatives, neighbors, friends, and enemies—would be Christian. All the governments of Europe were explicitly Christian and, with a few exceptions, for the purposes of everyday life had been Christian since time immemorial. The religious and secular institutions were almost always distinct, but the leaders of both professed the same faith and each felt obliged, at least in theory, to support the other. The boundaries between their spheres of authority were almost always fluid.

These days, the most common summary of the history of Christendom is an antagonistic narration of failure—when Christians had power, they abused it. It is frequently said that most of the time, popes, bishops, abbots, and priests were far more interested in land, wealth, and power than in anything spiritual. The Church was cruel and unjust to the few nonmembers it ran into, mostly Jews and Muslims, and to heretics, people who dissented from the official line. In this telling, the histories of the most important Catholic political institutions, the Holy Roman Empire and the Papal Curia with its directly controlled territories, alternated between tragedy and farce. In the least sympathetic versions of this narrative, the crusaders' sack of Constantinople in 1204 and the Church's persecution of Galileo four centuries later were all-too-typical examples of the institution's inherent flaws.

This entirely negative reading of history is exaggerated, but it reflects an undeniable truth. Fully Christian governments have been

148   CHAPTER 4

tried, over many years, in many different places and forms—and the mélange was clearly rejected. The end was slow enough that Christian rulers and their religious rivals and allies had centuries to stop the decline of Christian practice and the diminution of the Church's moral authority. They failed to do either. Direct Christian influence on government has been rejected in every formerly Christian polity. The last significant holdout lands, Ireland and Italy, are now almost as secular as France and Germany, which were the first to make a firm departure from the Christian political consensus.

Catholics have to admit they lost the historical battle, but they do not need to accept the purely negative narrative of the history of the Constantinian epoch. Indeed, they can tell almost the opposite story, a tale of progress followed by ingratitude for many of its actions. Leo XIII gave a quick summary of the first half of that positive story in 1885. "Christian Europe has subdued barbarous nations, and changed them from a savage to a civilized condition, from superstition to true worship. It victoriously rolled back the tide of Mohammedan conquest; retained the headship of civilization; stood forth in the front rank as the leader and teacher of all, in every branch of national culture; bestowed on the world the gift of true and many-sided liberty; and most wisely founded very numerous institutions for the solace of human suffering."[40] In less grandiose words, the undeniable political failings of the Church need to understood in their historical context and be set against the Church's significant contributions.

Leo also summarized the second portion of the pro-Christian narrative, the tale of de-Christianization. He blamed the Catholic defeat on the bursting forth of the new "tenets of unbridled license," which led to the rejection of the "authority, teaching, and counsels of the Church."[41] He was thinking primarily of the French Revolution, but almost a century and half after he wrote, the list of secular and Church-hostile political ideologies is much longer and more frightening. It includes nationalism, Nazism, and communism. Defenders of secularism sometimes try to disown the many awful regimes of the twentieth century as unrepresentative distortions of their nonreligious political ideal. However, even anti-Catholics mostly admit that all is far from right with the currently preferred secular form of government, the social democratic welfare state. I discuss its

---

40.   Leo XIII, *Immortale Dei*, 21.

41.   Leo XIII, *Immortale Dei*, 23, 22.

promotion of abortion and the denigration of the family in chapter 10, and but even secular observers often describe a political system stained by anomie, nihilism, and widespread depression and despair.

Considering the troubles of the post-Constantinian age, it might be tempting to ask whether the Constantinian model can be revived in some future time. Integralists, devout and optimistic Catholics, speculate that the Catholic Church could once more be fully integrated with civil authorities. For the purposes of the contemporary Catholic Social Teaching, the right response to such speculation is a clear deflection. Today's popes can only offer counsels of imperfection aimed at the world as it is. Not only does Christendom have no place in the world of today, but it is impossible to imagine how today's society can turn into one in which Christianity once again permeates all aspects of social life. Perhaps there will be a neo-Christendom someday, but daydreaming about how to create it is a waste of time, while fretting about how it should be organized is ridiculous. Any neo-Christendom could only come about after unforeseeable cultural changes, changes that would fundamentally alter the discussion.

Christendom, however, is still relevant to today's Catholic Social Teaching. The period of integration offers three relevant lessons.

First, Christians' political problems cannot be resolved simply by entwining church and state together. Even when the Catholic hierarchy was widely respected and the Christian faith was, so to speak, in the air people breathed, there was not much peace in the relations of the Church with the civil authorities. Christendom was almost always deeply divided by religious-political conflicts: popes and bishops against emperors, kings, and princes; popes pitting their worldly powers against the equally worldly powers of bishops and religious orders; governments supporting Western churches against those supporting Eastern churches; Catholic governments against Protestant governments; and popes backed by some rulers against antipopes backed by others.

The second lesson I would draw may be controversial and cannot be proven. However, I believe that the story of Christendom shows that a Christian society can help society as a whole be better by helping many people lead more godly lives. Christendom's fundamental alignment of people, Church, and rulers encouraged both rulers and people to pursue virtue. The undeniable flourishing of government-supported Christian art and architecture provides concrete evidence of this benefit. The evidence for the development of Christian spiritual life and charitable works is necessarily more debatable, but I am persuaded that on balance the Christian society helped the people become more Christian. In governing and guiding, the Church easily and frequently lost all humility, but Christ's good news never stopped to inspire reformers—monastic, mendicant, Protestant, Catholic counter-Protestant, and antisecular. These saintly men and women fought against the corruption of religious authorities and encouraged kings, princes, and peoples to live out their faith more fully. The persistent efforts at moral regeneration suggest an underlying political-religious cultural striving for holiness.

Finally, and perhaps somewhat less controversially, complacency about the faith is probably an inevitable structure of sin in any Christian society, because faith withers when it is taken for granted. Christendom certainly had a great deal of both complacency and withering among its rulers and throughout its religious structures. The fundamental Christian poverty of spirit and drive to perfection in all aspects of individual and social life were often compromised. From this perspective, the forced abandonment of temporal claims was one of the best things that ever happened to the Catholic Church.

Post-Constantinian

The third and current period is the *post-Constantinian*. It is an era of rejection, by the new world of the old Church and, partly in response, by the Church of the new world. It took some time before the confrontational nature of the epoch became clear. Officially Christian governments lasted in much of Europe for a century or more after the French Revolution. Regimes in some important countries remained vaguely Christian as late as the close of the twentieth century. In Italy, for example, Catholicism remained the official state religion until 1984. The lingering political power of Christianity was clear in Nazi Germany, where the government worried seriously about political opposition from both Catholics and Protestants. In the other direction, the right of Austrian emperor, as successor of the Holy Roman Emperor, to veto papal candidates was only revoked by Pius X in 1904. However, Christendom has now been fully gone for long enough to erase almost all traces of the Christian past. There are a few vestiges, including the state churches of England and

GOVERNMENT—CHURCH AND STATE 151

Scandinavia and the inclusion of some schools that are at least nominally religious in the state system in some countries. However, those churches are crumbling and most of those schools have lost almost all of their religion. The German government collects a church tax, but the churches use their ample money largely to pay for the works of the secular welfare state.

One sign of the finality of the change is the change in the Catholic response to its rejection in the former European stronghold. The predominant initial and almost instinctive reaction of the popes to the great modern hostility was a mix of horror and resistance. Catholics were ordered to fight any efforts to reduce Church influence in Catholic countries. The popes took the lead. For example, in 1861 Pius IX declared heretical the view that "the Roman Pontiff can, and ought to, reconcile himself and come to terms with progress, liberalism, and modern civilization."[42] Not only did he refuse to abandon the Holy See's claim of full political authority over the Papal States after the new Italian national government seized them, but he firmly condemned all official guarantees of religious freedom and any government's disestablishment of the Catholic Church from any area of civil and political life, castigating the error that "[i]n the present day it is no longer expedient that the Catholic religion should be held as the only religion of the State, to the exclusion of all other forms of worship."[43] Pius thought the Catholic world had broken faith with its Church. Christians should simply stay as far away as possible from the new, wicked authorities until the faith was restored and Catholicism was reestablished in its rightful place as the conscience of political life. Pius IX prohibited cooperation with the new Kingdom of Italy and promoted the doctrine of papal infallibility, which was designed to ensure that Catholics stayed loyal to their beleaguered leader.[44] Pius X, whose political-religious vision was much like his namesake's, could hardly have been clearer in 1910:

> [I]in these times of social and intellectual anarchy when everyone takes it upon himself to teach as a teacher and lawmaker . . . society cannot be setup unless the Church lays the foundations and supervises the work; no, civilization is not something yet to

---

42. Pius IX, *Syllabus Errorum*, Annex to Encyclical Letter *Quanta Cura* (December 8, 1864), proposition 80.

43. *Syllabus Errorum*, proposition 77.

44. For a summary of the history, see Aubert et al, *The Church in the Age of Liberalism*.

be found . . . it has been in existence and still is: it is Christian civilization, it is the Catholic City. It has only to be set up and restored continually against the unremitting attacks of insane dreamers, rebels, and miscreants."[45]

Both the fierce papal resistance and the blind antimodern fervor proved futile, in part because they were a deeply inadequate response to the serious challenges that modern thinking presented, as well as unchristian refusals to love the actual neighbors found on the road of history. Fortunately, or perhaps providentially, not all Catholics in the nineteenth century were persuaded by the papal "rejectionism." A substantial group argued for a more constructive engagement with the developing modern world. Some of their proposals were initially condemned as heretical, but the Magisterium gradually softened. In 1888, only two decades after Pius IX's firm refusal, Leo XIII admitted that "in the extraordinary condition of these times the Church usually acquiesces in certain modern liberties." However, he was clear that "it is contrary to reason that error and truth should have equal rights."[46] In his mind, as in his predecessor's, the list of errors certainly included any efforts by Catholic rulers to disestablish the Church.

However, as the world showed no sign of reversion, it was the Church that moved—to a more refined and less hostile analysis of modern ideas and to humbler position in its interactions with modern governments. The strength and distance of the movement was not always clear. During the Second World War, many leading French Catholics supported the traditionalist, Nazi-sympathizing government of Maréchal Pétain. Until as late as the Second Vatican Council (1962–65), Church authorities were often ready to condemn efforts by Catholics to absorb the insights of secular thinkers and were wary of all collaboration with secular political and social reformers.[47] The clergy and the lay faithful generally obeyed particular orders, since the Church's authority over its members was still great, but the trend to new thinking continued to gain momentum. The Council was a

---

45. Pius X, Encyclical Letter *Notre charge apostolique* (August 25, 1910).

46. Leo XIII, *Libertas Praetantissimum*, 34.

47. A quick and helpful summary of the political history in Paul Christopher Manuel and Margaret MacLeish Mott, "The Latin European Church: 'Une Messe Est Possible'" in *The Catholic Church and the Nation-State: Comparative Perspectives*, eds. Paul Christopher Manuel, Lawrence C. Reardon, and Clyde Wilcox (Washington, D.C.: Georgetown University Press, 2007), 53–69.

clear turning point. In one of its defining declarations, it promised that "to adapt more suitably to the needs of our own times those institutions which are subject to change."[48]

Since then, the papal and episcopal courting of potentially Catholic-friendly dictators has come to a welcome stop, but Church leaders still struggle to find the right balance of criticism, caution, and endorsement of government policies and new social norms. After the council, many Catholics took up the challenge of adaptation to modernity with excessive enthusiasm. Indeed, some of them adapted so thoroughly that they ended up endorsing pretty much everything about the modern world, from popular music to the sexual revolution. Their list of acceptable aspects of this world included many attributes of modern government: not only the separation of church and state but universal suffrage, extensive welfare states, leveling social policies, meritocratic government bureaucracies, multiparty democracy, and universal government-controlled education.

None of the popes from John Paul II through Francis have given anything like an unqualified endorsement to this sort of all-encompassing so-called spirit of Vatican II. While they have shown no inclination to call for a retreat from the council's nuanced but generally sympathetic response to modern governments and society, their tone is more wary than enthusiastic. That is surely right. As I point out in almost every chapter of this book, Christians should neither condemn the modern world unconditionally nor welcome it unquestioningly. The modern relations of church and state are no exception. On the positive side, in comparison to Christendom the church can be less sullied with worldly matters and the state can be less tempted to use the church for secular purposes. On the negative side, the new separation is a clear sign of society's rejection of faith, a rejection that is bad for everyone and that creates serious challenges for all who wish to live the Christian life.

What Now?

This last section of the chapter goes beyond the wary magisterial teaching. It presents my own evaluation of the current religious-political situation in the post-Constantinian West and my own

---

48.   Vatican Council II, Constitution on the Sacred Liturgy *Sacrosanctum Concilium* (December 4, 1963), 1.

recommendations of how Catholics should deal with this situation. The Western model is not limited to advanced economies. Almost every country in Latin America is very rapidly de-Catholicizing, while atheism and religious indifference are spreading quickly, from a low base.[49] Along with losing members, the Catholic Church has lost much of its social standing in most the region. Only in Africa do Christian religious authorities, including Catholic bishops, still retain a great deal of respect.

While the Western example is being followed elsewhere, the societies of Europe are certainly still the global leaders in secularization. In no European country are bishops or pastors regularly consulted about important political decisions. They are often not respected outside of their churches (and sometimes not very much inside) because their religion is not respected. Nor are churches feared. Few politicians, judges, or popular commentators believe that God will pass any judgment, let alone one of eternal damnation, on immoral or sacrilegious political and legal decisions. In none of these states is a test of faith required to take up political or civil service or to advance in any career. In most developed countries, atheists, agnostics, Jews, Muslims, and Buddhists have no more trouble fitting into the ruling class than do devout Christians. Indeed, atheists generally have less trouble. It is debatable whether the governments should be called predominantly humanist, rationalist, pragmatic, utilitarian, or nationalist, but they certainly cannot be called Christian, even when they technically preside over some vestiges of a Christian past—a state religion or state-supported religious schools and charities. In most countries identified as Western, the de-Christianization of government accurately reflects popular trends—declines in church membership, religious practice, and personal belief.

The United States was, and to some extent still is, a special case. It was the first country to endorse government neutrality in religious matters, with a neutrality that was, until the twentieth century, qualitatively different from the hostile "separation of Church and State" called for by European classical liberals. The country's culture remained largely Christian and religion flourished. Leo XIII described the situation, without naming any country, in which "by a fortunate inconsistency, the legislator is inspired by Christian

---

49.   See Pew Research Center, "Religion in Latin America: Widespread Change in a Historically Catholic Region" (November 13, 2014).

GOVERNMENT—CHURCH AND STATE 155

principles." His judgment was a clear counsel of imperfection: "[T]hough these advantages cannot justify the false principle of separation nor authorize its defense, they nevertheless render worthy of toleration a situation which, practically, might be worse."[50] However, the United States has been losing its religious exceptionalism. The government, especially the judiciary, led the way toward a more militantly secular approach to religion. At first, this was quite unpopular, but the American people seem to be catching up with the government in their disregard for religion as a moral guide and social anchor. The United States is not yet as secular as Europe, but it is heading rapidly in that direction.[51]

Post-Constantinian secularists do not think their governments pose any problem for religions and religious people. They say that individual consciences and beliefs are fully protected by the government-guaranteed freedom of religion and of religious practice; these amount to a legally enshrined commitment to leave harmless religious organizations alone. In this system, they say, religion's proper social role, as a potentially significant part of private life, is fully respected. Secularists may be sincere in this claim, but their tolerance of actual religion is limited, because they consider themselves obliged to constrain all beliefs and religious organizations that could damage society or undermine its values. These days, they often judge Catholics who are loyal to the Magisterium to be potentially dangerous fanatics.

Despite facing some intolerance, many Catholics in the West are comfortable with the secular ordering of religious-civil relations. They may seem to be supported by the Second Vatican Council's Declaration on Religious Freedom, which states that governments should avoid "all manner of coercion in matters religious."[52] However, the declaration does not only support religious freedom on its own. It ties that commitment with a reaffirmation of the traditional Catholic view that the state has positive religious obligations. "Government therefore ought indeed to take account of the religious life

---

50. Leo XIII, *Aux milieux des sollicitudes*, 28.

51. John Courtney Murray, S.J., was the classic defender of the traditional American approach to government and religion. He made a solid case for what had been this aspect of American exceptionalism. See "Leo XIII: Separation of Church and State," *Theological Studies* 14, no. 2 (1953): 145–214.

52. Vatican Council II, Declaration on Religious Freedom *Dignitatis Humanae* (December 7, 1965), 12.

of the citizenry and show it favor, since the function of government is to make provision for the common welfare."[53]

That doctrine is certainly not respected by contemporary governments in post-Christian societies. Their leaders do not merely deny that they have any obligation to promote religion; they often push in the opposite direction, promoting what Benedict XVI called "religious indifference or practical atheism." This religious policy mix—neutral-to-negative in the public sphere and mostly hands-off in private life—is far from respectful "to the transcendent dignity of men and women and . . . their innate yearning to 'be more.'"[54] At best, it effectively relegates religion to a secondary status in the polity, denigrating the spiritual essence of the common good. At worst, it leads to discrimination and persecution. I come back to the evil of the separate but unequal spheres of government and religion a little later in the chapter.

First, though, the council's defense of religious freedom deserves notice, as it was something largely new and truly valuable. The Magisterium had never before clearly declared that all state coercion in religious matters violates the inherent dignity of men and women. At most, the Church had in theory previously half-respected this principle, for example by allowing Jews in Christian countries freedom of worship within their own closed-in communities. In practice, the religious authorities encouraged drawing the line between coercion, which was not allowed, and promotion of the true faith, which was a central responsibility of rulers, in ways that created social disadvantages for any dissent from the Church and severe punishment for any religious dissent that was likely to undermine the faith and practice of the people.

The immediate cause of the new judgment was the weakening of the Church's political position in most formerly Christian countries. As long as Christendom still existed, or as long as the popes still thought it could be restored, Catholic leaders saw little virtue in promoting religious freedom. Theologians might admit that consciences should ideally not be coerced, but popes and bishops were much more concerned with the political responsibility of

---

53.   Vatican Council II, *Dignitatis Humanae*, 3. The meaning of entire declaration is parsed very carefully in David L. Schindler, "Freedom, Truth, and Human Dignity: An Interpretation of *Dignitatis Humanae* on the Right to Religious Liberty," *Communio: International Catholic Review* 40, no. 2–3 (2013): 209–316.

54.   Benedict XVI, *Caritas in Veritate*, 29.

GOVERNMENT—CHURCH AND STATE

protecting the community from religious error. Over the centuries, Catholic clergy encouraged many governments to suppress Christian heretics and schismatics. Conversely, Christian rulers often gained ecclesial support for restraining Jews, Muslims and, later, atheists.

As the Church lost temporal power, it gained in theological strength. Catholic thinkers embarked on an exploration of the anthropology of religion and the psychology of belief. Undoubtedly influenced and aided by the Romantic and existentialist focus on personal responsibility, scholars carefully studied the evangelical technique of Jesus. He invited people to the heavenly banquet and he offered himself to the world, but he never tried to command belief. They also studied Christian reflections from the pre-Constantinian era on the need for the Christian commitment of faith to be made freely. The scholars, and eventually the fathers of the Second Vatican Council, came to recognize the importance of the duty of the state to protect the religious freedom of those under its rule. They even accepted what was to Catholics the most disconcerting implication of this acceptance—that governments should respect the decisions of people "who do not live up to their obligation of seeking the truth and adhering to it."[55] In other words, the Magisterium admitted that error, or at least anyone upholding and promoting erroneous opinions, actually does have some civil rights.

The declaration called on all governments to respect and promote the full freedom of religion—to study, believe, practice, and convert. Religion, or more particularly conscience, was understood as a domain where the principle of subsidiarity held sway. The government should support but not impose religious understanding and expression. As another Vatican II document put it, the "exalted dignity proper to the human person" requires respect for "the upright norm of one's own conscience [and the] protection of privacy and rightful freedom even in matters religious."[56] In the subsequent decades, the defense of religious freedom has become a central tenet of the Vatican's political agenda and a leading practical theological sign of respect for personal dignity. John Paul II's praise in his encyclical about missionary activity is typical.

---

55. Vatican Council II, *Dignitatis Humanae*, 2.

56. Vatican Council II, *Gaudium et Spes*, 26.

> Religious freedom . . . remains the premise and guarantee of all the freedoms that ensure the common good of individuals and peoples . . . . The Church strives for [authentic religious freedom] in all countries, especially in those with a Catholic majority, where she has greater influence. But it is not a question of the religion of the majority or the minority, but of an inalienable right of each and every human person.[57]

It is always wonderful to peer more deeply into the mystery of God's love, but the historical context of this welcome development of doctrine can be a little embarrassing for Catholics. The Church now offers effusive praise for the same universal religious freedom that it previously rejected as irresponsible, especially in comparison to trusting the faith management of Catholic monarchs. At least putting the new doctrine into practice raises few practical issues. If, by some strange twist of history, the new respect for individual consciences had come during the era of Christendom, the Church would have been forced to balance this good with another, the continuing obligation of governments to support religion, especially the true religion of Catholicism. A good balance would have been hard to find. A too fervent dedication to religious promotion could interfere with freedom of conscience, while a too vigilant protection of religious freedom could undermine the common good that is served by the promotion of true Christianity.

In the post-Constantinian era, though, there is nothing to balance. All potentially Christian governments refuse on principle to give substantial support to any religion. On the contrary, dogmatic secularists offer a sort of antitype to the newly developed Catholic respect for the dignity and freedom of conscience. Where Catholics now want to share a lively public space, a "positive laïcité" in which the natural striving for the supernatural can flourish, secular governments promote what has been called "moral neutrality," that works by excluding religion as much as possible from the shared life of society. The secular leaders believe that religious matters are best kept inside each individual's conscience. If such concerns are allowed out in public at all, they should be limited to harmless and socially subservient religious clubs. For the semiofficially atheist state, there is something antisocial about grand spiritual movements, public

---

57. John Paul II, Encyclical Letter *Redemptoris Missio* (December 7, 1990), 39.

religious demands, and even religiously based arguments that might challenge conventional values.[58]

The secular monopoly on the public square in the former lands of Christendom leaves the Catholic Church and its members entirely on the defensive in their relations with ever more expansive states. Catholics should be grateful for whatever freedom of religion they are still allowed. These privileges are by no means guaranteed to last, since the antireligious secularists are in ever firmer control and are becoming ever less tolerant of all people who take any countercultural faith seriously.

For now, though, campaigns for minor concessions to beliefs that most legislators consider archaic can still work. For example, they can help retain the privilege of Christian medical personnel to stay away from anything to do with abortions. However, Christian objections and requests are increasingly swatted away like troublesome flies. Catholics do not face prison, let alone martyrdom, for presenting their arguments about the morality of homosexual acts and same-sex marriage, but they run a real risk of professional or even legal reprisal.

More generally, Christians in ex-Christendom must struggle to find a just, measured, and holy response to secular governments that are fundamentally hostile but usually not violently so. It is good to debate the right response. My personal judgment, much influenced by the papal writings, is that engagement is still preferable to withdrawal in post-Christian countries. I believe today's secular regimes retain enough residual goodwill, and perhaps enough of the legacy of their Christian heritage, that Christians should be willing to participate in governments and obey most laws and regulations. My reasoning is simple. While some parts of the political orthodoxy are totally unacceptable to Catholics, the ruling structures are not rotten to the core. They remain the legitimate authorities, and, as Saint Paul counseled,[59] those authorities come from God and should generally be obeyed.

Engagement is quite different from total endorsement. Discernment is crucial, because some laws and customs truly are morally

---

58. The quoted phrases are taken from International Theological Commission, *La libertà religiosa per il bene di tutti: approccio teologico alle sfide contemporanee* (March 21, 2019), 63 and 65. "Positive laïcité" is quoted from Benedict XVI, "Welcome Ceremony and Meeting with Authorities of State," Paris, September 12, 2008.

59. Rom. 13.1.

repugnant. In these cases, Catholics must choose some mix of avoidance, subterfuge, and open disobedience. Christians have to be like "sheep in the midst of wolves" and "wise as serpents and innocent as doves."[60] Engagement is also quite different from a lifelong marriage. As societies change, the right behavior will also change. The direction of social change is clearly toward more intolerance of Catholic principles. In response, the Catholic approach must become more critical and cautious. Sometime in the future, prudence might demand that Catholics withdraw from and resist unjust governments.

For now, though, I believe that governments still need Catholics who can preach the truth far more than most Catholics need to escape from governments' sway. The interaction requires messy compromises, but as Jesus indicates to Peter,[61] disciples regularly need to have their feet washed.

Here are five more specific suggestions for dealing with post-Christian governments. Obviously, these are mine and not the Magisterium's.

1. Where the Church still has any official standing, its privileges are generally worth defending. Any institutional Catholic presence is a gift to the world and a bastion for the faithful. The defense must be made shrewdly, because the historic tide is clearly running against public Catholicism. In most formerly Catholic countries, there are probably too few powerful, dedicated, and faithful Catholics left for an effective defense of every faith-friendly tradition and every Catholic school, university, hospital, charity, labor union, employers' group, and bank. Bishops, priests, and the laity may decide that it is prudent to sacrifice weaker or less important outposts.

2. Catholics should not delude themselves about intolerant secularism. The enemy should be recognized, condemned, and resisted. The secular praise of tolerance and openness in religious and moral matters almost always amount to the intolerant dismissal of some fundamental principle of Catholic teaching—the absolute truth of human nature, the God-given and inviolable dignity of every person, the reality of sin, the possibility of redemption, the wisdom of the Church, or the reality of grace. Cooperation with secularists is welcome and valuable whenever the Catholic and the dominant political agenda largely coincide, as in the promotion of economic

---

60. Mt 10:16.

61. Jn 13.10.

development, international peace, environmental responsibility, and humane laws. However, Catholics should always be on guard.

Because Catholics and secularists work from different starting propositions, they often come to the same conclusions through quite different reasoning. A small change in circumstances can lead to a sharp divergence of recommended policies. For example, when AIDS, a sexually transmitted disease, became a major issue of public health, many long-standing secular partners of Catholic organizations considered the promotion of condoms to be an obvious part of the antidisease strategy. Catholics rejected that response (or were supposed to), but the divorces from their long-term partners in charity were often painful. The faithful should be prepared for many similar separations of Catholic sheep from the secular goats.

3. Social democracy and welfare states are neither sure friends nor clear foes. As I discuss in chapter 6, most of the first organizers of modern intrusive and extensive governments were either believing Christians or under strong Christian influence, so the political and bureaucratic systems they created were generally oriented to the promotion of Christian virtues throughout the citizenry. Catholics should endorse whatever remains of that fine heritage, for example the commitment to help the weak and the wretched. Believers should be wary, however, because the Christian influence on governments and on the institutions of the welfare state is decreasing rapidly, as can be seen in the devaluing of marriage and the declining resistance to what is sometimes known as "assisted suicide."

4. The defense of the freedom of religion should be refined. The new emphasis on respect for the freedom to practice and change religion is sound. However, to beg for this religious freedom—Catholics are rarely politically strong enough to demand it—is quite different from endorsing the total separation of church and state. As I explained earlier, total separation is neither possible nor desirable. Advocating it is also unwise in many countries that have a dominant religion and a religious government. The authorities in such polities are less likely to endorse a total separation than they are to tolerate Catholics as a minority creed whose members respect the state's right to favor the majority religion. In contrast, in secular countries separation now amounts to a hidden attack on all religious practices and moral injunctions that are opposed to the supposedly higher virtues of tolerance and diversity. If Catholics have any hope of slowing

down this soft oppression, they will have to be bold and difficult, drawing attention to the state's duty to honor, rather than to ignore, the religious core of human nature.

5. Political campaigns to promote unpopular aspects of Catholic teaching are now mostly a waste of time. They will be crushed by the hostility of every relevant part of society—legislatures, voters, courts, professional association, and the media. Many, perhaps most practicing Catholics do not follow the Magisterium when it differs with wisdom of the secular world. The vast political efforts to restrict abortions in the United States provide a striking example. Despite spending a great amount of time and money on the least unpopular of the controversial Catholic causes in the least de-Christianized of the rich nations, the Church and its allies made almost no legal progress over more than forty years. That may now be changing, but any legal victory for the right of state legislatures to prohibit abortion is very likely to be followed by the majority of those legislatures legalizing the practice.

Instead of political striving, Catholics should work on evangelization, which is never a waste of time. Of course, in an uncomprehending world it is hard for Christians to get the attention of the secular society. Still, respectful conversations in which "truth is wedded to charity and understanding to love" will be far more effective than antagonistic political campaigns to protect Christians and their values. [62] Besides, an open dialogue is not merely defensive. It is the most appropriate sort of evangelical engagement with the critical, doubtful, and articulate modern world. To make the Christian side of this dialogue fruitful, believers must offer more than wise and clever words. They must strive to show holiness in their lives, to live in and by prayer, and to follow Mary's simple command at the wedding in Cana, "'Do whatever he tells you.'"[63] Only Jesus can turn the tasteless water of secular thinking into the wine of the heavenly banquet.

Will modern societies actually ever open the door at which he stands knocking?[64] Christians must live in hope, knowing that in time, in God's time, eventually "a little leaven leavens the whole lump."[65]

---

62. Paul VI, Encyclical Letter *Ecclesiam Suam* (August 6, 1964), 82.

63. Jn 2:5.

64. cf. Rv 3:20.

65. 1 Cor 5:6.

CHAPTER 5

Government—War and Peace

War is a moral paradox. It is barbaric and noble, fearsome chaos and precise discipline. It is the embodiment of unconstrained aggression and the final legal protection of freedom. It is a preeminent sign of both sin and sacrifice. It is against everything that Christians believe in and it has been part of Christian life from almost the earliest days.

War is unquestionably bad. It kills bodies, damages souls, and brings misery to almost all whom it touches. Still, military nobility and glory are more than dangerous deployments of excess testosterone in the body politic. The many statesmen, philosophers, poets, and soldiers who have praised war as a crucible in which characters are built and national greatness is tested are not completely wrong. In war, some great human moral dramas—life and death; courage, cowardice, and sacrifice; cunning and fate—are played out in the most concentrated way possible.

Christians experience war as all humans do. They hate its evil but often bear arms and generally prefer the glory of victory to the shame of submission. Christians, however, should do better, because the divine covenant and the promise of heaven cast a harsh light on all worldly disputes and ambitions. Rather than kill for the sake of justice and honor, they should suffer and forgive for the sake of peace. The history of the Catholic Church may seem to put it in a poor position to spread this message. Popes, bishops, and Christian rulers have often—probably much too often—endorsed wars. Cynics can accuse the Church of inconsistency or even hypocrisy—in favor of war when it suits, but always ready to fall back on high principles in the face of likely defeat. Still, while the record is discouraging, the Church is always called to the mission given to it by its founder, Jesus Christ, the Prince of Peace.

The chapter follows my standard pattern: brief discussions of biblical, philosophical, and historical considerations, leading to an explanation of the Church's current position. The basic story should already be familiar. Just as some innovations of the modern world challenged and somewhat changed the Catholic teaching on the elimination of poverty and others have provoked a reevaluation of the value of religious freedom, another set of "new things" have reshaped the emphases in the Catholic view of war. Like the old tolerance of the persistence of economic misery, the old tolerance of the many evils of war now looks morally inadequate.

The Biblical Background

The Bible is framed by peace. In the beginning, when man and woman were new, they lived in a profound harmony. Had Adam and Eve not succumbed to Satan's wiles, there would have been no killing of Abel by Cain, of brother by brother, of peoples by peoples. Alas. The flaming sword of the cherubim now keeps people away from Eden's peace.[1] Nonetheless, human beings cannot quite forget that "from the beginning it was not so" (as Jesus says in explaining why divorce has no place in the life of God's people).[2] Also in the end, it will not be so, after the demons and sin have been swept away from the world. Then, in the heavenly city where God is all in all, there will be a final and complete peace. The wolf will lie down with the lamb and God will wipe aware the bitter tears of human conflict. Death will be conquered by love.[3]

Between the peaceful beginning and end stretches the long, sad path of human history. As the people of God go along that path in the Bible, they look for peace: "Pray for the peace of Jerusalem: / May they prosper who love you! / Peace be within your walls / and security within your towers."[4] Kings search for the paths of Wisdom,

---

1. Gn 3:24.
2. Mt 19:8.
3. Is 11:6, Is 25:8, Rv 21.
4. Ps 122:6–7.

GOVERNMENT—WAR AND PEACE

"and all her paths are peace."[5] They can try to find these ways, but only God can grant wisdom and peace in this world: "In peace I will both lie down and sleep; / for thou alone, O LORD, makest me dwell in safety."[6] In this life, of course, the hopes and promises of divine peace often prove vain. Yet, at the end the Lord will keep his word: "I will make a covenant of peace with them; it will be an everlasting covenant with them."[7]

Jesus, the alpha and omega of humanity, brings together the peaceful beginning and end of human history. He is God's peace; he is the new and final covenant; he fills his Church with the perpetual peace that overshadows the many struggles of ecclesial history: "Peace I leave with you; my peace I give to you. Not as the world gives do I give to you."[8] Christians are to take Christ's peace and make it their own. "Do not resist one who is evil."[9] Paul tells them to "live peaceably with all," although he prefaces that stark command with an acknowledgment of the difficulty: "If possible, so far as it depends upon you."[10] Paul tells Christians in trouble to ask the Holy Spirit for help, so that "the peace of God, which passes all understanding, will keep your hearts and your minds in Christ Jesus."[11]

This Christian peace is more profound than the temporary cessation of hostilities. At best, such truces resemble the resurrection of Lazarus.[12] Although he will die again, his return from death at the hand of Jesus offers a foretaste of the divine life that Jesus both is and offers. Similarly, truces can offer a foretaste of the peace of heaven. True Christian peace, however, is more profound than any political arrangement. It is the perfect peace of the heart rather than the easily broken calm of the polity.

While the Bible is framed by and tinted with peace, it is filled with war. The Lord promises peace to the upright, but for now he is a fighter. Deborah sings: "The LORD is a man of war / the LORD is his name."[13] The Jews, the handpicked people of the Lord of Hosts

---

5. Prov 3:17.
6. Ps 4:8.
7. Ezek 37:26.
8. Jn 14:27.
9. Mt 5:39.
10. Rom 12:18.
11. Phil 4:7.
12. Jn 11.
13. Ex 15:3.

(usually understood as referring directly to the heavenly armies), are expected to fight for the divine name, under divine military protection. The formative tale of their political-theological history is a series of divinely ordained and highly successful battles: the destruction of the Egyptian army followed by the conquering of the seven Canaanite tribes. In times of peace, the Jews are to treat non-Jews with some respect. In war, the tone is often quite different. In the beginning, the Lord's fighters are often ordered to be ruthless. "And you shall destroy all the peoples that the LORD your God will give over to you, your eye shall not pity them."[14] Later in the story of the chosen people, Saul is punished for being insufficiently thorough in his destruction of the Amalekites.[15] At the end of the Old Testament history, Judas Maccabeus tells his soldiers that to "crush this army before us today" will be a sign that God "remember[s] his covenant with our fathers."[16]

The Old Testament takes war for granted. Military images permeate the text. In the Psalms, it is often unclear whether the Lord's aid is being requested for spiritual or physical battles. One of the main responsibilities of kings, both Jewish and gentile, is to fight. King David wages war from before the beginning of his rule until he is no longer strong enough to go to battle. He gets into trouble with the beautiful Bathsheba "in the spring of the year, the time when kings go off to battle."[17] Perhaps because war is considered as inevitable as the seasons—there is "a time for war, and a time for peace"[18]—it is rarely seen as unjust. Even those who conquer and enslave the Israelites are sometimes described as doing God's work in punishing the chosen people for their infidelity.

The New Testament treats war quite differently from the Old. Jesus is not warlike. His peacefulness is not limited to his choice of words, although war does hardly ever come up in either his discourses or the Gospel narrations. Much more significantly, his glory is shown fully in what might be called the antithesis of war, the unarmed and unconditional acceptance of defeat at the hands of soldiers. That approach is not supposed to stop with Jesus. As I

---

14. Dt 7:16.
15. 1 Sm 15.
16. 1 Mc 4:10.
17. 2 Sm 11:1.
18. Eccl 3:8.

GOVERNMENT—WAR AND PEACE

167

mentioned at the end of the previous chapter, he sends his disciples out as "sheep in the midst of wolves."[19]

Jesus is himself peace, but even he seems to accept war as a fact of life. He refers to himself as bringing a "sword."[20] That weapon may be symbolic, but the one carried by his disciple Peter is quite real. He uses it in the standard warlike way, cutting off a servant's ear—while Jesus is engaging in the distinctly nonstandard activity of not resisting arrest.[21] The virtuous centurion is a soldier who knows how to command. Jesus does not criticize his line of work; he just praises his faith.[22] Even the parables are not totally war-free. Preparation for a battle features in one, without any moral judgment.[23]

If silence is indicative, then the earliest Christians followed Jesus in accepting war as inevitable. Paul firmly condemns many varieties of conventionally accepted behavior but says nothing against (or for) military activity. He uses the armor of war to describe the Christians preparation in battle against evil.[24] James condemns the "passions that are at war in your members,"[25] which he says causes actual war, but he does not rail against the slaughter of war, as he does against wealth and faith without works.

In total, the Bible provides sufficient evidence to support many different evaluations of war. Selective readings have been used to support a wide range of judgments, from pacifism to committed militarism. Any extreme interpretation only discredits the intellectual integrity of the interpreter. The Bible is not simply a divine call to arms, a teacher of nonviolence, or a sourcebook for just war theory. It does, however, provide three lessons about war.

First, victory in war is not always the greatest good for God's people. It is true that the biblical narratives assume that any Israelite victory is a sign of divine favor, but the covenant and mission of the chosen people is not primarily military. In the divine plan, the Mosaic and Davidic military victories play a much lesser role than does the Babylonian exile, which followed a series of military defeats. Also, while wars, whether won or lost, do have an important

---

19. Mt 10:16.
20. Mt 10:34.
21. Jn 18:10.
22. Mt 8:5–13; Lk 7:1–10.
23. Lk 14:31–33.
24. Eph 6:10–18.
25. Jas 4:1.

role in the historical development of the Jews, they are much less important than either the Temple or the Law.

Second, God's way can include war, but his ultimate promise for his people is peace. The Bible has traces of a militaristic ideal, the belief that warfare allows noble men to test their valor and discover the will of the gods, but it has no more than traces. When the Lord of Hosts reveals himself to humanity, when the divine Word takes flesh, he bears the messianic title of "prince of peace"[26] and says, "Peace I leave with you; my peace I give to you."[27] Just as God formed man to be imperishable, "but through the devil's envy death entered the world,"[28] God formed humanity to be peaceful, but war is part of our fallen nature.[29] Mysteriously, war, like all the works of sin, is ultimately under God's control, so Christians believe that "in everything God works for good with those who love him."[30]

Finally, that divinely ordered peace is "not as the world gives."[31] Perfect peace can be found only in the world that will come after the end of the greatest war, the final battle of good and evil described in the book of Revelation. The prophets and Jesus teach that this war to end all wars is inevitable, but its timing is in the hands of God, not of humanity. People can only wait for the end of history. While waiting, they must live with the possibility of war. The Bible offers a consistent picture: all rulers and all subjects, no matter how peaceful their intentions or dispositions, must be prepared to fight.

The Philosophical Background

For the past few generations, philosophical discussions of war have largely been confined to two topics. The first is pacifism, which holds that the only appropriate response to all wars is to refuse to fight in them. Pacifism can be individual, the conscientious objection to bearing arms, or social, the refusal of governments to fight wars (declared or otherwise). Most contemporary philosophers of war and society

---

26. Is 9:6.

27. Jn 14:27.

28. Wis 2:24.

29. The thinking of René Girard helpfully ties together envy, violence, ritual conflict, and the full peace made possible and visible by the sacrifice of Christ on the cross. See René Girard, *The Girard Reader* (New York: Crossroad, 1996), especially chaps. 1 and 12.

30. Rom 8:28.

31. Jn 14:27.

reject total social pacifism, with some regret, but it is often taken as the obvious starting point for moral arguments. The second topic is "just war," the careful description of the conditions under which war might be permissible or even required for the sake of maintaining justice. The discussions of the justice of war also include the rules of fighting. Most contemporary philosophers accept that wars should only be fought for objectively just causes and in objectively just ways. Both parts of the "just war" debate can be traced back to the Catholic intellectual tradition. This is a rare example of a basically Christian idea that has entered the modern intellectual mainstream.[32]

After the great slaughters of the twentieth century, it is easy enough to present both of these ideas about war, endless peace as a goal and the strict need to justify fighting, as if there had never been and never could never be any rational or moral arguments for war as a necessary, let alone a beneficial, part of social life. Until very recently, however, it was the antiwar philosophies that had to be presented defensively and polemically. The commonsense judgment of war was usually something like "regrettable but splendid." Many philosophers and statesmen, including Christians, enthusiastically endorsed calls to arms and relatively few either opposed wars absolutely or even selectively. Times have changed, but Catholic arguments for shunning, avoiding, and limiting war should still be set against the traditional arguments in favor. In this section, I present three of the more persuasive prowar arguments: as an unavoidable fact of fallen human nature, as an acceptable remedy of injustice, and an agent of historical development. My intentions are peaceful; I want to recognize the merit of the philosophical case for war under certain conditions but do so to show that Christians are called on to rise to a higher standard.

---

32.   Michael Walzer, *Just and Unjust Wars* (New York: Basic Books, 2006 [1977]) is the standard modern secular work, much debated. Other helpful works include W. J. Sheils, ed., *The Church and War: Papers Read at the Twenty-First Summer Meeting and the Twenty-Second Winter Meeting of the Ecclesiastical History Society* (Oxford: Basil Blackwell, 1983); David Rodin and Richard Sorabji, eds., *The Ethics of War: Shared Problems in Different Traditions* (Aldershot, UK: Ashgate, 2006); Roland Bainton, *Christian Attitudes towards War and Peace, A Historical Survey and Critical Re-evaluation* (London: Hodder and Stoughton, 1960); Ronald G. Musto, *The Catholic Peace Tradition* (Maryknoll, N.Y.: Orbis Books, 1986); James Turner Johnson, *Ideology, Reason, and the Limitation of War: Religious and Secular Concepts, 1200–1740*, (Princeton, N.J.: Princeton University Press, 1975); G. E. M. Anscombe, "War and Murder," in *Nuclear Weapons and Christian Conscience*, ed. Walter Stein (London: Merlin Press, 1961), 45–62. In some of my arguments I have followed fairly closely Joseph E Capizzi, *Politics, Justice, and War: Christian Governance and the Ethics of Warfare* (Oxford: Oxford University Press, 2015).

All three moral arguments in favor of war start with the understanding that killing in war is not necessarily murder. If it were, the Christian debate would end almost before it began. Human life is a gift from God. It should be cultivated, not destroyed. In war, soldiers, who are people, willingly deprive other people of their lives. If war were nothing more than killing, then it would be bad in just the same way that other sorts of murder, including crimes of passion or greed, abortion, and euthanasia, are bad. However, Christian and non-Christian philosophers have generally seen much more in war than voluntary and organized mutual murder. It is perceived as an at least sometimes legitimate activity of governments. When the war is ordered by a ruler who is believed to be anointed or somehow approved by God, or if the fight is believed to be ordained by God, then the war receives divine approval and the soldier's mortal sacrifice brings him a sort of immortality. Claims that war can be God's work still ring true in some circles. These days, a few extremists among practicing Muslims and the professional "Islamophobic" community argue that the tenets of Islam call for unlimited Holy War, while many religious Americans and Russians would agree that God blesses their country's military endeavors.

With or without divine approval, war appeals to many people. The first argument in favor of war is that this appeal is natural in a good, or at least a largely good, way. Typically, the argument goes something like this: the desire for valor is noble and in a well-ordered society that noble desire can be put to good use in war.

If human nature were defined only by the way humans actually act, the argument would be invincible. War really is a fact of human social life and humans definitely find many virtues in it. The ubiquity of war is striking. There may have been peoples or tribes who never went to war, but if so, they have been scarce indeed.[33] Warlike behavior certainly seems to be ingrained in human nature, at least in fallen male nature. I discuss the natural differences between men and women in chapter 10, so here I will only say that boys and men are in practice much more physically violent than are girls and women. Leaving aside the questions of sexual difference, it is certainly true that almost all little boys fight with each other and love to play at doing battle. Many men love actually being soldiers. Engaging

---

33. Laurence Keeley, *War before Civilization: The Myth of the Peaceful Savage* (New York: Oxford University Press, 1996) summarizes the evidence from anthropological research.

in battle was often considered a necessary rite of manhood. The imagery of war permeates language—battles, weapons, armor, bulletproof, drill sergeant, and boot camp are found in a variety of contexts. This linguistic tribute to the experiences of war is matched by the widespread praise of actual acts of fighting, especially when the storied military valor brings victory or heroic defeat. Military men are generally admired, by men and women alike, and tales of combat are popular in fiction and film. It should be said that the massively destructive nature of modern war and its greater dependence on technology and economic resources than on personal valor have dimmed the enthusiasm somewhat. Few people want to read heroic war stories about atomic bombs, improvised explosive devices, or killing with drones.

The most destructive new technologies may have changed the practice of warfare, but wars certainly continue. With varying frequency and violence, men still do as they have always done. They gather up the best weapons they can make and go out to fight their neighbors. They make war exactly as they do most things. They use ingenuity, they invoke divine powers, they have a purpose, they work together, and they are supposed to follow rules. Sometimes the purpose is as simple as finding out which side is stronger. Usually, especially in the past few centuries, the stated purposes are more moral, whether the honor of king or country, the execution of justice, the restoration of durable peace, or the defense of their homeland.

In the dark and twisted logic of war, it often hardly seems to matter if the goals are not reached or reached but then lost again in a year or a century. War seems to make a human point that more peaceful endeavors cannot manage.

This justification from observation cannot simply be dismissed as irrelevant. A philosophy of war that is true to the human condition must recognize men's warlike nature. It is perhaps possible to go no further than merely recognize. It is perhaps possible to see no virtue in fighting, no original goodness mixed in with war's hatred and destruction. Catholic teaching, however, has always seen some goodness in rightly ordered military activity. It accepts the nobility of the soldiers' tasks. "If they carry out their duty honorably, they truly contribute to the common good of the nation and the maintenance of peace."[34] That acceptance is more than a sop to traditional

---

34. *Catechism of the Catholic Church*, 2310.

sentiments or to today's governments. It is a recognition that war is not completely outside of the domain of moral judgment. War is an activity in which some potential good is mixed up with much evil. Wars and the techniques of fighting can be judged as more or less good as well as more or less evil.

The argument from observations shows that war is natural in the sense that it is part of fallen human nature, but Christians should never forget that the Redemption allows men to do something better than fight. With the Holy Spirit's help, they can forgive their enemies (I come back to forgiveness later in this chapter). It is wrong simply to accept war as inevitable and then search out its nobility. Rather, the potential nobility of war should be noted and appreciated but considered far less significant than the glory of peace.

The second argument for war is that it can be the best path to peace, because military victories can bring a decisive end to disputes. The resolution may not always be just or kind to the vanquished, but over time victory can establish a new peaceful order in which justice can gradually grow and flourish, for victor and vanquished alike. The seeds of the new order are planted in the poisoned soil of death and oppression and the new peace is imperfect, but a clear victory may be better than bitterness without any prospect of an end. This argument has some historical support. Native Americans were in the right in their disputes with European settlers, but the Europeans' total military victory eventually led to a lasting peace. Wars and the threat of wars led to the unification of France and Germany, bringing internal, if not international, peace. The two terrible wars in the twentieth century led to something like the unification of Europe.

"War for the sake of peace" is sometimes defended on immoral grounds—some version of the argument that might makes right. That is completely unacceptable to Christians, who cannot argue for any evil because "good may come."[35] There is also, however, a defense of war-for-peace based on something like justice. War can be used to find a mutually acceptable end to an otherwise intractable dispute, as long as both sides can agree on the political meaning of victory. In other words, under certain circumstances, a trial by combat can reconcile men's warlike nature with their natural search for justice.

Of course, such agreements on the meaning of a war are often absent, are almost never articulated, and can easily be broken. In

---

35. Rom 3:8.

practice, each particular war is probably at least as likely to aggravate as to solve problems, even when the warriors on both sides initially intended to make peace. Those on the losing side of one war often decide that justice demands not only another war but a victory that will be more decisive than the last defeat. If that goal is reached, perhaps with the help of new allies, the winners-turned-losers may in turn look for an even greater victory. Alternatively, fear may lead the first winners to attack the disgruntled losers once more, before they can rebuild their strength or find new friends. This pattern can be seen as early as the Peloponnesian wars of the fifth century before Christ, described by Thucydides, and as recently as the three Franco-German wars between 1870 and 1945. War may have brought peace eventually but only after bringing more wars.

Christians might be able to accept the peace-promoting logic of war, but they should certainly be able to do better. There is a nobler path to reconciliation. They should remember that "God the LORD . . . will speak peace to his people . . . / Steadfast love and faithfulness will meet: righteousness and peace will kiss each other,"[36] and also that Jesus spoke of human forgiveness and divine justice. The peace that follows military victory and defeat is better than the tumult and destruction of war. It may even be better than the barely disguised violence of oppressive empires and the steady violence that lies behind that oppression that often accompanies unresolved political enmities. Those, though, are small claims. Forced peace is the brutal work of men, far from the peace of God. Military peace is rarely a triumph of justice. All too often, it is the peace of exhaustion, smoldering resentment, and unjust humiliation. It can turn into something more like true peace, but such peace can only be built over many generations and only if the children and grandchildren of victors and vanquished are willing to let charity overcome their inheritances of fear and just anger. It is better to let charity grow in less poisoned soil.

The third argument for war is that it helps men to advance through history. Hegel, who saw conflicts as fundamental to progress, argued that "[i]n peace . . . in the long run men stagnate. . . . As a result of war, nations are strengthened. . . . To be sure, war produces insecurity of property, but this insecurity of things is nothing but

---

36. Ps 85:8, 10.

their transience—which is inevitable."[37] In this view, war allows more advanced peoples and ideas to gain sway and speeds the healthy elimination of whatever is outmoded.

Once again, this argument cannot be dismissed out of hand. War had indeed accompanied many significant historical changes. The history of any people is in large part a history of war and most forward steps (however that direction may be defined) have been accompanied by violence. War allowed sophisticated Roman law to spread. War exposed more people to Christianity. War spurred the development of many technologies that later proved helpful in peacetime. The destruction of war has often been followed by the ambitious reconstructions of buildings, cities, nations, legal systems, and social mores. War has mingled peoples and created great nations. The U.S. Civil War ended slavery in that country and the Second World War destroyed Nazism.

Once again, though, Christians must try to do better. True conversions can only come from the heart, not at the point of a sword or a gun. Death should be left to God, not accelerated and made crueler by people. Humans, made in the image of the Creator, should follow the divine example by promoting order and beauty. They should not succumb to the diabolic temptation to wallow in destruction. The evil of war is not an unavoidable companion of progress. On the contrary, whatever progress war helps bring about is badly tainted by the accompanying destruction. If cultures are to be encouraged to change, persuasion and example are far preferable to the violent suppression of those judged to be history's losers. Perhaps the progress will be made more slowly by being made peacefully, but God is patient. People should be also.

The Historical Background

It is not just the Bible and most premodern philosophies that took war for granted. For almost two millennia, Christian men in every society lived with and died in wars, always without much surprise and often without much complaint. They fought steadily—before, during, after, inside, and outside Christendom. They sometimes fought for causes that they considered holy: to help spread the faith

---

37. G. W. F. Hegel, *Philosophy of Right*, trans. T. M. Knox (Oxford: Oxford University Press, 1942 [1821]), paragraph 324.

or to fight off infidels who were trying to uproot the faithful. They often fought for causes that modern observers might consider just—for Christian rulers resisting aggression, whether obvious or claimed, sometimes from infidels but most often from other Christian rulers or to defend just claims of sovereignty. Probably more often they fought for causes that now look unworthy of shedding blood—tests of military prowess, doubtful claims of pursuing justice, disputes over titles, revenge for minor slights to a ruler's honor, or simply for the manly pleasure of taking up arms.

The belligerence may have been nearly constant, but it never totally eclipsed the Christian calling of peace. Over the centuries, popes made many efforts to reduce the quantity and severity of wars. They promulgated mandatory truce days and rules for fair fighting. They tried to keep Christian kings from fighting each other, often by offering ecclesial mediation of disputes. They very gradually abandoned the idea the idea that God sometimes called people to a Holy War to promote the true religion. All these antiwar efforts were far from an unqualified success, but neither were they completely vain. Rulers sometimes paid attention to either specific exhortations or to the general Christian preference for peace. It is likely that Christian history would have been even bloodier if Christianity were not fundamentally a peace-loving religion.

Of course, such a counterfactual claim cannot be proven. What can be said with more confidence is that Christians neither ever fully endorsed nor completely abandoned the belief in the nobility of the battlefield. In cultures in which this belief is accepted unconditionally, peace is generally considered no more than a temporary period of preparation for the great and defining struggles of war. Saint Augustine expressed and solidified the Christian tradition by firmly rejecting that claim. He argued that the reverse was the case: "It is . . . with the desire for peace that wars are waged, even by those who take pleasure in exercising their warlike nature in command and battle. . . . For every man seeks peace by waging war, but no man seeks war by making peace."[38]

Later Christians accepted the essentially unnaturalness of war, for created and redeemed humanity. In the preaching and teaching, if not always in the hearts of soldiers and rulers, war was presented more as a sad sign of fallen human nature than as a vital activity for testing

---

38.   Augustine, *City of God* XIX.12.

176   CHAPTER 5

their character. Christians admired soldiers but venerated saints, who were almost exclusively men and women dedicated to peace. Christians who took up holy orders, the human calling considered to be the highest, were generally not allowed to bear arms. They accepted non-violence as they accepted celibacy—in anticipation of heaven. There was a clear consensus that a holy life was holier than even the holiest war.

Although the Church never completely endorsed the glamour of war, neither did it ever completely reject war as simply evil. There are few records of Christian challenges to the assumption of the necessity of war but a long history of Christian praise for military virtues. While clerics were not supposed to fight, they routinely held leading positions in societies in which military campaigns were considered a normal part of life. Not only did priests and bishops willingly provide spiritual succor to armies, but popes and bishop-princes frequently engaged in military alliances and marshaled armies of their own, with few if any signs of compunction. In the first centuries of the Church, the scanty evidence suggests some willingness to refuse military duties because warfare was unsuited to the Christian calling, but there was almost no ecclesial sympathy for pacifism, the response to war that most clearly and completely denies its nobility. That is still true, although the total refusal to bear arms is sometimes praised as being prophetic.

Despite papal and episcopal efforts to reduce warfare, Christians basically ruled as the non-Christians did, with ready recourse to arms. Starting in the sixteenth century, Catholic thinkers developed the long-established natural law into a Law of Nations. This universal framework, not merely applicable to Christian rulers and subjects, was supposed to limit both the number and viciousness of wars. However, there was neither intention nor expectation of eliminating war. Most theologians taught that military service was a potentially necessary part of life for every layman. The obligation to refuse unjust commands in warfare was upheld, but more in theory than in practice. As recently as 1956, Pope Pius XII went out of his way to say that a Catholic citizen of a legitimate government could not rely on "his own conscience to refuse to serve [in the armed forces] and to fulfil the duties fixed by law."[39]

---

39.   Pius XII, *Christmas Message of 1956* (December 23, 1956, my translation). For a helpful discussion of the history of the teaching on conscientious objection to fighting in wars in the context of the contentious deliberations of the Second Vatican Council, see *Commentary on the Documents of Vatican II*, Herbert Vorgrimler ed., vol. 5, *Pastoral Constitution on the Church in the Modern World*, trans. W. J. O'Hara (London: Burns & Oates, 1969), 353–54.

Starting with Saint Augustine, Catholic teachers did demand that wars be just. However, when Saint Thomas Aquinas set three standards that a decision to go to war had to meet to be just, they were not very constraining: a legitimate sovereign to declare war; a just cause, which could be nothing graver than making amends for "some fault"; and a rightful intention, which could be anything that worked for the "advancement of good or the avoidance of evil."[40] This thirteenth-century approach was somewhat modified over subsequent centuries. The Spanish Dominican Francisco de Vitoria's influential 1532 commentary on the Spanish war against the natives of South America expressed a strong preference for peace—"only under compulsion and reluctantly should he come to the necessity of war"—and provided higher standards than did Saint Thomas for a war to be just. "As, then, the evils inflicted in war are all of a severe and atrocious character . . . it is not lawful for slight wrongs to pursue the authors of the wrongs with war."[41] These higher standards, though, did not change the Magisterium's essential judgment of war—evil but inevitable, cruel but sometimes just. What might be called an enlightened realism remained the basic approach until well into the twentieth century. Then the emphasis of the doctrine changed dramatically.

A comparison of the two most recent official catechisms is instructive. In the 1566 offering, written in response to the Protestant Reformation, the discussion of war took up two short paragraphs. The first explained that a soldier who kills while serving his country in a "just war" is "guiltless." The second noted, without any apparent qualms, that God sometimes makes "special commands" for "carnage," that is the indiscriminate killing of noncombatants.[42] Biblical examples of that practice were provided. The writers did not

---

40. *Summa Theologica* II.ii.40. His acceptance, indeed his welcoming, of the use of military force under certain conditions is shown in several articles of II.ii.10. For an insightful analysis of his views, see Gerhard Beestermöller, "Thomas Aquinas and Humanitarian Intervention," in *From Just War to Modern Peace Ethics*, ed. Heinz Gehard Justenhoven and William A Barbieri (Berlin: de Gruyter, 2012), 71–99.

41. Francesco di Vitoria, *De jure belli Hispanorum.* Quotes are taken from pages 106 and 101, respectively, of John Eppstein, *The Catholic Tradition of the Law of Nations* (London: Burns Oates & Washbourne, 1935).

42. *Catechism of the Council of Trent (The Roman Catechism)*, "Manutian Text as Reflected in the Maredsous Edition of 1902, the Fourth Roman Edition of 1907 and the Turin Edition of 1914," translation and preface by John A. McHugh and Charles J. Callan (circa 1923), Fifth Commandment.

178   CHAPTER 5

even think it worthwhile to discuss Vitoria's careful cautions and considerations. The modern reader might well be surprised that such a text was written in the midst of a century of increasingly destructive religious wars.

In the 1997 *Catechism*, which largely reflects the approach of the Second Vatican Council of thirty years earlier, the discussion of war takes up twenty-seven paragraphs. Its approach, as the title "Safeguarding Peace" suggests, is strongly antiwar. "Because of the evils and injustices that all war brings with it, we must do everything reasonably possible to avoid it."[43] The only biblical references refer to the peace of Christ and the eschatological age in which "nation shall not lift up sword against nation."[44] The *Catechism* quotes Pius XII's statement that legitimate governments "have the right and duty to impose on citizens the obligations necessary for national defense."[45] However, the new guide to Christian behavior emphasized that "[a]ctions deliberately contrary to the law of nations and to its universal principles are crimes, as are the orders that command such actions. Blind obedience does not suffice to excuse those who carry them out . . . One is morally bound to resist orders that command genocide."[46] It also asked governments to offer "equitable provision for those who for reasons of conscience refuse to bear arms," directly reversing the teaching of Pius XII.[47]

As is always the case in the Catholic Social Teaching, the undeniable and significant changes in emphasis and policies hide an underlying consistency.[48] The Catholic response to war is and will always be a shifting and never completely successful effort to take into account two moral truths—war is evil and war can be noble—with some reference to a third empirical truth, war has always appeared to be inevitable. As with any attempt to reconcile the fallen human city with the Church's true home in the City of God, no advice can be more than a counsel of imperfection. The recommended types of imperfections vary with historical circumstances. It is easy to see any current counsel as finally wise and all former suggestions of how to

---

43.   *Catechism of the Catholic Church*, 2327.

44.   Is 2:4.

45.   *Catechism of the Catholic Church*, 2310.

46.   *Catechism of the Catholic Church*, 2313.

47.   *Catechism of the Catholic Church*, 2311.

48.   The discussions at the Second Vatican Council described in Vorgrimler, *Pastoral Constitution* demonstrate how great the change in attitude actually was.

deal with human sinfulness as practically misguided or unnecessarily distant from the Christian calling for perfection. That perception may sometimes be justified—I believe it is for the teaching on war—but there is no unchanging final solution to the sinfulness of people and society.

In any case, the Church's practical response to war changed from a perhaps too easy acceptance of its horrors to a perhaps unhelpfully unrealistic call for total avoidance. The reasons for a change of thinking of this sort can never be determined with any precision, but it is worth noting two historic innovations: more peaceful secular thinking and a new dimension of horror in wars. Both took place largely after the dissolution of Christendom.

The intellectual current leading toward peace promotion can be traced back to the strong antiwar streak in the Christian thinking of the Renaissance humanist Erasmus. He was followed a few centuries later by some barely Christian and non-Christian thinkers of the Enlightenment who argued that people needed no divine assistance to make life better in many ways, including the abolition of war. These optimists about human development believed that people did not need to wait for the eternal peace that God would provide sometime in the future. They could construct their own perpetual peace now, in this world. In 1795, Immanuel Kant proposed a federation of free European states to allow the "moral disposition" that is "slumbering in man" "to become master of the evil principle in himself."[49] He was certainly premature. Less than two decades later, Napoleon was leading his revolutionary armies in what was probably the most extensive and deadly European war up to that time.

The aspiration for permanent peace entered mainstream politics a century later, after the next, even larger, and more destructive war. A combination of residual Enlightenment optimism and modern technological dread inspired the creation of the League of Nations. After the even more destructive Second World War, the same combination helped inspire the formation of the United Nations. The consecutive failures to maintain peace seem only to have encouraged more ambitious efforts. The increased interest in economic prosperity has probably also amplified the abhorrence of war, which usually impoverishes everyone involved.

---

49.   Immanuel Kant, *Perpetual Peace: A Philosophical Sketch*, trans. Mary Campbell Smith (London: George Allen & Unwin, 1904), section 2.

Christians must always reject claims of human autonomy and perfectibility, as well as any utilitarian calculus, but as the secular belief in the possibility of semiperpetual peace became sturdier (despite the evidence of history), prudent religious temporizing over war looked both pusillanimous and excessively accommodating. Also, while Catholics are too conscious of sin to share earnest secularists' almost childlike confidence in any permanent pre-eschatological peace, the progressive intellectual current probably spurred bishops and popes to think more positively about what people can do. There are so many "new things" in the modern world that were previously considered impossible, from the potential elimination of material misery to the near-universal spread of literacy and the emancipation of women (to be discussed in chapter 9). The easy killing of millions of civilians in war (which I discuss shortly) is already on the list. Perhaps the more effective control of deadly combat could also be added.

Cynics can argue that the decline in the Church's worldly importance played a role in its increasing interest in peace. An institution that can neither raise an army nor expect others to fight on its behalf has little to gain from tolerating war. The Vatican finally signed away its claims over the Papal States in 1929, around the time that it accepted there were no longer any Catholic states it could call on. Under the circumstances, the enhanced idealism came relatively easily.

The cynical reading of doctrinal history is unfair, but even if it were completely justified the change of emphasis is a clear improvement. It is more Christian to praise peacemakers and to push recklessly for peace than to be reconciled, however sagely and reluctantly, to war. The Church is now better aligned with its mission.

The empirical case against war is clear and grim. While the devastation of wars has been increasing steadily for centuries, the terrible conflicts of the twentieth century set new standards in the death toll of soldiers, the deliberate murder of civilians, and the ease of killing. Nuclear weapons have changed the potential scale of killing, especially of civilians. The new level of man-made destruction could be described as no more than a continuation of the long-standing trend, but most modern observers think it amounts to something worse, something like a cancerous mutation in the already diseased essence of warfare. As long as the killing of everyone at hand was hard and personal work, men could rarely keep it up for very long. Massacres could perhaps be half-condoned as a particularly unfortunate part of war, or they could be, with more moral firmness, condemned as violations of the virtue inherent in the just military enterprise, but, whatever the judgment, they could be dismissed as exceptions, not taken as examples of what war was basically about.

Now, however, war does seem to be "about" mass destruction. Almost any conflict can easily turn into a sort of total war against civilians and soldiers alike. Many of them do. Machines allow massive slaughter from a distance, with no need to observe the victims' humanity face-to-face. Indeed, thanks to the ample supply of ready-to-use nuclear devices, one person or even one computer algorithm could order the immediate violent death of the majority of the human race. The annihilation of most of civilization would be complete in just a few hours. On a less apocalyptic but still grim scale, mechanical ingenuity makes possible all sorts of scientific slaughter, from death camps to chemical weapons to remotely controlled drones. Eventually robotic weapons might do all the killing, but for now people are still needed to operate murderous machines. There will always be enough obedient soldiers and civilians to carry out any desired atrocity, because modern ideologies have proven at least as effective as the fury of battle in stripping human beings of their moral sense.

The popes of the past half century have responded, unstintingly reiterating that peace is always a possible solution to any dispute. I discuss the current antiwar Catholic teaching at the close of this chapter. First, I examine the possible exceptions to this teaching, the hostilities that might be morally defensible. To receive even a tentative Church endorsement, an armed conflict must meet the new, much tougher standards for just war.

The Just War Doctrine

As I mentioned earlier in the chapter, Saint Thomas Aquinas provided standards for a just war. He was following the guidance of Saint Augustine, who in turn was influenced by Stoic philosophy, but the teaching is best understood as a practical application of Augustine's insight that a just peace is both always preferable to war and the only legitimate aim of war. With this priority of peace, a war can only be just if a just peace is otherwise impossible, whether because no peaceful alternatives are available or because all the available alternatives to war are unbearably unjust. Also, to be just, a war must be fought justly and solely for the sake of finding a durable and just peace.

While the Church's stated conditions that qualify a war as just have not changed much since Saint Thomas, the antiwar bias of interpreting them has been greatly strengthened. What once appeared to be a weary effort to keep away war's excesses—"the passion for inflicting harm, the cruel thirst for vengeance, an unpacific and relentless spirit, the fever of revolt, the lust of power," in Augustine's words[50]—has become the intellectual bulwark to the campaign in support of the universal Christian obligation to prefer peace to war: The *Catechism* states that "[a]ll citizens and all governments are obliged to work for the avoidance of war."[51] A look at the five conditions that must all be satisfied for a war to be just, according to the next paragraph of the *Catechism*, shows that the Church wants all leaders' instinctive response to suggestions of military action to be this: "We must in good conscience try everything to avoid taking up arms." It also shows that any decision to take up arms must be done with regret and with a clear and reasonable plan to use the destruction and slaughter to promote peace. A less friendly reading shows how easily consciences can be persuaded that war is actually the least unjust choice.

First, "[t]he damage inflicted by the aggressor on the nation or community of nations must be lasting, grave, and certain." The requirement that the damage of aggression be "grave" immediately excludes wars over minor disputes. The assumption that the "aggressor" is in the wrong implies that truly aggressive war is never just. The precondition of damage demonstrates that a war can only be just if it aims to right a clearly identifiable wrong.

Sadly, though, it is all too easy to believe that the enemy has terrible intentions. Invasions can be described as preemptive or as responses to especially aggressive and serious provocations.

Second, "[a]ll other means of putting an end to [the aggression] must have been shown to be impractical or ineffective." In other words, war must be a last resort. The justice of this demand is clear—military force should not be used until all peaceful means of settling a dispute fairly have been exhausted. This clause is meant to be

---

50. Augustine, *Contra Faustum* 22.74 cited by Thomas Aquinas, *Summa Theologica* II.II.40.

51. *Catechism of the Catholic Church*, 2308.

construed to require the acceptance of such a peace unless there are excellent reasons not to.

However, the practical matter of deciding whether all nonmilitary means of resisting aggression have been shown to be "impractical" is left open to interpretation. The proffered terms of peace often seem "impractical" and unjust to those who receive the offer, and thus they seem "ineffective" to those who offered them. The mutual incomprehension can lead to the judgment on both sides that all other means have indeed been tried but found inadequate.

Third, "[t]here must be serious prospects of success [in war]." In a strictly military understanding of this condition, the logic is similar to Jesus' own suggestions in his parable of preparation.[52] That view of battle is a direct challenge to the cult of military nobility, in which an apparently hopeless effort is always preferable to preemptive surrender. Actually, success should be understood as much more than the enemy's surrender. A war is only truly successful if it brings a peace that is more just and more durable than that which prevailed before the war started. A strict construal of this condition would eliminate all lopsided wars (since the losers would not bother to fight), all wars aiming only to show military prowess, and all wars in which the victor was unlikely or unwilling to bring lasting peace to the society of the vanquished. It would also lead to peace as soon the likely victor became reasonably clear.

In practice, it is all too easy for authorities to overestimate their prospects of success, both in fighting and in creating peace when the fighting is over. Even the decision to fight heroically to the bitter end in a clearly lost military cause can be justified as an inspirational sacrifice that is part of a larger military effort that can plausibly be expected to succeed over some length of time.

Fourth, "[t]he use of arms must not produce evils and disorders graver than the evil to be eliminated." This call for proportionality of gain and pain in war can also be read as an injunction against nearly all wars. After all, the direct evils of war are certain and grave. War kills, wounds, disrupts the civil order, and encourages violent retribution. All too often, there are also indirect evils: a debasement of moral standards, a hardening of enmities, and a diversion of resources from productive to destructive uses. It is hard to believe that the damages from not fighting could ever be greater. This

---

52. Lk 14:31–33.

standard should have become even more demanding in recent years, because, as the *Catechism* points out, "The power of modem means of destruction weighs very heavily in evaluating this condition."

All too often, though, debates about possible wars take place in a frenzy of fear and anger. In such a charged environment, peace without honor can often look more reckless than war.

Fifth, "[t]he evaluation of these conditions for moral legitimacy belongs to the prudential judgment of those who have responsibility for the common good." This condition is actually separated from the others in the new catechism, but it is found on most traditional short lists. It has two sides. As a guide to the justice of starting wars, it prohibits declarations of war by anyone who does not have the appropriate "responsibility," although it does not explain how to tell who actually has, or should have, this authority. A simple reading suggests that all forms of insurrection, private wars, and piracy are automatically unjust. However, "freedom fighters" of all sorts can claim that they actually represent a hidden but truly responsible government.

This condition should also guide those who actually fight in wars. The assignment of moral responsibility to leaders reduces the culpability of mere soldiers. All men should be prepared to serve their country and the hierarchy of command should be respected. Orders should generally be obeyed. However, the requirement that the leaders' judgment be "prudential" implicitly condones military disobedience whenever a particular war or strategy is clearly and seriously imprudent. As mentioned, the *Catechism* explicitly orders disobedience to commands that lead to the "extermination of a people, nation, or ethnic minority."[53]

When people fight wars, they can choose to fight in ways that either are or are not good. In other words, morality is not suspended in the strategy, tactics, and combat of warfare, so everything military is subject to moral analysis. The definitions of goodness in fighting differ from one culture to another and over time in each culture. In ancient Greece, good conduct in warfare included establishing and honoring truces to collect the bodies of the dead after the battle was over. In the modern world, there are other rules. For example, treaties should be honored, soldiers should not be disguised in civilian clothing, and soldiers who have surrendered should not be killed. The Church's teaching, which is in accord with international treaties,

---

53. *Catechism of the Catholic Church*, 2313.

GOVERNMENT—WAR AND PEACE

makes a special call for the just treatment of those not actively engaged in battle: "non-combatants, wounded soldiers, and prisoners."[54] The first group, the civilians, have fared particularly badly in modern wars. For example, the supposed moral superiority of the Americans and British in the Second World War, largely taken for granted by them at the time and too often subsequently, can be considered all but erased by the indiscriminate bombing of many cities in Germany and Japan. The willingness, however hypothetical, even to consider the use of "strategic" nuclear weapons suggests a deep disregard for civilian life.

The Current Teaching—The War against War

The clearest early magisterial recognition of the new moral calamity of warfare came at the beginning of the First World War. Benedict XV's first encyclical, written when the slaughter was just beginning, declared, "The combatants are the greatest and wealthiest nations of the earth; what wonder, then, if, well provided with the most awful weapons modern military science has devised, they strive to destroy one another with refinements of horror."[55] This condemnation, however, only took up two of the encyclical's thirty-three paragraphs. The rest were dedicated to the traditional Catholic concerns of the nineteenth century, starting with the decline in respect for the Church's authority.

After a year of brutal fighting, Benedict eloquently expressed his horror. Addressing the still nominally Christian leaders of Europe

> [i]n the holy name of God, in the name of our heavenly Father and Lord, by the Blessed Blood of Jesus, price of man's redemption," he asked them "to put an end at last to this horrible slaughter. . . . It is the blood of brothers that is being poured out on land and sea. . . . The abounding wealth, with which God the Creator has enriched the lands that are subject to You, allow You to go on with the struggle; but at what cost? Let the thousands of young lives quenched every day on the fields of battle make answer: the ruins of so many towns and villages, of so many monuments raised by the piety and genius of your ancestors. And the bitter

---

54. *Catechism of the Catholic Church*, 2313.

55. Benedict XV, Encyclical Letter *Ad Beatissimi Apostolorum* (November 1, 1914), 2.

186 CHAPTER 5

> tears shed in the secrecy of home, or at the foot of altars where suppliants beseech, do not these also repeat that the price of the long drawn-out struggle is great, too great?[56]

The pope also expressed the new urgency of lasting peace with evangelical intensity. "Lay aside your mutual purpose of destruction; remember that Nations do not die; humbled and oppressed, they chafe under the yoke imposed upon them, preparing a renewal of the combat, and passing down from generation to generation a mournful heritage of hatred and revenge. . . . Blessed be he who will first raise the olive-branch, and hold out his right hand to the enemy with an offer of reasonable terms of peace."[57] After the peace treaty was signed, Benedict surveyed the damage. "[I]f we look around where the fury of the war has been let loose we see immense regions utterly desolate, uncultivated and abandoned; multitudes reduced to want of food, clothing, and shelter; innumerable widows and orphans bereft of everything, and an incredible number of enfeebled beings, particularly children and young people, who carry on their bodies the ravages of this atrocious war."[58] A war of this sort was too destructive ever to be just.

In the judgment of his contemporaries, Benedict's papal diplomacy did not match the single-minded dedication to peace suggested by these quotations. The long-standing Vatican desire to defend its political interests, including the historically hopeless claim to the Papal States, got in the way.[59] His revulsion at the new ways of war received less attention. He was two generations, two tragic generations, ahead of his time. The full awfulness of modern war did not settle deeply into the thinking of the world and the Church until well after the Second World War. It took the loss of something like eighty million lives around the world in two great wars (with a twenty-one-year truce between them) and the deployment of vast arsenals of nuclear weapons for the Church's war teaching to turn strongly to peace.[60]

---

56. Benedict XV, Apostolic Exhortation *To the Peoples Now at War and to Their Rulers* (July 28, 1915).

57. Benedict XV, *To the Peoples Now at War.*

58. Benedict XV, Encyclical Letter *Pacem, dei Munus Pulcherrimum* (May 23, 1920) 10.

59. See John F. Pollard, *The Unknown Pope: Benedict XV (1914–1922) and the Pursuit of Peace* (London: Geoffrey Chapman, 1999).

60. I take the death tolls from http://necrometrics.com/20c5m.htm, which provides sources and a wide range of estimates.

Pope John XXIII set the current magisterial tone with his statement that the goal of diplomacy was "ultimately to abolish [armaments] entirely."[61] He explained the distinction between what was sometimes knows as a "balance of terror"[62] and a positive agenda of peace: "[T]he realization that true and lasting peace among nations cannot consist in the possession of an equal supply of armaments, but only in mutual trust."[63] I already mentioned Paul VI's succinct "no more war" and the peace-centered approach of the *Catechism* published during the pontificate of John Paul II. Both Benedict XVI chose his name partly as a tribute to the First World War's pope of peace. Francis has continued to deliver the pacific message, saying that a war "can be justified—in quotation marks—with many, many reasons. But . . . there is no justification. God weeps. Jesus weeps."[64]

Indeed, the current Catholic Social Teaching on war is not presented fairly by lingering on the latest iterations of the debate on the rules and regulations of just war. At the center of this doctrine are condemnations and remedies. The Magisterium's most pressing contemporary military condemnations are of countries with stockpiles of nuclear weapons, countries that build nuclear weapons, countries that sell arms indiscriminately, poor countries that spend too much on arms and too little on development, military strategies that willfully kill civilians and destroy nonmilitary buildings, and terrorism. In other words, cursed be the warmakers, the potential warmakers, the enablers of the warmakers, and the emulators of warmakers. In the simple and clear words of Francis, those "who work for war, who wage wars, are accursed, they are criminals."[65]

The remedy is peace. Catholic doctrine of war is now primarily a teaching about the need and the ways to tame humankind's warlike spirit, the need and the ways to promote, protect, and restore peace. Those great tasks are to be approached on two levels, the resolutely practical and the unapologetically spiritual.

In practice, the Church starts by asking peacemakers to strive against the provocations that lead to war. The Church urges fractious groupings—nations, tribes, ethnic groups, and religious

---

61. John XXIII, Encyclical Letter *Pacem in Terris* (April 11, 1963), 113.

62. See, for example, Albert Wohlstetter, "The Delicate Balance of Terror." RAND Working Paper 1472, Washington, D.C., 1958.

63. John XXIII, Encyclical Letter *Pacem in Terris*, 113.

64. Francis, Morning Meditation *The Way of Peace* (November 19, 2015).

65. Francis, Morning Meditation *The Way of Peace*.

organizations—to engage in respectful dialogue. It encourages nonviolent responses, including protest and civil disobedience, to injustices within states. It encourages governments to respect international agreements, to work with peaceful international organizations, and to search for and obey decisions of supernational arbitrators, including religious ones, for disputed claims. The popes have strongly supported the United Nations and other efforts to create global communities of communication and shared interest. While recognizing that war often pits brother against brother, the Church hopes that globalization of trade, politics, study, and labor can help reduce the ignorance and fear that can fan hostility at a distance.

The spiritual approach starts by asking what will inspire powerful and outraged governments to overcome "envy, distrust, and pride" without recourse to arms.[66] Catholics recognize that the fear of war, even of terrible modern war, will not suffice. The only full answer is a profound commitment to peace. That commitment is impossible without confidence that God not only wants people and peoples to live in peace but actually makes available the grace needed to do so. Once this primal trust is established, then, in the words of John Paul II, "peace is possible. Indeed, the Church does not tire of repeating that peace is a duty."[67] The peaceful orientation can be lived out if rulers and ruled support what the popes have called the four pillars of peace: truth, justice, love, and freedom.[58] The pillars are not simply a heap of practical policies. They are aspects of the worldview that holds all people to be of infinite value because each one is made and infinitely loved by God. Our common origin and nature make us, "a single family, built on the values of justice, equity, and solidarity."[69] To end conflicts and to maintain peace, all people must come to recognize this intimate universal bond and accept the obligations that it entails.

Of course, this recognition and acceptance are hard for fallen humanity. Every government, like every person, will sometimes fail to love. Injustice and the perception of injustice will inevitably set

---

66. *Catechism of the Catholic Church*, 2317.

67. John Paul II, *Message for the Celebration of the World Day for Peace 2004, An Ever Timely Commitment: Teaching Peace* (January 1, 2004), 4.

68. John Paul II, *Message for the Celebration of the World Day for Peace 2003, Pacem in Terris: A Permanent Commitment* (January 1, 2003), citing John XXIII, *Pacem in Terris*, 35.

69. John Paul II, *Message for World Day for Peace, Peace on Earth to Those Whom God Loves!* (January 1, 2000), 5.

GOVERNMENT—WAR AND PEACE

rulers against each other, leading peoples to mutual hostility. Struggles for power will last until the Second Coming, and when peace is created it will always be fragile, imperfect, and tainted with injustice. To keep and improve the peace that the Church proclaims, people must find ways to settle their disputes that avoid bloodshed. They must abandon violence for the sake of revenge, since the violence that is supposed to correct one perceived injustice only creates others. Peace, even the imperfect peace of the fallen world, requires rulers and people to be guided by a more loving understanding of justice. Christians can point them to the perfect model of this justice, the overflowing sacrificial love of Jesus. He loved us to the point of death "while we were yet sinners,"[70] and his sacrifice set aside our sins, with mercy but also with divine justice.

This love that sets aside sin is called forgiveness. Christians know that people are supposed to forgive each other, just as God has forgiven them.[71] Politically, as John Paul II explained with admirable succinctness, there can be "no peace without forgiveness."[72] With forgiveness, however, peace is truly possible. If each side in a dispute is willing to forgive the wrongs of the other and perhaps to ask for some forgiveness of its own wrongs, then—and only then—can mortal men and women create a peace that truly foreshadows the peace of heaven.

The Catholic Social Teaching's commitment to peace as a political and spiritual project is a clear improvement on any legalistic approach to the justice of war. It is also a theologically correct and psychologically attractive response to the failure of all earlier secular efforts to promote peace through negotiations and power games. Further, the Catholic peace project has neither beginning nor end, so it can be applied directly to the too numerous contemporary war projects that involve years or even decades of violent conflict.

The persistence of these interminable war projects in many parts of the world, from the Democratic Republic of the Congo to Mindanao Island in the Philippines, from the Kashmiri border to Yemen, could be interpreted as a sign that the any peace project, including the Catholic one, is futile. The large stockpiles of nuclear weapons in an increasing number of countries could be interpreted in the same

---

70. Rom 5:8.

71. Mt 6:12.

72. John Paul II, *World Day for Peace 2004*, 10.

way, on a larger scale. Such negative judgments are too hasty. Since, as Augustine said, war is always fought for the sake of peace, the promotion of the moral attitudes and social arrangement that fertilize peace can eventually bear fruit, even in the most scarred societies and even in the presence of the most terrifying and disgusting potential for destruction. Peace can indeed prevail, but only if people throughout society work for it with the same intensity that they have always prepared for war.

CHAPTER 6

The Church Adrift in a Secular World

IN THE VERY BEGINNING, not only did Christians live in a pagan world, but they made pagan words and ideas their own. The New Testament is a Jewish book in many ways, but it is written in Greek, the pagan intellectual vernacular of the time, rather than in Aramaic or Hebrew, the languages of the Jews of Palestine. In the prologue to John's gospel, Jesus is called the *logos*, a word some Greek philosophers used to mean something like "reason." Paul offers Christianity to the pagan philosophers in Athens in their own terms. He tells Christians about their "mystery," using a word borrowed from pagan cults. Scholars argue over just how much and in what ways the earliest Christian thought was shaped by Platonism, stoicism, and other intellectual currents of the time and place, but the existence of a sometimes-uneasy intellectual mélange is incontestable. Believers, trusting that the Holy Spirit will straighten out any confusion of intellectual idioms, can see a theological point: Jesus not only fulfils the prophecies of the Jews, he also answers the yearnings of all people and completes the speculations of all thinkers.

This point may have sometimes been almost forgotten to by those who lived safely within an all-encompassing Christendom. At the intellectual and cultural frontiers, however, Christian history is a story of challenges: from Gnostics, Stoics, Neoplatonists, Muslims, the rediscovered Aristotle, and (later and to a lesser extent) the religions and philosophies of the East. Each encounter left Christianity contaminated, because some alien ideas were accepted with too much enthusiasm, but eventually each also purified the religion, as the refutation and discernment of the strange and the different deepened the understanding of the unchanging Christian revelation.

The interaction continues in the post-Constantinian era, but for the past few centuries the leading challenges to the one, holy, and apostolic Catholic Church have not come from alien civilizations but from its own world, first from dissident Christian voices and then from nonbelievers in what had become formerly Christian societies. The Catholic Social Teaching is largely a response to some of these challenges, to aspects of what can be called the modern worldview. This modernism is a developing tradition. It has been influenced by ancient and Eastern thinking, but it is primarily a child of the Christian world. Many modern ideas are expressions—some insightful, some flawed, some diabolically twisted—of the truly central Christian notions of freedom and human dignity. Indeed, the modern rebellion against the Catholic Church at first often resembled that of a child who wishes to protest against his parents' genuine hypocrisy and perceived limits. The modern revolt gradually expanded, both in scope and popularity. After Catholicism, all Christianity was rejected, then all organized religion, and finally everything supposedly transcendental. This modern refusal to respect the literally awesome ways of God is, like its earliest ancestor in Eden, evil, but unlike that primordial Fall, the contemporary evil has been mixed with much good: both a virtuous frustration with the unchristian social and intellectual constraints that had developed in Christendom and a hope—sometimes possibly realistic, sometimes totally misguided—that earthly life can be made more like the kingdom of heaven.

It would be easier for Christians to deal with these modern ideas if they were either all simply fruitful developments of Christianity or all simply incompatible with the faith. However, as I never tire of repeating, the modern potion is a mix of good and bad that should be neither drained to the dregs nor condemned as undrinkable. The intoxicating drafts of modern worldly and Titanic flavors have often been poisonous, but some of the ingredients have led to deeper faith, more generous action, and a greater humility in the face of the divine. Many of the Church's holiest men and women of the past two centuries—for example, Frédéric Ozanam, Thérèse of Lisieux, Benedicta of the Cross (Edith Stein), and Maximilian Kolbe—have been thoroughly modern.

Modern denials of the existence of anything beyond the material world are unacceptable to Christians, but equally modern calls for more just societies and for more sympathy for the wretched of the earth should resonate with them, as should proposals for universal moral values, improvements in education, and the end of various types of social and psychological oppression. Even extreme modern individualism and materialism should be considered distorted developments of the truly Christian ideas of God's infinite love for each person and God's command to humans to take charge over God's creation.

As I have already noted several times, the Christian responses to modern ideas have often been excessive—too negative when the non-Christian elements received too much attention and too positive when they were downplayed. Overreaction in one or both directions can be seen in the Church's response to five of the six secular ideas I am about to discuss. For democracy and human rights, the magisterial response shifted from too much hostility to too little caution. For the welfare state, the Church was probably too friendly in the beginning and is still struggling to find a coherent mix of welcome and wariness. The Church has consistently been too optimistic about modern approaches to crime and punishment. It was tragically late in its theological and cultural renovation of relations with the Jews. Only on migration has the Church been roughly right from the beginning.

The six challenges discussed in this chapter are not chosen arbitrarily. Along with freedom of religion (discussed in chapter 4) and the privatization of family issues (discussed in chapters 9 and 10), they are almost a catalogue of the most distinctive features of modern polities. The Jews may not seem to belong on the list, as their role and status are now rarely seen as political issues, although there are some alarming recent signs. However, the vile response to the challenge of finding an acceptable place for Jews in modern society was one of the black marks of the twentieth century in what had fairly recently still been Christendom.

I apologize for leaving some worthy topics unmentioned, but a longer list would make for even briefer discussions of each issue. As it is, while I try to provide the usual mix of biblical, historical, philosophical, and theological background, the analyses are painfully abbreviated.

Democracy

There is no democracy, in any sense, anywhere in the Bible. The patriarchs in the book of Genesis are portrayed as tribal chiefs. The "judges," the rulers who succeeded them, were chosen by God, not by the people. The people eventually rejected the judges, but they did not call for anything like representative government. They asked God to give them a king, "like all the nations."[1] During the rest of the biblical era, the Jews were ruled by kings, either Israelite and foreign, or by royally appointed surrogates, carrying titles such as governor and high priest. The Jews were unique neither in the predominance of royalty nor in the claim that rulers should have some sort of divine approval. Until perhaps a century ago, regal or aristocratic governments were the norm almost everywhere. Around the world, this form of government always had a religious aura. When the kings and princes were not considered half-divine themselves, they were almost always thought to have received some sort of sanctification by priestly blessing, anointing, or rite. Even in premodern republics, rule rarely slipped out of the hands of a self-selected, largely hereditary elite group whose authority was endorsed by religious leaders. Rule on behalf of all "the people," the uneducated mass of peasants, slaves, servants, and manual laborers, was almost unheard of. Even the ruling *demos* of ancient Athenian *demo*-cracy excluded a large population of slaves. The elite uniformly considered the majority of the population unfit to govern, an attitude that persisted well into the modern era. Until the middle of the nineteenth century, all but the most radical reformers recommended limiting the vote to property owners or literate men.[2]

Defenders of contemporary democracy often claim the system is the heir to one or both or two striking exceptions to the usual anointed royalty, the just-mentioned democracy of ancient Athens and the republic of ancient Rome. Considering the social differences between both those societies and any polity existing in the Christian or post-Christian worlds, this claimed filiation necessarily involves a good deal of cultural appropriation and creative imagination. For the Church, these historical arguments are of only academic interest. The only relevant issue is its response to the political system that is currently known as democracy. That name, along with its cousin (so to speak) the republic, has been

---

1.   1 Sam. 8.5.

2.   Giorgio Agamben, *Homo sacer: il potere sovrano e la nuda vita* (Turin: Einaudi, 1995) provides a helpful discussion of the role of "the people" in the Western political imagination. Pierre Manent, *Cours familier de philosophie politique* (Paris: Fayard, 2001) offers a more conventional and less negative summary.

applied to various types of governments over the past three centuries. In its current meaning, a full democracy has universal adult suffrage, frequent elections of one or more representative assemblies, some sort of constitution that defines and limits the government's power, legitimacy derived solely from the people (rather than in any way from God or the Gods), a theoretical rejection of all senseless tradition, a theoretical commitment to rely on agreed rational principles, extensive nonpartisan bureaucratic administrations, effective religious tolerance or government neutrality in religious matters (now sometimes government hostility to all public religious activities), and a stated commitment to reducing various sorts of social inequality. Some democracies retain remnants of the nineteenth-century political liberals' mistrust of the masses, for example, legislative houses selected by merit and legal guarantees of certain rights, but these have faded steadily in importance.[3]

This modern democracy is a recent construction. The definition is too flexible for a firm count, but any sort of popular rule was fairly rare until after the Second World War. In its European homeland, democracy seemed to be losing ground to secular authoritarian rule as late as the 1930s. Now, however, modern democracy is accepted globally as the normal form of government. Even the few remaining Communist Party governments and the new authoritarians I mentioned in chapter 3 mostly rule in states that remain formally democratic. This practical triumph has rather occluded the unresolved philosophical debates over the value of the whole democratic concept.

Philosophers have many objections, one of which is particularly relevant to Christians—a government exclusively from, of, and for the people has no intrinsic responsibility to rely on or uphold any absolute and transcendental truth. To Christians, this absence is an

---

3. For a good introduction to the history and philosophies of democracy, see David Held, *Models of Democracy*, 3rd ed. (Cambridge, UK: Polity, 2006). Also, Pierre Manent, *La cité de l'homme* (Paris: Fayard, 1994); Robert A. Dahl, *Democracy and Its Critics* (New Haven, Conn.: Yale University Press, 1989) and James Bohman and William Rehg, eds., *Deliberative Democracy: Essays on Reason and Politics* (Cambridge, Mass.: MIT Press, 1997). *Illiberal democracy* was coined by Fareed Zakaria, "The Rise of Illiberal Democracy," *Foreign Affairs* 76, no. 6 (1997): 22–43. None of secular books cited even mentions contemporary Catholic political teaching. On the Catholic response to democracy, see the nicely complementary studies of Emile Perreau-Saussine, *Catholicism and Democracy: An Essay in the History of Political Thought*, trans. Richard Rex (Princeton, N.J.: Princeton University Press, 2012) and Jay P. Corrin, *Catholic Intellectuals and the Challenge of Democracy* (Notre Dame, Ind.: University of Notre Dame Press, 2002). Corrin's chapters 12 and 13 on Franco's Spain are particularly illuminating.

196   CHAPTER 6

invitation to disaster. The checks and balances of modern democracies can perhaps protect the people from some abuses of power, but they do not anchor authority to any fundamental respect for the inalienable, God-given dignity of every person or to any other truth of human nature. This leaves a gap. Unless democratic rule is restrained by and anchored to some higher concept of the good, whatever group or party is in control will have the freedom to define its own "truth." John Paul II explained the danger of such a system. "[I]f there is no ultimate truth to guide and direct political activity, then ideas and convictions can easily be manipulated for reasons of power. As history demonstrates, a democracy without values easily turns into open or thinly disguised totalitarianism."[4] Just before being elected John Paul's successor, Joseph Ratzinger went further, suggesting that modern democracies actually oppress the absolute truth and all people who wish to find and follow it. "We are building a dictatorship of relativism that does not recognize anything as definitive and whose ultimate goal consists solely of one's own ego and desires."[5]

When Christendom was starting to crumble, popes, most bishops, and many Catholics abandoned their own long-standing battles with each other to bond together in opposition to the new political ideas. They correctly saw political liberalism, nascent industrial capitalism, and revolutionary socialism as inimical to the Church's traditional social position. They also assumed, with much less justification, that these rising cultures were essentially inimical to all Christian values. This almost instinctive antipathy led many Catholic leaders and thinkers to ignore the religious sympathies of some of the early political liberals. On the contrary, popes included democracy, especially the most radical sort, on their lists of dangerous new ideas. The 1832 encyclical *Mirari Vos* expressed this general disdain in clear and harsh language. Gregory XVI wrote it in response to a request for approval from Félicité de Lamennais, a leading French Catholic priest who had become sympathetic to some of the new liberal ideas. Gregory, who did not allow railroads and gas lighting in the Papal States, did not oblige. Instead, he rolled off a series of condemnations. Indifferentism, the belief that "it is possible to obtain the eternal salvation of the soul by the profession of any kind

---

4.   John Paul II, Encyclical Letter *Centesimus Annus* (September 1, 1991), 46.

5.   Joseph Ratzinger, Homily in "Mass 'Pro Eligendo Romano Pontifice'" (April 18, 2005).

THE CHURCH ADRIFT IN A SECULAR WORLD   197

of religion" was described as a "perverse opinion . . . spread on all sides by the fraud of the wicked."[6] Then comes "liberty of conscience [that] spreads ruin in sacred and civil affairs . . . transformation of minds, corruption of youths, contempt of sacred things, and holy laws—in other words, a pestilence more deadly to the state than any other,"[7] followed by "freedom to publish any writings . . . monstrous doctrines and prodigious errors . . . disseminated far and wide."[8]

The new ideas of popular rule, which are guilty of "separating the church from the state,"[9] finish off the list. Gregory is firm. "Therefore both divine and human laws cry out against those who strive by treason and sedition to drive the people from confidence in their princes and force them from their government."[10] Those who are disloyal to the current order, which in practice meant to the royal leaders of Europe, were like the Waldensians and other heretical groups, "sons of Belial . . . the sores and disgrace of the human race."[11] In their "detestable insolence and improbity . . . consumed with the unbridled lust for freedom, [they] are entirely devoted to impairing and destroying all rights of dominion while bringing servitude to the people under the slogan of liberty."[12]

Lamennais was very disappointed, but the pope's strong feelings are a mirror image of those of many of his philosophical opponents. A wide and deep anti-Catholic streak marked modern political thinking. From John Locke to Karl Marx, all the leading proponents of new political ideas vehemently rejected what they perceived to be the unjust, authoritarian, and retrograde Catholic worldview. Jean-Jacques Rousseau, who is sometimes considered a father of modern democracy and sometimes a father of modern dictatorships, provides a perhaps extreme but certainly influential example. In his *Social Contract* of 1761, he endorsed a Christianity of the heart, but the Church of priests who claimed political powers was a "most bizarre sort of religion that gives men two codes of law, two rulers, and two countries, imposes contradictory duties on them, and prevents them from being devout and citizens at the same time. The

---

6.   Gregory XVI, Encyclical Letter *Mirari Vos* (August 15, 1832), 13.

7.   Gregory XVI, *Mirari Vos*, 14.

8.   Gregory XVI, *Mirari Vos*, 15.

9.   Gregory XVI, *Mirari Vos*, 20.

10.   Gregory XVI, *Mirari Vos*, 17.

11.   Gregory XVI, *Mirari Vos*, 19.

12.   Gregory XVI, *Mirari Vos*, 19.

198   CHAPTER 6

religion of the Lamas is like that, and so is the religion of the Japanese. Another example is Roman Catholic Christianity. This can be called the religion of the priest."[13]

Anti-Catholicism and democracy flourished together. By the time England became an exemplar of democracy, the fear of papist subterfuge had been deeply ingrained in the established culture for centuries. The danger of the papacy was widely accepted among the political establishment during the first century of the existence of the United States, which had added some democratic modifications to the British system. The French revolutionary republic, the greatest eighteenth-century effort to create democracy almost entirely from first principles, first disestablished the Catholic Church in France, then tried to close it down, and went on to expel the pope from Rome. Later in the nineteenth century, the leading political parties of the newly established constitutional monarchies of Germany and Italy were, at least at first, firmly anti-Catholic.

Did Catholic leaders hate democracy because it was anti-Catholic, or were leading proponents of democratic rule anti-Catholic because the Church resisted them so fiercely? I will not try to answer the question of priority. What is indisputable is that until the death of Pius X in 1914, Catholic political thinkers who gained papal favor were almost all as mistrustful of the ideology of democracy as most enthusiasts of democracy were hostile to the priestly cult, the wicked cardinals in Rome, and the oppressive Magisterium. In 1885, Leo XIII warned against laws written to please the "delusive caprices and opinions of the mass of the people" and held that the advent of popular sovereignty had led to the "risk of public disturbance . . . ever hanging over our heads."[14] In 1901, he said that proponents of "Social Democracy" tended "to maintain that there is really nothing existing above the natural order of things, and that the acquirement and enjoyment of corporal and external goods constitute man's happiness. [Social Democracy] aims at putting all government in the hands of the masses, reducing all ranks to the same level, abolishing all distinction of class, and finally introducing community of goods."[15] Leo's successor Pius X was even less sympathetic to the egalitarian claims that he thought were inherent to modern democracy. On the

---

13.   Jean-Jacques Rousseau, *Du contrat social, ou Principes du droit politique*, (Paris: Union Générale d'Éditions, 1963 [1762]), book 4, chap. 8 (my translation).

14.   Leo XIII, Encyclical Letter *Immortale Dei* (November 1, 1885), 18, 31.

15.   Leo XIII, *Immortale Dei*, 5.

THE CHURCH ADRIFT IN A SECULAR WORLD   199

contrary, his first encyclical included a call "to restore equilibrium between the different classes of society according to Christian precept and custom."[16]

A careful reading of such magisterial texts shows no conceptual objection to elected governments, as long as they rely on Christian moral foundations and respect the authority of the Church. Leo XIII declared, "[I]t is not of itself wrong to prefer a democratic form of government, if only the Catholic doctrine be maintained as to the origin and exercise of power."[17] In practice, however, for many decades this qualification ruled out warm endorsements of any actual democracies. Even alliances with leading groups in favor of majority rule and universal suffrage were difficult. In 1892, Leo did tell French Catholics to work with the existing republic rather than dream of restoring a monarchy. However, his goal was that "upright men should unite as one to combat, by all lawful and honest means" to fight against the democratic majority's anticlerical legislation. Otherwise, "God alone can measure the abyss of evil into which she [France] will sink if this legislation . . . will stubbornly continue in a course which must end in plucking from the minds and hearts of Frenchmen the religion which has made them so great."[18]

The French monarchists were hardly the only devout Catholics who resented the new political ways. Many European bishops were highly suspicious and sometimes directly hostile to democratic innovations. Catholics in the United States, both lay people and bishops, were always an exception. Catholic migrants to the New World did not expect a Catholic state, Catholics were able to worship freely there, and there was relatively little discrimination against the closely knit Catholic communities. American Catholics were well enough integrated into American democracy that they did not feel the need to found their own political party. Elsewhere, there were deeper cleavages between religions and between the religious and the secular forces, so the acceptance of Christian democratic groups as legitimate Catholic political forces in most countries was very gradual. Catholics had valid political and cultural reasons to distrust most democratic, popular, and socialist movements. Still, I think it is fair to say that many Catholic leaders, both clerical and

---

16. Pius X, Encyclical Letter *E Supremi* (October 4, 1903), 9.

17. Leo XIII, Encyclical Letter *Libertas Praetantissimum* (June 20, 1888), 44.

18. Leo XIII, Encyclical Letter *Aux milieux des sollicitudes* (February 16, 1892), 24, 33.

lay, unhelpfully exaggerated the strength of the theological and philosophical objections to the new political reality.

As the times changed, so did the leaders of the Church. At first the endorsement of popular rule was tepid. Leo XIII accepted a carefully defined politics of "Christian Democracy" in 1901, but he also warned that Catholic enthusiasts for the "cause of the people" should be sure "to keep aloof on all occasions from seditious acts and seditious men; to hold inviolate the rights of others; to show a proper respect to superiors; to willingly perform the work in which they are employed . . . to keep to their religious practices above all."[19] It took a great war, or perhaps two of them, before the popes and most of the bishops fully and finally accepted that the old order had disappeared forever, so that the Church should help believers make realistic choices in the world they actually had to live in.

The choices were hard in the 1930s and 1940s. In most countries, for Catholics the realistic alternatives were constitutional democracies, with or without nominal monarchs, and various sorts of dictatorships, most of them even more fundamentally anticlerical than the decreasingly ideological democracies. Democracy was clearly preferable. In his Christmas address of 1944, Pius XII spoke warmly of "the people" who were "waking as from a long torpor."[20] This "people" was composed of the descendants of the ill-educated rabble whom the popes of the nineteenth century had so feared, but times had changed. If the pope was still afraid of truly popular rule, the fear had diminished with the spread of education and the decline of total misery. Besides, the wicked absolutist governments of both left and right, which relied on and manipulated "the masses," were far more threatening.

Like Pius XII, his successors have all emphasized the need for moral foundations in democracy. However, the Magisterium has basically joined the modern consensus that democracy is the normal and preferable form of government. Prodemocratic teaching has become so accepted that, when Benedict XVI wrote that increasing social inequality places "democracy at risk,"[21] he took it as obvious

---

19.　Leo XIII, Encyclical Letter *Graves de Communi Re* (January 18, 1901), 24. For background, see Paul Misner, *Social Catholicism in Europe: From the Onset of Industrialisation to the First World War* (London: Darton, Longman and Todd, 1991), 189–212. Thomas Bokenkotter, *Church and Revolution: Catholics in the Struggle for Democracy and Social Justice* (New York: Doubleday, 1998) goes over the history from a self-consciously progressive perspective.

20.　Pius XII, *Christmas Radio Message of 1944* (December 24, 1944).

21.　Benedict XVI, Encyclical Letter *Caritas in Veritate* (June 29, 2009), 32.

that democracy is something that should be protected. National bishops do not hesitate to invoke democratic principles when recommending this or that change in policies or governments. The Church also shares the general enthusiasm for free elections. Bishops call on citizens to vote, even when no candidate who has any chance of being elected accepts fundamental Catholic teachings on such morally sensitive topics as abortion, marriage, and the prevention of war.

Still, the Magisterium has certainly not officially endorsed democracy as the best form of government in theory, and its approach to the actual democracies on offer is very cautious. John Paul II spoke warmly of "authentic democracy" but warned of the tendency to "claim that agnosticism and skeptical relativism are the philosophy and the basic attitude which correspond to democratic forms of political life."[22] He described the legalization of abortion in many democracies as a sort of totalitarian expression of the power of the strong against the most vulnerable.

Catholics should recognize that, while democracy may currently be the most acceptable form of government, any magisterial endorsement can be only a counsel of imperfection, subject to review. Catholic principles and practices have been challenged in democracies by both the tyranny of the majority and the dictatorship of relativism. The legalization of abortion is indeed the leading current example, but Catholic positions on most sexual and many cultural matters are often marginalized. Worse, these doctrines of the faith are increasingly held to be illegitimate expressions of intolerance that have no place in a modern democracy. It is easy to compile a collection of alarming incidents—courts and legislatures that have been willing to sacrifice democratically guaranteed freedoms of religion and of speech for the sake of the democratically guaranteed freedom to avoid the "hate rhetoric" of anyone who condemns sin. The acceptance of same-sex marriage and transsexual rights and the lack of protection for those who do not want to endorse either are the latest signs of democratic polities' hostility to the Catholic Social Teaching.

Fortunately, there are still few legal restrictions on or punishments of Christians and Catholics. Indeed, although Catholicism has often been considered incompatible with democracy by both Catholics and anticlericalists, today's democratic governments are currently a much less active threat to the Catholic faith than are the

---

22. John Paul II, *Centesimus Annus*, 46.

indifference of the baptized, the general thrust of secular society, and the violent power of more directly authoritarian regimes. In modern democracies, Catholics can at least worship freely and live by their moral principles without much trouble. The position of believers could certainly be better, but it could be, any may well become, much worse. I say a few words about this worrying prospect in the final chapter.

I have just discussed democracy in some detail, but I should add that the Church's somewhat confused historical response to democracy is unfortunately not the only misreading of the signs of the political times. It is safe to say that the Magisterium has been slow to master the political idioms of post-Christendom. Of course, any collection of policies will always look flawed in retrospect—that is the way with an imperfect world. Still, the list of what now look like Catholic mistakes (not always papal) is depressingly long. In the nineteenth century, it includes repeated alliances with aristocratic political movements (for example the anti-Dreyfusards in France), a frigid response to all popular political movements, and the virulent condemnation of the new Italian state. In the twentieth century, the Vatican signed a concordat with Hitler and a treaty with Mussolini (although the latter did finally resolve the "Roman question" of the Papal States). Later, the hierarchy maintained what now looks like too close relations with elitist and oppressive governments in South America (see the discussion of liberation theology in chapter 3). On the other side, the official Catholic response to the twentieth-century communist governments in Europe after the Second World War was arguably too accommodating until the papacy of John Paul II, a man with direct experience of one of those regimes. All of these decisions were undoubtedly justifiable at the time. The intentions were good, and there can never be a clearly best way for the Church to work for all of its political goals—protecting its own members, defending the common good, and criticizing the evils of cruel and vindictive authorities. Still, it is reasonable to hope that the Magisterium has become more discerning in its observations and responses.

Human Rights

Whatever human rights may be, they are not easily found in the Bible. The drama of Israel and the Incarnation does not include

THE CHURCH ADRIFT IN A SECULAR WORLD   203

anything resembling the rights to "life, liberty, and security of person," the first rights listed in the United Nations' 1948 Universal Declaration of Human Rights,[23] let alone freedom of opinion, expression, and assembly, which come later in that declaration. The humans described in the Scriptures all inherit from Adam the dignity of the divine image and from Jesus they all receive the potential to be temples of the Holy Spirit,[24] but God has all the rights. He gives the Israelites a covenant and gives all humanity love, laws, and duties. Divine right, absolutely—human rights, not so much.

The twentieth-century *Catechism* does not accept this surface reading. Rather, it identifies human rights hidden in the Ten Commandments. The affirmations that people should not be killed, robbed, tricked in court, or deceived in marriage "indirectly" shows the "fundamental rights inherent in the nature of the human person."[25] That is true enough in its way but historically misleading. The whole modern approach to "rights" would have puzzled everyone throughout all biblical times, from the earliest Israelites to the first Christians. It would also have puzzled everyone else in the Middle East in the long biblical era and indeed everyone everywhere in the world until sometime after 1500. They would all have found the concept of subjective rights—rights that people have just for being human—almost incomprehensible. They would have hardly been persuaded by an explanation that led to claims of such innate rights as freedom from slavery and freedom to protest against legitimate governments, let alone such more recent purported universal human rights as the right to access to the internet.

Still, the *Catechism* is correct to suggest some convergence. God told the Israelites to protect the weak and be fair to everyone, both within and outside of their own community. The earliest Christians were called on to love everyone and to treat others as they would wish to be treated. Such injunctions lead more naturally to lists of duties than of human rights, but communities built on these divinely given norms would respect some modern human rights, for example, the rights to life and to just trials and punishment. More significantly, the Jewish and Christian understanding of the tremendous dignity of human nature—each person is created in the image and likeness of

---

23.   "The Universal Declaration of Human Rights" (New York: United Nations, 1948).
24.   cf. cf. Gen. 5:1, 1 Cor 6:19.
25.   *Catechism of the Catholic Church*, 2070.

an omnipotent, just, and loving God—was the foundation of the concept of human rights. Indeed, the concept developed from the ideas of quite orthodox Christian thinkers. Intellectual historians trace the ancestry of the contemporary meaning of human rights back to the sixteenth-century Spanish philosophers who wrote in defense of the human dignity of the indigenous non-Christian peoples of South America. These thinkers thought more in terms of natural law than of natural or human rights, but they argued that the natural law of nations provided humans, including the indigenous population of the Americas and Africa, with what would subsequently be called rights, which Christians could not justly abrogate.[26]

These new ideas expanded and modified the traditional thinking of Christendom, in which justice was in large part defined in the social terms of privileges or rights granted by higher authorities and expressed as particular duties to social superiors, equals, and inferiors. After a few centuries of increasingly individualistic social philosophy, philosophers of universal human rights came to ascribe a list of rights to every individual, without any reference to a social setting and with only occasional references to corresponding duties.

The increasingly secular understanding of human nature and society effectively swept away the religious foundations of the earlier justifications of natural rights. Although it is certainly hard and probably impossible to explain why being human would come with anything like God-given rights unless every person has something like a God-approved nature, by the end of the eighteenth century most of the leading proponents of human rights were reluctant to

---

26. Almost everything about "rights thinking" is highly controversial. For a largely sympathetic approach to the historical background, see Brian Tierney, *The Idea of Natural Rights: Studies on Natural Rights, Natural Law and Church Law 1150–1625* (Atlanta: Scholars Press, 1997); Brian Tierney, "The Idea of Natural Rights: Origins and Persistence," *Northwestern Journal of International Human Rights* 2, no. 1 (2004): Article 2. Ernest Fortin provides a more skeptical historical narrative, for example, in "On the Presumed Medieval Origin of Individual Rights," in *Ernest L. Fortin: Collected Essays*, vol. 2, ed. J. Brian Benestad (Lanham Md.: Rowman and Littlefield, 1996), 243–64. The philosophical discussion of "human rights" has been deepened and transformed by Alasdair MacIntyre. See his *After Virtue: A Study in Moral Theory*, 2nd ed. (London: Duckworth, 1985). A narrower philosophical critique can be found in chap. 8 of John Finnis, *Natural Law & Human Rights*, 2nd ed. (Oxford: Oxford University Press, 2011). For some explicitly Catholic analysis of the contemporary issues, see Edmond Malinvaud and Mary Ann Glendon, eds., *Conceptualization of the Person in Social Sciences. Acta 11* (Vatican City: Pontifical Academy of Social Sciences, 2006) and John Witte Jr. and Frank S. Alexander, *The Teachings of Modern Roman Catholicism on Law, Politics, and Human Nature* (New York: Columbia University Press, 2007).

rely too heavily on divine authority. The 1776 American Declaration of Independence did mention God as the source of its enumeration of rights, but the divine connection was immediately supplemented with the far from transcendental claim that the existence of these rights is "self-evident." Such a combination of naked intellectual assertiveness and philosophical sleight of hand lays the groundwork for any number of purely subjective claims to rights—"It is self-evident (to me) that I have a right to X." When the idea of a God-given human nature become intellectually suspect, it became increasingly easy to create rights to suit the whims—or sins—of the moment.

Even without any such secular adulterations, the standard thinking about human rights is significantly different from the Christian teaching about human nature. Consider the same Declaration of Independence's list of "inalienable" rights: "life, liberty, and the pursuit of happiness" ("happiness" possibly having been substituted for "property" fairly late in the drafting of the document[27]). There is no mention of sin, which sometimes makes it better for people not to pursue happiness as they define it and which is sometimes best punished by the restriction of liberty or perhaps even by the deprivation of life. There is also no reference to any responsibilities and duties that these rights might entail. Nor is there any hint of how truth, love, or the service of God fit into the picture. As a statement of moral or political philosophy, the Declaration's enumeration of rights can perhaps be reconciled with a Christian description of human dignity, but it is certainly not where Christians would want to start.

Indeed, the use of rights in political discourse raises several problems for Christians. I have just mentioned the first and most important one, the philosophical incoherence of the concept. Without a fairly extensive preexisting doctrine of the human nature to which rights naturally accrue—the obvious example of such a doctrine is the Christian one—there is no reasonable way to justify or deny the existence

---

27. The two rights, to pursuing "happiness" and possessing "property," were listed in the 1776 Virginia *Declaration of Rights* (section 1, accessed at http://avalon.law.yale.edu/18th_century /virginia.asp). As Carol V. Hamilton points out in "The Surprising Origins and Meaning of the 'Pursuit of Happiness,'" History News Network, (2008), Thomas Jefferson, who drafted the U.S. Declaration of Independence, was influenced by what he perceived to be an Epicurean ethic: "Moral.—Happiness the aim of life./ Virtue the foundation of happiness./Utility the test of virtue." For a reasonable summary of the Lockean and eighteenth-century legal ideas behind the phrase, see Carli N. Conklin, "The Origins of the Pursuit of Happiness," *Washington University Jurisprudence Review 195 (2015): 195–262*.

of this or that right or to decide which rights should take preeminence when they conflict. The incoherence has recently been raised to a new dimension with the conflating of animal rights to the human variety.

I have also discussed the second problem, the incoherence of rights without corresponding responsibilities or duties. The right to, for example, adequate nutrition, is meaningless without a specific assignment of the responsibility to ensure this right is respected. However, in contemporary political philosophy responsibility discourse is rarely connected to rights discourse.

Third, Christians have to be suspicious about many of today's generally accepted human rights. Some provide too much amoral freedom, as in the right to access to artificial contraception. Others in practice give too much control to the state, because only the government can define which the rights to, for example, education and health care mean in practice.

Fourth, simple enumerations of human rights almost entirely ignore God's rights. That gap is not seen by atheists and is admired by most secularists for its religious neutrality, but it is crippling for any believer.

Fifth, it is almost senseless to assign rights to individuals without any reference to the communities and common good that are the prerequisite and the location of all personal flourishing. While rights can be interpreted in a social sense, as John XXIII certainly intended, it is close to impossible to shake off their original taint of antigovernmental and almost antisocial individualism.

Finally, all rights talk is morally simplistic. It always ignores the existence of sin and shows no respect for the complexity of moral choices.

The almost instinctual recognition of these intellectual problems helps explain why the Church was not initially friendly to the notion of human rights. In the eighteenth and nineteenth centuries, there was also one strong practical reason for not focusing on the ultimate Christian origins of rights-thinking or the many areas of congruence of rights-talk with Christian moral and social teaching. The thinkers and statesmen who were most enthusiastic about human rights almost always wanted to limit the legal rights, along with the moral authority and social prestige of the Catholic Church. Unfortunately, the Catholics' legitimate philosophical objections to these ideas were sometimes too closely entwined with what amounted to, or sounded like, self-interested pleading for Catholic institutional authority.

While the Church's original negative judgment on the concept of human rights was not wrong, it was too crude. Catholics eventually realized that the philosophical weaknesses of the concept of human rights, like those of democracy, did not prevent the concept from being used to give political meaning to the truly Christian idea of God-given human dignity. The historical experience in the United States was instructive. Anti-Catholic sentiment was common there, but in practice the rights enumerated in the country's constitution, particularly the right to the "free exercise" of religion,[28] allowed the Church to flourish. More generally, in many countries the guarantee of rights helped promote a Catholic vision of society by protecting the weak and by limiting the sway of potentially oppressive governments. In painful contrast, the horrors of the great wars and persecutions of the middle of the twentieth century were propagated in the name of ideologies that were thoroughly modern but contemptuous of anything like human rights (at least in practice—communists often paid lip service to rights).

For human rights, as for democracy, these mid-century tragedies changed the Church's approach. As late as 1937, Pius XI could declare, "It is not true that all have equal rights in civil society."[29] After the Second World War, though, Catholic thinkers attempted to reconcile the Enlightenment rights tradition with its Christian and Christian-compatible Stoic antecedents. Jacques Maritain, a leading French Catholic philosopher, helped draft the Universal Declaration of Human Rights endorsed by the nascent United Nations in 1948.[30] At the time, most leading Catholics warmly welcomed this political-philosophical charter for the modern world. They saw rights as a sort of common moral language that could not only be shared by Christians and secularists but that could be used to challenge inhumane practices in non-Christian and post-Christian cultures.

By 1963, rights had become sufficiently Catholic that John XXIII offered a dauntingly long list of them—"universal, inviolable, and

---

28. From the First Amendment to the *Constitution of the United States of America*, ratified on Dec. 15, 1791.

29. Pius XI, Encyclical Letter *Divini Redemptoris* (March 4, 1979), 33.

30. See Jacques Maritain, *Man and the State* (London: Hollis & Cater, 1954) and *Les droits de l'homme et la loi Naturelle* (Paris: Paul Hartmann, 1945 [New York, 1942]), both texts that now seem tinted with excessive optimism about the virtues of the liberal democratic state. On his contribution to the Declaration of Independence, see Andrew Woodcock, "Jacques Maritain, Natural Law and the Universal Declaration of Human Rights," *Journal of the History of International Law* 8, no. 2 (2006): 245–66.

inalienable"—in his encyclical *Pacem in Terris*.[31] His enumeration, influenced by Maritain's work,[32] extends to thirteen main and nineteen subsidiary rights, by my count. Like most such lists, John's combines quite different sorts of rights—those that the law should be able to protect in any law-abiding society (e.g., the right to freedom of worship), those that require prosperity as well as a strong legal system (e.g., the right to necessary social services), those that government cannot protect without widespread social support (e.g., the right to exercise personal initiative at work), and one or two rights that probably cannot be guaranteed fully outside of heaven ("to choose for themselves the kind of life which appeals to them,"[33] admittedly listed in the narrowed context of the right to found a family or join the priesthood).

Unlike most secular philosophers of human rights, Pope John XXIII emphasized that rights cannot be separated from duties, but it soon became clear that this qualification was not enough to bridge the gap between the Christian and secular understandings. Only a decade after *Pacem in Terris*, the United States Supreme Court declared that bans on abortion violated the newly discovered right to privacy. Catholics were appalled to discover that such a doubtful right could be judged more important than the right to life, the right that expresses in the most fundamental way the dignity of the human condition.[34]

Sadly, the "right to privacy" was only the firsts of several morally erroneous rights to gain legal and popular acceptance. Within a few years, secular thinkers and courts around the world started to claim a "reproductive right" to artificial contraception as well as to abortion. Reproductive rights have expanded to include, according to some philosophers, the right of infertile or unmarried women to have children. The right to privacy was extended to protect many sinful sexual activities. The social good of marriage came to be considered far less important than the right of disgruntled spouses to pursue individual happiness. The rights of children have been expanded to

---

31.   John XXIII, Encyclical Letter *Pacem in Terris* (April 11, 1963), 145.

32.   See Drew Christiansen, "Commentary on *Pacem in Terris*," in Kenneth B. Himes, ed., *Modern Catholic Social Teaching: Commentaries & Interpretations* (Washington, D.C.: Georgetown University Press, 2004), 236.

33.   John XXIII, *Pacem in Terris*, 15.

34.   See, for example, Susan E. Wills, "Ten Legal Reasons to Reject Roe," (Washington, D.C.: United States Conference of Catholic Bishops, 2003).

deprive parents of the responsibility for their offspring's moral and religious education. Indeed, it seems that almost any personal preference or social policy, good or bad, can be justified by the extension of an old right or the discovery of a new one.

Some Catholics have been alarmed by the rights inflation. In the words of an article published by the Pontifical Academy of Social Sciences, "[t]hese negative trends, with their injurious consequences, must be condemned in the name of the rational coherence of human rights."[35] However, official Church documents have been slow to abandon Catholic rights talk. The *Compendium of the Social Doctrine* has more than a hundred references to rights and *Caritas in Veritate* used the word twenty-four times. In both documents "rights" is mostly used in a positive way. However, Benedict XVI was not naïve, writing that "unlimited and indiscriminate" claims of individual rights can amount to a supposed "right to excess, and even to transgression and vice."[36] Francis seems to have adopted a more cautious approach. In *Laudato Si'*, many of the mentions of rights are in quotations or criticisms of unjustly claimed rights, although the pope does say, for example, that, "access to safe drinkable water is a basic and universal human right."[37]

Francis might not be cautious enough. Human rights may no longer be part of a moral language that is mutually comprehensible by Catholics and non-Catholics. They may have become just another domain of irreconcilable religious-secular disagreement. Still, the original effort to "rebaptize" rights was well intentioned. The Church should try to speak as much as possible in a language that outsiders can understand. As with democracy, however, the Church has been clumsy in its approach to rights. In both cases, it was initially too hostile, then too friendly and confident. Now, there is still work to be done to make clear that the Catholic understanding of human rights is no longer automatically or even easily compatible with current conventional wisdom. There is a fairly strong case that rights talk should play a lesser role in future enunciations of the Catholic teaching.

---

35.   From Roland Minnerath, Ombretta Fumagalli Carulli, and Vittorio Possenti, *Catholic Social Doctrine and Human Rights, Acta 15* (Vatican City: The Pontifical Academy of Social Sciences, 2010), 16.

36.   Benedict XVI, *Caritas in Veritate*, 43.

37.   Francis, Encyclical Letter *Laudato Si'* (May 24, 2015), 30.

210   CHAPTER 6

The Welfare State

Like democracy and rights, the welfare state is an idea so distinctly
modern that no direct biblical guidance is available. There is almost
nothing in the Old or the New Testament that sheds light on the
key principles of contemporary government welfare programs: the
universal provision, within politically determined borders, of carefully measured benefits following detailed allocation rules; various
types of care provided through administrative systems designed and
implemented by agencies of governments that are explicitly nonreligious; and a government commitment to provide a high level of economic security for all the governed. Scattered biblical readings can be
collected to justify any particular view on such massive government
structures, but no one before the eighteenth century, let alone in biblical times, could even have imagined most of the building blocks of
the welfare state: tremendous prosperity, ubiquitous cash economies,
statistical and secular thinking, and sociological analysis.[38]

My lists of the key components of the welfare state would not
gain universal assent. Indeed, it is hard to know just what the welfare
state really is. It has changed almost beyond recognition in its century and a half of existence.

In extent, the programs have become steadily larger and more
ambitious, moving from the minimal provision of economic security
for the most vulnerable to vast and intrusive programs that fund and
regulate many aspects of life for rich and poor alike. Using my broad
definition, the constituent programs of today's welfare states control
most education, set many of the terms and conditions of employment, compensate many working-age people who are not employed,
organize and provide health care for all, pay pensions to the elderly,
and ensure special treatment for anyone qualified as needy by some
rule-implementing agency. In quality, the social vision behind the
seemingly ever-increasing array of programs has also changed significantly. Programs that used to focus on the intermediate organizations of families, respecting the principle of subsidiarity, have
increasingly created direct, Hegelian State-individual relationships.

---

38.   A few sources: Christopher Pierson and Francis G. Castles, *The Welfare State Reader*
(Cambridge: Polity Press, 2000); Francis G. Castles, Stephan Leibfried, Jane Lewis, Herbert
Obinger, and Christopher Pierson, eds., *The Oxford Handbook of the Welfare State* (Oxford:
Oxford University Press, 2010); Gøsta Esping-Andersen, *The Three Worlds of Welfare Capital-
ism* (Princeton, N.J.: Polity & Princeton University Press, 1990). None of these books pay much
attention to the questions about the welfare state that are most pertinent to Catholics.

This proto-Hegelian approach is also seen in the willingness of governments to set precise rules and define controversial objectives.

Despite the many changes, a threefold constancy in the vision of the welfare state can be traced from the beginning in the mid-nineteenth century, with the passing of the first meager worker protection laws (limiting the hours of factory work for children less than twelve years old, for example), all the way to the most recent initiatives, the massive programs of health and child care. First, there is an unwavering belief in the value of "social engineering"—organized plans to deliver justice to all. Second, there is a Hegelian confidence in the wisdom of the State. Finally, there is the preference for detailed and supposedly fair rules over arbitrary judgments that might be more loving.

For the most part, Catholic authorities have been much better disposed toward both individual social programs and the entire vision of the welfare state than they have been to democracy and the Enlightenment expressions of human rights. Chronology is probably the best explanation for the difference. By the time most of these programs were passed into law, the Church had retreated from its fierce resistance to the de-Christianization of public affairs. With this more accepting attitude, initial doubts and persistent worries did not stop bishops in most countries from lobbying to influence the new laws and cooperating with them when they were passed.[39] Some leading Catholics would have preferred to address the social misery that accompanied industrialization and urbanization with a return to a more agrarian, aristocratic, and Church-influenced social order, but from Leo XIII onward the Magisterium basically welcomed the expanding role of government.

Rerum Novarum set the tone. Leo did condemn the intrusive socialist-Hegelian approach: "[T]he State must not absorb the individual or the family; both should be allowed free and untrammeled action so far as is consistent with the common good and the interest of others." That restriction was, however, followed immediately by an injunction to do almost exactly that. "Rulers should, nevertheless, anxiously safeguard the community and all its members."[40] A few paragraphs later, he asks explicitly for arrangements that would

---

39. For a detailed one-country study of the historic Catholic response, see Peter Coman, *Catholics and the Welfare State* (London: Longman, 1977).

40. Leo XIII, Encyclical Letter *Rerum Novarum* (May 15, 1891), 35.

eventually develop into the welfare or social assistance state, as John Paul II would later call it.[41] "[T]he mass of the poor have no resources of their own to fall back upon, and must chiefly depend upon the assistance of the State. And it is for this reason that wage-earners, since they mostly belong in the mass of the needy, should be specially cared for and protected by the government."[42]

Subsequent popes and bishops have endorsed various government plans to protect workers, the unemployed, the aged, the poor, and the ill. With more or less enthusiasm, they often allowed secular civil servants to take over the traditional responsibilities of many Church charitable organizations. In retrospect, there probably should have been more doubts about the move from organizations that were inspired by the charity of Jesus and integrated into the sacramental life of the Church—"one of her essential activities, along with the administration of the sacraments"[43]—to heavily bureaucratic administrations that relied on regulations and excluded religion. For these duties of social love, religious organizations are increasingly relegated to filling in the relatively small gaps created by programs that are poorly designed or particularly ungenerous.

However, even in retrospect the warm response cannot be considered entirely foolish. The welfare state promised to fulfil the basic Christian demands to feed the hungry, clothe the naked, cure the ill, and care for the weak. It can be argued that the financial model of welfare programs—take from those who have (in taxes) and give to those who need (in cash benefits or in services)—supports the basic Catholic principles of the universal destination of goods, the preferential option for the poor, and solidarity. In the 1881 words of the German emperor Wilhelm I to the national legislature, the funding and operating of welfare programs is "is also one of the highest tasks of any community that rests upon the moral foundations of a Christian national life."[44]

There was perhaps another factor in the favorable magisterial response to secular welfare programs. The calls for the various programs that would develop into the welfare state, unlike the calls for democracy and human rights, did not come almost exclusively from

---

41. John Paul II, *Centesimus Annus*, 48.

42. Leo XIII, *Rerum Novarum*, 37.

43. Benedict XVI, *Deus Caritas Est*, 22.

44. Wilhelm I, Emperor. "Address to German Parliament 17 November 1881" (my translation).

opponents of all things Catholic. There were certainly anticlerical secularists among the leading nineteenth- and twentieth-century European and American social reformers, but there were also many devout Christians, both Protestant and Catholic. After the Second World War, Christian Democrat political parties often cooperated with their Social Democrat counterparts in the construction of welfare states. Less charitably, the continuing positive Church response might be influenced by the decline in religious vocations, which depleted the resources that the Church itself could dedicate to social relief.

The welfare state approach—pass laws, set up programs, levy taxes to pay for them, monitor progress—has worked well enough to deserve much Christian praise. In terms of housing, food and other basic material goods, no societies in history have been more effective than have modern welfare states at satisfying the biblical injunctions to care for our weaker neighbors. Desperate poverty has been all but eliminated in all advanced economies and in many middle-income ones. Welfare states have also sharply reduced the economic uncertainties brought by age, ill health, and technological change and have helped spread widely the vast wealth of modern industrial economies. My positive Catholic judgment of some parts of the modern economy, offered in chapter 2, is quite dependent on the accomplishments of the welfare state.

In offering this Catholic praise, I do not wish to suggest that all is well with every welfare system in every affluent country. On the contrary, as many bishops frequently point out, in almost every country there are far too many people "left behind"—desperately poor by local standards, socially isolated, poorly cared for, or stunted in their economic lives. The bishops are undoubtedly right to call for expansion of many traditional government programs and for the development of innovative new government programs to deal with new or particularly recalcitrant issues.

Still, as I suggested in the discussion of subsidiarity and solidarity in chapter 2, Catholics should increasingly have more concerns with the excesses of welfare systems than they should with their deficiencies. To start, as the gigantic state bureaucratic programs become more extensive, they increasingly do just what Leo said they should not: "absorb the individual or the family."[45] In true Hegelian fashion, government welfare programs have gradually reduced the role once

---

45. Leo XIII, *Rerum Novarum*, 25.

played by various organizations of civil society, including various sorts of families and familial groupings, parishes, monastic orders, confraternities, and organized Christian charities. Also, unchristian Hegelian themes run through many features of the welfare state. Its structure and operations reflect the Hegelian socialist's dislike of private property and privately sponsored culture, the Hegelian psychologist's desire to give the government prime responsibility for child rearing, the Hegelian economist's enthusiasm for letting government or government-guided programs take the family's role in providing for the weak, and the Hegelian sociologist's confidence in the ability of government programs to straighten out the wayward.

Catholics should also have noticed an unattractive utilitarian tint to the welfare state. Utilitarians want to maximize pleasure and minimize pain by social engineering, without making moral judgments. The welfare state attempts to do that with complex rules that sometimes embody a conscious effort to eliminate both the moral virtue of personal generosity and the motivations provided by social shame. Children can be especially harmed by programs that provide material rather than spiritual support and by those that support their parents' bad choices. Catholics know that any type of social utilitarianism is bound to fail, because all societies and all people need a moral and transcendental orientation to flourish. And, as might be expected, the purely worldly welfare state, which ignores or discourages the transcendental urge, too often ends up subsidizing antisocial behavior.

In the history of the welfare state, Catholic analysis did not diverge from the secular mainstream until well after the Second World War. Especially in Europe, any Catholic fears of excessive government meddling were countered by the hope the welfare state could provide a political bulwark against the popular appeal of communism, which was a more extreme and antispiritual manifestation of Hegelian thinking than was any democratic welfare program. Communism was totally unacceptable to Catholics in its politics, economics, ethics, and enforced atheism. In any case, it could be argued that as long as Christian Democratic parties and Christian politicians had a strong influence on their governments, the state programs were not likely to move too far away from a Christian agenda.

In the past few decades, however, many welfare policies have become less acceptable to Catholics. Government programs now

THE CHURCH ADRIFT IN A SECULAR WORLD 215

sometimes subsidize indolence, illegitimacy (as it used to be called), and inappropriate health care. Abortions and artificial contraceptives are made readily available. Adoption agencies are often intolerant of unacceptable Christian religious beliefs. Homosexual marriage has been legitimized. The rules of benefits programs often force mothers away from maternal vocations. Other rules discourage marriage or make divorce less unattractive. The political desire to maintain generous welfare programs within rich societies has encouraged antagonism toward immigrants from poor societies, in direct opposition to the Christian call for global solidarity (as I discuss later in this chapter).

In response to these developments, the Magisterium has become much more cautious. John Paul II observed that "the Social Assistance State leads to a loss of human energies and an inordinate increase of public agencies, which are dominated more by bureaucratic ways of thinking than by concern for serving their clients."[46] He called for more volunteer work and "intermediate communities"—in other words, for greater subsidiarity. Benedict XVI went even further: "[T]he State which would provide everything, absorbing everything into itself, would ultimately become a mere rule-based and impersonal bureaucracy incapable of guaranteeing the very thing which the suffering person—every person—needs: namely, loving personal concern. We do not need a State which regulates and controls everything."[47]

The modern ideas and practices of both democracy and human rights sometimes create problems for Catholics, but most of the difficult issues either concern attitudes and principles or affect relatively few people. The weaknesses are rarely sufficiently noxious for the only moral response to be civil disobedience, although there are significant exceptions and the trends are undoubtedly discouraging. In contrast, the challenges presented by the expansive welfare state are sometimes quite direct. The main danger is not policies that are incompatible with the Catholic understanding of the good, although such policies are indeed becoming more prevalent, but a sort of asphyxiation of the charitable impulse that is central to any social manifestation of Christianity.

Leo XIII presciently and beautifully described the spiritual-practical economy of charity. "No one is so rich that he does not need

---

46. John Paul II, *Centesimus Annus*, 48.
47. Benedict XVI, *Deus Caritas Est*, 28.

another's help; no one so poor as not to be useful in some way to his fellow man; and the disposition to ask assistance from others with confidence and to grant it with kindness is part of our very nature."[48]: Benedict XVI explained that this economy of charity was integral to the life of the Catholic Church: "For the Church, charity is not a kind of welfare activity which could equally well be left to others, but is a part of her nature, an indispensable expression of her very being."[49]

When the government imposes its own rule-based model on all sorts of social aid, the growth of the important expression of Christian love will be stunted. Fortunately, as Benedict pointed out so energetically, love, which casts out fear and is as powerful as death, can triumph over even the most ingenious wiles of the welfare state. "There is no ordering of the State so just that it can eliminate the need for a service of love. . . . There will always be suffering which cries out for consolation and help. There will always be loneliness. There will always be situations of material need where help in the form of concrete love of neighbor is indispensable."[50] However, a great deal of effort is now required for Christian love to breathe in societies that are increasingly smothered by an administrative simulacrum of true generosity.

Crimes and Punishment

Unlike the first three topics of this chapter, the law and the punishments for wrongdoing certainly are discussed in the Bible, in both the Old and New Testaments. Indeed, the God-given law of Moses, one of the central expressions of the old covenant, includes some quite specific commands. For example, "If a thief is found breaking in and is struck so that he dies, there shall be no bloodguilt for him; but if the sun has risen upon him, there shall be bloodguilt for him . . . When fire breaks out and catches in thorns so that the stacked grain or the standing grain or the field is consumed, he that kindled the fire shall make full restitution."[51] The new covenant is not "legalistic" in the sense of listing crimes and punishments, but in is in its essence one simple law—the divine code of pure and total love.

---

48. Leo XIII, Encyclical Letter *Graves de Communi Re* (January 18, 1901), 16.
49. Benedict XVI, *Deus Caritas Est*, 25.
50. Benedict XVI, *Deus Caritas Est*, 28.
51. Ex 22:2–3, 6.

THE CHURCH ADRIFT IN A SECULAR WORLD   217

The admixture of Roman law in the intellectual and practical discussions in Christendom did not fundamentally loosen the biblical anchor. Even in fully secular societies, debates about justice, law, and legal punishment are marked by biblical Christian concepts of justice, personal responsibility, the common good, and the possibility of redemptive reform.

Still, there is a fundamental difference between the biblical and the modern approaches. The revealed law in both the Old and New Testaments is essentially a description of how "you shall love your God with all your heart, all your soul, and all your mind." The biblical emphasis is overwhelmingly on this "great commandment," which seems to subsume or imply the second command that "is like it," to "love your neighbor as yourself," as Jesus sums up the meaning of "all the law and the prophets."[52] In this conception of law, the rules of worship are totally integrated with the rules of behavior in society and the rules of purity in what moderns would consider "private" life.[53]

How much of this unity of cult and society was preserved in the various legal systems of Christendom is an interesting question, but the answer is not relevant to the Church's modern, post-Christendom Social Teaching. What is relevant is the entirely secular character of modern criminal law (outside of a few Islamic polities). In effect, Jesus' two great commandments are firmly separated, with the legal systems showing no interest in the first, greater one. For Christians, this draining of religion from the legal arrangements is spiritually impoverishing. It diminishes the grandeur of the law, the dignity of criminals as God-created and God-imaging persons who have, at least from the perspective of the community, failed in their divine calling, and the spiritual meaning of punishments. However, the Social Teaching has to deal with a world in which punishments are secular, so in searching for biblical sources it can only rely on a partial and inevitably distorted reading of the Law given to Moses.

In the Old Testament, the only directly expressed penal philosophy in human-to-human justice is the thrice repeated injunction to

---

52.   Mt 22:36–38.

53.   The immense scholarship on the three law codes of the Torah is not directly relevant to my point, which is simply that in the final composition of the texts cultic, social, and criminal rules were all included in the Law. For a clear introduction to the scholarly and some of the exegetical issues, see Dale Patrick, *Old Testament Law* (London: SCM Press, 1986) and Frank Crüsemann, *The Torah: Theology and Social History of Old Testament Law*, trans. Allan W. Mahnke (Edinburgh: T&T Clark 1996 [1992]).

take "life for life, eye for eye, tooth for tooth, hand for hand, foot for foot."[54] That principle might be helpful, but its meaning is contested. It has been interpreted as a demand that punishments and penalties are proportionate to the offenses, as a call to avoid excessive punishments, and as an injunction against lax ones. In such uncertainty, it is better to look for more general principles of biblical criminal justice. The Old Testament yields two that are relevant to the Christian response to the secular legal order.

First, there should be a firm response to evil. In a typical injunction, God tells the Israelites, "You must show no pity" to false witnesses.[55] Second, there should be a willingness not to persist in revenge and ill will. God also tells the Israelites not to "exact vengeance" on each other but, as mentioned, to "love your neighbor as yourself."[56] The two principles are not exactly contradictory; God himself can follow both perfectly. In human practice, however, they are often hard to reconcile. Punishment should be considered a necessarily imperfect human effort to be both just and merciful. Clearly, any teaching on punishment will have to be a counsel of imperfection.

The New Testament teaches Christians to be merciful, leaving the harsh side of justice to God. Jesus tells his followers to reject the old penal principal of equivalence of crime and punishment in favor of forgiving and loving wrongdoers.[57] Paul tells the first Christian communities that "love is the fulfilling of the law."[58] The criminal punishment at the center of the gospel, the crucifixion of Jesus, provides a deeply unsettling example of the potential iniquity of any human penal judgment. Still, neither the command to love unconditionally nor the profound fallibility of our judgment implies punishment should have no place in our societies. Jesus enjoins mercy on his followers, but he also tells Pontius Pilate that his authority to punish comes from God and he seems to have no problem with putting debtors in prison.[59] Paul is even clearer, explicitly praising the government's ability "to execute [God's] wrath on the wrongdoer."[60] Neither Paul nor Jesus goes into any detail about what sort of

---

54. Ex 21:23–24; also Lv 24:17–20 and Dt 19:21.

55. Dt 19:21.

56. Lv 19:18.

57. cf. Mt 5:38–42.

58. Rom 13:10.

59. Jn 19:11; cf. Lk 12:57–59: Mt 18:23–35.

60. Rom 13:4.

THE CHURCH ADRIFT IN A SECULAR WORLD   219

human retributions should be considered just. They are much more concerned with God's eternal justice.

The biblical discussion of punishment is too scanty to provide guidance on the central philosophical-practical questions of modern criminal justice: What is the goal of punishment? What combination of rehabilitation, equitable retribution, deterrence, or restorative justice is desirable or reasonable? The Bible is just as unhelpful in addressing the modern sociological-psychological debates: How should responsibility be divided between criminals and the family or society that helped shape them? How should wrongdoers be treated? These omissions, like the failure to give insight into democracy or the welfare state, are inevitable. Extensive prison systems, long sentences, and a philosophy of corrections did not exist in biblical times. Still, there were prisons. The Bible often refers to them in symbolic or almost symbolic terms, as places where men are isolated from God's love and protection. For example, Isaiah declares that the prophet of the Lord will "proclaim liberty to the captives and the opening of the prison to those who are bound, proclaim the year of the LORD's favor, and the day of vengeance of our God."[61]

Jesus identifies himself explicitly with Isaiah's liberating prophet.[62] In his list of saving Christian acts of mercy,[63] he also identifies himself with all imprisoned people. Unlike the other good deeds on that list—feeding the hungry, giving drink to the thirsty, clothing the naked, and welcoming the stranger—visiting prisoners does not seem to have precedents in the Jewish tradition of charitable acts.[64] For Christians, however, this identification makes theological sense. Jesus comes to retrieve the lost and the outcasts. In their emulation of their Lord, Christians should take a special interest in reclaiming those who found themselves physically cut off from the rest of society. The forgiveness and grace of God is most relevant to these lost sheep.

The literal injunction to visit prisoners was not entirely ignored in the history of Christianity. There was especially great interest in preparing the condemned for a good death. However, until a few centuries ago, neither Christian mercy nor what is now called

---

61.   Is 61:1–2.

62.   cf. Lk 4:18.

63.   cf. Mt 25:36.

64.   So says W. D. Davies and Dale C. Allison, *A Critical and Exegetical Commentary on the Gospel According to Saint Matthew*, vol. 3 (London: Bloomsbury, 1997), 428, citing only Hebrews 10.34 and 13.3 as comparable passages.

rehabilitation was a guiding principle in the treatment of Christendom's miscreants. At best, the system of punishment was guided by various fairly harsh standards of justice—retribution for past crimes and prevention of future ones, through restraining or executing actual criminals and frightening potential ones. At worst, it was guided by unjust or at least unchristian fury and vengeance. While both civil and church leaders occasionally called for what would now be called more humane treatment of wrongdoers, Christian judges and rulers had no problem ordering painful executions, torture, harsh physical punishments, and long confinements in fetid and often fatal prisons.

Monasteries, which can be considered prisons into which inmates enter voluntarily and for life, eventually adopted an approach to punishment that was less concerned with vengeance than with the rehabilitation of the moral capacity of the reprobate and his or her restoration to the normal life of the community. In effect, errant members of religious communities were sentenced to harsh extensions of their normal spiritual and physical discipline—lengthy periods of confinement, physical deprivation, carefully controlled activities, and extensive spiritual guidance. There are not enough surviving records to judge how much individual spiritual reform these monastic punishments actually produced, but they were attractive enough to serve as model for modern rehabilitative prisons, in both their architecture (cells build around a central courtyard) and their commitment to reforming as well as punishing wrongdoers.[65]

The Christian influence on the penal reform movement that came into prominence in the nineteenth century was not limited to providing examples of what was hoped would be good prison architecture. As in some other campaigns for social improvements, both religious and secular thinkers worked to institute more humane systems of punishment, systems that were also supposed to be more just, less vindictive, and more effective at reducing crime. The Catholic contribution started early. Jean Mabillon, a seventeenth-century Benedictine monk who is best known as a pioneer in modern

---

65. For various sorts of background on criminal justice, see Andrew Skotnicki, *Criminal Justice and the Catholic Church* (Lanham, Md.: Rowman & Littlefield, 2008); Marcello Maestro, *Cesare Beccaria and the Origins of Penal Reform* (Philadelphia: Temple University Press, 1973); Richard R. Follett, *Evangelicalism, Penal Theory and the Politics of Criminal Law Reform in England, 1808–30* (Basingstoke, UK: Palgrave, 2001). The editors' introduction to R. A. Duff and David Garland, eds., *A Reader on Punishment* (Oxford: Oxford University Press, 1994) provides a good, although totally secular, outline of the modern sociological and philosophical debate on the numerous issues of criminal justice and penology.

techniques of editing manuscripts, helped design what was then a modern Roman prison. That institution much impressed Cesare Beccaria, a deist who condemned the death penalty and torture and who praised rehabilitation. Beccaria inspired Jeremy Bentham, the renowned utilitarian atheist, who designed what he thought would be an ideal prison.

This transmission of ideas across the religious-secular border was not unusual. Believers and secularists shared the convictions that the human dignity of criminals should be respected and that many, if not all, of them could be reformed through the appropriate mix of discipline and inspiration. Christians were evidently more interested than were atheists in Christian inspiration, in particular in opening prisoners up to divine grace, but most atheists were willing to countenance or even counsel prayer if it helped bring the wicked to their moral or prosocial senses.

The religious-secular partnership among prison reformers and workers has persisted. Secularists generally welcome the work of Christians with current and former prisoners. The secular reasoning is usually pragmatic. Christian preaching and care have been at least as effective as secular alternatives. In general, secularists involved in prison work get along so well with Christians that the current approach to crime and punishment can be considered a modern innovation that has not disconcerted or embarrassed Catholics. Conversely, most secularists would be perfectly happy with John Paul II's ideal for prisons: "Punishment cannot be reduced to mere retribution, much less take the form of social retaliation or a sort of institutional vengeance. Punishment and imprisonment have meaning if, while maintaining the demands of justice and discouraging crime, they serve the rehabilitation of the individual by offering those who have made a mistake an opportunity to reflect and to change their lives in order to be fully reintegrated into society."[66]

The comforting conclusion of Catholic modernity and ecumenical social unity has to be qualified in two ways. First, while it is good to see a Catholic Social Teaching that is not rejected by secular authorities, the treatment of criminals has never been a major theme in the magisterial teaching. The *Catechism* dedicates only one brief paragraph to the topic and the slightly longer discussion in the

---

66.   John Paul II, *Homily in Regina Caeli Prison* (July 9, 2000).

Compendium of the Social Doctrine cites no encyclicals,[67] only two addresses to relevant groups by John Paul II.[68] Second, the rehabilitative goals of the new techniques—correction, remorse, and rehabilitation—are too frequently not reached. Despite two centuries of conscientious and increasingly expensive efforts, in most countries a distressingly large number of released prisoners return to incarceration and many never become, as John Paul II wished, "fully reintegrated into society."[69] Among those whose behavior does improve, the calming effects of age seem often to have been at least as effective as the punishments and programs of the law. The lack of success has encouraged some antiestablishment intellectuals to postulate that prisons are actually designed to fail as part of a nefarious social plot.[70] That model of conscious and unconscious malice is vastly exaggerated, but prison systems do often seem to suffer from one old and two typically modern flaws. The old issue is the desire to punish rather than to help. The new ones are excessive optimism about people's ability to become virtuous and excessive trust in the power of carefully designed but emotionally and spiritually impoverished processes of behavioral engineering.

I have already discussed how the first new issue, the refusal to countenance the powerful lure of sin, has encouraged simplistic economics and excessive trust in democracy and human rights. In penology, it can lead to unrealistic expectations about the ease of changing the hearts and behavior of prisoners, who are generally morally weak and frequently psychologically troubled people forced to live together for many years. The second new issue, the exaggerated faith in pure process, blights the welfare state and undermines some of premises and promises of democracy. Such rule-based systems are particularly unlikely to help prisoners, who can only change under the influence of love and loving discipline, both antithetical to inflexible rule-based behaviorism.

The history of the penal reform movement is not very encouraging. Many of the movement's nineteenth-century pioneers were

---

67.   *Catechism of the Catholic Church*, 2266.

68.   *Compendium of the Social Doctrine of the Church*, 402–4.

69.   Some background from a U.S. perspective in Carolyn W. Deady, "Incarceration and Recidivism: Lessons from Abroad" (Newport, R.I.: Pell Center for International Relations and Public Policy, 2014).

70.   The classic text is Michel Foucault, *Surveiller et punir: naissance de la prison* (Paris: Gallimard, 1975).

keen on solitary confinement, which was supposed to leave the criminals alone with their consciences, but actually led to more madness than repentance. Since then, various mixes of harshness, gentleness, work, idleness, education, recreation, evangelization, shame, rewards, and who knows what else have been tried, none with more than intermittent, temporary, or very partial success. The same can be said of the specific techniques, which include training, rules, parole boards, harsh sentences, gentle sentences, private ownership, and both formal and informal procedures. It sometimes seems that the most significant accomplishment of contemporary prisons is the transmission of the quintessentially modern skill of manipulating rules and officials to some of the roughest and most lawless members of the community.

It is possible that the future will be better than the past. A few countries, mostly in Scandinavia, have quite low recidivism rates. They rely on expensive and extensive programs of rehabilitation that continue well after release into the community. However, they also have had the advantage of working in relatively closed and homogenous societies, which criminals are likely to want to rejoin. Whether these nations' success can be maintained or duplicated is not clear. All too often it seems that the wisdom of the psalmist prevails: "Transgression speaks to the wicked, deep in his heart. / There is no fear of God before his eyes."[71]

Actually, many people enmeshed in the criminal justice system are not so much wicked as lost—some combination of poorly raised, ill-treated, undereducated, mentally unstable, and damaged by alcohol or drugs. Christians recognize people who suffer from extreme cases of the modern social pathologies of loneliness, alienation, and the separation from the divine. The current standard prison life is certainly not designed for such people. Arguably, the so-called prison abolition movement seems to offer a more appropriate approach to punishment. It calls for policies of social support to help people stay out of prison in the first place, for using punishments to restore or develop the criminals' sense of moral and social responsibility, and for providing them with continuing social and psychological help. Some Catholic thinkers about crime, mostly residents of the disproportionately prison-reliant United States, have endorsed versions of

---

71. Ps 36:1.

this approach.[72] This is certainly in accord with the advice Pius XII gave to prison visitors—to desire that the friends and family of the prisoner forgive him sincerely, to believe in his goodness, and to love him as the Lord loved.[73]

Overall, or at least in aspirations, the current arrangements of criminal punishments have a more Christian outlook than those of the officially Christian societies of Christendom. Contemporary Christians usually see prisoners as people whom God wishes to re-form, reform, and save. Progressive secular thinkers about penology would basically agree, just leaving God out of the description. That is a significant change from almost every premodern society, in which punishment was aimed almost exclusively at exacting vengeance and protecting the civil order. The officially Christian societies of Christendom were hardly any kinder to their prisoners. It is safe to say that this particular group of the least of Christ's brothers has gained something from the modern age and that modern secular thinking deserves some credit for helping the Church find a more deeply Christian approach.

Capital punishment deserves a few paragraphs, even though few governments currently execute anyone and almost all those that do use the penalty rarely. Symbolically and morally, however, the death penalty is and will remain significant, because one of the marks of a legitimate government is the legitimate use of violence, including mortal violence, against some of the people it governs. The willingness or unwillingness to kill people legally is an important sign of how a government understands justice, mercy, and responsibility.

The Bible does not really consider the possibility of a society without capital punishment. Legal executions were authorized in God's injunction to Noah, "Whoever sheds the blood of man, by man shall his blood be shed; for God made man in his own image."[74] The subsequent law given to Moses was replete with capital crimes. In the New Testament, the penalty was simply taken for granted. The execution of Jesus was unjust, but there is no suggestion that executions are unjust in themselves. Even the "good thief" crucified

---

72.   See Katie Walker Grimes, "From Slavery to Incarceration," *Church Life Journal* (March 7, 2019); Kathryn Getek Soltis, "Can Justice Demand Prison Abolition?," *Church Life Journal* (March 12, 2019); Kathryn Getek Soltis, "The Christian Virtue of Justice and the U.S. Prison," *Journal of Catholic Social Thought* 8, no. 1 (2011): 37–56.

73.   Pius XII, Speech *Discorso ai giuristi cattolici circa l'aiuto ai carcerati* (May 26, 1957).

74.   Gn 9:6.

next to him described his "condemnation" as a "due reward" for what he has done.[75]

Some early Christians struggled to reconcile Jesus' teaching of forgiveness with any killing, in peace as in war. A few condemned executions absolutely. Over time, members of the clergy were forbidden to participate in the shedding of human blood, but within Christendom executions, like war, were always considered a necessary evil. Just as states could engage in the evil and killing of war against outside enemies, they could legitimately deprive their own subjects of their lives. The *Catechism* of 1566 was unequivocal. "Another kind of lawful slaying belongs to the civil authorities, to whom is entrusted power of life and death, by the legal and judicious exercise of which they punish the guilty and protect the innocent."[76] That statement expresses some of the philosophical arguments in favor of capital punishment. The criminal's death is a just penalty for a heinous crime, instils fear in other potential wrongdoers, and keeps a dangerous person from doing more harm to the community. In addition, for the condemned criminal the prospect of imminent death could lead a soul-saving repentance. In practice, of course, legal executions were often carried out without the solemnity and seriousness that these philosophical arguments mandate. On the contrary, careless and excessively harsh judgments, uncontrolled fury, and undignified cruelty were all too common.

I already mentioned the Italian Enlightenment thinker Cesare Beccaria, who published the first influential modern argument against the death penalty in 1764. In response, the government of Grand Duchy of Tuscany prohibited the practice in 1786. During the nineteenth century, some social liberals and Christian reformers included abolition of the death penalty on their agendas. As a result of the new thinking, the penalty was abolished or allowed to fall into disuse in a few countries, most notably Russia. Some Catholics also joined the abolitionist cause. They argued that legal executions are an insult to the dignity and sacredness of every human life, besides

---

75. Lk 23:40, 41.

76. *Catechism of the Council of Trent*, Fifth Commandment. A survey of the history of the Church's teaching on capital punishment is included in Howard Bromberg, "Pope John Paul II, Vatican II, and Capital Punishment," *Ave Maria Law Review* 6, no. 1 (2007): 109–54. The article has extensive bibliographic references. For a more informal but philosophically informed treatment, see Avery Dulles, "Catholicism & Capital Punishment," *First Things* 112 (April 2001): 30–35.

depriving the criminal of every possible chance to repent and reform. Christians could also endorse the practical argument that the ultimate penalty cannot be reversed, so its use carries the risk of literally fatal miscarriages of justice. Those long-standing arguments have been buttressed in recent decades by widespread revulsion at the tremendous scale of government-sponsored killing during the twentieth century and, quite probably, a widespread disbelief that secular governments really have been "entrusted," as the old *Catechism* said, with the "power of life and death." Leo XIII said that "the ruling powers are invested with a sacredness more than human . . . and obedience is . . . submission to the will of God, exercising His sovereignty through the medium of men."[77] It is hard to imaging Francis saying anything similar.

Whatever the reasons, the abolitionists have basically won the debate. This once universal and standard punishment has become rare. For example, in the most recent five years for which full data is available, there have been almost four hundred times more murders than legal executions in the United States.[78]

Catholics have moved with the times. As recently as 1953, Pope Pius XII defended the penalty: "[The] public authority limits itself to depriving the offender of the good of life in expiation for his guilt, after he, through his crime, deprived himself of his own right to life."[79] However, John Paul II took the Magisterium in a different direction. He pointed out that God, "who is always merciful even when he punishes," spared the life of Cain, the first murderer in the Bible. The lesson from that divine choice is that "[n]ot even a murderer loses his personal dignity, and God himself pledges to guarantee this."[80] The pope then said that people should emulate God in preferring life over death. In the modern world, they can do so more thoroughly than in the past, because of the new presence of "a system of penal justice ever more in line with human dignity." He might have added the persistence of some of the old injustices of the penal system—the tendency to hasty and biased judgments and excessively harsh sentences. His conclusion was that cases in which the death penalty is

---

77.   Leo XIII, *Immortale Dei*, 18.

78.   Murders from https://ucr.fbi.gov/crime-in-the-u.s/2015/crime-in-the-u.s.-2015/tables /table-1. Executions from https://deathpenaltyinfo.org/executions-year.

79.   Pius XII, *Address to the First International Congress of Histopathology of the Nervous System* (September 14, 1952).

80.   John Paul II, Encyclical Letter *Evangelium Vitae* (March 25, 1995), 9.

justified are "very rare, if not practically non-existent."[81] Francis has gone further, revising the relevant text of the new *Catechism* in 2018 to include a full condemnation: "[T]he death penalty is inadmissible because it is an attack on the inviolability and dignity of the person."[82]

The relatively recent strong Catholic opposition to the death penalty is a change, for the better in my view. It continues the line started with the calls for more humane treatment of all prisoners and it echoes the roughly simultaneous move from discouraging war to actively promoting peace. Still, a small note of caution is needed. The condemnation of capital punishment is a social teaching, a counsel of imperfection. The arguments in favor of capital punishment have not been proven false. They have only been found weaker than have the arguments against in current social and political conditions. The teaching could be modified if those conditions change. For example, if the number of murders increases dramatically, then the virtue of visible expiation and the good of providing a social witness of the horribleness of some crimes may be judged more important. Under those circumstances, the magisterial opposition to the death penalty could once again become less absolute.

Anti-Semitism

The Catholic Church "decries hatred, persecutions, displays of anti-Semitism, directed against Jews at any time and by anyone." Further: "The hostility or diffidence of numerous Christians toward Jews in the course of time is a sad historical fact and is the cause of profound remorse for Christians." All Catholics, indeed all people, should wish these declarations had been made much earlier than they actually were—in 1965 and 1999, respectively, the first at the Second Vatican Council and the second by the influential International Theological Commission.[83] Had the Catholic Church produced such a strong official condemnation and such a clear self-recrimination a century earlier, it is conceivable that fewer Jews might have been slaughtered

---

81.   John Paul II, *Evangelium Vitae*, 9.

82.   "New Revision of Number 2267 of the Catechism of the Catholic Church on the Death Penalty—Rescriptum 'Ex Audientia SS.MI,'" August 2, 2018.

83.   Vatican Council II. *Nostra Aetate, Declaration on the Relation of the Church to Non-Christian Religions:* (October 28, 1965), 4; International Theological Commission, *Memory and Reconciliation: The Church and the Faults of the Past* (December 1999), 5.4.

228   CHAPTER 6

during the Second World War, especially if this putative document had been backed up by vigorous canonical action against Catholics who endorsed or tolerated anti-Semitic ideas and political movements.

Such a historical contrafactual is sadly far from reality. In fact, the Magisterium was tragically slow. It waited until well after the Holocaust to make a realistic appraisal of the "quite negative" balance of relations between Christians and Jews over the previous 1900 or so years.[84] Any history of the Catholic Social Teaching should include the admission that the Church responded poorly to this important "new thing," the changing position of Jews in the rapidly de-Christianizing societies of the nineteenth and early twentieth centuries. A purification of the traditional Christian attitude toward Jews in society was needed, as was a refinement of the traditional theological treatment of Judaism. Neither was forthcoming.

There were two important social changes that the Church did not take note of. On one side was the civil emancipation of Jews in increasingly secular societies. On the other was the widespread negative response to that emancipation. Christians and secularists alike transferred the traditional religious arguments against Jews into new dimensions. Jewish behavior, businesses, and rootlessness were condemned as threats to national unity and modern values, while pseudobiological cultural analysis was used to explain that the supposed Jewish race threatened to all that was good about Europe or America. None of this stirred much critical reflection from the Magisterium or from Catholic intellectuals. Many believers easily accepted the new ways of disliking Jews.

The popes did not abandon their long tradition of trying simultaneously to respect Jewish communities and to condemn Jewish practices and beliefs, a balance that often failed in the direction of more condemnation and less protection. Benedict XIV, the first pope to write encyclicals, anticipated the secular anti-Jewish arguments in 1751. Writing about the Jews of Poland, he said that, "by means of their particular practice of commerce, they amass a great store of money and then by an exorbitant rate of interest utterly destroy the wealth and inheritance of Christians."[85] He could have been quoted in the entry on "anti-Semitism" published in 1930 a

---

84. Commission for Religious Relations with the Jews, *We Remember: A Reflection on the Shoah* (January 25, 1998), III.

85. Benedict XIV, Encyclical Letter *A Quo Primum* (June 14, 1751), 3.

distinguished German Catholic encyclopedia. The article described the "dark aspects of the Jewish soul expelled from its homeland," manifested in movements such as "global plutocracy and Bolshevism" which were "destructive of human society."[86] A hostile approach to the Jews was encouraged by the most prevalent Catholic teaching about how Christians should love their neighbors. The most popular text of moral theology in the late nineteenth and early twentieth centuries stated clearly that in the practice of love, blood relations deserve preference over people who do not share "our religious confession, homeland or the like."[87] Even when secular anti-Semitism was blended with some variety of anti-Christianity, as in the philosophies of Feuerbach, Schopenhauer, and Nietzsche, Catholic condemnations of these thinkers rarely included any defense of the specifically Jewish contributions to the common good. The significance of the absence became clear when too many Christians failed to object to the transformation of anti-Semitic ideas into murderous policies of cultural purification.[88]

Some twentieth-century Catholics did feel differently about the Jews, well before horror at the Nazi's "final solution" forced others to rethink their prejudices. In 1926, a fervent Dutch Jewish convert to Catholicism inspired the foundation of a clerical organization, the Friends of Israel. Its goals were to end the Church's anti-Jewish thinking and rhetoric and to use kindness and respect, rather than

---

86. In this account, I have relied heavily on an excellent article by Martin Rhonheimer, "The Holocaust: What Was Not Said," *First Things* 137 (November 2003): 18–27 and Thomas Breuer, "Die Haltung der katholischen Kirche zur Judenverfolgung im Dritten Reich," PSM Geschichte (May 22, 2003). https://www.zum.de/psm/ns/k_kirche.php. The sources for all the quotations can be found in the Rhonheimer article. See also John Connelly, *From Enemy to Brother: The Revolution in Catholic Teaching on the Jews, 1933–1965* (Cambridge, Mass.: Harvard University Press, 2012); Eli Lederhendler, ed., "Jews, Catholics, and the Burden of History," *Studies in Contemporary Jewry XXI* (Oxford: Avraham Harman Institute of Contemporary Jewry, Hebrew University of Jerusalem, 2005) and, on a technical question, Menahem R. Macina, "Essai d'élucidation des causes et circonstances de l'abolition, par le Saint-Office, de l'« Opus sacerdotale Amici Israel » (1926–1928)," *Travaux Recherches de l'Université*, (Lille: l'Université Charles-de-Gaulle - Lille 3, 2003): 87–110.

87. From J. P. Gury, *Moraltheologie* (Germany: Regensburg and Mainz, 1869), 102, cited in Connelly, *From Enemy to Brother*: 38.

88. See the discussion by Henri de Lubac in his "Note Historique" *Affrontements Mystiques* (Paris: Témoignage chrétien, 1950), reprinted in vol. 4 of *Oeuvres Complètes* (Paris Cerf, 2006), 336–46. That short essay is well complemented by Christian Joseph K. Gordon, "Ressourcement Anti-Semitism? Addressing an Obstacle to Henri de Lubac's Proposed Renewal of Premodern Christian Spiritual Exegesis," *Theological Studies* 78, no. 3 (2017): 614–33. Gordon is justly harsh on de Lubac's blindness to the Christian contribution to anti-Semitism.

pressure and insults, to lead more Jews to Christianity. Nine cardinals and many priests signed on, but the Holy Office closed the group down after two years. Although the motivations for that decision are unclear, the ban reflects badly on the Church. The decree announcing the decision did manage to condemn "the hatred which is today customarily known as anti-Semitism," but a commentary on the affair in the semiofficial *La Civiltà Cattolica* explained that "Jews are a danger to the whole world because of their pernicious infiltration, their hidden influence, and their resulting disproportionate power which violates both reason and the common good." In effect, radical racial anti-Semitism was considered bad, but "reason" still supported the Church's long tradition of anti-Judaism.

Once the Nazis started to kill members of the supposed Jewish "race," many Catholics, including Pope Pius XII, worked with heroic fervor to save lives. In Italy and the Netherlands, the whole Church came together for the cause. (In some other countries, there were many brave individuals, but the hierarchies did little.) Nonetheless, the Magisterium remained reluctant to condemn unequivocally all civil discrimination against Jews. Even in 1946, when anti-Semitism inspired the massacre of a group of Jews who had returned to the Polish town of Kielce, the responses of both the Catholic hierarchy in Poland and Pius were tepid and equivocating.[89] It took almost another two decades before the Church officially repudiated the hatred of Jews with the requisite firmness.

The term anti-Semitism is properly assigned to a purely secular analysis, generally based on biology or culture, of the "Jewish question." However, the use of scientific and social arguments cannot hide the Christian roots of all-Semitism. The ideology would never have flourished if there had not been centuries of Church denigration of Jewish "Christ-killers," innumerable examples of hostile social exclusion of Jews, a willing exaggeration of any actual offences by Jews, and the easy acceptance of totally false accusations of evil Jewish actions and attitudes. By the twentieth century, Jews were often

---

89.   Jan T. Gross, *Fear: Anti-Semitism in Poland after Auschwitz* (Princeton, N.J.: Princeton University Press, 2006), 134–53, gives a thorough account, including an illuminating footnote on p. 140 on the response of the Vatican. Michael Phayer, *Pius XII, The Holocaust, and the Cold War* (Bloomington, Ind.: Indiana University Press, 2008) provides some papal context on p. 168. For a defense of the Church response, see Mark Paul, "The Catholic Church and the Kielce Tragedy," in *Kielce - July 4, 1946: Background, Context and Events* [no named editor] (Toronto: Polish Educational Foundation in North America, 1996), 105–16. The defenders seem to assume that anti-Jewish sentiment was justified because many leading Communists were Jews.

considered troubling in many, often contradictory ways. They were too poor or too rich, too strong or too weak, too isolated or too anxious to belong, too clever or too ignorant.

In retrospect, it is painfully clear that the original problem was a dualistic theology of potentially good Christians and inevitably bad Jews. As long as this duality dominated the thinking of most Christians, no sort of anti-Jewish prejudice, from suspicions of ritual murder to racist pseudoscience, could seem sufficiently horrible to be denounced unconditionally.

The revision of this simplistic theology was not easy, because it required the recognition of a serious error. Just as Peter had betrayed Jesus in his moment of greatest need, those who spoke for the heavenly Church on earth had consistently offered "forms of counter-witness and scandal" to God's chosen people.[90] Such magisterial admissions of error, especially on theologically significant topics, were almost unheard of before the second half of the twentieth century. The near-destruction of the European Jews made this one urgent.

One biblical text had done a great deal of harm. Matthew's account of the crucifixion, in which the Jews take the "blood" of Jesus "on us and on our children,"[91] was used to hold all Jews for all time responsible for the death of the Savior. The idea of inherited guilt was prevalent enough in the mid-twentieth century that the fathers of the Second Vatican Council judged it necessary to provide a formal renunciation of the accusation. "[W]hat happened in His passion cannot be charged against all the Jews, without distinction, then alive, nor against the Jews of today. Although the Church is the new people of God, the Jews should not be presented as rejected or accursed by God, as if this followed from the Holy Scriptures."[92]

In a slightly less determinist interpretation of the text, the Jewish priests who, at the crucial moment, were "slow of heart to believe all that the prophets have spoken,"[93] were thought to have set a dire pattern of disbelief that was passed on, like the "mercy" of the Lord to Mary, from "generation to generation."[94] Jesus, as the angel Gabriel explains to Mary, will sit on "the throne of his father David, and he will

---

90.   International Theological Commission, *Memory and Reconciliation: The Church and the Faults of the Past* (December 1999), 3.

91.   Mt 27:25.

92.   Vatican Council II. *Nostra Aetate*, 4.

93.   Lk 24:25.

94.   Lk 1:50.

reign over the house of Jacob forever,"[95] and yet the Jews of his time rejected their king. All Jews who subsequently refuse to accept him as their king and savior commit the same error, of stubbornly rejecting the full revealed truth of their religion. The continuing Jewish obduracy in the face of the Church, "the children of the promise,"[96] might well be worse than the hostility of pagans to Christianity. Those gentiles, after all, did not have Sacred Scriptures to teach them to accept the Messiah who had arisen from their own people.

Modern biblical scholars have qualified the declaration of the Jewish leaders in Matthew in various ways. Most profoundly, Pope Benedict XVI pointed out that the Jews were unwittingly expressing their need for the "purifying power of love which is in [Jesus'] blood."[97] However, reasoned theology may not be the main issue. The fervor of anti-Jewish teaching and feeling often seemed and seems to transcend even the harshest Christian theological logic. The exaggerated hatred may be better analyzed by calling on recent theorizing about "pariah people" and other barely tolerated resident groups. The list of relevant theories includes the important social role of scapegoats, the use of social exclusion to support social cohesion, and the too ready willingness of Christians to write off some of "the least of these my brothers"[98] as eternally damned.[99] Such approaches suggest that fallen human nature is more relevant than solid theology to the Christian choice to use the line in Matthew to demonize people living centuries later or to exclude them from normal society because of what might be considered a somewhat tendentious interpretation of their own religious text.

Whatever the value of such speculations, the factual history is clear enough. Long before Christians controlled any societies, distinguished theologians were vigorously expounding the theme of Jewish infidelity to God. They elaborated the contrast between the true

---

95.   Lk 1:32–33.

96.   Rom 9:8.

97.   Benedict XVI, *Jesus of Nazareth: Part Two, From the Entrance into Jerusalem to the Resurrection* (London: Catholic Truth Society, 2011), 187–88.

98.   Mt 25:40.

99.   For pariah people, see the very critical Arnaldo Momigliano "A Note on Max Weber's Definition of Judaism as a Pariah-Religion," *History and Theory* 19, no. 3 (1980): 313–18. For scapegoats, see René Girard, *The Girard Reader*. For exclusion, see, for example, Giorgio Agamben, *Homo sacer*. For the theological tendency, see Hans Urs von Balthasar, *Dare We Hope "That All Men Be Saved*," trans. David Kipp and Lothar Krauth (San Francisco: Ignatius, 1988 [1986]).

THE CHURCH ADRIFT IN A SECULAR WORLD   233

Church of Christ and the superseded "synagogue of Satan."[100] When Christianity became the state religion, kings and other leaders often and easily turned the hostile theology into public policy. Restrictions on Jewish roles in society could be justified by a core principle of Christendom—error has no rights. For the many defenders of such policies, there was nothing unfair about them, since all Jews needed to do to shake off the curse that they had accepted at the time of Jesus was to accept sincerely the full truth of their own religion. Of course, it might take a few generations to wash away completely the taint of Jewish thinking.

The theology endorsed by the Second Vatican Council is built primarily on a different biblical text, chapters 9 to 11 of Paul's epistle to the Romans. The apostle explains that God's love for the Jews is "irrevocable"[101] and that Christians are uniquely dependent on them in what would later be called the economy of salvation. He does not exculpate Jews for the rejection of the Messiah, saying that their sin darkens their relationships with both God and Christians. Still, Christians are not authorized to reject the people of the Lord. On the contrary, non-Jewish Christians should be grateful that they, "a wild olive shoot, were grafted in their place to share the richness of the olive tree."[102] The Jews remain "the root that supports you."[103] The ultimate reversal of the initial Jewish rejection, their "full inclusion"[104] in the new Israel, is central to the "mystery"[105] of God's universal saving love. Paul states emphatically that God has not rejected the Jews and that "my heart's desire and prayer to God for them is that they may be saved."[106]

Christians often ignored that prayer for most of the next two millennia, or they interpreted it as an incitement to treat Jews harshly for the sake of their conversion. Expropriations, expulsions, and sometimes murders were depressingly common, especially from the thirteenth century onward. It is unfair to criticize kingdoms and states for not giving Jews secular civil rights, since such rights were literally inconceivable in any society anywhere before the seventeenth

---

100.   Rv 2:9; Rv 3:9.
101.   Rom 11:29.
102.   Rom 11:17.
103.   Rom 11:18.
104.   Rom 11:12.
105.   Rom 11:25.
106.   Rom 10:1.

century and almost unheard of in practice for another two centuries. However, it is perfectly fair to criticize supposedly Christian societies for persecution.

That persistent injustice set an ominous standard. Adolf Hitler was all too close to correct in the historical summary he provided one German Catholic bishop in 1933: "The Catholic Church considered the Jews pestilent for fifteen hundred years." There is no record of any disagreement with this claim, probably because what would now be considered shocking anti-Semitism was common among leading Catholic intellectuals and politicians throughout Hitler's life (he was born in 1889). With that cultural background, the then-new German Führer could count on some episcopal sympathy in portraying himself as restoring a traditional value of Christian society: "In the epoch of liberalism the danger [from the Jews] was no longer recognized . . . perhaps I am doing Christianity a great service by pushing them [Jews] out of schools and public functions."

Hitler's final approach was actually much more radical than that of any Christian ruler. No Catholic or Protestant could ever endorse anything like the indiscriminate murder of members of the supposedly inferior and dangerous Jewish race, let alone considering such slaughter to be an objective, hygienic good. Ideologically, the distance between the Church's traditional anti-Jewish thinking and the Nazi's racial anti-Semitism was sufficiently great that, as I said, many Catholic leaders objected strenuously to the latter. Sadly, the distance was not great enough for more than a handful of influential Christians to condemn all anti-Judaism and anti-Semitism in anything like the firm words first used officially in 1965.

Since then, Catholic theologians have paid far more attention to the Jews' irrevocable call described in Romans than to the self-curse in Matthew. The rebalancing cannot completely resolve the Jewish theological question for Christians. Nothing can, until God reveals the full truth of the mystery discussed by Paul in Romans. The Jews will always be, as John Paul II said, the "older brothers"[107] of the covenant, with all the ambiguity that the Bible gives to that relationship. After all, while "every male that opens the womb shall be called holy

---

107. John Paul II, Speech *Incontro con la comunità ebraica nella sinagoga della città di roma* (April 13, 1986).

THE CHURCH ADRIFT IN A SECULAR WORLD 235

to the Lord,"[108] in the history of the Covenant God consistently favors younger brothers over their older siblings, from Abel over Cain to the parable of the prodigal son.[109]

While waiting for the full elucidation of this mystery, the new Catholic approach to it is clearly a gargantuan improvement over the old, practically as well as theologically. Christians and Jews now routinely engage in fruitful and respectful religious dialogue, often cooperate in dealing with social and political challenges, and sometimes band together as co-carriers of the monotheist Judeo-Christian heritage. In sharp contrast with the Church that condemned the "Friends of Israel," Catholic bishops around the world now consistently condemn all sorts of anti-Jewish sentiments, open or veiled, from any source. Of course, it may take a few more generations to eliminate the stain of anti-Jewish thinking among Catholics.

Migration

After discussing what has probably been the Catholic Social Teaching's greatest failure, I end this long chapter with a topic that shows the Church in a much more flattering light. As usual, the Church has not fully understood the secular world's response to the topic, but in this case it is the Magisterium that has consistently advocated policies that all in accord with Christian morality and that make social and economic sense in modern societies. For once, there is no need to tell of retrograde Catholics scrambling to adjust to the helpful parts of the reality of the modern world or to worry that the Church has endorsed some imperfectly purified version of confused secular ideas. The topic is migration.

Migrants and Jews are similar in several ways. Both groups often live at the margins of their societies. Both have lost their ancestral homelands. Historically, everyone in their host societies, from the most powerful to the weakest, has been prone to be harsh with both groups. However, while until very recently the Catholic responses to Judaism and Jewish communities have rarely been better than ambiguous, the Church's teaching on migration has always been direct and positive. In a sentence, the Church teaches that, as long as there are just reasons, all people should be free to leave their old,

---

108. Lk 2:23, citing Ex 13:2 and 13:12.
109. Lk 15:11–32.

unpromising, or dangerous homes and that Christians should, as much as they possibly can, welcome migrants into their new homes, looking at them as strangers in need of active love.

The view is strong and clear in large part because the appreciation of something very similar to modern migration is a central biblical theme. That direct relevance is extremely unusual. For almost all of the topics I discuss in this book, biblical guidance is either scarce, dated, or hard to interpret. On migration, the scriptural teaching is ample and consistent. This is not surprising, because migration was one of the formative experiences of the people who actually wrote, rewrote, or selected the Old Testament texts that have come down to us. Many of the people who were striving to put God's word into human speech were trying to make religious sense of the experience of exile. Some of them were concerned with the half century during which many leading Jews were forced from Jerusalem to Babylon. Others were more concerned with the subsequent scattering (diaspora) of the Jews away from the temple in Jerusalem to locations all around the Mediterranean Sea.

The basic lesson, taught at least as much by the prophets and wisdom books as by the more directly historical narratives, is that migrants are people who are or might be following God's orders. Their exile may be a punishment, but it is holy to stay close to God and his law in exile, even when the Temple is distant or destroyed. Reciprocally, the exile's weakness is an opportunity for those who host migrants to do God's work.

The pattern is found in nascent form at the very beginning of the holy book. Fallen human history begins after God expels Adam from his original home, "therefore the LORD God sent him forth from the garden of Eden."[110] Adam and Eve learn that God does not abandon them in exile. He makes them "garments of skins."[111] He counteracts the death that sin has brought by giving them fecundity. A new generation comes, made "with the help of the LORD."[112] A little later in the narrative, the theme is expressed more directly. God orders the first patriarch, Abraham, to leave his paternal home, "Go from your country and your kindred and your father's

---

110. Gn 3:23.

111. Gn 3:21.

112. Gn. 4:1.

THE CHURCH ADRIFT IN A SECULAR WORLD   237

house to the land that I will show you."[113] God's people are defined by their status as recent migrants. The lesson is reinforced with the story of exile into and later from Egypt. This story, particularly the Israelites' escape from the cruel pharaoh and their subsequent wandering in the desert, is treated throughout the scriptures as the foundational story of Jewish history. It is told and retold as a two-part story of migration—of one good pharaoh who welcomes Jacob's famished immigrant family and of a later Egyptian ruler who is punished for his attempt to restrain the emigration of Jacob's oppressed descendants.

In all the recensions of the Law, the Lord draws an explicit lesson about migrants and migrations from this experience: "The stranger who sojourns with you shall be as the as the native among you, and you shall love him as yourself; for you were strangers in the land of Egypt."[114] For the people of God, themselves so often called or forced into exile, welcoming the exiled is part of their duty to their Creator and Redeemer. This firm command is not contradicted elsewhere in the Old Testament. Christians looking for biblical support for anti-immigrant policies are forced to turn to texts that are not actually very supportive. They most commonly rely on the frequent condemnations of Jewish assimilation with foreign peoples, but nonassimilation is quite different from nonsettlement.

While migration is not as major a theme in the New Testament as in the Old, the approach is remarkably consistent. Two passages in particular reinforce the Old Testament's message. First, a temporary migration saves the life of the infant Jesus. In an echo of Jacob-Israel's move to safety in Egypt, Jesus leaves Judea for Egypt as what would now be called a refugee.[115] Second, in the great injunction to charity that comes at the end of his teaching, Jesus identifies himself with all outsiders, including migrants: "I was a foreigner and you took me in."[116] Theologically, the incarnation is itself a sort of migration, the obedient departure of the Son to do the will of the Father in a distant and not very pleasant land.[117] Christians must welcome the divine migrant, in part because, as they are reminded in the letter to

---

113.   Gn 12:1.

114.   Lv 19:34; see also Dt 10:17–19, Dt 16:9–12, and Ex 23:9.

115.   Mt 2:13–23.

116.   Mt 25:35, my translation.

117.   Cf. Phil 2:7–8.

238   CHAPTER 6

the Hebrews, they are themselves always exiles, with "no lasting city" in this life.[118]

As with the Old Testament, the New Testament ground is also remarkably unfertile for Christians who would restrict migration on principle. The most helpful text for them is Paul's injunction to obey the legitimate government.[119] This can reasonably be interpreted as condemning illegal immigration but not as condoning making immigration illegal in the first place. The Pauline injunction certainly does not justify obedience to manifestly unjust laws, and, as I suggested earlier in the discussion of the welfare state earlier in this chapter, Catholics have an obligation to question the justice of today's expansive and intrusive governments. Paul cannot legitimately be read as endorsing blind obedience to laws that contravene the Church's teaching on an important social manifestation of human dignity.

Along with being clear, the biblical teaching remains relevant. While modern developments in transport, communications technology, and government have made migration easier in many ways, they have not essentially changed the phenomenon. When the popes of the nineteenth and early twentieth centuries looked at the vast Italian migration to the New World, they naturally and legitimately saw the spiritual heirs of the Jews migrating from Egypt or exiled from Jerusalem. The same is true of more recent popes looking at other migrants—whether the streams of Second World War refugees, driven out by bombing and political decrees, or today's poor Africans and war-scarred Syrians trying to get to rich Europe, and today's poor Latin Americans trying to get to the rich United States. Pius XII said it explicitly in 1952: "The expelled Holy Family of Nazareth, fleeing into Egypt, is the archetype of every refugee family. Jesus, Mary and Joseph, living in exile in Egypt to escape the fury of an evil king, are, for all times and all places, the models and protectors of every migrant, alien, and refugee of whatever kind who, whether compelled by fear of persecution or by want, is forced to leave his native land, his beloved parents and relatives, his close friends, and to seek a foreign soil."[120]

---

118.   Heb 13:14. For brief and helpful discussion to the biblical context, with references, see Susanna Snyder, "Biblical and Theological Perspectives on Migration," in *Fortress Britain: Ethical Approaches to Immigration Policy for a Post-Brexit Britain*, ed. Ben Ryan (London: Jessica Kingsley, 2018), 94–113, especially 96–99.

119.   Rom 13:1–7.

120.   Pius XII, Apostolic Constitution *Exsul Familia Nazarethana* (Aug. 1, 1952), Introduction.

THE CHURCH ADRIFT IN A SECULAR WORLD   239

The fundamental teaching on migration has been constant, but it has developed. At the beginning of the modern social teaching, the prime papal concern was the aid, primarily spiritual but also material, of displaced Catholics. Pius XII took a broader approach. He noted with satisfaction that during the Second World War organized Catholic charity had been extended not only to "our sons" but also to "displaced Jews who were victims of the cruelest persecutions" and to "the Christians and the non-Christians" who suffered in the wars in Palestine.[121]

The next pope removed religion entirely from the discussion of migration. Migration was one of the many universal human rights recognized by John XXIII. "[E]very human being has the right to freedom of movement and of residence within the confines of his own State. When there are just reasons in favor of it, he must be permitted to emigrate to other countries and take up residence there. The fact that he is a citizen of a particular State does not deprive him of membership in the human family, nor of citizenship in that universal society, the common, world-wide fellowship of men."[122] John Paul II integrated the spiritual with the worldly. The Polish pope, who called himself a migrant to Italy, said the "ultimate source" of migration was the universal "longing for a transcendent horizon of justice, freedom, and peace," a longing that "testifies to an anxiety that, however indirectly, refers to God, in whom alone man can find the full satisfaction of all his expectations."[123]

Francis has made the support of migrants a central theme of his pontificate, calling on a mix of Christian theology, universal solidarity, and practical concern.

> Every stranger who knocks at our door is an opportunity for an encounter with Jesus Christ, who identifies with the welcomed and rejected strangers of every age. The Lord entrusts to the Church's motherly love every person forced to leave their homeland in search of a better future. This solidarity must be concretely expressed at every stage of the migratory experience—from departure through journey to arrival and return. This is a great responsibility, which the Church intends to share

---

121.   Pius XII, *Exsul Familia Nazarethana*, Part II.

122.   John XXIII, *Pacem in Terris*, 25.

123.   John Paul II, *Letter to Artists* (April 4, 1999), 1.

240   CHAPTER 6

with all believers and men and women of good will, who are
called to respond to the many challenges of contemporary
migration with generosity, promptness, wisdom, and foresight,
each according to their own abilities.[124]

Francis turned words on migration into deeds in 2016, when he
dramatically brought twelve Syrian Muslim refugees back to Italy at
the end of a trip to a Greek refugee camp.[125]

The teaching on migration is one of great gems of the Social
Teaching. It is worth restating more fully. Since a person's home and
homeland inevitably play significant roles in the basic human task
of searching for the fullness of life, there is a fundamental injustice
in restricting the freedom to look for a good home. In other words,
the pilgrimage of life, the journey toward heaven, can sometimes be
helped along by a physical pilgrimage across the politically imposed
borders that separate one earthly homeland from another. This transcendental argument elevates migration from a mundane question
to a transcendental one. The debate should not be about how best to
balance some practical considerations, such as greater safety, better
opportunities, higher income, and lower crime rates, against others,
for example social disruption and inadequate resources. Rather, it
should be about how best to fulfill the duty of communities and governments to promote the highest gift and responsibility of human
nature, the vocation to the divine life of love. John Paul II and Francis have eloquently demonstrated that both for those who leave and
those who receive, migration expresses solidarity and true freedom.

The imperfections of the world, including the borders imposed
by welfare states, the great global inequality of wealth, and the widespread dislike of foreigners, preclude totally free migration, at least
for the moment. In practice, without limits on the free flow of people,
enough of them would probably change jurisdictions to weaken sub-
stantially some of today's strong societies. Appropriately, the Magisterium offers counsels of imperfection to modify its endorsement of
the concept of borderless movement. Today's intrusive regulatory
states have a great deal of responsibility. "It is obviously the task of
Governments to regulate the migratory flows with full respect for

---

124. Francis, *Message for the 104th World Day of Migrants and Refugees 2018* (August 15,
2017).

125. Jim Yardley, "Pope Francis Takes 12 Refugees Back to Vatican after Trip to Greece," *New
York Times* (April 16, 2016).

THE CHURCH ADRIFT IN A SECULAR WORLD 241

the dignity of the persons and for their families' needs, mindful of the requirements of the host societies."[126]

The balance of "respect for dignity" and "mindful of the requirements" has been translated into some fairly simple guidelines. The reasons for leaving or choosing a particular destination should not be frivolous, settlers should respect and fortify the culture of their new homelands, migration should be of whole families rather than only of breadwinners, and the governments of both sending and receiving countries have a responsibility to regulate the flow of people for the sake of the national and universal common good.[127] In addition, the Church recognizes a sort of unpaid debt that emigrants have to the country they are leaving. In the words of John Paul II, migration "is the loss of a subject of work, whose efforts of mind and body could contribute to the common good of his own country, but these efforts, this contribution, are instead offered to another society which in a sense has less right to them than the person's country of origin."[128]

Many sincere Catholics seem to emphasize the teaching's qualifications, but any claim of a preferential option for control should be treated with suspicion. While there is certainly room for legitimate debate in every situation, the transcendental good and charity that the popes have identified in migration set a high bar for any argument in favor of tight restrictions. Again, John Paul II is clear. "Migration can in fact facilitate encounter and understanding between civilizations as well as between individuals and communities . . . This happens when . . . every possible means is used to promote the culture of acceptance and the culture of peace that smooths out differences and seeks dialogue . . . This openness in solidarity becomes a gift and condition of peace."[129]

---

126. John Paul II, *Message for the 90th World Day of Migrants and Refugees 2004* (December 15, 2003), 3.

127. See *Compendium of the Social Doctrine of the Church*, 298, with references. For the duty of migrants, see John Paul II, *Message for the 89th World Day of Migrants and Refugees 2003*, 4.

128. John Paul II, Encyclical Letter *Laborem Exercens* (September 14, 1981), 23. The Catholic teaching is well summarized in Michael A. Blume, "Migration and the Social Doctrine of the Church," *People on the Move*, (December 2002), 88–89. Michael Dummett, *On Immigration and Refugees* (London: Routledge, 2001) provides a less overtly Catholic and more philosophical presentation, while the last chapters of Joseph H. Carens, *The Ethics of Immigration* (Oxford: Oxford University Press, 2013) provide a secular, liberal justification for something similar to the basic Catholic position.

129. John Paul II, *Laborem Exercens*, 5.

Arguments against migration that are based on racial and cultural differences do not cross that papal bar. They are anathema to Christian principles. In the Church's theological anthropology, which is reflected in contemporary magisterial proclamations, the bonds of common humanity are considered far stronger than are any differences created by race (there should none of those whatsoever), nationality, or cultural history. Indeed, John Paul argued that Christians should see migration as "opportunities of living the experience of catholicity, a mark of the Church expressing her essential openness to all that is the work of the Spirit in every people." Noting that "[o]ften, solidarity does not come easily," he called for "parents and teachers to combat racism and xenophobia by inculcating positive attitudes based on Catholic social doctrine."[130]

Economic arguments against immigration also generally fail, on both practical and ethical grounds. Practically, migration has little effect on incomes and wealth in the receiving country. The logic is simple. For migrants as for everyone else, the value of the labor they contribute to the community is roughly the same as the value of the consumption extracted from it. Empirical studies suggest that this logic is sound. At the worst, an influx of immigrants into rich countries sometimes pulls down some wages for some workers in the receiving countries for some time. In countries with welfare states, migrants on the whole generally contribute more money than they take out.[131] However, any simple calculations of wage and job gains and losses require an elevating moral adjustment. Any economic losses of the richer natives have less moral weight than the economic gains of the much poorer immigrants.

There is also a religious argument, which Christians today apply almost exclusively against Muslims. They fear that members of the traditional enemy of the faith will undermine the religious cultures of Europe and the United States. The protection of existing communities is an acceptable reason for limiting migration, but John Paul II preferred to see the arrival of "non-Christians . . . in traditionally

---

130. John Paul II, *Message for the 89th World Day of Migrants and Refugees 2003*, 2,3.

131. See, for example, Lant Pritchett, "Alleviating Global Poverty: Labor Mobility, Direct Assistance, and Economic Growth," Center for Global Development, CGD Working Paper 479, Washington, D.C., 2018; Michael Frenkel, "Is Migration Good for an Economy? A Survey of the Main Economic Effects," *Journal for Markets and Ethics/Zeitschrift für Marktwirtschaft und Ethik,* 5 no. 1 (2017):13–22; OECD Migration Policy Debates, "Is Migration Good for the Economy?" (May 2014); World Bank, "Impact of Migration on Economic and Social Development: A Review of Evidence and Emerging Issues" (2010).

Christian countries [as] creating fresh opportunities for contacts and cultural exchanges, and [as] calling the Church to hospitality, dialogue, assistance and, in a word, fraternity."[132] In any case, the major premise of the argument, that there are Christian cultures to defend, is false. The once Christian prosperous societies that are the desired destinations for many migrants are now, for better or for worse, secular. It might perhaps be appropriate to fear that too many Muslim, Hindu, Buddhist, or Confucian migrants would undermine the values of a predominantly Christian society, although I doubt it. However, that possibility is currently irrelevant.

Defenders of secular society can argue that the firm religious beliefs of migrant Muslims will weaken the remaining social bonds in contemporary nation-states. Cultural mixing is always challenging. In this case, it is easy to find Islamic texts and a few actual Muslims arguing that depraved Western values justify militant or even armed hostility to migrants' new homelands. However, in the overall debate over cultural depravity Catholics are more naturally allied with Muslims than they are with secularists. An increase in the number of Muslims would strengthen the voice of monotheists and moral non-relativists in society and would provide allies to Christians resisting further cultural secularization and religious marginalization.

The most persuasive moral argument against immigration has nothing to do with the receiving countries. It is one that I already mentioned: that emigration can deprive poor and poorly governed countries of many of the people most qualified to improve conditions. Also, these countries' social fabric is frayed by numerous departures, even when the Church's injunction to support family unity in migration is respected, as it rarely is today. Still, sociological research in the actual patterns of movement suggest that this concern is often exaggerated, because the people who leave countries often bring benefits to those left behind, through monetary remittances, eventual return, commercial connections, or merely by stimulating emulation and education in the homeland.[133]

In any case, the right solution to excessive migration is not to restrict personal freedom. It is to reduce the desire to leave by improving life at home. As Francis put it, "The Church stands at the

---

132. John Paul II, Encyclical Letter *Redemptoris Missio* (December 7, 1990), 37b.

133. Michele R. Pistone and John J. Hoeffner, *Stepping Out of the Brain Drain: Applying Catholic Social Teaching in a New Era of Migration* (Lanham, Md.: Lexington Books, 2007) provides evidence and arguments.

side of all who work to defend each person's right to live with dignity, first and foremost by exercising the right not to emigrate and to contribute to the development of one's country of origin . . . [I]t is necessary to avert, if possible at the earliest stages, the flight of refugees and departures as a result of poverty, violence, and persecution."[134] The source countries bear most of the responsibility for keeping residents at home, but potential receiving countries can help with various forms of aid and perhaps with more generous offers of temporary permission to live and work.

Rich countries should be careful about using the legitimate responsibility to control migration as an excuse to shirk the weightier responsibility to help the poor, the wretched, and the stranger. As Pius XII wrote, "[T]he sovereignty of the State, although it must be respected, cannot be exaggerated to the point that access to this land is, for inadequate or unjustified reasons, denied to needy and decent people from other nations, provided of course, that the public wealth, considered very carefully, does not forbid this."[135]

The message is simple. Christians should not search eagerly for the practical limits to generosity. Rather, they should work diligently and imaginatively to extend those limits, to welcome as many migrants as possible. Welcome is owed to the promising and the unpromising alike and to settlers from both familiar and strange lands. Christians should chafe at the modern legal division between migrants fleeing persecution, who are theoretically always welcomed, and migrants in search of opportunity, to whom the law gives no protection. Of course, migration offers great practical challenges, for both those who come and those who receive. These are challenges that Christians should rise to, as John Paul II explained: "The path to true acceptance of immigrants in their cultural diversity is actually a difficult one, in some cases a real Way of the Cross. That must not discourage us from pursuing the will of God, who wishes to draw all peoples to himself in Christ, through the instrumentality of his Church, the sacrament of the unity of all mankind."[136]

---

134. Francis, *Message for the World Day of Migrants and Refugees 2016* (September 12, 2015).

135. Pius XII, *Letter to American Bishops* (December 24, 1948), quoted in Pius XII, *Exsul Familia Nazarethana*.

136. John Paul II, *Message for the 89th World Day of Migrants and Refugees 2003*, 4.

Looking Forward

For the first few centuries of the modern era, the Catholic analysis of intellectual and social novelties was internally coherent and in many ways wise, but it did not lend itself to a useful discernment of the steady stream of new ideas that might be entirely, partly, barely, or not at all compatible with Christian teaching. Only gradually did popes, bishops, theologians, and lay Catholics recognize just how far and how fast the world was moving away from the social order and preconceptions of Christendom. As the Church gained a more realistic perspective, its response to the new social challenges became more helpful.

Has the Church finally found a voice that is both strong in the proclamation of Christian values and able to judge how those values are faring in an indifferent or hostile world? Much of this chapter might suggest a negative answer. The solid teaching on immigration is not really evidence for a positive one, since the teaching emerged pretty much unchanged from the treasure store of the Church's tradition. Still, there are reasons to be hopeful. John Paul II, Benedict XVI, and now Francis spent their adult lives in fully post-Christian nations. The first two dedicated much of their intellectual efforts to exactly the sort of critical fusions—of Christian with secular, of old and true with new and doubtful, of reason with faith and love with truth—that the Church needs if it is to speak authoritatively about the modern world (and to it, if it will listen). Francis is continuing on the same path.

The most recent popes' worldview has gradually permeated the Curia and the rest of the Church. Subsequent popes will undoubtedly be influenced by the needs and thoughts of new generations of Catholics, people who never experienced the old arrogant Church of the dying and dead Christendom. The future is of course unknown, but I will venture a prediction. Many of the rising generation of Catholics, especially those in Latin America, Africa, and Asia, will be less interested in accommodating the modern spirit than the Catholic hierarchies have been since the Second Vatican Council. Instead, these Catholics will look to the Church for a distinctively Catholic anchor to keep them from drifting in, or sinking under, dangerously enticing modern cultural currents. The mostly quite new teaching on the environment, the subject of the next two chapters, provides a good example of how well the Magisterium can satisfy that desire.

CHAPTER 7

The Care of Creation

THE WORD *POLLUTION* WAS originally used to describe the desecration of holy objects. By the end of the nineteenth century, its meaning had been extended from the sacred to the profane, to the dirtying of rivers by factory effluents. As industry expanded and populations increased, the degradation spread to the seas, soil, and atmosphere. Despite some subsequent scattered and intermittent efforts at industrial purification, by the 1960s human activity had killed almost all life in some rivers and was making breathing hazardous in many cities.

The pollution of nature then became an important political and social issue, in most rich countries. A broad consensus on the need to address the problem led to new laws, practices, and approaches. Although the changes could have been faster and deeper, enough was done to makes the physical environment much less toxic, in rich countries. In rich countries, emissions of noxious substances are now at tiny fractions of their levels a half century ago and many formerly fouled rivers and land areas have been made safe for living things. Further declines are likely, in rich countries, since the social consensus against pollution still holds and the knowledge that helps to satisfy this aspect of the common good continues to increase. (The American presidency of Donald Trump is undoubtedly a contrary indicator, but even his friends would not like a return to the flammable rivers of the 1960s.)

My repetition of "rich countries" in the preceding paragraph was not merely bad writing. It was an awkward reminder that in environmental matters, there has been nothing like a preferential option for the poor. On the contrary, poor lands still mostly suffer from worsening industrial pollution, a trend that significantly widens the generally narrowing economic divide with rich countries. Somewhat paradoxically, the increase in overall wealth in many poor countries has also increased the environmental misery caused by pollution, because in those countries the control of noxious emissions, like the ordering of life in rapidly expanding cities, is almost always treated as a far less important social goal than is the crude increase of production. As most of the people in the world live in poor countries, the global result is tragic. Pope Francis, who comes from relatively poor Argentina, describes the situation with his usual rhetorical flair. "The earth, our home, is beginning to look more and more like an immense pile of filth."[1]

On environmental issues, the Church has, or at least seems to have, a message that is popular in the secular world. I counsel some caution over this enthusiasm, because the secular tributes often do not recognize either the Catholic teaching's moral foundation or its social implications. In its critique of the polluting society, the Church is far more radical in many ways than most mainstream activists could accept, while the teaching, correctly understood, contains too much praise of the industrial economy to please most radical environmentalists. I shall try to bring out these depths in this chapter and the next, starting, as always, with biblical teaching.

The Biblical and Theological Base

Religious environmentalists who claim a clear biblical mandate exaggerate the evidence. The Bible offers no simple, direct teaching on the distinctly modern problem of the human pollution of nature. The Scriptures are very concerned with the relations of people with each other and with the God who creates and controls the natural world, but they pay relatively little attention to the relations of humanity and the rest of creation. The neglect is basically intentional, since ignoring the natural world serves to emphasize that the God of creation, who is the God of the patriarchs and the Father of the only-begotten Son, is not to be confused with any pagan divinity of sky, mountain, river, or land. The Holy Spirit is quite different from the pagan spirits that are supposed to inhabit the world's sacred places and infuse

---

1.   Francis, Encyclical Letter *Laudato Si'* (May 24, 2015), 21.

248 CHAPTER 7

everything in nature with some hints of holiness.[2] Still, the Bible, in its overall narrative and in its scattered and indirect references to what is currently known as the environment, can justly be read as a great story of the creation, fall, and redemption of nature, as well as of humanity.

The story starts with the brief biblical description of creation in its prelapsarian condition and then as it was altered by the covenant given to Noah after the Flood.[3] Two themes can be teased out.

The first is the original harmony of the natural world, both in itself and with the intentions of God. The world was made by the good God in divine order. He judged it "very good."[4] Pope Francis explains: "Creation is of the order of love. God's love is the fundamental moving force in all created things . . . Every creature is thus the object of the Father's tenderness, who gives it its place in the world. Even the fleeting life of the least of beings is the object of his love, and in its few seconds of existence, God enfolds it with his affection."[5] Or, on a larger scale, as God explains to Jonah, "And should not I pity Nineveh, that great city of in which there are . . . much cattle?"[6]

The details of the curse God puts on Adam and Eve after their sin suggests a little more about the nature of paradise, in particular about the original harmony between created human nature and the rest of the natural world. Adam's disobedience led the ground to be "cursed" so that its produce would be eaten of "in toil" with the "sweat" of the harvester.[7] That suggests that the pre-Fall gift of using "every plant yielding seed which is upon the face of all the earth" as food had made (or would have made) the fruits readily available.[8] There would have been nothing like toil if non-sinning humanity had followed God's instruction "to till . . . and keep" the abundantly watered garden of Eden.[9]

It also seems that there was no need for violence between people and animals. The permission to eat flesh does not come until the

---

2. e.g., Victor Hamilton, *The Book of Genesis: Chapters 1–17* (Grand Rapids, Mich.: Eerdmans, 1990), 126–41, emphasizing the distinctness and polemical intention of the biblical narrative.

3. Gn 1–2; 7-9.

4. Gn 1:31.

5. Francis, *Laudato Si'*, 77.

6. Jon 4:11.

7. Gn 3:17–19.

8. Gn 1:29.

9. Gn 2:15.

covenant of God with Noah,[10] which appears to follow the covenant with Adam as a fuller divine concession to the needs and desires of ever more sinful humanity. Even after the Fall and the Flood, God promises to keep nature reasonably friendly. "I will never again curse the ground because of man, for the imagination of the human heart is evil from his youth: neither will I ever again destroy every living creature as I have done."[11]

The second pre- and postlapsarian theme is domination. The two creation accounts and the Noahic covenant all emphasize humankind's leading role in nature. In the first account, humans, made in the image of the creating and sustaining God, are given "dominion" over all animals, even those that do not serve them directly.[12] Humanity is to "fill the earth and subdue it."[13] In the second account, the animals are named by the first man,[14] a process that scholars interpret as offering the namegivers some sort of control or authority over the named,[15] then rejected as partners because of their difference and, implicitly, inferiority. In the covenant with Noah, God says, "The fear of you and the dread of you will fall on all the beasts of the earth."[16] In nature, human beings were created to be rulers.

The fall from paradise damaged but did not destroy both the harmony and the dominion. Even as he curses and expels, God makes "Adam and his wife garments of skins,"[17] expressing his continuing approval of the natural world's service of humankind's new needs. The divine willingness to provide worldly aid to people in their fallen state is even clearer in the rescue of Noah, who receives detailed instructions on how to build an ark that will allow God's creatures to survive God's wrath against the God-created world. From a modern environmental perspective, this divinely designed craft looks like a sign of the potential holiness in the human effort to make use of the nonhuman portion of creation. Not only the ark but the divine gift of meat in the post-Flood covenant with Noah and later the gift

---

10.   cf. Gn 9:3.

11.   Gn 8:21.

12.   Gn 1:26.

13.   Gn 1:28.

14.   cf. Gn 2:19–20.

15.   e.g., Kenneth A. Mathews, *Genesis 1–11: An Exegetical and Theological Exposition of Holy Scripture, New American Commentary*, vol 1A (Nashville, Tenn.: B&H Publishing Group, 1996).

16.   Gn 9:2.

17.   Gn 3:21.

of God's own body, "food indeed,"[18] show that God's concern for human well-being in the natural world mysteriously only deepens as sin increases the distance between the Creator and his creatures.

This theological observation, based on the biblical narratives of the Creation and the Fall, has readily visible practical implications. God sustains the fundamental harmony of human needs and desires with the sometimes-hidden gifts of nature; God has ordained nature to provide people with both what they need and what they justly desire. Tragically, the fall of humanity and the divine curse of the ground have disturbed creation's original friendly balance. Since the Fall, hostility, sometimes a deep hostility, has marred the support-ive relations of nature and humans. In other words, nature's bounty remains available to people, but it is no longer readily and easily avail-able. The Fall also seems to bring hostility within nature, although the Bible only alludes to this shift indirectly, by describing all animals as vegetarian before the fall and by promising a supernatural peace in nature when the Fall is finally reversed in messianic times.

In that time beyond normal time, "the wolf shall dwell the lamb and the leopard shall lie down the kid."[19] Then, too, when "the earth shall be full of the knowledge of the Lord,"[20] it seems the hostility of nature to people will also cease—"the suckling child shall play over the hole of the asp."[21] Until then, though, there have been and will be problems, including the pollution of nature. The attempt to build a tower in Babel that reaches to heaven[22] is a model for the industrial age's damage. Disaster ensues whenever people try to make nature serve them without paying any heed to their responsibility to God.

These biblical hints of a theological history of environmental bounty, damage, and responsibility are complemented by a few scrip-tural indications of the correct position of fallen humanity in nature. On one side, people should be humble, waiting "in patience" for the full redemption of earth and heaven, for which "the whole creation has been groaning in travail together until now."[23] On the other side, they should continue to exercise their God-given dominion over the earth. They remain "little less than God," creatures who rule over "all

---

18.   Jn 6:55.

19.   Is 11:6.

20.   Is 11:9.

21.   Is 11:8.

22.   cf. Gn 11:1–9.

23.   Rom 8:25, 22.

THE CARE OF CREATION   251

sheep and oxen, and also the beasts of the field, the birds of the air, and the fish of the sea."[24] This domination brings some worldly glory, as expressed by the king who speaks in the book of Ecclesiastes: "I built houses and planted vineyards for myself. . . . I bought male and female slaves . . . had also great possessions of herd and flocks . . . silver and gold and the treasure of kings and provinces."[25] The writer ultimately denigrates such mastery of nature as a "vanity," but Job, in another wisdom book, does not dismiss the grandeur of the humanization of the created world, when "man puts his hand to the flinty rock, and overturns mountains by the roots."[26] In this power over the rest of creation, people are indeed a little like God, whose hands control "the depths of the earth; the heights of the mountains are his also."[27] However, while humanity has dominion inside creation, it is only the Lord (*dominus* in Latin) who actually creates and ultimately sustains.

Environmental pollution fits perfectly into the fallen phase of the implicit biblical history of creation. It comes from the sinful human neglect of the responsibility of dominion, a pervasive mistreatment that has done widespread, severe, and enduring damage. As Pope Francis put it, "Never have we so hurt and mistreated our common home as we have in the last two hundred years."[28] Conversely, the many successes in the struggle against pollution belong to the history of redemption. They are encouraging signs of a still strong desire in modern societies to follow God's desire to restore human harmony with nature.

Any good account of biblical environmentalism is incomplete without an eschatological conclusion. After all, Christian believe that the human story that began with Adam will not end until Jesus Christ, who is the omega as well as the alpha of creation,[29] comes again to provide the fullest possible harmony of humanity in all "three fundamental and closely intertwined [human] relationships: with God, with our neighbor and with the earth itself."[30] In anticipation of the fullness of the kingdom of heaven, we are called to imitate the sacrificial love that Jesus showed us in his time as a man.

24.   Ps 8:7–8.
25.   Eccl 2:4–8.
26.   Jb 28:9.
27.   Ps 95.4–5.
28.   Francis, *Laudato Si'*, 53.
29.   cf. Rv 1:8.
30.   Francis, *Laudato Si'*, 66.

For the environment, this eschatological vocation requires a consecrated dedication to the good of the created world, to the point of willingly sacrificing personal ease and comfort. The goal is heavenly, nothing less than the renewal of the purity of earthly paradise. Like any other aspect of the City of God, it will never be reached in the fallen world, but it is the responsibility of humanity to journey in the right direction.

In the industrial world of today, even the smallest steps of that journey often require a profound purification, both of action in creation and of personal and social priorities. True sacrificial environmental love cannot be set out completely with mere worldly rules and laws. In the midst of the swarm of carefully designed technical measures, Christians should always remember that "[t]he ultimate destiny of the universe is in the fullness of God . . . [A]ll creatures are moving forward with us and through us toward . . . that transcendent fullness where the risen Christ embraces and illumines all things. Human beings . . . are called to lead all creatures back to their Creator."[31]

The Teaching in Context

It is fair to say that the Catholic Church responded to rather than initiated modern environmental concerns. With the possible and at best partial exception of Saint Francis of Assisi (1181–1226), until the middle of the twentieth century no leading Christian theologian, philosopher, or political leader expressed much interest in the correct practical human attitude to the natural world. The neglect was hardly surprising. In practice, there was little to worry about before the coming of modern industry. In any case, the first encyclical to mention environmental questions was Paul VI's *Octogesima Adveniens* in 1971, a few years after industrial pollution had already become a serious political issue.[32] He expressed the problem forcefully. "Man is suddenly becoming aware that by an ill-considered exploitation of nature he risks destroying it and becoming in his turn the victim of this degradation. Not only is the material environment becoming a permanent menace—pollution and refuse, new illness and absolute destructive capacity—but the human framework is no

31.   Francis, *Laudato Si'*, 83.

32.   For some secular background on the development of environmentalism, see Robert Gottlieb, *Forcing the Spring: The Transformation of the American Environmental Movement*, rev. ed. (Washington, D.C.: Island Press, 2005).

THE CARE OF CREATION 253

longer under man's control, thus creating an environment for tomorrow which may well be intolerable. This is a wide-ranging social problem which concerns the entire human family."[33] The integration of ecology into the Catholic Social Teaching increased in the following years. In 1989 John Paul II proclaimed Saint Francis as the patron saint of ecology and dedicated his New Year's letter for 1990 to the theme. Pope Francis used line from a poem by Saint Francis as a title and a theme for *Laudato Si'*, his 2015 encyclical on ecology.

There are two directly opposed ways of interpreting the delay. Critics have argued that Christians were slow to catch on to this issue because the religion's "anthropocentrism," the conviction of the absolute human superiority over everything else in creation, was the founding principle of the industrial economy. According to this view, post-Christian and anti-Christian moderns have inherited the fundamental Christian dismissal of nature's spiritual dignity, so Christianity is in large part responsible for the wanton human pollution of the natural world.[34] Among early secular environmentalists, it was widely believed that Christianity was antinature in a way that other religions were not.[35] The Catholic Church was especially condemned for its unwillingness to endorse the goal of limiting the human population to protect the nonhuman world. The animus against Christianity has diminished, in part because so many Christians have become environmentalists and in part because the Christian views have lost so much political influence.

More realistically, defenders of the Church point out that by its historic standards of dealing with new social challenges, the response to pollution was extremely rapid. This relative nimbleness can be credited to a latent but deep respect of the natural world as a manifestation of God's loving will. Modern people can easily

---

33.   Paul VI, Apostolic Letter *Octogesima Adveniens* (May 14, 1971), 21.

34.   This critique was made powerfully by Lynn White Jr., a distinguished medieval historian of science, in a 1967 article "The Historical Roots of Our Ecologic Crisis," *Science* 155 (1967): 1203–7, reprinted in *Ecology and Religion in History*, eds. David Spring and Eileen Spring (New York: Harper & Row, 1974), 15–31. In the same volume, the historian Arnold Toynbee calls for "reverting from the *Weltanschauung* of monotheism to the *Weltanschauung* of pantheism." ("The Religious Background of the Present Environmental Crisis," 137–49, quote at 148). See also the editor's introduction to Todd LeVasseur and Anna Peterson eds., *Religion and Ecological Crisis: The "Lynn White Thesis" at 50* (Abingdon, UK: Routledge, 2017).

35.   Many of the essays in May Evelyn Tucker and John A. Grim, eds., *Worldviews and Ecology: Religion, Philosophy and the Environment* (Maryknoll, N.Y.: Orbis Books, 1994) are infused with this "worldview."

appreciate the poetic enthusiasm of Saint Francis, but Saint Thomas Aquinas, whose influence over Christian teaching was greater, validates the importance of the cosmos with his assumption that everything in creation has a reality and purpose that comes from and heads toward God.[36] Besides, the popes had long been suspicious of the archetypical modern desire to reshape nature crudely and aggressively in the image of humankind. (I come back to this objection to one of the central tenets of modern thinking in the next chapter.) In effect, the Church was just waiting to be asked to explain why people's approach to nature was wrong—and what the right approach was.

The Catholic approach combines the two biblical themes of harmony and dominion into a single concept: "responsible stewardship over nature, in order to protect it, to enjoy its fruits."[37] In a single word, people have a responsibility. Human beings are responsible for protecting the fundamental harmony of all creation, but that responsibility makes us less absolute rulers than shepherds or stewards who obey the one Lord and Creator.

What is this harmony of creation? It cannot be described in simple or straightforward terms, because it is a material manifestation of a transcendental order and beauty. However, Christians can say that people have a distinct, elevated, and responsible position in this beautiful order. God created the heavens and the earth and all that is in them for the benefit of human beings, who are integral parts of creation but who are also stewards of it. Benedict XVI summarized this idea in some rather dense philosophical-theological language. "Nature expresses a design of love and truth. It is prior to us, and it has been given to us by God as the setting for our life . . . [It is] a gift of the Creator who has given it an inbuilt order, enabling man to draw from it the principles needed in order 'to till it and keep it."[38] Francis expresses the same judgment more poetically, "our common home is like a sister with whom we share our life and a beautiful mother who opens her arms to embrace us."[39]

---

36. For a somewhat exaggerated but basically sound ecological reading of Thomas, see Willis Jenkins, *Ecologies of Grace* (Oxford: Oxford University Press, 2008), 133–52.

37. Benedict XVI, Encyclical Letter *Caritas in Veritate* (June 29, 2009), 50.

38. Benedict XVI, *Caritas in Veritate*, 48, citing Gen 2:15.

39. Francis, *Laudato Si'*, 1. For some background, see Drew Christiansen and Walter Gracer, eds., *"And God Saw That It Was Good": Catholic Theology and the Environment* (Washington, D.C.: United States Catholic Conference, 1996); Daniel P. Scheid, *The Cosmic Common Good:*

It is not necessary to take up paganism to understand that the natural world has something sacramental about it. The earth and what it contains, the air, the occult forces of life, the energies of the cosmos, and the secret harmonies of the physical world—all those are visible or discoverable signs of divine love. They are all a call to worship, as the hymn of creation in the biblical book of Daniel explains. This litany ties all the components of the created world—the earth, mountains and hills, everything growing, dolphins, birds, beasts—to the Jewish priests of the Lord, with the repeated exhortation to each part of creation, nonhuman and human, gentile and Jewish, to "sing praise to him and highly exalt him forever."[40] The praise includes the appreciation of the awesome and awful beauties of nature, an appreciation that often takes the form of restraint before nature's mysteries and power, in recognition of the limits to human knowledge, strength, and judgment. In other words, people should not "view other living beings as mere objects subjected to arbitrary human domination."[41] Rather, they should have a "disinterested, unselfish, and aesthetic attitude that is born of wonder in the presence of being and of the beauty which enables one to see in visible things the message of the invisible God who created them."[42] The dignity of animals deserves special respect, because they share with humankind more of the gifts of God than do plants or inanimate objects.

Of course, the natural world is not merely offered for sacramental appreciation. It also provides the raw material and the tools of human life. Humankind's physical, intellectual, and moral nature compels all people to make both much use and considered use of the physical world in which they live. We cannot survive without forcing somewhat recalcitrant nature to yield some of its bounty—food, minerals, water, and energy. There is an inevitable tension between creation as sacrament and nature as raw material, nurturing womb, and tool, but the necessary exploitation and manipulation is not an excuse for "sacrilegious" irresponsibility. In Francis's words, domination should not be confused with "tyrannical anthropocentrism unconcerned for

---

Religious Grounds for Ecological Ethics (Oxford: Oxford University Press, 2016) and Celia Deane-Drummond, "Joining in the Dance: Catholic Social Teaching and Ecology," *New Blackfriars*, 93 (2012): 193–212.

40. Dn 3:29–90.

41. Francis, *Laudato Si'*, 82.

42. John Paul II, Encyclical Letter *Centesimus Annus* (September 1, 1991), 37.

other creatures."[43] The responsibility is universal. "The natural environment is a collective good, the patrimony of all humanity and the responsibility of everyone."[44] The universality extends in time as well as space. Authentic development requires that patrimony to be repaired when it has been damaged so it can be passed on in good condition.

Francis writes of sin's dire effect on the natural "harmony between the Creator, humanity, and creation."[45] The restoration of this triple harmony, to the extent that this is possible in a fallen world, is the central goal of Christian ecology.[46] The environmental aspect of that harmony is seen when human society flourishes in the physical world, when people respect the divinely imposed limits on their physical worldly human ambitions, and when the world is allowed to make manifest both its divinely provided richness and its divinely ordained beauty. In the words of Benedict XVI, we have the responsibility of "being guardians of creation and developing its gifts; of actively collaborating in God's work ourselves, in the evolution that he ordered in the world so that the gifts of Creation might be appreciated rather than trampled upon and destroyed."[47]

The judgment of the goodness of any particular human interaction with nature is often hard. Many acts can be described as either the virtuous promotion of human flourishing through altering creation or as the sinful trampling of the created environment for the sake of spiritually meaningless human convenience. Conversely, inaction may be a virtuous human respect for creation—or a sinful failure to promote human flourishing. The difficulty of judgment has been increased by the vastly greater human mastery of nature that has accompanied the development of modern industry. People can do more, so they have to think harder. "We must become wiser," as John Paul II put it.[48] (I discuss the moral responsibilities that come with progress in the final chapter.)

---

43.   Francis, *Laudato Si'*, 68.

44.   Francis, *Laudato Si'*, 95.

45.   Francis, *Laudato Si'*, 66.

46.   The triad of God, humankind, and the world (with the world understood as the human community rather than as nonhuman creation) predates environmental thinking. Oliver Davies, *The Creativity of God: World, Eucharist, Reason* (Cambridge: Cambridge University Press, 2004) presents a similar idea in a more modern form, although his interest is not directly ecological.

47.   Benedict XVI, Speech *Meeting with the Clergy of the Diocese of Bolzano-Bressanone* (August 6, 2008).

48.   John Paul II, Speech in Hiroshima, Japan *Address to Scientists and Representatives of the United Nations University* (February 25, 1981), 6.

Contrary to the accepted wisdom among many radical environmentalists, the increased human power has not been used solely to damage the humanity-God-nature harmony. Increased life expectancies and the many comforts of modern life show that in many ways nature has been trained to serve people better than ever before, while the vast division of labor and the global coordination of economic and scientific activity show that people have learned to work better together to take greater advantage of what nature has to offer. In thinking of the relations of God to humanity, the more successful harvesting of the world's riches has brought what might be considered a theological uplift. The Creator now looks less harsh with the human race than he did in the preindustrial age, since it turns out that far more material generosity was hidden in creation than was previously suspected. In sum, nature has become more of what it should be, both as a sign of God's generosity and beauty and as a loyal servant to its human master. The Magisterium has recognized these accomplishments: "[A]s people who believe in God, who saw that nature which he had created was 'good,' we rejoice in the technological and economic progress which people, using their intelligence, have managed to make."[49]

Still, the gains in harmony have to be set against significant losses. John Paul II summarized the situation, with a moral-psychological explanation: "In his desire to have and to enjoy rather than to be and to grow, man consumes the resources of the earth and his own life in an excessive and disordered way."[50] The vast amount of pollution so carelessly created over so much time in so many places clearly shows sin at work. So does the degradation of natural beauty, the wasteful use of many physical natural resources, the dangerously excessive homogenization of cultivated plants and animals, the reduction of biodiversity in the wild, the careless use of fresh water, and the helter-skelter approach to industrialization, especially in the developing world.

The popes have spoken firmly and clearly about the disordered relationship to the created world that is found in so much of modern economy. People who succumb to the temptation to abuse God's gifts in nature try to act "in place of God." They risk "provoking a rebellion [against man] on the part of nature, which is more tyrannized

---

49. *Compendium of the Social Doctrine of the Church*, 457, quoting John Paul II, Speech in Hiroshima, Japan, *Address to Scientists*, 3.

50. John Paul II, *Centesimus Annus*, 37.

than governed by him."[51] Francis, who sees an "intimate relationship between the poor and the fragility of the planet,"[52] speaks of the dire and differentiated social consequences of ecological neglect, creating an "ecological debt" that the rich countries owe to the poor lands whose natural resources they have so carelessly exploited.[53]

The Catholic Social Teaching's quest for a triple harmony presents the moral challenge of the environment is terms that are realistic, respectful of both human nature and the rest of creation, and ultimately religious. Humans, who are made in God's image, must find the right way to live in the beautiful, fruitful and, after the Fall, sometimes hostile world that God has created for them.

In my judgment, this perspective is one of the triumphs of the Catholic Social Teaching. I rank it with the universal destination of goods (discussed in chapter 2) and the defense of the dignity of migration (discussed in chapter 6). The Catholic environmental approach does not merely stand somewhere between the opposing extreme claims—the purely human-centered view of the world that people can do whatever they want with everything found in nature and the purely nature-worshipping view that people should leave nature alone as much as possible. It stands above both, by assuming that the responsible use of creation is part of the human obligation to the divine. The teaching intimately ties the almost heavenly beauty of nature with the apparently mundane debate about the management of resources and the efficiency of technology. It also ties the respect for humanity and its transcendental calling with the respect for the physical world in which people live.

Catholic environmental teaching never strays far from the underlying and overarching cultural questions raised by the blight of pollution. Why did and do societies rush into industrialization and urbanization with so little heed for the whole of creation? Why have they waited until so much damage has been done before changing their ways? Why is there often so much resistance to every effort to reduce environmental damage and so much willingness to repeal environmental restrictions? The magisterial answers to all these questions can ultimately be reduced to a simple failure, the disregard of the God-human-nature triangle of gift and responsibility.

---

51.   John Paul II, *Centesimus Annus*, 37.

52.   Francis, *Laudato Si'*, 16.

53.   Francis, *Laudato Si'*, 51.

The Church's teaching encourages people to do better, to follow their vocation to serve God in creation.

It does that in a positive way by calling for respect for nature, its awesome power and beauty, and also its potential benefit to humanity. The teaching is also negative, presenting a warning, or even a threat. Human arrogance, recklessness, and greed will inevitably damage the environmental common good. If we ignore our true environmental vocation, the world will end up hideous and perhaps uninhabitable. The evangelization through fear is timely, because the environment in most of the world is currently suffering greatly from depredations brought by careless industrialization. The call is also almost timeless, because the technologies the future will undoubtedly give people the power to do even greater environmental damage and the temptation to use that power will endure as long as this fallen world lasts. The triple harmony will presumably be perfect when paradise is restored. All will be well when there is "a new heaven and a new earth."[54] Until then, we must be reminded constantly to "choose life."[55]

This truly elegant and beautiful teaching has one great disadvantage. It does not lead to clear practical judgments in most environmental controversies. Consider, for example, nuclear power. The technical facts are hotly disputed, allowing Catholics to argue both sides of the question with the firm conviction of support from the environmental Magisterium. If nuclear power is seen as a relatively inexpensive, nonpolluting, and safe source of energy, then the Church is in favor of its use. If, however, nuclear power production is considered to be highly risky, hugely expensive, and unnecessary, then Catholics are resolutely opposed. It can only be hoped that all the Catholic proponents of the two contradictory views have all reflected on the concerns raised by the teaching, including the capacity of humanity in general, and of each particular society at any particular time, to be responsible stewards of this especially hidden and especially potent force of nature.

Catholics against the Mainstream—Four Issues

At first glance, the Church's environmental teaching might look close to useless. Not only does this beautiful approach rarely lead

---

54. Rv 21:1, referring to Is 65:17.

55. Dt 30:19.

to clear policy recommendations, but when it does point in a particular direction, the Catholic conclusion is often practically identical to that reached by the less elevated, nonreligious analyses of secular environmental activists. The frequent practical convergence of Catholic and secular thinking should not be surprising. Theologically, this is an example of the basic Thomistic principle that grace perfects nature without contradicting or denigrating it. A grace-filled approach to the created world can deepen a shallow nonsupernatural understanding, but the lesser secular approach is often basically right, just incomplete. More pragmatically, since Christian and many secular environmentalists work with the same facts, share a single scientific method, and, as I explain a little later, have similar visions of the flaws of industrial society, their arguments tend to end up in similar places.

The congruence of policy recommendations helps explain the relatively warm secular response to Catholic environmental pronouncements, so different from the bitter rejection of so much of the Church's social and sexual teaching. However, as I suggested at the beginning of this chapter, the differences between secular and Christian environmentalism are actually profound. The rest of this chapter and a large portion of the next one are dedicated to topics that are, or in my opinion should be, signs of contradiction.

The Body

Secular environmentalists typically think of humans as essentially quite separate from the natural world and in their modern behavior often intrinsically opposed to welfare of nature. Bound by this ideology of separate and basically unequal, such environmentalists have rarely considered issues of human biotechnology and bioethics to be their concern. The Catholic Social Teaching, which looks at people as the apex of creation, is quite different. Living human bodies are seen as integral parts of the created physical world, so their correct treatment is an environmental challenge. Indeed, it is a particularly important challenge, because these bodies have a special place in the triple harmony of humanity, God, and nature. The ensouled body is made in God's image, and God himself takes on bodily life in this world the Incarnation of Jesus. The living person is "a manifestation of God in

THE CARE OF CREATION 261

the world, a sign of his presence, a trace of his glory,"[56] as John Paul II put it.

Most of chapters 9 and 10 are dedicated to some of the many ways in which these bodies are abused in the modern social environment. In this chapter, I want to mention the sharp debates on a few highly contested medical-environmental issues. In all these cases, the Catholic Social Teaching is almost directly opposed to the conventional secular wisdom. Christians believe that bodies deserve reverence. They also believe that God's wish for people to "have life ... abundantly"[57] includes the healthy life of the body and indeed the God-desired lives all human bodies, healthy or unhealthy. Humans can and should cooperate with the divine will in this bodily intention. Finally, in the Christian view of human nature, people have enough of heaven in them that only our heavenly Father can rightfully decide who is worthy of life in this world and for how long. Most notably, God has not given people enough wisdom to judge that a person's life should be snuffed out through a medical procedure, that the quality of a particular life, actual or potential, is unacceptably low, or that alternative genetic and procreative arrangements are better than the divinely provided ones.

Before complaining about contemporary antilife medical practices, I should provide a few sentences of warm praise. In many crucial ways, modern medicine is environmentally sound. The human body is reverenced as it should be in most of the careful attention paid to the ill, in the praise of physical fitness and healthy diets, and in the many, mostly new techniques and arrangements that help people with disabilities live longer, more dignified, and more fulfilled lives. For healthy people, the modern medical respect for human bodies has made a significant contribution to one of the great accomplishments of modern society: the environment of prosperous countries promotes lives that are longer and less troubled by disabling illnesses than ever in history. As John Paul II declared, "people today pay ever great and closer attention to the sufferings of their neighbor, seek to understand those sufferings and deal with them with ever greater skill."[58]

Still, serious complaints are necessary, because just as we have felt free to pollute the divine gifts of air, earth, and water, we have

---

56.   John Paul II, *Evangelium Vitae*, 34.

57.   Jn 10:10.

58.   John Paul II, Apostolic Letter *Salvificis Doloris* (February 11, 1984), 29.

felt free to insult the sacramental dignity of some human bodies. As with the rest of creation, more hubris than reverence is visible in several vital domains. The worst practices come mostly around birth and death, when "[h]uman life finds itself most vulnerable."[59] At the beginning of life, there is the widespread acceptance of abortion, the voluntary killing of undesired or unhealthy children. There is also the well-established industry of in vitro fertilization, which produces embryos in laboratories and keeps many of them alive for years in a sort of suspended animation. Then there is the developing science of designing new and supposedly improved bodies. Both genetic engineering, in which the material that determines inherited characteristics is modified, and therapeutic cloning, in which unborn children are created and killed for the sake of their organs, are already closer to reality than to fantasy.

At the other end of life, there is a broadening acceptance of euthanasia, the voluntary killing of people deemed unworthy of further life. The practice has been legalized in several jurisdictions and in some of them the decision to kill can be made without the consent of the to-be-killed person. Death-on-demand is still mostly presented as morally challenging, but the idea that the practice is reasonable or even virtuous seems to be gaining ground. Conversely, what might be called life-on-demand may also sometimes be an environmental issue, when vast quantities of resources are dedicated to fighting off what could well be God's will to end a life.

There are also some serious corporal medical abuses in the years between birth and death. Prescription drugs that modify moods and behavior are sometimes helpful, but they are too often used without attention to the true interest of the whole person in his or her physical, emotional, and spiritual environment. Similarly, the medical skill and knowledge that is so valuable in difficult births is often invoked for no good reason. The Vatican has not yet dealt with such problems in any detail, but it has spoken out against another abuse, the medical treatment given to people who do not accept their biological gender. The use of hormones and surgery to try to turn men into women, and vice versa, is doomed to fail. The notion that it might succeed reflects a sinful belief in a human right to tell God how their people's bodies should work. As Francis explained, "The biological and psychological manipulation of sexual difference, which

---

59. John Paul II, *Evangelium Vitae*, 44.

biomedical technology can now make appear as a simple matter of personal choice—which it is not!—runs the risk of dismantling the energy source that feeds the covenant between man and woman, making it creative and fruitful."[60]

On some of these issues, Catholics and mainstream environmentalists are on the same side. Most notably, environmentalists who mistrust all human efforts to reshape nature are instinctively uneasy about the genetic manipulation of human life. Catholics should be grateful for these allies but wary of their often-flawed logic. Any sound argument against these practices will include a clear recognition of the distinctly different moral status of people and lesser forms of life. Without that distinction, it will be almost impossible to condone any selective breeding of animals and plants, practices that are often excellent examples of the wise human use of the gifts of nature.

When arguing against many other abuses of the human body, Catholic environmentalists cannot count on their mainstream peers to take their side. On one crucial issue, abortion, they can expect a fight, as "Green" activists are almost always enthusiastic supporters of legal abortion.[61] This view is incompatible with true respect for creation, since an outrage on the womb, the most intimate part of the human environment, is a profound violation of the natural order of people living in the world. Environmentalism is not worthy of the name if it does not protest against this abuse. (This accusation of environmentalist inconsistency mirrors that of proabortion campaigners who decry any opponents of abortion whose concern for life that does not extend fully to human life outside of the womb.)

On other medical environmental problems, the Catholic and secular environmentalists may not fight, but they may struggle to engage. For example, Catholics cannot expect their secular peers to understand, let alone to support, their campaigns against the vicious practice of legal euthanasia. Similarly, the separation of the creation of human life from human sexual life-giving act is a topic of almost no concern to mainstream campaigners, but Catholic environmentalists should be appalled. In vitro fertilization and surrogate motherhood violate the God-given physical order of creation. (I come back to this topic in chapter 10.)

---

60.   Francis, *Address to the Participants in the Congress on Child Dignity in the Digital World* (October 6, 2017).

61.   For example, Gabby Bess, "Reuse, Reduce, Reproductive Rights: How Abortion Can Help Save the Planet." *Vice* (October 6, 2015).

264 CHAPTER 7

The Catholic-secular conflicts in medical environmentalism rarely come to the fore, largely because Catholic environmental activists almost always ignore the tie between the "ecological question and "'human ecology,' properly speaking."[62] In this separation, they lose the seamless connection expressed by John Paul II in one of his lists of threats to human life: "the spreading of death caused by reckless tampering with the world's ecological balance, by the criminal spread of drugs, or by the promotion of certain kinds of sexual activity which, besides being morally unacceptable, also involve grave risks to life."[63] The division can make sense politically, as long as more can be accomplished by keeping secular friends who share some environmental views than by alienating them with unwelcome proselytizing on other environmental topics. However, anything less than the integral Catholic view of environmental responsibilities is dangerously incomplete. The evil of trying to wrest from God the full control of the creation and termination of human life is essentially the same evil as trying to ignore the divinely given responsibility to be good stewards of land, sea, and air.

The Ideal of Wilderness

One of the earliest and most persistent strands of secular environmental thinking is the veneration of all nature that is untouched by human hands. This respect for the world's raw beauty, often described as wilderness, is usually combined with an instinctive dislike of humankind's alteration of nature. This tie, which has become accepted wisdom in much of the secular environmental movement, can be traced back to the immensely popular early nineteenth-century naturalist and nature philosopher Alexander von Humboldt. Although he was not opposed to the "enlightened employment" of the "products and forces of nature," he drew a sharp contrast between the pure power and beauty of untouched nature and the "incalculable" damage so often done to it by people's "insatiable avarice."[64] The case against human mismanage-

---

62.   John Paul II, *Evangelium Vitae*, 42.

63.   John Paul II, *Evangelium Vitae*, 10.

64.   Alexander von Humboldt, *Personal Narratives*, vol. 3, 2, cited in Andrea Wulf, *The Invention of Nature: Alexander von Humboldt's New World* (London: John Murray, 2015), 103. See also, Aaron Sachs, *The Humboldt Current: A European Explorer and His American Disciples*, (Oxford: Oxford University Press, 2007), 73–108. The Romantic appreciation is put into historical context in the very fine Roderick Nash, *Wilderness and the American Mind*, 3rd ed. (New

ment of the natural world was particularly strong in Latin America, where Humboldt formed much of his view of the cosmos. That was the name of his huge book on the philosophy of nature. Significantly, while he wrote in *Kosmos* about the "sublimity" and "grandeur" of the world, he did not mention God. Nature itself seemed to be his divinity.[65] Later in the nineteenth century, the American wilderness enthusiast John Muir expressed a similar sentiment, comparing "the galling harshness of civilization" to the "great, fresh, unblighted, unredeemed wilderness" that is "the hope of the world." People were merely "part of wild nature, kin to everything." Like people, "all the rest of creation" had rights.[66] Perhaps under the influence of demographic arguments for eugenic limits on human breeding, some protoenvironmentalists in the middle decades of the twentieth century seemed to delight in arguing for harsh measures to control the human "population explosion" that they were certain was destroying the natural world.[67]

This essentially pantheistic view, with or without the addition of nonhuman rights, is in explicit opposition to Christian teaching. Believers see humanity as the divinely ordained steward of nature and have traditionally seen wild nature, untamed by humanity, as disordered and threatening. In contrast, Humboldt saw wild nature as pure and godlike and humans as destructive intruders into the world's divine places. The contemporary environmental movement remains colored by Humboldt's enthusiasm for raw nature, his suspicion of human industry, and his indifference, if not outright hostility, to Christianity. His most extreme intellectual heirs endorse so-called deep ecology, going as far as rejecting all agriculture as oppressive to nature.

Secular environmentalists are generally much more moderate, but most of them desire, at least in some vague way, to minimize the human "footprint" on the natural world. In line with Humboldt, their praise of pure wilderness is frequently combined with doubts about the value of all human cultures, with more severe doubts about

---

Haven, Conn.: Yale University Press, 1982), although Nash does not actually mention Humboldt.

65.   Alexander von Humboldt, *Kosmos: The Physical Phenomena of the Universe* (London: Hippolyte Baillière, 1845), 1:10.

66.   Quoted in Nash, *Wilderness* 128–29.

67.   For a quick summary of this distasteful aspect of environmentalism, see Jedediah Purdy, "Environmentalism's Racist History," *The New Yorker* (August 13, 2015), and Donald T. Critchlow, "Birth Control, Population Control, and Family Planning: An Overview," in Donald T. Critchlow, ed., *The Politics of Abortion and Birth Control in Historical Perspective* (University Park, Penn.: The Pennsylvania State University Press, 1996), 1–21.

more sophisticated cultures. They are prone to suspect that what Catholics consider to be the natural and beneficial human activity of harvesting the good things of the earth is actually an undesirable although perhaps unavoidable disruption of the cosmic harmony of nonhuman nature. In the words of Colin Fletcher, who popularized backpacking in the 1960s, people should learn to abandon "the crass assumption that the world was made for man."[68]

Catholics should have a mixed response of to the praise of wild pure nature and the concomitant denigration of artificial civilization. They can certainly support the preservation of something like raw nature in national parks, which were created partly in response to Humboldt's warnings. They should, as Francis recommends, recognize the value to humanity of protecting both natural beauty and biodiversity. "The loss of forests and woodlands entails the loss of species which may constitute extremely important resources. . . . It is not enough, however, to think of different species merely as potential 'resources' to be exploited, while overlooking the fact that they have value in themselves. . . . Because of us, thousands of species will no longer give glory to God by their very existence, nor convey their message to us."[69]

However, believers should be wary of environmentalists' too enthusiastic praise for the intrinsic value of purely nonhuman nature, because the praise is often matched with an unduly low view of humanity, not just their current behavior in unwild cities but their place in the universe (or creation) as a whole. God undoubtedly provides all the natural world with its own beauty and meaning—as God explains to Job, he provides "water to a land where no man is . . . to make the ground put forth grass."[70] However, a disproportionate appreciation of the value of nature relative to the value of human flourishing leads to "undesirable attitudes of neo-paganism or a new pantheism,"[71] as Benedict XVI explained. Similarly, Francis warns against a "divinization of the earth which would prevent us from working on it and protecting it in its fragility."[72]

---

68. Cited in Nash, *Wilderness* 256. The essays in Dale Jamieson, ed., *A Companion to Environmental Philosophy* (Oxford: Blackwell, 2001) provide a range of contemporary views on the relative value of humanity and the natural world. The Catholic position is presented only sporadically and never clearly or favorably.

69. Francis, *Laudato Si'*, 32–33.

70. Jb 38:26–27.

71. Benedict XVI, *Caritas in Veritate*, 48.

72. Francis, *Laudato Si'*, 90.

Nature is not God, but God's hand is seen in all of nature, including human nature, which includes the unique ability and desire to approach, appreciate, and guard the grandeur of all creation. "The natural environment is a collective good, the patrimony of all humanity and the responsibility of everyone,"[73] a human responsibility that includes the cultivation of sublime landscapes. However, such cultivation does not necessarily require the preservation of vast amounts of absolute wilderness. Indeed, preservation of nature in total isolation from humankind may show less respect for God's unsearchable generosity than would modifying the natural world so that people can more easily use, visit, and appreciate it. In the Catholic understanding, nature is fundamentally more natural when it is being guided by people than when it is inaccessible to its natural, God-given human stewards. It is noteworthy that the preservation of wilderness, of nature untouched by human hands, receives no mention in the numerous papal discussions of environmental matters. At most, it might be implied in a comment such as, "contemplation of [nature's] magnificence imparts peace and serenity."[74] Even there, though, what is valued is the human interaction with nature, not the conservation of a natural world that is imagined as independent of humanity.

Like the attitude toward the human body, the attitude toward wilderness is a good touchstone for differentiating Catholic concern for the environment from a fundamentally antihuman approach to nature. In the pure-nature creed of Humboldt, nature is different, better, and closer to the divine when we leave it alone. For Catholics, the purity and otherness of raw nature is not inherently any more beautiful or divine than the fields, forests, and cities that humanity has shaped.

Climate Change

In my judgment, the approach of Catholic environmentalists to anthropogenic climate change should be different from that of their secular peers. I recognize that this view is unpopular among concerned Catholics and that Francis does not seem to share my belief in the value of keeping an intellectual distance. Nonetheless,

---

73. Francis, *Laudato Si'*, 95.
74. John Paul II, *Message for the Celebration of the World Day of Peace* (January 1, 1990), 14.

268   CHAPTER 7

an important facet of the Social Teaching is at stake—the Catholic willingness to hope and even to expect that human ingenuity will find the "new things" needed to address the problems created by new manifestations of human sin and that humans organizations will be flexible enough to make use of novel technologies and social arrangements without any radical social changes.

It is certainly reasonable to argue that global warming is the inevitable penalty for a careless disregard of the good and integrity of creation. There is, however, a gap between that historical moral judgment and the technological and social despair shown in accepting that the warming is so powerful and so devastating that the only reasonable response is the dismantling of some central practices of the contemporary economy. The last two popes, though, seem to have joined most mainstream environmentalists in accepting both claims.

Francis could have been speaking for one of the more radical Green groups when he wrote, "Many of those who possess more resources and economic or political power seem mostly to be concerned with masking the problems or concealing their symptoms, simply making efforts to reduce some of the negative impacts of climate change. However, many of these symptoms indicate that such effects will continue to worsen if we continue with current models of production and consumption."[75] The Green campaigners would probably also endorse his papal remedy: "Humanity is called to recognize the need for changes of lifestyle, production, and consumption, in order to combat this warming."[76] Later in that encyclical, Francis quotes the equally strong words of his predecessor, Benedict XVI, "[T]echnologically advanced societies must be prepared to encourage more sober lifestyles, while reducing their energy consumption and improving its efficiency."[77]

The unity of secular and Catholic thinking on this topic not only reflects a shared interpretation of the scientific evidence. It also springs from common intellectual and cultural preconceptions. I already mentioned the influence of Alexander von Humboldt on secular environmental thinking. Catholics reject his almost pantheistic appreciation of nature, but they can be almost as critical as he was of the modern approach to physical creation. For example,

---

75.   Francis, *Laudato Si'*, 26.

76.   Francis, *Laudato Si'*, 23.

77.   Francis, *Laudato Si'*, 193, citing Benedict XVI, *Message for the Celebration of the 2010 World Day for Peace: If You Want to Cultivate Peace, Protect Creation*, 9.

the early twentieth-century German Catholic theologian Romano Guardini argued that industrial society, with its resolute denial of the any sacred meaning in creation and its relentless striving for efficiency and power, is inherently disrespectful of the nuanced ways of nature.[78] Francis planned to write a doctoral dissertation on Guardini and quotes him several times in *Laudato Si'*.

Guardini is perhaps extreme in his condemnation of the modern desecration of the natural world, but, as I try to explain in the next chapter, orthodox Catholic teaching is quite sympathetic to both his underlying vision and to his sharp criticisms of a spiritually moribund, recklessly destructive, and potentially self-destructive industrial society. The Guardini vision, even watered down, is close enough to Humboldt's for many Catholics to accept almost unquestioningly secular campaigners' cataclysmic claims about climate change. It is almost too easy for them to discover in it a subtle but especially dangerous type of spiritual-physical pollution that has been caused by humanity's crude misuse of nature.

There is, though, a key difference between the secular and Catholic positions. For climate change activists who reject the current popular vision of industrial society, this issue has become paramount. Their campaign against economic excess in developed countries would be severely damaged if the science or technology related to climate change turned against them, because in rich parts of the world industrial production is increasing while most nonclimate-related sorts of dangerous emissions are declining. For Catholics, though, man-made climate change is only one of many types of environmental damage, so no new scientific facts or technical developments can falsify their whole analysis. In other words, the basic Catholic teaching about integral human ecology (a concept I discuss in more detail in the next chapter) would remain intact even if it turned out that human activity is not actually warming the world to a dangerous degree or if people manage to find ways to deal fairly easily with the problems caused by their warming activities. The overall disregard of the human duty to use nature respectfully would still be creating severe problems in the humanity-nature-God triangle.

Indeed, in some ways the Catholic teaching would be fortified if humanity manages to deal with this challenge without any

---

78. See Romano Guardini, *Letters from Lake Como: Explorations on Technology and the Human Race*, trans. Geoffrey W. Bromiley (Edinburgh: T&T Clark, 1994 [1927])

impoverishment or significant change in lifestyles. As I hinted a moment ago, such an accomplishment would justify the long-standing papal confidence in the capacity for goodness in God's creation, both in human nature and in the nonhuman natural world. As I have discussed several times, the goodness was scarred and damaged by the fall of humanity into sin, but it was not erased. The residue of goodness in created nature, which is brought to fruition in redeemed nature, is what allows the Social Teaching's prophetic hope to complement and sometimes to overcome its prophetic gloom. From Leo XIII onward, the popes have believed that, with the help of God's grace and guided by the truths of faith, modern people can solve the serious social problems that they have caused and that these Christian solutions would bring social changes, but neither disastrous disruptions nor revolutionary convulsions. It is theologically reasonable for Christians to hope that anthropogenic climate change is such a solvable problem.

Of course, the Magisterium's prophetic voice cannot speak with precision about science and technology, so popes will always be learning more than they are teaching about climate science and the related practical issues of warming. This ignorance should lead to some caution, even when the scientific consensus is strong. Prelates have little to lose in being discreet in their contemporary scientific interventions. The credibility of the Church's environmental teaching does not ultimately depend on the truth of any particular set of scientific models and technological assumptions, but a too strong endorsement of the current accepted wisdom could leave the whole Church teaching on the environment unnecessarily subject to an embarrassing correction. As Thomas Aquinas warned when discussing an earlier scientific controversy, "if further progress in the search of truth justly undermines this position, we too fall with it."[79] It seems wiser to avoid excessive magisterial attention to any one issue and to pay more attention to the many other types of physical and spiritual damage caused by the careless exploitation of nature.

Pessimism

The papal rush to pessimism on global warming is a particularly

---

79. From Thomas Aquinas, *Sentences* 2.2.d.12.a.2, translated in Ralph McInerny, *Thomas Aquinas: Selected Writings.* The question is whether the six "days" of creation should be taken literally. Thomas argues that there is no orthodox teaching on the matter, and that too much false confidence could lead to "the mockery of unbelievers."

THE CARE OF CREATION   271

topical example of an unfortunate general tendency toward a lopsid-edly negative teaching on pollution. For several decades, the mag-isterial writings have rarely if ever suggested that the soiling of the environment is either an unwanted by-product of basically welcome increases in affluence or a problem that can probably be addressed successfully with further scientific-technical effort and a few rela-tively minor cultural tweaks. Rather, it is almost taken for granted that disastrous levels of pollution are inevitable in the flawed mod-ern culture and that the battle against this scourge will be lost with-out massive cultural changes. Francis mocked a "superficial ecology which bolsters complacency and a cheerful recklessness." He then dismissed all who "doggedly uphold the myth of progress and tell us that ecological problems will solve themselves simply with the application of new technology and without any need for ethical con-siderations or deep change."[80]

Such harsh judgments help keep Catholics close to the environ-mentalist mainstream, perhaps too close. There is a good case that Catholic pessimists have both misread the history of environmen-tal damage and misunderstood the relevant parts of the culture of industrial economies.

To be fair, the papal discussions have never offered pure gloom. Paul VI, the first pope to comments on the subject, was almost opti-mistic in 1970, when he said, "It took millennia for man to learn how to dominate nature. . . . The hour has now come for him to dominate his domination; this essential undertaking requires no less courage and dauntlessness than the conquest of nature itself."[81] It sounds like he thought that the next epoch in the history of human domination of nature can be a good one, because it can take fuller advantage of the courageous and dauntless modern spirit. It was that same con-fidence in human capacity that led him to argue against what his successor would call "a certain panic deriving from the studies of ecologists and futurologists on population growth."[82] Paul's 1965 words to the United Nations show his conviction that modern peo-ple can address their modern problems. "It is in your Assembly, even where the matter of the great problem of birth rates is concerned, that respect for life ought to find its loftiest profession and its most

---

80.   Francis, *Laudato Si'*, 59, 60.

81.   Paul VI, *Visit to the FAO on the 25th Anniversary of Its Institution* (November 16, 1970), 4.

82.   John Paul II, Apostolic Exhortation *Familiaris Consortio* (November 22, 1981), 30.

reasonable defense. Your task is so to act that there will enough bread at the table of mankind and not to support an artificial birth control that would be irrational, with the aim of reducing the number of those sharing in the banquet of life."[83]

Paul was quite right in his confidence that a much larger population could be adequately fed. Since he wrote, the world's population has more than doubled, while the proportion of people suffering from malnutrition has declined.[84] Even on pollution, he was certainly not totally wrong. His successors have all noted progress in dealing with pollution. Even Francis dedicates one paragraph in *Laudato Si'* to the "positive examples of environmental improvement" that show "men and women are still capable of intervening positively."[85]

However, that paragraph reads like a token concession. Francis is overwhelmingly pessimistic. He immediately undercuts his modest praise with a forlorn warning that "[t]hese achievements do not solve global problems." The overall text is weighted heavily to a detailed and dark list of environmental depredations. Besides climate change, he cites the reduction of biodiversity, wasteful consumerism, and damage to the water supply. Seeing a firmly established culture of denial and inaction, he declares that the future will be dire unless a dramatically new culture is established. "[T]he pace of consumption, waste, and environmental change has so stretched the planet's capacity that our contemporary lifestyle, unsustainable as it is, can only precipitate catastrophes."[86] He seems to think the world is in the position of Nineveh in the days of the prophet Jonah— it is doomed unless the king and people change their wicked ways.

The bleak analysis may show genuine prophetic insight. Poor countries often seem stuck in an unfortunate limbo, with economies that are well enough organized to create toxic pollution but societies that are too poorly organized to fight back. This limbo leaves most of the world's people admiring the declines in pollution in prosperous countries from an increasingly poisoned and embittered distance. Without a significant change, catastrophe is, as Francis says, probably unavoidable.

History, however, is a narrative of change. In the book of Jonah,

---

83. Paul VI, *Address to the United Nations*.

84. The relevant data can be found at Ourworldindata.com.

85. Francis, *Laudato Si'*, 58.

86. Francis, *Laudato Si'*, 61.

Nineveh was not destroyed, because the king and people actually did convert. A similarly successful but less traumatic change in the fight against pollution is certainly possible. It has already happened in all rich countries. Today's environmental pessimists should learn from the mistakes made in the 1960s by their intellectual ancestors, many Catholics among them. Their Humboldt-Guardini style of analysis led them to conclude that the profit-oriented capitalist economic system was structurally incapable of undoing the environmental damage it had caused. The whole arrangement, they claimed, was so oriented to private greed that neither powerful producers nor the consuming public would be willing to pay the cost of purification. Also, many of the pessimists were sure that the scientific challenges were insurmountable. They believed that modern science, like the sorcerer's apprentice of the Goethe poem, could invoke great powers but could not then control them.[87] The only reasonable expectation was a collapse, either of the environment or of capitalism.

In fact, neither fell apart. The environment in rich countries was cleaned up and the economic system was only tweaked, not destroyed or transmogrified. The industrial culture fairly easily added the new value of environmental respect. That value was turned into pollution-reducing polices by the scientists and engineers who rose to the technological challenges and by the governments that introduced ever stricter technical standards along with extensive bureaucracies to enforce them. The additional business objective did introduce a new tension in corporations, between emission control and profit maximization, but that conflict proved no more difficult to manage than other existing tensions, for example the stress caused by corporate commitments to both low prices and fair wages.[88]

The fearful environmentalists of the 1960s would have been more optimistic if they had paid more attention to Catholic theory and historical practice. The theory, the theological anthropology sketched out at the beginning of this chapter, is both encouraging and sobering. It is encouraging that God does more than give weak and sinful humanity dominion over creation. He also gives them the means to take on the responsibility, an aid symbolized by a story that I have already mentioned several times, God's fabrication of clothing

---

87. Johann Wolfgang von Goethe, "Der Zauberlehrling" (1799). Retrieved from http://germanstories .veu.edu/goethe/zauber_dual.html.

88. See Andrew J. Hoffman, *From Heresy to Dogma: An Institutional History of Corporate Environmentalism* (San Francisco: Stanford University Press, 2001).

for the expelled Adam and Eve.[89] The theory is sobering because the ubiquity of sin ensures that even with divine support the balance between the skills needed to keep the environment sound and the human capacity to steward is shaky. A too sinful society could be destroyed, just as a too sinful person risks damnation.

However, the history of industrial development is basically encouraging. The new environmental challenge was not so different from the worker challenge that inspired the creation of the modern Catholic Social Teaching in the nineteenth century. Karl Marx and his followers were confident that the exploitation of apparently powerless workers by rapacious factory owners could only be changed by a communist revolution that would overthrow the values and culture of bourgeois society. He was wrong. Once the problem was taken seriously by established and new social authorities, it was dealt with effectively by new labor laws and improvements in standard employment practices. Similarly, for some decades rapacious captains of industry gauged customers and ignored product safety. After some delay, laws, regulations, and technology all responded, adding to the complexity of the modern economy but also to its quality and justice. In both cases, the materialist and individualist culture remained intact, as did the typically modern reliance on powerful guiding laws and detailed regulation.

In developed economies, the response to the environmental challenge has followed a similar pattern. Elsewhere, the story is far from over, but it would be surprising if the increased affluence that accompanies increased industrial production did not eventually produce a similar alteration in environmental desires and practices. As pollution and wealth increase, the leaders and residents of poor countries are likely to decide that shunning pollution is really important. Then the changes will come fairly easily, since the needed technology can be imported and the antipollution regulations can be copied. There is no need for a cultural revolution. Consumerism and other materialist values can thrive along with cleaner air, water, and soil.

Jonah was a bit miffed that Nineveh was left standing, but as I said about man-made global warming, good news on pollution is not bad news for prophetic Catholic Social Teaching. Indeed, a global change of social practice on pollution would only enhance the wisdom of one part of the teaching: the recognition that modern societies can

---

89. Gn 3.21.

often find enough virtue inside them to solve serious problems. This relatively optimistic strand of observation and prophecy is entirely absent from many strains of the purely secular versions of the Humboldt-Guardini critique, which amount to a prediction of ineluctable doom for industrial civilization. That harsh judgment—that the system's inhumanity and unnaturalness will eventually lead to physical destruction—ensures that most mainstream environmentalists remain unregenerate pessimists, no matter how good the current news on pollution may be.

Catholic environmentalists can be far more nuanced. They should of course continue, in the style of Jonah, to criticize modern societies for allowing pollution to become and remain such a curse, but they should also praise the ability of these same corrupt societies to repent and revive. This dual narrative is not only more Catholic and more historically realistic than is a purely bleak account. It also brings out the fundamental difference between the Catholic and secular approaches. The religious teaching's cautiously optimistic premise shows more respect for all three sides of the environmental triangle. The premise is that despite sin, God, humanity, and the world all fundamentally "want" the industrial society to succeed. God has created humankind and the world so both can flourish. Humans have enough dignity and freedom to be good stewards of the world, and the world is resilient and rich enough to safely provide imperfect humanity with the raw material of industrial civilization.

A more balanced approach to pollution has another advantage. It would allow the Church to deliver its most important environmental message more clearly. The message is that that the modern mistreatment of creation harms societies and souls at least as much as it damages the physical world. This critique of what Pope Francis calls integral ecology is the subject of the next chapter.

CHAPTER 8

Integral Ecology

EVEN IF ENVIRONMENTAL POLLUTION soon becomes a largely technical issue (as I suggested it could in the previous chapter), past technological inadequacy cannot explain why noxious emissions ever came to be a serious threat to human well-being. Technically, it would have been relatively easy to control emissions while simultaneously increasing industrial and agricultural production. However, before the 1960s few influential scientists and engineers were very interested in this challenge. Political leaders were hardly any more concerned and corporate bosses were generally indifferent or even hostile to expanding their environmental responsibilities. In the establishment view, the worst environmental challenges—supplying clean water and clean sources of energy, while removing waste in a sanitary way—had already been met. To make a serious effort to reduce dangerous discharges was seen as excessive. It might, as Philadelphia's chief engineer had said in 1890s, "interfere with the large manufacturing interests which add so greatly to our permanent prosperity."[1]

The problem was not evil intent. If the elite had really been malicious, they would not have responded so effectively when they finally accepted the gravity of the problem. Rather, they seemed almost blind to the severity of the damage to the environment, only noticing when rich countries were in danger of becoming unlivable.

Why did so many basically well-intentioned people ignore this seemingly obvious problem? Catholic Social Teaching offers a

---

1. Quoted in Robert Gottlieb, *Forcing the Spring: The Transformation of the American Environment,* rev. ed. (Washington, D.C.: Island Press), 90.

profound explanation—the predominance of a fundamentally wrong way of looking at the human position in the world. I described the problem in the previous chapter as not living up to the humanity-God-world triangle of responsibility. Pope Francis refers to this error, a mistake that has implications that extend far beyond noxious emissions, as disrespect for "integral ecology."[2]

I think it is fair to divide the papal analysis of this disrespect into two parts, each with its own descriptive phrase from Francis. One of the identified problems is very old and the other is quite new.

The Big Old Idea—Misguided Anthropocentrism

The old problem is what Francis calls "misguided anthropocentrism."[3] This is the belief that people should take as full control as possible of their entire environment, without any reference to or reverence for the Creator who has given them the world and their privileged place in it. They are to be masters rather than stewards. This mistaken worldview long predates the modern world. Indeed, it can be seen as the original sin of Adam and Eve, who believed the diabolical promise that people could be like God. However, Christians and other cultural critics have identified the quasi-worship of humanity and the unlimited desire to shape the world to serve human desires as distinctly modern ideas—the dangerously optimistic central conceit of Enlightenment progressivism or intellectual liberalism and the dangerously reductive justification of pure individualism.

According to Francis, modern anthropocentrism "leads to a misguided lifestyle."[4] In this judgment of cause and effect, he is not only rejecting the modern environmentalist criticism of old-fashioned human-centered Christianity, which I mentioned in the previous chapter. He is casting the blame back on the modern presumptions of total power over everything in nature. In this critique, Francis directly follows his predecessor Benedict XVI, who explained that, when "we ourselves [humankind] are the ultimate standard," then "matter is henceforth only material for us" and "we no longer recognize any judgment superior to our own, but see only ourselves. . . . [T]here is no longer any concept of life beyond death," so "in this

---

2. Francis, Encyclical Letter *Laudato Si'* (May 24, 2015), 10, and nine other times in that document.

3. Francis, *Laudato Si'*, 118.

4. Francis, *Laudato Si'*, 122.

life we must grab hold of everything and possess life as intensely as possible."[5] In the papal analysis, such a worldly attitude necessarily generates pollution, since people are so intent on taking whatever they can from the world that they pay no attention to the damage their grabbing does to the world.

There is something profound about this analysis. An unduly great sense of human entitlement and a lack of belief in eternal responsibility might well lead to a degrading treatment of the world, just as entitlement and irresponsibility lead men to mistreat women and colonists to mistreat their native subjects. However, there is also something doubtful about tying the moral sin of misguided anthropocentrism to the social damage caused by grievous environmental damage. The anthropocentrics whom the popes condemn—they tend to call themselves secular humanists—can make a reasonably strong case that their principles are not fundamentally hostile to the good of the natural world.

Their humanism is guided, they say, by the truth of human nature. People can and should use their reason and strength to take as full charge as possible of their destiny, their lives, and their physical environment. Whatever the value of religion for individuals or nations (the humanists differ on this question), the popes are wrong to blame a lack of transcendental values for pollution. On the contrary, the humanists claim, in the same way that religious considerations add nothing to the fully human and scientific analysis of the organization of virtuous, flourishing, and just societies, these considerations are irrelevant to the rigorous analysis of the damage to and protection of the environment.

Their secular analysis shows that environmental damage is an unhappy accident, an unwanted by-product of the confident, imaginative, and largely successful modern human effort to build a flourishing technological civilization. The cure of pollution is not to give religion and religious values more respect, they say, but to redirect more of people's civilizing ingenuity and energy from one set of worthy goals, producing more and better products, toward another equally worldly and equally worthy goal: cleaner air and water. God has nothing to do with it.

Needless to say, Francis and his predecessors reject secular humanism and all its empty promises. Equally needless to say, the

---

5. Benedict XVI: Speech *Meeting with the Clergy of the Diocese of Bolzano-Bressanone* (August 6, 2008), translation slightly modified, partially quoted in Francis, *Laudato Si'*, 6.

popes do not dismiss human ingenuity and energy or condemn all of their modern fruits. As Benedict explains, the desire for technological development is natural, as human nature "is constitutionally oriented toward 'being more.'"[6] However, the Magisterium judges the secular version of humanism to be dangerously incomplete. "A humanism which excludes God is an inhuman humanism. Only a humanism open to the Absolute can guide us in the promotion and building of forms of social and civic life—structures, institutions, culture, and ethos—without exposing us to the risk of becoming ensnared by the fashions of the moment."[7] In other words, good social policies and good personal lives require a vision that goes beyond the worldly and material, because the human condition actually transcends the world. Without these good policies, pollution cannot be tamed.

Theologically, the popes are certainly right. The truest humanism is Christian, based on Jesus Christ, who is both the perfection of humankind and the divine Son of God. Christians believe that people are most completely themselves when they live in the world as Jesus did, in perfect obedience to the will of the Father. This obedience includes respect for the nature of humanity and for the nature of the rest of creation. The pollution caused by prideful and earth-exploiting anthropocentrism can justly be seen as a good example of what happens when people do not respect the nature of the world God gives them.

Still, in environmental matters, I think some caution is needed before jumping from theology to policy analysis. Although Catholics should accept the argument that Christian humanism is in fact more human than is its secular counterpart, they are not obliged to believe that atheist anthropocentrism is solely or primarily responsible for pollution, any more than they must accept that atheist thinking is primarily responsible for the good things about modern economies and societies. This papal analysis is part of a counsel of imperfection, which must be tested against experience. As the conclusion to the previous chapter implies, following my reading of past experience and current trends, for example, the dramatic efforts to reduce pollution in highly anthropocentric China,[8] it is far too early to declare Francis and Benedict unconditional victors in the debate with the

---

6. Benedict XVI, Encyclical Letter *Caritas in Veritate* (June 29, 2009), 14.

7. Benedict XVI, *Caritas in Veritate*, 78.

8. For a recent, largely optimistic report on pollution trends in China, see B. Silver et al., "Substantial Changes in Air Pollution across China during 2015–2017," *Environmental Research Letters* 13 (2018):114012.

secular humanists over pollution. Pollution may actually be best understood as the secular humanists do—a problem that can be solved by the normal political, economic, and cultural developments of modern secular societies.

The Big New Idea—The Technocratic Paradigm

In my judgment, Francis's second idea, which he calls the "technocratic paradigm," is more pertinent to pollution and to the whole Social Teaching. It describes a distinctly modern expression of misguided anthropocentrism. This paradigm, which he describes as "omnipresent" in today's technically sophisticated societies, provides the intellectual framework for the highly pragmatic "cult of unlimited human power," a cult that leads "to environmental degradation and social decay."[9] Unfortunately, Francis's own explanation of the paradigm is somewhat murky. He describes "the tendency, at times unconscious, to make the method and aims of science and technology an epistemological paradigm which shapes the lives of individuals and the workings of society."[10] He adds that this model of reality is a "reductionism" in which "[l]ife gradually becomes an abandonment to situations conditioned by technology, itself viewed as the principal resource for interpreting existence."[11]

I think Francis is trying to claim that there is a close, mutually reinforcing relationship between the modern world's technological excellence and its spiritual and moral emptiness. The idea of this tie is not exclusively Catholic. Indeed, the moral criticism of what is now called the technological culture can be traced back several centuries, at least to the vaguely Christian and anti-Christian Romantics. More recent commentators, Christian and secular, have expressed disquiet at everything surrounding technology—the effects of the social fascination with endless technological improvements on individual striving; the effects on society and individuals of the apparently endless technological advances in so many domains, including transportation, communications, comforts, entertainment, and medicine; and the effects on the spiritual and intellectual life of the scientific service to and dependence on technology. The German-American

---

9. Francis, *Laudato Si'*, 122.

10. Francis, *Laudato Si'*, 107.

11. Francis, *Laudato Si'*, 110, translation modified.

philosopher Hans Jonas provides a nice summary: "The sheer grandeur of the [technological] enterprise and its seeming infinity inspire enthusiasm and fire ambition. Thus . . . technology as a grand venture tends to establish *itself* as the transcendent end . . . To become ever more masters of the world, to advance from power to power . . . *can* now be seen to be chief vocation of mankind."[12] In the minds of these secular critics, the many gains from technology, from longer lives and more learning to recorded music and fresh fruit out of season, must be set against a fundamental dislocation of the human position in the world.

Francis does not mention Jonas in *Laudato Si'*, but, as I noted in the previous chapter, he does quote the German priest-philosopher Romano Guardini. Jonas would probably have some sympathy for Guardini's idea that, instead of working respectfully with God-given nature, modern people strive to overpower it with a violence that is both intellectual and practical. Certainly, several contemporary Christian philosophers have developed the idea that technology has become a sort of modern antisacrament, a visible sign of an invisible absence of grace in the way people think of humanity, God, and the world. Without grace, there is a profound disharmony, leading to, among other evils, the destruction of the good and the beauty of the natural world.

This practical damage is the almost inevitable result of a theological-philosophical error. Technology becomes a dominant standard because modern secular thinking has purposely sucked the wonder of being out of human experience and removed the ultimate reality of selfless, trinitarian love from human thought, replacing both with a mechanistic and exploitative understanding that is inevitably restless and ultimately destructive of truth and goodness. In the words of one of these Christian thinkers, Michael Hanby, "The essence of modernity . . . is the technologization of being, wherein . . . *nature* is conflated with artifice, and contemplation is conflated with action . . . [T]he knowledge of nature is essentially engineering . . . the truth of that knowledge is whatever is technically possible. And since the

---

12. Hans Jonas, "Toward a Philosophy of Technology," *Hastings Center Report 9/1* (1979), reprinted in Robert C. Scharff and Val Dusek, eds., *Philosophy of Technology: The Technological Condition*, 2nd ed. (Chichester, UK: Wiley Blackwell, 2014), 215. The anthology is a good introduction to the questions raised by the "technocratic paradigm," particularly the selections from Lewis Mumford and Jacques Ellul, as well as the text and comments of Martin Heidegger's "The Question Concerning Technology." Tellingly, there is no discussion of a Catholic approach to technology.

ultimate limits of possibility can only be determined by transgressing the present limits of possibility, a thoroughly technological society . . . will establish revolution as a permanent principle."[13]

Francis is developing a tradition of magisterial thought about the inhuman manifestations a dangerously amoral modern technological spirit. Pius XII dedicated most of his 1953 Christmas message to the "serious spiritual danger" created by what he called the "technical spirit." He denounced the spiritual damage done by the "intoxicating" confidence in human power over the material world. The result is the "secret fears of modern man, rendered blind by willingly surrounding himself with shadows."[14] A few years later, John XXIII lamented that "our age is marked by a clear contrast between the immense scientific and technical progress and the fearful human decline."[15] Like Pius, he was referring specifically to the nuclear weapons that had brought the world to the brink of self-immolation, but the judgment certainly had, and has, a wider application. The Second Vatican Council was explicit. "[T]he methods of investigation which these sciences use can be wrongly considered as the supreme rule of seeking the whole truth. . . . [T]he danger is present that man, confiding too much in the discoveries of today, may think that he is sufficient unto himself and no longer seek the higher things."[16]

Paul VI noticed the decline of "ideologies," primarily communism, but warned of the rise of a "new positivism: universalized technology as the dominant form of activity, as the overwhelming pattern of existence, even as a language, without the question of its meaning being really asked."[17] He identified just such an unmerited belief in technological self-sufficiency in the promotion of artificial contraception, which did not show the "reverence due to the whole human organism and its natural functions."[18]

The rejection of a technocratic approach to the biology of reproduction in Paul's *Humanae Vitae* was matched with an equally firm dismissal of any technocratic approach to the sociology of population. The pope accepted the scientific consensus of the time that "a

---

13.   Michael Hanby, "Technology and Time," *Communio: International Catholic Review* 43, no. 3 (2016): 360.

14.   Pius XII, *Christmas Message of 1953* (December 24, 1953, my translation).

15.   John XXIII, Encyclical Letter *Mater et Magistra* (May 15, 1961), 243.

16.   Vatican Council II, *Gaudium et Spes*, 57.

17.   Paul VI, Apostolic Letter *Octogesima Adveniens* (May 14, 1971), 29.

18.   Paul VI, Encyclical Letter *Humanae Vitae* (July 26, 1968), 17.

INTEGRAL ECOLOGY

too rapid increase in the population too often adds new difficulties to the problems of development"[19] and that governments "can and should solve the population problem."[20] However, he rejected the calls from leading scientists and social theorists, including some Catholics, to overpower people's sexual nature by imposing technological and Hegelian solutions—government-mandated sterilizations, government-guaranteed ready access to abortions, and, as would be practiced in China a decade later, legal limits on the number of children. Rather, he suggested that "educating the people wisely" would encourage couples to practice true "responsible parenthood."[21] The last phrase had been used by proponents of "zero population growth" as a code for having few or no children, but Paul said, while responsibility included physical and sociological matters—"biology, psychology, demography or sociology"—it went much further, into "the whole man and the whole mission to which he is called . . . both its natural, earthly aspects and its supernatural, eternal aspects."[22]

As mentioned in the previous chapter, Paul also brought pollution into the Social Teaching. He explained that the problem was caused by a blind reliance on technology, the "dramatic and unexpected consequence of human activity." The effect of this "ill-considered exploitation of nature" is that "the human framework is no longer under man's control, thus creating an environment for tomorrow which may well be intolerable."[23] He was perhaps less worried than his successors were that excessive trust in technology was itself a sign of a dangerous social disorder. However, he understood well that higher technology set a higher moral standard. "The most extraordinary scientific progress, the most astounding technical feats and the most amazing economic growth, unless accompanied by authentic moral and social progress, will in the long run go against man."[24]

---

19.   Paul VI, Encyclical Letter *Populorum Progressio* (March 26, 1967), 37 (translation altered).

20.   Paul VI, *Humanae Vitae*, 23.

21.   Paul VI, *Humanae Vitae*, 23.

22.   Paul VI, *Humanae Vitae*, 7. For some background on the debate, mostly but not exclusively from an American perspective, see Donald T. Critchlow, *Intended Consequences: Birth Control, Abortion, and the Federal Government in Modern America* (New York: Oxford University Press, 1999), chap. 4; John Sharpless, "World Population Growth, Family Planning, and American Foreign Policy," in Donald T. Critchlow, ed., *The Politics of Abortion and Birth Control in Historical Perspective*, (University Park, Penn.: The Pennsylvania State University Press, 1996), 103–27.

23.   Paul VI, *Octogesima Adveniens*, 21.

24.   Paul VI, *Visit of Pope Paul VI to the FAO on the 25th Anniversary of Its Institution.* (November 16, 1970), 4.

John Paul II brilliantly widened his predecessors' social-technological analysis. In *Centesimus Annus*, he first provided a pithy philosophical recapitulation of the "anthropological error," basically the "misguided anthropocentrism" of Francis. "Man, who discovers his capacity to transform and in a certain sense create the world through his own work, forgets that this is always based on God's prior and original gift of the things that are."[25] He then explained that the God-given environment that people are despoiling is not limited to the earth, water, air, and nonhuman living things. The natural environment includes people themselves—"man too is God's gift to man. He must therefore respect the natural and moral structure with which he has been endowed."[26] For John Paul, the error of believing that people should take absolute power over all that is given to them, the fundamental error of the technocratic paradigm, leads not only to pollution but also to poor urban planning, the weakening of family ties, and the industrial economy's many moral and psychological troubles.

In turn, John Paul's successor, Benedict XVI, expressed the scope of the technological disorder in more poetic language. "The book of nature is one and indivisible: it takes in not only the environment but also life, sexuality, marriage, the family, social relations: in a word, integral human development. Our duties toward the environment are linked to our duties toward the human person, considered in himself and in relation to others."[27]

The order and disorder of this book of nature constitute what Francis calls integral ecology. It is indeed a big book. For Catholics, one of the principal chapters concerns the proper respect for family ties. That is the topic of the following two chapters. For the rest of this one I discuss four more directly environmental issues.

Before starting in, two cautionary notes are in order. First, these discussions are less an ordered explanation of established doctrine than a collection of almost personal reflections on officially stated themes. The various agencies of the Vatican and many loyal Catholic thinkers have mused on these issues, as they have on other contemporary problems of integral ecology, but authoritative teaching is scanty.

Second, I admit to being nervous about the papal tendency to portray a clear and total opposition between well-guided and

---

25. John Paul II, Encyclical Letter *Centesimus Annus* (September 1, 1991), 37.

26. John Paul II, *Centesimus Annus*, 38.

27. Benedict XVI, *Caritas in Veritate*, 51.

misguided anthropocentrism, between totally spiritual and totally materialist visions. Of course, the idea of a battle between purely good and purely evil choices is completely Christian. As mentioned, Adam and Eve were the first to fall onto the wrong side, and the book of Revelation assures us that the conflict will last until the coming of a new heaven and a new earth. The twentieth-century Swiss theologian Hans Urs von Balthasar provided a helpful summary. "The course of history is . . . determined by . . . the interaction of two mysteries: . . . 'the wisdom of God in a mystery' . . . and that of the great Whore of Babylon, 'on whose forehead is written a name of mystery.'"[28]

Still, it is also a basic truth of Catholic anthropology, mentioned in chapter 1, that the spark of eternity and the wonder at the divine light are always present in each person. This is even true of men and women who claim to be firm atheists and to have a purely materialist worldview and of the societies that they form and that form them. The spark and the wonder can never be extinguished, so no person, no social practice, and no technological development can ever be purely worldly, sinful, or technocratic. The highly developed modern technocratic culture is no exception. The divine light may sometimes seem to be totally absent, but actually there is always at least a faint glow, bright enough to affect every thought, action, and organization. John XXIII understood this universal striving for goodness when he recommended that Catholics work together with nonbelievers to promote the common good: "[W]ho can deny the possible existence of good and commendable elements in these undertakings, elements which do indeed conform to the dictates of right reason, and are an expression of man's lawful aspirations?"[29]

This admixture of goodness helps explain why the fundamentally misguided technocratic paradigm has produced so many true goods. There are far too many of them for everything about this way of thinking to be dismissed as simply diabolical. Rather than offer blanket condemnations, the Catholic Social Teaching, at its best, responds to each development of our excessively technological and dangerously secular culture with subtle—and usually mixed—judgments.

---

28.   1 Cor 2:7; Rv 17:5. Hans Urs von Balthasar, *Theo-Drama: Theological Dramatic Theory, Volume IV: The Action*, trans. Graham Harrison (San Francisco: Ignatius Press, 1994 [1980]), 442.

29.   John XXIII, Encyclical Letter *Pacem in Terris* (Encyclical letter April 11, 1963), 159.

286   CHAPTER 8

Food Production—People in Nature

The production of food was enjoined as the basic human activity in the
Garden of Eden. Until a century or so ago, the labor of that production remained central to the life of the vast majority of people in every
part of the world.[30] History largely recounts the deeds of warriors,
kings, priests, and scholars, but in even the most sophisticated preindustrial societies most of most people's labor was directly concerned
with feeding people, while a substantial portion of the remaining labor
went to provide food producers with fairly simple goods and services.
Despite this demographic dominance, however, preindustrial farming
created few problems of integral ecology. A few philosophers complained that agriculture was an affront to Mother Nature (although
they complained more vociferously about the rape of nature needed
for mining), but in fact human power was not great enough to do
much more than nudge nature gently in desired directions.

Industrial agriculture changed that. People can now push creation quite hard, making use of the many technologies embodied in
powerful mechanical equipment, manufactured fertilizers and pesti-
cides, the enhanced breeding of crops, intensive farming of animals,
inexpensive transport, and a host of other tools and techniques. For
integral ecology, the result has been wonderful in many ways. The
relationship of humanity to the food-producing part of creation has
improved so much that billions more people than ever before are
well fed, while the smallest proportion ever of the world's population is malnourished. The integral ecology of labor in this domain
has also improved. The easy life of the Garden of Eden has not been
regained, but industrially aided food workers produce more than
ever with less human labor than ever and with much less physically
debilitating labor.

Still, there are problems. Probably the most urgent is that there
is not yet enough industrial agriculture. Although downtrodden and
barely surviving peasants are gradually fading into history, they are

---

30.   Roughly 70 to 75 percent of the population in nonindustrialized economies of the early
twentieth century worked in agriculture, according to Simon Kuznets, *Economic Growth of
Nations* (Oxford: Oxford University Press, 1971), 250–54 (especially table 38). Fewer than 10
percent of the population of advanced agrarian societies lived in cities, following the estimates in
chap. 7 of Patrick Nolan and Gerhard Lenski, *Human Societies: An Introduction to Macrosociology*, 10th ed. (Boulder, Colo.: Paradigm, 2004), 146–73. For a gathering of some European data,
see Robert C. Allen, "Economic Structure and Agricultural Productivity in Europe, 1300–1800,"
European Review of Economic History 4, no. 1 (2000): 1–25.

disappearing far more slowly than they should. Hundreds of millions of farmers remain in traditional rural misery, plagued not only by the real possibility of destitution but also by continuing ignorance, isolation, and political oppression. The persistence of inefficient food production and debilitating agricultural poverty is scandalous. Pope Francis is completely right when he says, "The fact that today, well into the twenty-first century, so many people suffer from this scourge [of food shortage] is due to a selfish and wrong distribution of resources, to the 'merchandizing' of food."[31] Any qualified technocrat could easily design economically realistic arrangements to ensure both a decent supply of food for everyone in the world and a decent life for everyone producing that food. The bad current practices are protected by the ignorance of the powerless, the selfishness of the powerful, and the lack of generosity of outsiders.

The popes, including Francis, have quite rightly drawn attention to this distorted ecology of food production. *Laudato Si'* asks for "investment in rural infrastructures, a better organization of local or national markets, systems of irrigation, and the development of techniques of sustainable agriculture."[32] Francis might also have called for the faster and more thorough spread of advanced equipment, seeds, and chemicals, as well as the knowledge and economic structures needed to take full advantage of the potential increases in yields. Christians can help improve this side of agricultural ecology by working to educate the poor, to inspire the elite, and to subvert unjust social and ecological practices. In particular, they can use the Catholic Social Teaching to point out two truths. First, "the earth is essentially a shared inheritance, whose fruits are meant to benefit everyone,"[33] so mistreatment of the earth and the inability to help it serve humanity appropriately are offences to to all people. Second, righting these wrongs is a "duty [that] concerns first and foremost the wealthier nations."[34]As I explained in chapter 2, all property comes with a "social mortgage," a debt to society, and rich people have particularly large balances to pay off. One type of repayment for that debt could be personal and institutional economic sacrifices to help poor farmers.

---

31.   Francis, *Address to the 2016 Annual Meeting of the Executive Board of the World Food Programme (WFP)* (June 13, 2016).

32.   Francis, *Laudato Si'*, 180.

33.   Francis, *Laudato Si'*, 93.

34.   Paul VI, *Populorum Progressio*, 44.

However, the problems in the food chain are certainly not all of the not-enough-good-stuff variety. There are also some bad practices, starting with the great damage to creation done by intensive modern agricultural techniques. Environmental neglect remains standard practice for farmers in much of the world, so the physical environment is more often desecrated than reverenced. As a Vatican representative explained in 2018, "It is not a question of opposing the results achieved by scientific and technological research with an attitude of rejection toward innovative . . . production systems, but rather of establishing an orderly balance of the said systems and the adequate prevention of risks that may cause suffering to people or ecosystems. . . . This will also make it possible to recognize the sustainability of agricultural production and the protection of the environment."[35]

The destructive standard practices may change as farmers become richer and more sophisticated. They may gradually learn that environmental responsibility will ultimately help themselves, their societies, and the natural world. There have already been significant improvements in agricultural ecology in rich countries, although agriculture lags other industries in the integration of environmental concerns into standard business practice.

More generally, there are intractable problems in the integral ecology of food that stretch through the entire food chain, from farm to table (or perhaps farm to mouth, considering how much food is eaten on the run). In my judgment, the common theme is a too-blind acceptance of the technological paradigm. The problems are most severe in rich countries, where the production of food is now almost entirely guided by the utilitarian logic of industrial organization. At best, this thinking produces food efficiently, as measured in nutrition-adjusted calorie output per unit of labor and purchased energy, but it often sacrifices the true welfare of customers, farmers, farm animals, and farmland for the sake of lower costs, higher revenues, or larger immediate profits.

At the beginning of the chain, creation would serve humanity better if much farming were less oriented toward maximizing production and minimizing expenses and more toward sustaining quality and treating natural resources with respect. Currently, the beautiful variety of the natural world is too often sacrificed for the sake of

---

35.   Holy See Permanent Observer at the FAO, *Intervention at the 31st Regional Conference of the FAO in Europe* (Voronezh, Russian Federation, May 16, 2018), 3.

efficiency and the actual treatment of farm animals often seems to violate their God-given dignity. As then-cardinal Joseph Ratzinger said in an interview, "a sort of industrial use of creatures, so that geese are fed in such a way as to produce as large a liver as possible, or hens live so packed together that they become just caricatures of birds, this degrading of living creatures to a commodity seems to me in fact to contradict the relationship of mutuality that comes across in the Bible."[36] Ratzinger could certainly have added pigs and cows to the list of mistreated species.

The paradigm problems certainly do not stop at the farm. Manufacturers often manipulate flavors and add large amounts of sugar, salt, and other quasi-addictive ingredients to tempt consumers to buy and eat more food than they would otherwise want. Quality is sacrificed and basic nutrition is abandoned to allow for greater convenience in preparation and consumption. The food industry, including the restaurant and catering trades, long encouraged unhealthy diets. They have finally started to retreat, although without much haste.[37]

More subtly but more profoundly, the contemporary culture seems too worldly to recognize the spiritual and psychological value of food. The preparation of "the fruit of the earth and the work of human hands" for family and friends used to be understood universally as an act of love. The "breaking of bread" should be a sign and ratification of communion, in households just as at Mass.[38] In prosperous modern societies the factories, businesses, and farms are ever more efficient, so people can work fewer hours to produce more. While using this potential additional time away from the job, they could take advantage of appliances that have made cooking easier and industrial efficiency that has made ingredients readily available in more convenient forms (compare the packaged yeast of today to the home-gathered leaven of a century ago). In short, there is potentially more time than ever to dedicate to the loving preparation

---

36. Joseph Ratzinger, *God and the World: A Conversation with Peter Seewald* (San Francisco: Ignatius Press, 2002), 78–79. Edward N. Eadie, *Understanding Animal Welfare: An Integrated Approach* (Berlin: Springer, 2012), especially chap. 3, provides a reasonable secular summary of the modern history and ethical arguments about the treatment of animals on modern "industrial" farms.

37. Joanna Blythman provides an appropriately indignant account in *Swallow This: Serving Up the Food Industry's Darkest Secrets* (London: Fourth Estate, 2015). See also Michael J Maloni and Michael E Brown, "Corporate Social Responsibility in the Supply Chain: An Application in the Food Industry" *Journal of Business Ethics* 68, no. 1 (2006): 35–52.

38. cf. Lk 24:35.

and eating of homemade food, while the domestic labor involved has never been easier. Nonetheless, both shared family meals and careful cooking have become less common. They have given way to individualized "grazing" on prepared concoctions and to a fast-food approach to cooking, both in and out of the home. While restaurant chains sometimes tout their family atmosphere, the approach to eating that these institutions actually embody and encourage is essentially drained of the love—of the earth, of eating, of sharing, of family, of entertaining—that should drench everything to do with food.

The Catholic Social Teaching about the technocratic paradigm explains why the production, processing, and consumption of food have all become more inhumane. The social approach the whole process has moved in the wrong, technocratic direction. That analysis lies behind the comment of Pope Francis, "At times we are no longer able even to see the just value of food, which goes far beyond mere economic parameters."[39] I would go further. Too many people do not see that the beauty and fecundity of the land come from God, so they abuse the earth, looking only to produce as much as possible as fast as possible. Too many people do not see that animals are God's creatures and not merely human tools, so they are bred in unhealthy ways and kept in miserable conditions. Too many people do not see that the produce of the earth is a valuable gift from God, so they pay more attention to the price of food than to its quality. Too many people do not see that good food served with love nourishes and delights both souls and bodies, so they treat eating as no more than a chore or, worse, as a source of fleeting and merely sensuous pleasure. Too many people do not recognize that the traditions of recipes and feasts tie families and communities together, over the years and through the generations. These "too many people" constitute and are influenced by a society, so the sum of individual disordered desires and inclinations creates what might be called a technocratic structure of sin.

In the technocratic mindset, the only answers to social problems are technological—in this case meals that are even easier to prepare or the rearrangements of working hours. Those shifts might be welcome, but what may not be true for global warming and environmental pollution is certainly true for food. A truly healthy integral ecology of food is impossible without a reconsideration of everything

---

39. Francis, *Address to the World Food Programme.*

involved with the production and consumption of the fruits of the earth. Unless a new godly way replaces the godforsaken values of the food industry, its suppliers, and its customers, people will continue to treat food as no more than a typical consumer product and to look on farmers as just another supplier of raw materials. Too many farmers will accept this classification, so the integral ecology of food, the staff of life, will remain broken.

The Life of Cities—The Poor and the Rich

The decline of agricultural life has been matched almost exactly by the rise of urban and suburban life. More than half the people in the world now live in cities, towns, or nonagricultural villages.[40] In these communities, the degree of human control of the physical world is far greater than anything even today's highly mechanized farmers can achieve. While the work of plow, tractor, herd, and forest plantings can reshape nature for human purposes, the environment of city dwellers is so close to entirely man-made that the raw work of God is often all but invisible. The skies are often polluted and the earth is mostly covered with buildings and roads. In the gardens and parks where plants are allowed to grow, almost everything is arranged to suit people's convenience and desires. When the look is "natural," it is still carefully cultivated. Even the invisible underground world of cities has been remade to serve human purposes—it is crisscrossed by tunnels, pipes, and cables. Residents of these man-made environments can only thrive with a truly integral human ecology.

The ecological challenges vary because contemporary urban life varies. The needs of affluent commuting suburbs are different from those of impoverished shantytowns. High-rise apartment developments differ from street after street of row houses, drone work in factories and offices differs from the brain work of artists, and the ample consumer comforts of the affluent differs from the precarious living of the poor. With so many differences, there can be no simple answer to the question of whether today's cities overall encourage or discourage true human flourishing.

---

40.   The United Nations Department of Economic and Social Affairs estimates that 55 percent of the world's population lived in urban areas in 2018, although the definition of "urban" varies by country. See United Nations Department of Economic and Social Affairs, Population Division. Population Facts. December 2018. Accessed at https://population.un.org/wup/Publications/Files/WUP2018-PopFacts_2018–1.pdf.

Certainly, as with so much in the modern world, cities could be much worse. Contemporary cities house more people with more comfort and dignity than any premodern city did. The success is clearest for the more than a billion people who live in reasonably prosperous urban neighborhoods. These communities include almost every part of every city in developed countries as well as many areas in developing countries. In them, the urban environment is friendly, at least in most worldly respects. The residents of these neighborhoods can count on heat in the winter, clean running hot and cold water, sewage services, ample electricity, and various sorts of telecommunications, not to mention adequate food, reasonable health care, and education for their children. The streets are generally safe enough to walk around freely and unarmed. As recently as two centuries ago, none of these urban goods was readily available anywhere.

There are another two or three billion city dwellers who have it worse materially, sometimes much worse. In the worst slums of poor cities, the typical life is probably almost as deprived and dangerous as that of a landless peasant today or that of a city day laborer in a poor region a few centuries ago. Most of the world's urban poor, though, are not in such desperate straits, at least by material standards. They have fairly good access to the basic amenities of modern life, from decent food to advanced telecommunications. Also, they can reasonably live in hope, at least in material terms. In general, both the poor and the very poor can expect their children to have a better material life than they do. Only in a few failed states has the typical city life actually moved backward over the past few decades, in material terms.

In spite of this, as with the decline of industrial pollution and the rise of industrial agriculture, progress in the material urban development certainly could have been, and thus definitely should have been, much faster. The knowledge needed to provide all of the world's poor people with much better housing, schooling, transport, and so forth is readily available now. It would only take a few decades of concerted global commitment to find the needed physical resources, train the needed laborers, and complete the work. What stands in the way of faster improvements is ultimately, as always, sin. The details vary, but the themes are always the same. Poor countries are plagued by disorganization, excess respect for the existing unjust social order, and selfishness, especially among the elite. Rich countries lack the charity required for effectively spreading their excess and their expertise among poorer lands.

As is right and should be expected, the popes of the modern Catholic Social Teaching have consistently decried the social structures of sin that keep poor cities down. The popes have not only worried about cities' material poverty. Without neglecting that physical deprivation, they have increasingly turned their attention to spiritual deficits. There is something deeply wrong with the integral ecology of modern cities, something that statistical indicators of poverty and prosperity do not capture. Francis writes of the "social anonymity" that can create "a sense of uprootedness which spawns antisocial behavior and violence."[41] While he is referring explicitly to poor cities with their "overcrowding" and "areas lacking harmony, open spaces or potential for integration," much the same criticism can be directed at more affluent areas. There the anonymity is less likely to spawn violence than despair, seen in the prevalence of broken families, substance abuse, and mental illness.

In my judgment, the underlying problem is technocratic. Cities and urban lifestyles are built around machines and the mechanical comforts and conveniences that they create. The overall design and the individual features often isolate residents and despiritualize city life, rather than ennobling souls and strengthening communities. This spiritual urban blight can be seen almost everywhere. Contemporary housing, whether purely functional apartment blocks inhabited by strangers or widely separated gigantic suburban houses, is generally well designed to provide technological creature comforts but so self-sufficient that it can easily encourage mistrust and an unneighborly self-reliance. In particular, the automotive culture separates work from home, buildings from their human purpose, and people from each other.

Cars, at least, have a certain sleek beauty. Overall, beauty is rare in modern cities. They are designed for technological ease, often leaving soul-damaging ugliness. Architects and planners do know how to create a comfortable life, but even that is often left behind in the search for high revenues and low costs. When they actually want to do something inspirational, they are almost always at a loss. Spaces and buildings that provoke reverence or that promote social intimacy are rare. The greatest achievement is often no more than

---

41. Francis, *Laudato Si'*, 149.

a crude grandeur. As societies have become wealthier, houses and apartments have generally become larger (Britain is an exception to this trend) and the number of bathrooms has increased, but beauty remains slighted. Residents can try to humanize their housing with decorations. Private commercial buildings and public spaces often lack even that human touch. Today's stores, warehouses, offices, and factories rarely offer any tribute to the richness and spiritual ambition of human nature. Rather, they are places where technological efficiency and human alienation thrive. Francis explains: "If architecture reflects the spirit of an age, our megastructures and drab apartment blocks express the spirit of globalized technology, where a constant flood of new products coexists with a tedious monotony."[42]

The whole urban experience is worse than the sum of its parts. A trip down a six-lane American road lined with shopping centers and apartment developments, or through a similar but somewhat less grandiose European suburb, is a voyage to an environment that mixes technological accomplishment and commercial acumen with cultural vacuity. A visit to a sprawling megacity in the developing world offers a series of lessons about the inability or unwillingness of people to create a living environment that is pleasing, let alone uplifting. The spiritual emptiness of the new cities helps explain the widespread enthusiasm for preserving as many old buildings and old parts of cities as possible. For all the technical skills of modern people, they seem to have lost the ability to create urban environments that express and respect the traditions of civilizations and the fullness of human nature.

Francis is onto the problem. "It is not enough to seek the beauty of design. More precious still is the service we offer to another kind of beauty: people's quality of life, their adaptation to the environment, encounter, and mutual assistance."[43] He is certainly right about the quality of life, but attention to beautiful designs would already be a significant improvement over current practices. If even a small fraction of the effort dedicated to cheaper construction and more physically comfortable buildings were given to the promotion of beauty in buildings and urban planning, the quality of city life and the adaption of people to their environment would improve greatly. Today's public art is better than nothing, but it too often seems more

---

42. Francis, *Laudato Si'*, 113.

43. Francis, *Laudato Si'*, 150.

to reflect a culture of nihilism rather than to offer a vision of something great and grand.

The technocratic dominance of soulless cities both reflects and encourages spiritually deprived lifestyles. Of course, anonymous decadence often flourished in premodern cities, but modern cities almost invite social decay. The many solitary residences allow too many people to live by themselves, without any support from friends and family. The ease of transport and lack of traditions remove many of the restraints that help keep families and communities intact. It is too easy for broken families to find shards of housing to inhabit. Too many jobs are located family-damaging distances from homes. Too many friendships are rendered temporary by the ease of mobility, of both employment and housing. Too much time every day is spent amidst total strangers. Too little time is spent with anything beautiful, either raw or man-made.

In his critiques of modern society, the German philosopher Martin Heidegger identified a distinctly modern spiritual emptiness that he called "homelessness." He said that this "destiny of the world" is connected to the lack of what might be called a transcendental or religious home, a rootlessness that leaves modern people unable to find a solid base in their daily lives. They cannot truly "dwell," by which he means living in a way and place that join earth to heaven, of awaiting "the divinities as divinities." Instead, they turn to "technology," which provides only a "dry, monotonous, and therefore oppressive" expression of the world.[44] Heidegger does not discuss urban planning, but it is fair to think his spiritual homelessness is relevant to cities with no character, housing that is merely functional, and daily lives dominated by the limited and ultimately inhuman logic of technological efficiency. Benedict XVI captured something of this idea in a poetic image: "Today we can illuminate our cities so brightly that the stars of the sky are no longer visible. Is this not an image of the problems caused by our version of enlightenment? With regard to material things, our knowledge and our technical accomplishments are legion, but what reaches beyond, the things of God and the question of good, we can no longer identify."[45]

---

44.   All quotes from Martin Heidegger, *Basic Writings*, rev. ed., ed. David Farrell Krell (London: Routledge, 1993). In order, from "Letter on Humanism" 243, "The Question Concerning Technology" 323, and "Building Dwelling Thinking" 352. I include this extremely difficult philosopher because I believe his insight into the fundamental flaws of technological thinking is very close to that of the most recent popes.

45.   Benedict XVI, *Homily for Holy Saturday* (April 7, 2012).

The Catholic Church used to be something of a bulwark of resistance to the deterioration of the human ecology of cities. Its parishes helped hold communities together, its buildings and worship usually strove for beauty, and its traditions anchored otherwise worldly and changing cities to both history and eternity. In the rapidly expanding cities of North America, explicitly Catholic organizations were leaders both in the practice of many sorts of community activities, from education to organized charity, and in the development of a sort of applied theology for the development of humane and religiously vibrant communities. Much of this has been lost in the past half century. Too many new churches feel like shopping centers, too many parishes have become anonymous, and too much of the worship has become banal. The increase in affluence probably bears some responsibility for this spiritual ecological decline. Jesus did warn that riches and holiness are in fundamental conflict.[46] The problem is also cultural. A too secularized Catholic culture cannot resist the powerful technocratic paradigm that leads to cities built to reach such goals as increasing the efficiency of machines and adding to the residents' worldly comforts.

While the popes have spoken out on various urban issues, I believe the Catholic Social Teaching has more to offer. Its balanced attention to the interweaving of the worldly and the transcendent in the human good is particularly pertinent for the man-made environments of cities. The specifically Catholic approach can bring great insight into urban planning, neighborhood strengthening, intergenerational solidarity, beautification, intercommunal relations, both literal and cultural homelessness, loneliness, economic isolation, and many other small and large issues of contemporary urban life.

The Life of Leisure

Whatever leisure is, it is not exactly a modern invention. If leisure is defined as the suspension of normal labor or as periods without any necessity to labor for survival, there has always been some of it. If leisure is considered to be a set of activities traditionally reserved for aristocrats, such as scholarship, fighting on horseback, and hunting for pleasure, then it has been around for about as long as there have been aristocrats. If leisure is a set of very common activities that are

---

46. cf. Mt 6:24.

defined as somehow nonserious, for example drinking, gambling, singing, and perhaps worship, then leisure must be considered part of the human condition in society. Another way of thinking about leisure is historical, looking backward from contemporary practices that are considered leisure activities. All of them have some premodern antecedent. There were always games, celebrations, entertainments, journeys, studies, religious services, and entertaining pastimes.

However, like modern technology, modern leisure is in many ways entirely new. It is certainly different in quantity—there is a great deal more of it than ever before, especially in rich countries. It is probably different in quality—it somehow works differently from anything that came earlier and it somehow has different meanings in society and in people's lives. I briefly sketch out these changes, starting with quantity.[47]

In the most advanced economies, the provision of leisure services—from tourism to hobbies to video games to exercise to spectator sports and even to some sorts of optional education—probably employs more people than does manufacturing (the claim is only probable because the definition of leisure jobs is disputed). All these activities take up a great deal of time—during the years of schooling and retirement, the weeks of paid holidays, the weekends off, and the evenings at home. Many of these activities have become massive. The tourism industry allows millions of people to be amused or instructed in great comfort, in places far from their homes. Films and television programs are often watched by millions of people. About nine hundred million people, about one out of eight people in the world, watched the World Cup final in 2018. Almost twenty-one million people went in person to Walt Disney's Magic Kingdom in 2017.[48]

The social importance of leisure in modern lives cannot be measured, but it certainly seems to be significant. On the providers' side,

---

47. For some background in a field that has only relatively recently started to receive serious academic study, see Peter Borsay and Jan Hein Furnée, *Leisure Cultures In Urban Europe, c. 1700–1870: A Transnational Perspective* (Manchester: University of Manchester Press, 2016); Hugh Cunningham, *Time, Work and Leisure: Life Changes in England Since 1700* (Manchester, UK: University of Manchester Press, 2014) and Rudy Koshar, *Histories of Leisure* (London: Bloomsbury, 2002). The classic critical study of modern leisure, particularly the entertainment industry, is the chapter "The Culture Industry: Enlightenment as Mass Deception" in Max Horkheimer and Theodor Adorno, *Dialectic of Enlightenment*, trans. Edmund Jephcott (Stanford, Cal.: Stanford University Press 2002 [1947]).

48. From Elsa Keslassy, "Global Broadcasters Score Big with Live World Cup Final Ratings," *Variety* (July 18, 2018) and https://disneynews.us/disney-parks-attendance/.

the development of leisure as a factory-style product has been one of the many remarkable and unprecedented endeavors of the modern economy. The combination of mass production and customization required for contemporary media, travel, and sports rivals the accomplishments of modern agriculture and manufacturing. On the users' side, for many people and many families, leisure contributes a significant part of the "meaning of life." Recreational dining out, watching or playing sports, hobbies, and travel are likely to be highlights of their weeks, months, and years. Whether for better or for worse, most people's access to the true, the good, and the beautiful is largely mediated by the media industry, through leisure products that shape consciences and influence social values. In retirement, the various types of leisure activities are sometimes almost all there is to life, besides the pains to trying to stay alive.

This modern flowering of leisure could be a wonderful thing for the human condition. All people are responsible for developing their God-given and society-enhanced talents, and the vast increase in time and resources dedicated to leisure could certainly allow far more of this development. There is more time and there are more resources that could be dedicated to enhancing life with more beauty, worship, knowledge, love, social solidarity, and deep personal friendships. More people than ever before can now afford the spiritual enhancement that comes from the more ample study of the finest works of people and of the multiple graces of God. In comparison to this practical potential, the choices made in reality are disappointing. Too small a portion of the newly available time and wealth is used well. Much has been squandered on more or less ignoble activities.

The squandered possibilities, along with the massive scale, incessant planning, and constant innovation of leisure industries, immediately bring to mind the papal strictures on the technocratic paradigm. As leisure becomes more important in individual lives, the economy, and social arrangements, it becomes a battleground in "today's cultural struggle between the supremacy of technology and human moral responsibility."[49] The stakes are high for integral ecology. The technological amplification of almost every type of leisure activity increases both the ability to flower and ease of spiritual self-destruction. Benedict XVI mentioned one prominent example

---

49. Benedict XVI, *Caritas in Veritate*, 74.

of the danger, the relentless interconnectedness made possible by social media. "Today many young people, stunned by the infinite possibilities offered by computer networks or by other forms of technology, establish methods of communication that do not contribute to their growth in humanity. Rather they risk increasing their sense of loneliness and disorientation."[50] A few years later, Francis was even stronger when speaking about a related problem, the damage done to children by sexual material on the internet: "We rightly wonder if we are capable of guiding the processes we ourselves have set in motion, whether they might be escaping our grasp, and whether we are doing enough to keep them in check."[51] There is a clear echo of the technocratic paradigm.

The warnings are certainly apt but perhaps inadequate. In my judgment, the popes and the Church as a whole have not yet given contemporary leisure the full attention it deserves. The Social Teaching has not provided much guidance on how to use leisure time well, either in general or in detail, or on how to judge the human value of most leisure activities. Pornography for children is bad, but what about adults reading erotic novels, watching violent television programs, or going on luxury cruises? The challenge to provide wise and relevant counsels on leisure, even quite imperfect ones, should stimulate the talents of many Catholic social teachers.

To be fair, the quotes I just provided are the specific fruits of some broader efforts. As far back as 1965, the Second Vatican Council's pastoral constitution *Gaudium et Spes* noted that "the leisure time of most men has increased." However, it managed to provide only a quite vague invocation: "May this leisure be used properly to relax, to fortify the health of soul and body through spontaneous study and activity, through tourism which refines man's character and enriches him with understanding of others, through sports activity which helps to preserve equilibrium of spirit even in the community, and to establish fraternal relations among men of all conditions, nations, and races. Let Christians cooperate so that the cultural manifestations and collective activity characteristic of our time may be imbued with a human and a Christian spirit."[52] The council also dedicated

---

50.   Benedict XVI, *Address to Participants in the Plenary Assembly of The Pontifical Council for Culture* (November 13, 2010).

51.   Francis, *Address to the Participants in the Congress on Child Dignity in the Digital World* (October 6, 2017).

52.   Vatican Council II, *Gaudium et Spes*, 61.

Inter Mirifica, a decree (less authoritative than a constitution), to "the means of social communication." Unfortunately, the document did not address any of the ways in which mass media can change individuals, communities, and societies. Since then, various Vatican offices have taken on various bits of the leisure culture. Still, no pope has given leisure as a whole anything like the broad attention that Francis gave to the physical environment in *Laudato Si'*.

For example, tourism is studied primarily by one branch of the Pontifical Council for Pastoral Care of Migrants and Itinerant People. The office's basic approach is uplifting, if simple. As the council's website explains, "Man has an innate desire to go beyond his everyday horizons. In an age where the communications media bring the wonders, traditions and cultures of the whole world into our homes, the desire to leave becomes irresistible in order to know and admire other lands and to venture into the unknown."[53] The actual reports, though, tend to be bland and have fully addressed few of the many issues raised by mass modern tourism, which range from the exploitation of the poor by the rich to the uglification of natural beauty and the degradation of man-made treasures.

I would particularly like to see more magisterial work on popular entertainment. The excellences of beauty and ritual have certainly not vanished in the leisure entertainments of modern societies. However, a distressing portion of the output is soul deadening and society sapping. From pornography to the blatant and often cruel sexuality promoted in rap music, from violent video games to self-indulgent extreme exercise programs, there is too much pandering to base pleasures and selfish satisfactions. "The right to wholesome recreation of a kind that also fosters family values,"[54] a right claimed by John Paul II, is all too rarely respected. If anything, the makers and users of entertainment often seem to assume a right to promote vice.

The weakness of popular culture is not surprising in a world "marked by the absence of God and often by opposition to God,"[55] as John Paul II described the challenge for contemporary artists. Indeed, today's expensively materialist, spiritually superficial, and humanly isolated pleasures can seem like offerings to the anti-Gods of our world. Even when the content is not unsound, the consumption

---

53.   Pontifical Council for Pastoral Care of Migrants and Itinerant People, *Pilgrims of Beauty and Faith* (No date, translation altered).

54.   John Paul II, Apostolic Exhortation *Familiaris Consortio* (November 22, 1981), 46.

55.   John Paul II, *Letter to Artists* (April 4, 1999), 10.

INTEGRAL ECOLOGY 301

increasingly takes place in a solitary, almost antisocial, environment. People sit alone and watch something on a screen. In addition, too much entertainment is merely chemical. Artificially mind-numbing and stimulating substances have been around for a long time. They may well be used less in modern than in preindustrial societies. Still, the use of legal and illegal substances is sufficiently intense and widespread to suggest a mass desire to escape from this world. The direction of psychological travel is not toward the kingdom of heaven.

Benedict XVI provided a fine initial guideline. What he said of the media, that it "must avoid becoming spokesmen for economic materialism and ethical relativism, true scourges of our time," is true for all sorts of entertainment.[56] However, in that message he gave no hints on how to evaluate particular works. Perhaps he is put off by the embarrassing memories of "The Index of Prohibited Books" mentioned in chapter 1. He may have been right to be cautions. Cardinal Joseph Ratzinger's prepapal description of all rock music as "completely antithetical to the Christian concept of redemption and freedom"[57] is, at least in my judgment, greatly exaggerated.

In a different direction, Catholic leaders and thinkers should be particularly concerned by the trends in the inherently spiritual parts of life that are or that overlap with leisure activities. Unlike so much of the contemporary world of leisure, these have mostly become smaller and duller. I already mentioned the aesthetic decline of religious architecture and liturgy. I can add the reduced respect for religious holidays, the fading of popular religious rituals, and the substitution of shopping and sports for worship on the Sabbath. The public calendar and public spaces in rich countries used to be marked out in ways that were consciously designed to encourage frequent pauses for the recognition of the divine. As I have already pointed out, Catholics see such an integration of transcendental markers into mundane time and space as a mark of social strength. Of course, the markers never indicated anything like deep and universal public faith, but even the shared desire to appear spiritual is a sign of social respect for higher goods. Now, though, the supernatural is increasingly restricted to private time, private spaces, and private choices, so the ecology of public social life is generally secular and unspiritual.

---

56. Benedict XVI, *Message for the 42nd World Communications Day* (January 24, 2008), 5.

57. Joseph Ratzinger, "Liturgy and Church Music," a lecture given at the Eighth International Church Music Congress (Rome, November 17, 1985).

In my opinion, the broad despiritualization of leisure currently presents at least as great threat to integral ecology as environmental pollution. Pollution is an evil that has been recognized by almost everyone, while fierce critics of the leisure economy are still widely dismissed as cranks. Pollution can be tamed without shaking modern society to its foundations, or so I believe, while the leisure economy expresses all too clearly some of this society's most firmly held and most spiritually destructive principles. Pollution mostly harms the mortal body, but the damage from the depravities and distractions of the leisure industry can easily tarnish people's immortal souls. In addition, the spiritual losses from the abuse of leisure are harder to reverse than all but the most severe physical soiling of the world. At best, the misuse of so much modern leisure time amounts to a great wasted opportunity. At worst, too many of today's practices do significant damage to both individuals and communities.

Without a cultural change, the problem is set to worsen. Each year, more people can afford more expensive ways to spend their leisure time. The popes would certainly like to foment a needed cultural revolution, but the Catholic Church cannot realistically be expected to create a sounder ecology of leisure on its own. It can only comment and exhort, which it does on some issues with some degree of fervor. As I suggested earlier in the chapter, it could and should do much more. Indeed, I fear that future generations may wonder at the relatively little attention paid by today's Catholic Social Teaching to this distinctly modern manifestation of the technocratic paradigm, a major source of cultural confusion and spiritual impoverishment.

The Denigration of the Domestic

The integral ecology of the home will always be troubled, in any society at any time. In households, people usually live out the relations of the two sexes, of several generations with each other, and of the private family with the public community. All of these pairings are inevitably both stained by sinful selfishness and troubled by conflicting legitimate desires and responsibilities. When the Magisterium refers to the home as the "domestic church" (for the first time at the Second Vatican Council[58]), there is a certain irony. Like the pilgrim

---

58.   Vatican Council II, Dogmatic Constitution on the Church *Lumen Gentium* (November 21, 1964), 11.

Church on earth, the home is always in need of profound reform. This universality of woe does not, however, exempt the Catholic Social Teaching from the responsibility to discuss the most prevalent and virulent current weaknesses of home life. On the contrary, the need for discernment of the situation in this always troubled part of human experience is always particularly acute. John Paul II said, "The future of humanity passes by way of the family,"[59] and no place is more important for the family of humanity than the family home.

Traditionally, the largest ecological problem in the home was almost certainly physical. Almost all people in premodern societies lived their frequently short lives in great discomfort. Statistics and even anecdotes are scarce, but the picture that emerges in most cultures features widespread desperate poverty—frequent life-threatening shortages of food along with inadequate fuel, shelter, and clothing. Then there was extremely hard physical labor, many early deaths, nearly universal illiteracy, widespread violence, and frequent recourse to intoxicants. Women's work was particularly harsh and relentless.[60]

These troubles of physical ecology have faded away in rich societies, which now offer almost every resident an unprecedented supply of consumption comforts, along with ample living space, by preindustrial standards, and many labor-saving tools and appliances. Desperate material deprivation is rare , a dozen years of childhood is typically dedicated to education, domestic violence is much diminished, and lives in these comfortable homes are typically longer and healthier. Whether or not the use of intoxicants has declined, they are much less likely than in the past to be resorted to in response to material misery.

Unfortunately, these many physical successes and their many helpful social ramifications are far from the only story. The great new material comforts are too often matched by a largely new spiritual hollowness, a disregard for anything higher than daily pleasures and worldly accomplishments, and all too often, a more psychological sort of degradation of women. Indeed, today's typical "domestic church" may be as dysfunctional as the typical contemporary parish church is ugly. The two suffer from the same basic illness. Both organized

---

59.   John Paul II, *Familiaris Consortio*, 86.

60.   A classic introduction to some of the everyday misery of the ancien régime is Fernand Braudel, *Les structures du quotidian: Le possible et impossible* (Paris: Armand Colin, 1979). See also Our World in Data charts on literacy and homicides: https://ourworldindata.org/literacy and https://ourworldindata.org/homicides#homicide-rates-in-five-western-european-regions-1300–2010-max-roserref.

religion and the home and family space have lost much of their spiritual resonance in a secular age. Human ecology has been badly wounded.

Of course, religious people always and everywhere complain about the excess of worldliness in domestic life. Declarations that the writer lives in the most grasping and least spiritual of all ages can be found throughout history, often combined with generous praise of some bygone era. I may be guilty of the same mistaken perception, but I do think there has been a dramatic spiritual emptying in home life over the past few generations in rich countries. In Christendom, generous familial love, especially for the weakest members and sometimes for neighbors, was almost everywhere the accepted standard. The standard was not often kept, but at least it was generally respected as a noble and not entirely unrealistic ideal. Now, the home life is often lived as if the God of love does not exist.

I have already mentioned one relevant sign of this spiritual emptying, the deterioration in the domestic ecology of food. That decline is all too typical. Consider the treatment given to four types of people—the young, the ill, the troubled, and the old. They all benefit greatly from careful care and personal loving concern at home, and in rich societies they increasingly fail to receive these gifts of domestic love. These are problems of affluence, as discussed in chapter 3. Many of these problems are spreading around the world at least as quickly as wealth is increasing.

Start with the young. Leaving aside the legal "right" to kill children before they are born, those who come into the world are often not welcomed very lovingly. Legal, administrative, and economic systems are geared toward autonomous adults, not families that nurture new human life. Francis criticizes the unwillingness to protect "the rights of the family [as such] and not only those of individuals"[61] an unwillingness that takes such social forms as expensive housing, unfavorable tax treatment for parents, and family-unfriendly employment arrangements, especially for mothers. Most potential parents have absorbed the social standard. The maternal labor of childcare is usually delayed for years, in large part because future mothers give it lesser priority than they do both the emotions of their romantic lives and their paid labor outside the home. During courtship, both men and women often fail to think of children as the natural fruit of their sexual love, thanks to "the growth of a mentality

---

61. Francis, Post-Synodal Apostolic Exhortation *Amoris Laetitia* (March 19, 2016), 44.

that would reduce the generation of human life to one variable of an individual's or a couple's plans."[62]

If and when children finally do arrive, they are often met with what might be described as mixed feelings. While their medical care is excellent, their bedrooms are generally well stocked, and they benefit from the latest expertise on child psychology, contemporary societies have certainly not heeded the command of John Paul II: "The mentality which honors women more for their work outside the home than for their work within the family must be overcome."[63] (I discuss the distinct maternal role in the next chapter.) On the contrary, the great prosperity of affluent countries is rarely used to ensure children receive ample supplies of maternal, or indeed parental, time. Rather, many children are entrusted to poorly paid outsiders for the majority of their waking hours during the first years of life. Mothers who wish to stay with them as full-time carers find society set firmly against them. Most of them must make significant sacrifices, both economic and social. They are routinely described as "nonworking."

Children also need fathers, and the paternal situation is also mixed. Lower levels of commitment and higher levels of divorce have led to a vast increase in both fatherless homes and often tense blended families. On the other hand, when fathers are around, they do generally provide more practical assistance and childcare than their male ancestors did. The stronger emotional ties within families are a real gain, but they come at some human ecological cost. For one thing, the male contribution at home, whether considered in hours or in effort, is generally not enough to compensate for the female contribution to the paid labor force, so women often end up taking on more emotional and physical strains than did their mothers or grandmothers. Both fathers and mothers are often disconcerted by the fluid and sometimes conflicting responsibilities.

More psychologically or spiritually, the new male role both reflects and reinforces what Francis calls the "ideology of gender that denies the difference and reciprocity in nature of a man and a woman and envisages a society without sexual differences, thereby eliminating the anthropological basis of the family."[64] Francis writes quite clearly about the importance of mothers, who are "even in

---

62. Francis, *Amoris Laetitia*, 82.

63. John Paul II, *Familiaris Consortio*, 23.

64. Francis, *Amoris Laetitia*, 56.

306   CHAPTER 8

the worst of times witnesses to tenderness, dedication, and moral strength." He declares that the results of not living up to the "specific mission" of "womanhood" are dire: "The weakening of this maternal presence with its feminine qualities poses a grave risk to our world."[65] (In the next chapter I say more about the importance of sexual differentiation in the economy of family love.) His warnings are even less likely to be heeded than is the order of John Paul II.

As children in affluent societies get older, their typical situation improves in many ways, especially in comparison to the standard premodern harsh discipline and early entry into hard labor in the field or workshop. All contemporary children get many years of education. Elaborate toys and electronic devices are ubiquitous, and many children are trained in sports and other pleasant activities. Still, the material gains are at least somewhat undercut by significant emotional and spiritual losses. Some difficulties come from outside, from "today's cultural reality and the powerful influence of the media."[66] The public and social media threaten children's psychological equilibrium and encourage premature sexualization. Other difficulties come from within the family. As mentioned, a substantial minority of children in rich countries grow up in broken or deeply troubled homes. Even when families are intact, modern school-aged children are often plagued with isolation. To judge from sociological studies, church attendance trends, and anecdotal evidence, relatively few children in rich countries are raised in families with a shared spiritual life and a tiny proportion get the benefit of a lively, church-oriented, morally guided religious upbringing.[67] (I also return to the relations of parents and children in the next chapter.)

The seriously ill of all ages are often left bereft of the most natural sort of loving support. The dramas of illness were traditionally largely domestic stories of practical love, sacrifice, and possibly redemptive suffering. Such tales are increasingly rare. Although affluent societies dedicate vast resources to health care and specialized residential facilities for people who cannot take care of themselves, the process is overwhelmingly institutional. Not only are medical systems

---

65.   Francis, *Amoris Laetitia*, 173.

66.   Francis, *Amoris Laetitia*, 84.

67.   For a reasonable summary of fairly recent evidence, see the first four chapters of part 7 of Peter B. Clarke, ed., *The Oxford Handbook of the Sociology of Religion* (Oxford: Oxford University Press, 2009) 599–670. For some data and analysis from Europe, see Yves Lambert, "Trends in Religious Feeling in Europe and Russia," *Revue française de sociologie*, 47, no. 5 (2006): 99–129, and David Voas, "The Rise and Fall of Fuzzy Fidelity in Europe," *European Sociological Review* 25, no. 2 (2009): 155–68.

strongly biased in favor of technological intervention and skilled labor, and equally biased against simple loving care, but societies' economic and social arrangements reflect and usually amplify that bias. Living arrangements and career obligations all too often prevent the creation of the most natural and spiritually comforting situation for the ill person—to suffer and recover or decline at home, under the loving care of relatives. Even death now mostly takes place in an impersonal environment, although family care of the dying is having a welcome revival in some countries. That bright spot does not change the general trend toward ever less practice of and praise for the domestic gratuitous love for sick people.

The tendency to separate the ill from their families is part of a broader trend to narrow active family responsibilities to members of a small community of well-functioning, closely related individuals. There are numerous counterexamples, but government agencies and the dominant models of family life ease or even encourage the exclusion of various types of potentially difficult people. Unmarried relatives are likely to end up living on their own. Few families are willing to share their homes with distant relatives, neighbors, or strangers who are in need of being taken in. Even children with fairly mild problems are sometimes "institutionalized" or "medicalized" into docility. The result is a culture of limited-care families and a society marred by what John Paul II called the "phenomenon of social and cultural exclusion, which seriously affects the elderly, the sick, the disabled, drug addicts, ex-prisoners, etc."[68]

Old people who are not seriously ill still often need substantial practical support. When they are too physically weak to leave their dwellings with ease, it is especially good for them to live in spaces that are suffused with personal love. Traditionally, older people were primarily taken care of in just this type of domestic space by their own children or, if there were no living offspring, by other relatives. Now, though, social norms increasingly encourage parents not to be "a burden" on people who love them. The state's policies reflect these norms. Governments provide, subsidize or supervise impersonal systems of pensions and social care. The final destination before death is very often some residential institution. Even when the care in these "homes" is technically excellent, residents are forced to rely primarily on people with whom they have no natural ties of love or

---

68.   John Paul II, *Familiaris Consortio*, 41.

duty. The loss of true home care for older people amounts to bad human ecology. The situation has only worsened since 1981, when John Paul II criticized "cultures [that] have both in the past and in the present set the elderly aside in unacceptable ways. This causes acute suffering to them and spiritually impoverishes many families."[69]

When comparing paid and family care, the technocrats of the age and their defenders often point out that mothers, wives, husbands, and children lack the training and skills of professionals. This lack, sometimes significant and sometimes largely imagined, helps explain why the decline of loving familial care within the home has been matched by the rise of depersonalized professional care outside of it. Decisions to favor skills over love are not necessarily wrong. For example, teachers with expertise provide children above a certain age with better instruction than most parents can manage. In medicine, skilled care is often invaluable. Still the social trend away from the flexible, familiar, and above all loving ecology of the home reflects a hierarchy of values that should make Christians uncomfortable. Love struggles to flourish in a doctor's office visit that is one of twenty in a day, in a hospital with hundreds or thousands of employees or in a specialized residence where the staff must follow countless well-intentioned technical rules. All too often, care professionals live in Francis's technological paradigm, in which "a subject . . . using logical and rational procedures, progressively approaches and gains control over an external object."[70] In other words, instead of seeing a person who craves love they observe a living "object" in need of skilled manipulation.

The Magisterium has noted and criticized some aspects of the decline in domestic ecology. I have noted the papal defenses of the distinctly feminine gifts that flourish in domestic labors of love. However, there has not yet been a comprehensive look at the wounded and unspiritual ecology of the modern home, the physical and spiritual location of the domestic Church. Indeed, it sometimes seems that the opportunity to do so is missed. In John Paul's messages for the World Day of the Sick, for example, he almost never mentioned the carers inside the family or the virtue of struggling to keep ill people at home. At least Francis has filled in some of that gap by noting that "a wife can care for her sick husband and thus, in drawing near to the Cross, renew her commitment to love unto

---

69. John Paul II, *Familiaris Consortio*, 27.

70. Francis, *Laudato Si'*, 106.

death. In such love, the dignity of the true lover shines forth."[71]

In domestic matters, the Magisterium has done best in what I call Catholic family teaching. As I discuss in the next two chapters, the popes have explained how the new modern approach to love, sexuality, and sexual relations have damaged the always fragile respect for family responsibilities.

Cautionary Conclusion

The Catholic Church has too often struggled to catch up with what is good in modern thinking and has sometimes misidentified what is bad. The treatments of the environment and integral ecology have not completely escaped these problems, in my judgment. To give the Church due credit, it was fairly quick to identify the environment as a social and spiritual issue as well as a technical one, and the Magisterium has been emphasizing technology's need for moral guidance for decades. However, there are serious issues of both commission and omission. Although the scale and scope of environmental damage is undeniably great, the fervor of the campaign against man-made climate change, the unrelenting pessimism on pollution, and the strict dichotomy between the godly and ungodly ways of integral ecology all seem exaggerated. As for omissions, I would like to see much more analysis and radical criticism of some of the distinctly modern weaknesses in integral ecology, especially the problems that plague most affluent societies.

If I had time, I would add five more aspects of contemporary society to my Vatican to-study list for integral human ecology. First, the culture of relentless and restless technical innovation deserves serious attention on its own, not merely mention as one part of consumerism or one aspect of the technocratic paradigm. Second, modern administrative systems—with their institutional rejection of subsidiarity, their meritocratic bureaucracies staffed with necessarily imperfect human bureaucrats, and their vast quantities of rules with vaster quantities of authoritative interpretations—have a significant effect on social ecology. Third, the various contemporary approaches to education, so many of them humanly debasing, deserve fuller study. Fourth, although John Paul II was deeply aware of the corrosive effects of "bureaucratic and aloof" health care, much more can be written about how to "draw on a transcendent vision of man which stresses the value and sacredness

---

71.   Francis, *Amoris Laetitia*, 162.

of life in the sick person as the image and child of God."[72] Finally, the Church's Christian humanism could provide valuable insights into the tense relations of economic globalization, ethnic and regional identity, and political nationalism.

The foundation of my list of specific potential topics for study is a single suggestion—a more thorough and lively discussion about integral ecology. In my opinion, this rubric covers much of what is now most distressing about the modern world. The decline in so many aspects of the human environment, in the midst of the greatest prosperity and, since the end of the Second World War, some of the most peaceful societies in history, may well be the greatest challenge to the true success of modern civilization. The Church has long taught well about the changes in one aspect of daily life—at the workplace. For the life outside of work, however, in leisure, the life at home, and the life of cities, the Catholic Social Teaching is still underdeveloped. As with its discussions the new things of labor and the many social issues surrounding them, the faith-filled Church has much to offer.

Those judgments are of course personal. The negative ones may seem impudent, but they are offered with a loyal heart and mind. Indeed, I think Catholics have a duty to proffer faith-motivated criticism of this necessarily tentative part of the Magisterium. After all, the Catholic Social Teaching consists of counsels of imperfection, so it is always possible to make them less imperfect.

A cautionary note is needed here. I want to shift and add to the teaching, not subtract anything from it. I am not certainly saying that the greatest issues of the previous decades of Catholic Social Teaching—economic misery and injustice, shifting political systems, crude and cruel ideologies, the unprecedented destruction of modern warfare—have all been sorted out fully. If only that were the case! Even where there have been significant improvements in the world, there is never room for complacency, for sin "always prowls around like a roaring lion."[73] As I hope I have made clear, it is essential that the Church keep supporting the weakest members of the human community. Francis explains: "Blessed, therefore, are the open hands that embrace the poor and help them: they are hands that bring hope. Blessed are the hands that reach beyond every barrier of culture, religion, and nationality, and pour the balm of consolation over the wounds of humanity."[74]

---

72.   John Paul II, *Message for the First Annual World Day of the Sick* (October 21, 1992), 4.

73.   1 Pt 5:8.

74.   Francis, *Message for the First World Day of the Poor* (November 19, 2017), 5.

CHAPTER 9

The Human Family—I

COMPLAINTS THAT FAMILIES are in bad shape are probably are old as fallen humanity, so it should not be surprising that many biblical families are in terrible condition. Cain kills his brother Abel one generation after creation. Not that much later, two of Noah's children behave shamelessly and, in more historical times, David's families are chaotic and rebellious. The advent of Christianity did not obviously change things for the better. Starting in Corinth in the days of Paul, where members of the new Church were accused of incest,[1] Christian families have kept on misbehaving, around the world and in all parts of society.

The dismal record might suggest that contemporary complaints about the situation of families, including those from the Catholic Magisterium, can be no more than current versions of a bitter and timeless truth. If that were the whole story, then the complaints and accompanying exhortations to do better would still be worthwhile, since the familiarity of sin is no excuse for abandoning the good fight against it. However, the modern approach to the family is part of a historically unique assault on many traditions of integral ecology. Much as the technocratic paradigm has changed people's relations with the rest of creation, the cults of radical individualism, the modern ideas of Hegelian uniformity, Lockean individualism, and Romantic self-expression (I discuss all of these later in this chapter) have created a series of novelties—in the relations of the family to other social organizations, in the social relations of men and women, in the dominant social attitude toward

---

1.   1 Cor 5:1.

old people and children, and in social expectations and judgments of sexual behavior.

The Catholic Church has been or has become enthusiastic about some of these new family arrangements—a less social and more personal view of marriage, less sexually determined divisions of social roles, and the increased separation of economic from family life (I also discuss all of these). However, the novelty in family ways is quite different from many of the distinctly modern challenges discussed in earlier chapters. While those have led the Church to change some of its counsels, often quite radically, the key teachings of the Magisterium on the ideals and obligations of family life have not altered. There have been some purifications, particularly about the social position of women, and some changes in vocabulary and presentations, but the core teachings remained constant.

Before discussing the contemporary form of those teachings, I offer three personal judgments. These are, of course, not part of the Magisterium in any way.

First, the shift in family structures and values is, on balance, one the least successful aspects of the modern experiment. The failure was not immediate and it is not total. If it were either, then this part of the modern experiment would presumably have been abandoned long ago. In reality, the new ways are experienced as genuinely liberating and fulfilling by many young adults in rich Western countries and by some people of all ages everywhere. A social order based almost entirely on choice and desire in family matters is undoubtedly freer than the old way of obligation, according to the modern standard of freedom as morally indifferent choice. Still, few people would speak out in favor of such related contemporary social phenomena as the high prevalence of divorce, the large number of children raised by a single parent, the large number of fertile women who are unwillingly childless or have fewer children than they would like, and the popularity of pornography. Even those who angrily reject traditional arguments for well-ordered families are often uncomfortable with the actual trends in family life.

Second, of all aspects of the Catholic Social Teaching, the guidance on family structures and values is the most unpopular. Many people find everything about the family teaching simply incomprehensible, while those who do understand the reasoning often reject it as some combination of superseded, incoherent, and cruel. The response to the Church's teaching on artificial contraception is particularly extreme. It is ridiculed by non-Catholics and ignored by the vast majority of otherwise practicing Catholics. Teachings on marriage, divorce, and the complementarity of the sexes may not be as despised as that teaching, but they are certainly not welcomed. On the contrary, they typically irritate or baffle the relatively few people who bother to think about them. Appropriately, the antipathy is mutual. Despite the conciliatory remarks about good intentions included in most presentations of Catholic family teaching, the heart of the teaching is fundamentally hostile to central modern beliefs about the integral ecology of the family.

Third, the unacceptability of this teaching explains much of the popular disdain for the Church as a whole. Attacks on the Catholic Church frequently assume that any organization that promotes what are thought to be crazed and oppressive ideas about sex and family life must itself be crazed, oppressive, and fundamentally untrustworthy. The family teaching repels intellectuals who might respect many other aspects of the Catholic Social Teaching. It also drives many baptized Catholics from the Church. They see no reason to abandon the common sense of their peers in favor of obeying the Magisterium's odd demands.

Of course, I would not dedicate two chapters to this Catholic family teaching unless I was persuaded that the Magisterium is right and rest of the world wrong. I shall try to explain my confident judgment in this chapter and the next, starting with the unexpected and distinctly unmodern wisdom of the biblical teaching, proceeding through a critical exposition of the nature of the modern vision, first in practice and then in theory, concluding with a restatement of the Catholic understanding of the family in society.

The Family in the Bible

At first glance, the Bible might seem to be an odd place for contemporary Christians, let alone for contemporary nonbelievers, to look for guidance on family matters. In many ways, it is hopelessly old-fashioned. Women are sometimes portrayed as passive recipients of men's orders and almost always as socially inferior to men. There is far more discussion of family obligation than of emotional fulfilment. Families are often treated as tribes, rather than divided into the standard contemporary "nuclear" unit of parents with their own children. There is often no clear border between familial and social authority. The Bible also seems to be inconsistent. Within the Old Testament polygamy is at first treated as standard practice, at least for patriarchs and kings. By the time the New Testament was written, polygamy is assumed to be wrong. The contradiction on divorce is explicit. In the Old Testament, God not only permits the practice but sets up rules for it, while Jesus rejects those rules and bans the practice completely. Then there is marriage. In the Old Testament, the practice is considered clearly desirable (the about-to-be sacrificed daughter of Jephthah "bewails her virginity"[2]) and infertility is a curse. The New Testament begins with a similar judgment, as Elizabeth declares that her pregnancy has "taken away my reproach among men,"[3] but her prophetic son John does not marry and both Jesus and Paul seem to endorse celibacy as superior to any sort of family tie. As for filial obligations, family duties are paramount in the Old Testament, while Jesus tells his followers to "hate" their parents.[4]

The distance and discrepancies are real, but, as always, biblical teaching is actually profound and ultimately consistent—it just needs to be interpreted. I believe the Bible offers four crucial ideas about families, each of which has been denied by many modern thinkers.

The first idea is that sexual difference is significant. God does not create a sexually undifferentiated "humankind." Rather, he makes people "male and female."[5] That description of the two sexes might look almost accidental in the first chapter of Genesis, but it is crucial in the story of Adam and Eve, told in the following two chapters. Pope John Paul II provided a brilliant, profound, and detailed analysis of the narrative.[6] His hundred or so pages do not deserve to be reduced to a few paragraphs, but I shall nonetheless try to do so.

In John Paul's retelling, God creates men and women to be both the same, as humans, and essentially different, in their sexual nature. Even before considering sin, the combination of identity and difference leads inevitably to a complex relationship filled with wonder, distinctness, and unity. The tie between men and women is the primal

---

2.   Jgs 11:37.

3.   Lk 1:25.

4.   Lk 14:26.

5.   Gn 1:27.

6.   The account takes up the first third of John Paul II, *Man and Woman He Created Them: A Theology of the Body*, trans. Michael Waldstein (Boston, Mass. Pauline Books, 2006 [1986]).

and primary social relationship. The wonder at the mysterious other, different and also the same, is first seen in Adam's initial response to the newly created Eve—"bone of my bones, flesh of my flesh."[7] This wonder and the concomitant desire for the restoration of the original unity touch every encounter between men and women and, ultimately, every human relationship. The distinctness of the inevitable differences between men and women are the source of human fruitfulness. Each generation experiences the distinctness anew as a new invitation to sexual union: "Therefore shall a man leave his father and his mother, and shall cleave unto his wife."[8] The distinctness is metaphysical as well as physical. Men and women are different in their thinking, feeling, and labor in the world, as well as in their bodies. The metaphysical difference becomes unity in the physical act of sexual union: men and women "become one flesh."[9] That union is also metaphysical; men and women are bound together by far more than physical sexual desire and physical sexual union. The physical and spiritual intercourse is used by people as the foundation of the family and by God for the creation and nurturing of new human life. In procreation, men and women come about as close as they can in the physical world to acting in the likeness of God.

Just as sexual difference is particularly closely connected to the human calling to the divine, so is it particularly deeply stained by sin. After the first sin of pride, Eve's expression of discontent with the divine order, came the sin of sexual disorder—Adam divides himself from his wife by blaming her for his own disobedience. According to the biblical account, this sexual discord made the body shameful and made sexuality, which was created in glory, into a source of disorder, both individual and social. According to the Christian doctrine of original sin, the effects of that first sexual sin are still felt today. Sin always threatens to poison the life of the family, which should be created out of the pure and totally mutual love of men and women. The effect of sin on families is clear enough in the Bible—the first human brothers are fratricidal, the all-encompassing personal union of one Adam with one Eve quickly declines into oppressive polygamy, and the due order of family life is so easily distorted and forgotten that it has to be enjoined in the Ten Commandments.

---

7. Gn 2:23.
8. Gn 2:24.
9. Gn 2:24.

It might seem hard to deny this first biblical teaching. Men and women are clearly different, and the relations between the sexes are clearly troubled in every society and potentially between each man and each woman. However, both claims, of difference and inevitable trouble, have become controversial. In contemporary thinking, sexual differences are increasingly considered to have no fundamental importance. Law and custom increasingly treat men and women indifferently as citizens, as workers, and even as family members. Although the popular culture still generally recognizes, and often celebrates, some sexual differences, the desexualization of gender has led to a widespread acceptance that all sexual arrangements are good, provided that those involved and society as a whole judge them to be nonexploitative. I come back to this troubling notion in the next chapter.

Even the most naïve modern person will admit that in practice sexual relations are often troubled. However, many contemporary social customs work on the expectation that, men will, when asked, treat all women with sexual respect. Unmarried men and women who study, work, play, or live together are expected to get along without any sort of sexual misbehavior. Couples, married or not, are expected to respect each other emotionally and sexually all the time. There is a chorus of totally merited social disapproval and totally unrealistic surprise when men do not live up this standard. (Woman sometimes also fail, perhaps more often than in the past, but assertive sexual sins are still overwhelmingly male.)

The commandment to "honor your father and your mother"[10] expresses the second central biblical idea about families, that there is a natural hierarchical order in families. Children are supposed to respect their parents simply because these people brought them into the world. The commandment does not suggest that bad parents deserve less honor than do good ones or that the honor is only appropriate as long as the children are physically, emotionally, or socially dependent on their parents. Rather, it implies that the honor should be built into the nature of the relationship. There cannot be parents who do not deserve honor and there cannot be children who are not obliged to honor. Within the historical narrative of the Bible, the sins of both parents and children often complicate the determination of how the honoring is best accomplished, but the principle is unshakeable.

---

10.   Ex 20:12 and Dt 5:16.

THE HUMAN FAMILY—I   317

In the Old Testament, marriage is also often presented as a hierarchical relationship, with men clearly above women. After the Fall, the original imperfect symmetry of Adam and Eve—while they are portrayed as equal in their humanity and full companions for each other, Adam does come first and Eve does sin first—is massively magnified. Men marry many women, men institute divorce, and men's rights over children are paramount. Jesus, however, will explain that this part of the old Law is given as a concession, as a reflection of the "hardness of heart" of those ordered to obey it.[11] He presents marriage as a reciprocal rather than a hierarchical relationship. A close reading of Saint Paul, whom modern readers often accuse of misogyny, shows that he is scrupulously symmetrical in his injunctions—women's obedience is to be matched by men's sacrificial love.[12] He does not discuss families in any detail, but his view seems to be typical of the time—they are by nature both ordered and hierarchical.

Some contemporary thinkers deny this second teaching. Following Rousseau, who said that "men are born free," they argue that children and parents have only a contractual relationship.[13] (Rousseau was himself developing the ideas of John Locke, as I explain later in this chapter.) As soon as a child pays off the contractual debt incurred for being raised, a debt that is reduced if the upbringing was poorly managed, he or she has no further obligation. Such practices as asking parents' approval for marriage and taking care of elderly parents are at best voluntary, at worst fundamentally unnatural. To these thinkers, an adult has no obligatory ties to his or her parents, other relatives, or, once suitable practical arrangements have been made, to spouse and children. Nor is there any hierarchy. The dependence of children on their parents is considered temporary and basically unnatural. People are expected to find their own order in family life.

The third biblical idea about the family is that the relations of God to humanity are familial as well as individual. The first covenants are with Adam and with Noah, who are presented as representatives of the whole human family. God tells Abraham that the

---

11. Mt 19:8.

12. Eph 5:21–33.

13. Jean-Jacques Rousseau, *Du contrat social, ou Principes du droit politique* (Paris: Union Générale d'Éditions, 1963 [1762]), chap. 1. He explains: "The most ancient of all societies . . . is the family: yet the children are only tied to the father for as long as they need them to stay alive. As soon as the need ceases, the natural tie is dissolved."

covenant is with "you and your descendants after you throughout their generations."[14] The membership of that covenant is determined by circumcision, a sign that shows God's presence in the creation of each next generation. Whatever the historical accuracy of this tribal telling of God's relation to his people, the theological significance is undeniable. The people of God are actually the family of God. Conversely, the obligations of worship and religious virtue are assigned through family ties, from the sacrifice of Isaac to the royal descendants of David. In Jeremiah, all Judah is told "you have played the harlot with many lovers,"[15] an infidelity that has lasted generations. In Isaiah, God promises to marry the purified Israel.[16] The family becomes even more theologically important in the New Testament. Paul argues that Christians, including pagans, have been adopted into the family of God.[17] Supplanting the old Israel, the new Church is portrayed as the bride of Christ.[18]

The notion that families, which essentially date from the indefinite past and will live into the indefinite future, should be considered the basic unit of humanity is distinctly nonmodern. For more than two centuries in the West, there has been a steady erosion of the role of families in society and a steady rise in the importance of isolated individuals. I mentioned Pope Francis's complaint about the legal enshrinement of this new order in the previous chapter. In many cases, the law has come ahead of practice, but the trend is undeniable. As in the Bible, heredity was long considered a just basis for social or professional position. That idea now seems so ridiculous that even the advantages children inadvertently inherit from well-connected or well-educated parents are often considered suspect. Until a few generations ago, it was taken for granted in all societies that one man, whether the husband or the paterfamilias, would naturally represent an entire family in all legal and monetary matters. That notion now seems worse than oppressive. It sounds bizarre. More recently, the increased interest in the rights of children, which are guaranteed by the society as a whole, reflects an increased discomfort with the traditional assumption that parents, aided by the extended family,

---

14. Gn 17:9.

15. Jer 3:1.

16. Is 62.

17. cf. Rom 8:23.

18. Eph 5:21–33.

THE HUMAN FAMILY—I

319

should be totally responsible for the raising of children. Similarly, the rise of communal and state pensions corresponds with a decline in the obligations of children to take care of their own parents.

Finally, there is the difference between the visions of the family in the Old and New Testaments, which I think should be read as both a sign and an invitation. In marriage, the central axis of the family, Jesus explicitly demands that his followers live up to a higher standard of social morality than the old Law requires. He rejects divorce and equates all lust with adultery.[19] As he explains the permission for divorce, "it was not this way from the beginning,"[20] that is before the advent of sin in the world. Saint Paul is loyal to this higher standard when he demands that the Church, the bride and body of Christ, be "without spot or wrinkle or any such thing."[21] Jesus also replaces the old willingness to go to court with a brother with a command to make peace.[22] He also moves from the old family of the Lord, the Israelites whose ties were based on heredity and obedience, into a new one, the Church, based on faith, love, and service. In each of these transitions, the new idea that family relations should be perfect—"as your father in heaven in perfect"[23]—is a sign of the power of the Redemption: through and with Jesus we can overcome the effects of sin. There is always an invitation to this higher family life, this wedding banquet with the Lord.[24]

In modern society, the Christian vision of a redeemed family is often accepted but in a distorted form. Marriage is indeed expected to be perfect, so much so that it is thought wise and kind to delay marriages until the couples are mature enough to make a perfect commitment and to dissolve them when husband or wife fall sufficiently short of this standard. Similarly, parents and children often feel that the other's imperfections justify the rejection of obligations. Love, although understood largely in a non-Christian sense as an emotion, is so elevated as a standard of social relations that it is allowed to disrupt families and override duties. In effect, the teachings of Jesus are accepted but without recognizing the need for the grace of God to carry them out in a sinful world. (I say more about

19.   Mt 5:28.
20.   Mt 19:8.
21.   Eph 5:27.
22.   cf. Mt 5:23–24.
23.   Mt 5:48.
24.   cf. Mt 22:1–14.

these topics in the course of this chapter.) As might be expected from a society that largely rejects all transcendental intuitions and aspects of experience and reality, people are expected to reach perfection by simply overpowering anything in the physical or emotional world that gets in their way.

The Modern Shift, in Practice

In the standard secular narrative, the modern history of families and marriage is a simple tale of progress, with the addition of each "new thing" in family life accepted as a clear move forward, from restraint toward freedom, from arbitrary and constricting conventions to a more honest and genuine attempt to have life "abundantly."[25] Because the Christian idea of a full life is quite different from the secular one, the Christian version of the story is much more complex.

In one way, the Christian recounting is actual simpler. Where many anthropologists and sociologists see many quite different pre-Christian arrangements, Christians see a single primordial organization of the family. The arrangements were undoubtedly varied in many ways, but they almost all shared five features that are particularly relevant for understanding how marriages and families have changed.

First, primordial families, which were themselves entities that transcended the individual members, couples, and nuclear families, were closely set into broader social arrangements. The working of any of the smaller family and tribal unit can only be understood in the context of the orientations, symbols, and structures of wider communities. Second, women and men had distinct roles in both family and society. The social and family roles were intimately connected, and both were assumed to reflect and express what were assumed to be inherent sexual differences. Third, intrafamily relationships, sometimes known as kinship, were inseparable from what modern people might call personal identity. In other words, the question "Who are you?" would always be answered, at least in part, by something like, "I am the daughter of X and Y, wife of L, cousin of F through M," and so forth. Fourth, children had a clearly defined and central place in families. Families were in large part structured to help them through their lives, from conception until well after they joined the adult world, and those lives were always

---

25. Jn 10:10.

a central social concern. Finally, the arrangements and practices of marriage were central to the organization of society. At the center of those marriage practices was the "marriage act," sexual intercourse that carried a religious aura and had a distinct social function. In effect, marriage gave both divine and social legitimacy to both the act itself and the children who would naturally spring from it.[26] The divine validation also affirmed the transcendental nature of procreation.[27]

The Christian idea of marriage does not contradict any of these primordial characteristics, but it develops and deepens them, based on the teaching of Jesus as it came to be understood over the centuries. His clear and consistent words on marriage and divorce can be understood as articulating one of the familial implications of his "new commandment" to "love one another even as I have loved you."[28] The current family teaching was almost fully developed by the time Leo XIII started the modern Catholic Social Teaching. Below I list the nine important features of the Christian understanding of marriage, citing both Leo's 1880 encyclical *Arcanum* and the more modern articulation in John Paul II's 1981 apostolic exhortation *Familiaris Consortio* (a document that carries less authority but is more contemporary). The combination can provide insight into the evolution of the teaching, or more accurately of the expression of a consistent understanding of the essence of Christian marital love.

First, Christian marriage is inherently Christian, in the highest possible sense. In Leo's words, it is "an example of the mystical union between Himself and His Church" that "made the naturally indivisible union of one man with one woman far more perfect through the bond of heavenly love."[29] John Paul is more effusive: "Spouses are therefore the permanent reminder to the Church of what happened on the Cross; they are for one another and for the children witnesses to the salvation in which the sacrament makes them sharers. Of this

---

26. For some insightful descriptive analysis with helpful historical background, see Maurice Godelier, *The Metamorphoses of Kinship*, trans. Nora Scott (London: Verso, 2011 [2004]), 101–104.

27. "[I]n all known societies, the making and birth of a baby are the outcome of a series of gifts that human being, but also ancestors, spirits or gods, have made in order to assemble and unify the components of a new human being." Godelier, *Metamorphoses* 105.

28. Mt 5:27–32; Mt 19:1–9; Mk 10:1–12; Lk 16:18; Jn 13:34.

29. Leo XIII, Encyclical Letter *Arcanum* (February 10, 1880), 9

salvation event marriage, like every sacrament, is a memorial, actuation and prophecy."[30]

Second, marriage is a psychological and spiritual bond. Leo says the couple is "to have such feelings for one another as to cherish always very great mutual love."[31] John Paul combines psychology, grace, and theology. "The gift of the Spirit is a commandment of life for Christian spouses and at the same time a stimulating impulse so that every day they may progress toward an ever richer union with each other on all levels—of the body, of the character, of the heart, of the intelligence and will, of the soul—revealing in this way to the Church and to the world the new communion of love, given by the grace of Christ."[32]

Third, marriage is spiritually oriented to procreation and to the continuation of the Christian community. Leo, who wrote before any respectable thinker endorsed artificial contraception, merely says that marriage "not only looks to the propagation of the human race, but to the bringing forth of children for the Church."[33] John Paul is more extravagant and perhaps more defensive and less triumphalist. "According to the plan of God, marriage is the foundation of the wider community of the family, since the very institution of marriage and conjugal love are ordained to the procreation and education of children, in whom they [marriage and conjugal love] find their crowning. . . . [C]onjugal love . . . does not end with the couple, because it makes them . . . co-operators with God for giving life to a new human person. . . . [Children] are a living reflection of their [parents'] love, a permanent sign of conjugal unity and a living and inseparable synthesis of their being a father and a mother."[34]

Fourth, marriage automatically creates a spiritual and practical community of man and women. Leo explains that this union makes "the lives of husbands and wives . . . better and happier . . . by their lightening each other's burdens through mutual help . . . by having all their possessions in common."[35] John Paul frames the idea biologically, psychologically, ethically, and theologically. "This conjugal communion sinks its roots in the natural complementarity that exists

---

30. John Paul II, Apostolic Exhortation *Familiaris Consortio* (November 22, 1981), 13.

31. Leo XIII, *Arcanum*, 11

32. John Paul II, *Familiaris Consortio*, 19.

33. Leo XIII, *Arcanum*, 10

34. John Paul II, *Familiaris Consortio*, 14.

35. Leo XIII, *Arcanum*, 26

THE HUMAN FAMILY—I 323

between man and woman, and is nurtured through the personal willingness of the spouses to share their entire life-project, what they have and what they are: for this reason such communion is the fruit and the sign of a profoundly human need. But in the Lord Christ God takes up this human need, confirms it, purifies it and elevates it, leading it to perfection through the sacrament of matrimony."[36]

Fifth, marriage is a lifelong union. Leo basically restates canon law: "[N]o power can dissolve the bond of Christian marriage whenever this has been ratified and consummated."[37] John Paul provides a rich psychological and theological background for this doctrine, which shocked those listening to Jesus and continues to shock today. "Being rooted in the personal and total self-giving of the couple, and being required by the good of the children, the indissolubility of marriage . . . is thus the supreme realization of the unconditional faithfulness with which God loves His people . . . The gift of the sacrament is at the same time a vocation and commandment for the Christian spouses, that they may remain faithful to each other forever, beyond every trial and difficulty, in generous obedience to the holy will of the Lord: 'What therefore God has joined together, let not man put asunder.'"[38]

Sixth, sacramental marriage is monogamous, between one man and one woman. Leo sets out the historical novelty of this demand: "Christ our Lord condemned the long-standing practice of polygamy."[39] John Paul provides a more theological explanation: "[T]he new communion of love, given by the grace of Christ . . . is radically contradicted by polygamy: this . . . is contrary to the equal personal dignity of men and women who in matrimony give themselves with a love that is total and therefore unique and exclusive."[40]

Seventh, marriage is sexually exclusive, so adultery is contrary to its nature. Leo only states the fact. Spouses are "ever faithful to their marriage vow."[41] John Paul puts it in theological context. The married couple's "bond of love becomes the image and the symbol of the covenant that unites God and His people. And the same sin that can harm the conjugal covenant becomes an image of the infidelity

---

36. John Paul II, *Familiaris Consortio*, 19, quoting Mt 19:6.

37. Leo XIII, *Arcanum*, 41

38. John Paul II, *Familiaris Consortio*, 20.

39. Leo XIII, *Arcanum*, 21.

40. John Paul II, *Familiaris Consortio*, 19.

41. Leo XIII, *Arcanum*, 11.

of the people to their God: idolatry is prostitution, infidelity is adultery, disobedience to the law is abandonment of the spousal love of the Lord."[42] In his teaching on the "Theology of the Body." John Paul II points out that Christian marital fidelity is not limited to the body, but extends all the way to "the depth of the human person."[43]

Eighth, marriage involves a divinely ordained structured relationship of husband and wife. In this part of the doctrine there has been a change since Leo's time, certainly of emphasis and perhaps of substance. Leo describes the relationship of the sexes as hierarchical but respectful. "The woman . . . must be subject to her husband and obey him; not, indeed, as a servant, but as a companion."[44] When he wrote that, the obedience was largely taken for granted while the demand for companionship would have been somewhat controversial. A century later, the situation is more than reversed. Christians, at least in secularized societies, generally ignore the clear biblical endorsement of female subjugation—"Your [the woman's] desire shall be for your husband, and he shall rule over you."[45] John Paul does exactly that in *Familiaris Consortio* (he discusses and basically softens the meaning of the relevant biblical texts elsewhere). He states that marriage and family are based on "the equal dignity and responsibility of women with men" that is manifested "in that reciprocal self-giving by each one to the other and by both to the children that is proper to marriage and the family." Each sex has its own "inalienable rights and responsibilities proper to the human person."[46] In this formulation, "inalienable" refers to the distinctly male and female ways of being in the "image" and "likeness" of God.[47]

Ninth, the only central attribute of Christian marriage omitted in both *Arcanum* and *Familiaris Consortio* is the free consent of the spouses. Early theologians established the principle that the husband and wife, not the parents or any social superior, are the contractors of the marriage and the ministers of the sacrament, but the practice was so contrary to the dominance of social considerations in primordial family marriages that it took centuries to become accepted. Still, it was well enough established by the nineteenth century that Leo

42. John Paul II, *Familiaris Consortio*, 12.
43. John Paul II, *General Audience* (October 8, 1980), 6.
44. Leo XIII, *Arcanum*, 26.
45. Gn 3:16.
46. John Paul II, *Familiaris Consortio*, 22.
47. Gn 1:26.

did not feel the need to mention it. Indeed, the principle was quite well accepted in the sixteenth century, when the Council of Trent affirmed the validity of past clandestine marriages, even though they were often hidden precisely to deny the parents' will. The council tried to eliminate the practice by requiring the publication of banns, but the goal was only to ensure that the existence of a marriage was indisputable, not to allow the imposition of marriage by force.[48] The current *Catechism* is unequivocal. "The Church holds the exchange of consent between the spouses to be the indispensable element that 'makes the marriage.' If consent is lacking there is no marriage. . . . The consent must be an act of the will of each of the contracting parties, free of coercion or grave external fear. No human power can substitute for this consent. If this freedom is lacking, the marriage is invalid."[49]

In comparison to the Christian ideal, even the best Christian marriages fall short. In this fallen world, a lifetime of perfect and peaceful union is impossible, even though the grace of the sacrament strengthens Christian spouses in both perseverance and forgiveness. The worldly reign of sin often stains deeply the social arrangements of marriage. Leo, writing of non-Christian societies, said, "[M]anifold [are] the vices and so great the ignominies with which marriage was defiled."[50] John Paul emphasized the sins of the strong against the weak, criticizing "that persistent mentality that considers the human being not as a person but as a thing, as an object of trade, at the service of selfish interest and mere pleasure: the first victims of this mentality are women."[51]

The presence and prevalence of sin explains why all premodern societies, Christian and otherwise, endorsed or tolerated many deviations from and debasements of Christian marriage norms. They had arranged marriages, polygamy, concubinage, brutal sexual conquest, semilicit fornication, or even royal incest. Christians trying to purify marriage only slowly recovered from the confusion of the first

---

48.   When the Council of Trent required a priestly witness and public announcement of marriage, it specifically confirmed the validity of previous clandestine unions. "[I]t is not to be doubted that clandestine marriages made with the free consent of the contracting parties are valid." (*Council of Trent*, session 24, chap. 1). Chap. 9 of the same session specifically banned pressure from "lords or magistrates" to "compel men and women . . . to contract marriage against their will."

49.   *Catechism of the Catholic Church*, 1626, 1628.

50.   Leo XIII, *Arcanum*, 8.

51.   John Paul II, *Familiaris Consortio*, 24.

followers of Jesus. "The disciples said to him, 'If such is the case of a man with his wife, it is not expedient to marry.'"[52] The full adoption of his norms required many steps, each of them slow and initially tentative or controversial. The highlights, in roughly chronological order, are the recognition of infant baptism as an initiation of a new family member into God's redeeming love; the understanding of Christian marriage as a sacrament of the Church; the reasonably effective banning of polygamy, concubinage, divorce, and remarriage (the latter two prohibitions eventually softened in Protestant countries); the condemnation of male as well as female adultery (practice lagged particularly far behind teaching in this crucial affirmation of sexual equality); the requirement of genuine spousal consent to marriage; the recognition of the ramifications of women's dignity and spiritual freedom; and the expectation that marriage should promote not only the social position and material good of the spouses but also their emotional and spiritual lives, as well as those of their children and of the whole community.[53]

By the time Leo XIII wrote *Arcanum*, European marriage and family structures had been sufficiently Christianized that anthropologists considered the comparable rules and customs of the "primitive" tribes that they studied to be greatly different from, and clearly inferior to, their own arrangements. In some ways, though, the family structures of even the most secular society in 1880 had more in common with those of the most peculiar primitive tribe than with today's arrangements. Non-Christians and eventually anti-Christians have brought marriage and family a long way in new directions.

The milestones are well known. The most important ones mark the gradual emancipation of women from their sex-specific and family-dominated roles—freedom to own property, to sue for divorce, to marry solely for love, to receive some education, to receive the exact same education as men, to participate in government, to pursue careers, to pursue careers after having children, to pursue the exact same careers as men, to use birth control, to have somewhat legitimate sexual relations outside of marriage, to cohabit with nonspouses, to determine their own sexual morality, to initiate

---

52. Mt 19:10.

53. A sample of the historical issues, from a Catholic perspective, can be found in Glenn W. Olsen, ed., *Christian Marriage: A Historical Study* (New York: Crossroad, 2001). An interesting, more specialized study is David d'Avray, *Medieval Marriage: Symbolism and Society* (Oxford: Oxford University Press, 2005).

divorce in tragic circumstances, to initiate divorce for emotional reasons, to maintain custody of children after divorce, to choose freely to have abortions, to choose freely to have childless marriages, to have children without anything like a "marital act," to separate pregnancy from motherhood. There are a few corresponding male milestones—to share parenting responsibility, to refrain from physical violence against wives, to ask for divorce because of emotional discontent, to share custody of children with estranged mothers, to choose to work in what used to be women's caring professions (e.g., nursing)—but they are best understood as necessary adjustments to the women's journey.

Families advanced along with women. The direction of causality can be disputed. Did liberated women change family structures, did changed family structures liberate women, or were the changes of both women's roles and family structures propelled by the common forces of social, economic, and cultural modernization? Whatever the answer, the direction of change for families is clear, toward groups that are smaller, less structured, less socially integrated, and less religious. Smaller—kinship and other communal relations were increasingly treated as secondary to the concerns of the nuclear family of parents and their own children. Less structured—integral nuclear families were often broken apart by divorce, while new alternative quasi-families became common. Less socially integrated—familial relations, both between the sexes and between the generations, were increasingly separated from political, cultural, economic, and other social structures. Less religious—the civil marriages that Leo XII condemned as "the fertile source of much detriment and calamity"[54] are treated as equal or superior to the ties created by religious vows, while mere cohabitation—"those unhappy persons who, carried away by the heat of passion, and being utterly indifferent to their salvation, live wickedly together without the bond of lawful marriage"[55]—is considered almost a social equivalent to any sort of marriage.

The dis-integration reached within marriage and sexual relations. Couples felt free to have sex without marriage, to the extent that both members basically now consider themselves free to switch sexual partners at will, perhaps after some declaration of an emotional justification for separation. The once universal and divinely

---

54. Leo XIII, *Arcanum*, 24.

55. Leo XIII, *Arcanum*, 44.

blessed tie of marriage with procreation and child rearing has been dissolved. Children outside of marriages and marriages without any desire for children both became acceptable. The integration of parents and children remains but has become more fragile, as many fathers have deserted their children and many mothers end up balancing "life" (their maternal responsibilities and joys) with "work" (their paid labor) in ways the favor the latter over the former.

In sum, marriage is increasing treated as an optional and merely legal arrangement, reproduction as pure biology (with some Lockean property rights thrown in), and the family task of child rearing as an aspect of work-life management. Marriage and family have lost much of their social and almost all of their divine connotations and controls.

The legitimation of same-sex marriage is the latest milestone on the family road, which is now turning away from the liberation of women. It amounts to a ratification of the modern, emotional idea of marriage and a denial of the traditional Christian and premodern non-Christian assumption that marriage is essentially procreative. I say a little more about the social meaning of the social acceptance of homosexual relations and same-sex marriage in the next chapter.

We may not yet have reached the end of the road of family and sexual redefinition, but we have come far enough to be able to survey the new arrangements. Christians should find five innovations particularly challenging. I genuinely mean challenging, as each of them is neither simply horrible nor totally wonderful. Rather, in the typical modern way, each is both troubling and in some respects an improvement over what came before.

The New Roles and Image of Women

The first challenging innovation is the center of the historical narrative: the new role and image of women. Much of the old picture has been erased. The chattel approach to marriage has all but disappeared in post-Christian societies, as has the attitude that led men to praise women in such terms as the fair sex, the better half, icons of purity, self-sacrificing mothers, the geniuses of the household, and the world-ruling hand that rocks the cradle. Leo XIII's description of women now sounds insulting: "[A] woman is by nature fitted for home-work, and it is that which is best adapted at once to preserve her modesty and to promote the good bringing up of children and the well-being of the family."[56]

Women may in practice still do most of the housework, child rearing, and general family support, but in the law, in the lessons taught in school, and in the presentation of the mainstream media, women and men are expected to have virtually identical personal natures and social roles. "Unisex" is supposed to rule in education, employment, financial arrangements, and legal positions. It has even made some headway in fashion and personal adornment. Actual practice is gradually catching up with this vision of "gender neutrality." For almost a century, each generation of women has been more professionally ambitious than their mothers and each generation of men has been expected to do more traditionally female labor than their fathers did.

Explicitly Christian ideals did not motivate many of the leaders of the most recent stages of the feminist journey—and they were likely to identify the Catholic Church as a bastion of oppression—but Christians should nonetheless welcome much of the new attitude toward womanhood and a good portion of the actual changes. The Christian respect for the equal dignity of women before God helped start society on the new path, by exposing many old attitudes and practices as unworthy of women's fully human nature. Few Christians before the twentieth century would have anticipated what was going to happen, but it is in accord with that feminine dignity to reject unjust and erroneous assumptions and practices—considering women intellectually inferior to men; keeping them socially inferior, not developing their intellectual, artistic, and professional gifts; excluding them from social and economic opportunities; and imposing a double standard for sexual behavior (although no one's dignity is enhanced by lifting that standard through devaluing virginity and chastity for both sexes).

However, as mentioned in the previous chapter, something important has been lost in the decline of what used to be considered distinctly feminine roles in families. Modern sexual freedom is a less suitable ideal for young womanhood than the purity that it replaced. Asexual parenthood is an inferior substitute for maternal love. The "neutering" of both men and women is forced and unnatural. Catholics should find the new order especially jarring, since it cannot easily

---

56.   Leo XIII, Encyclical Letter *Rerum Novarum* (May 15, 1891), 42.

be reconciled with either the biblical imagery of men and women or the symbolic sexual relations in the history of salvation—of Mary and Jesus and of Christ and his Church. (Of course, most Christians do not notice these problems; they share the general feeling that, if such symbolism stops the Catholic Church from ordaining women as priests, then it is time for new symbolism.) I come back to the Catholic view of men, women, and women's social roles a little later in this chapter.

The Triumph of Feelings

The second challenging idea is what I call the triumph of feelings. In the old order, emotions, especially Romantic sentiments, were often considered weak and "womanly" (not a compliment). In all personal and familial matters, people, especially men, were supposed to ignore or overcome any feelings that did not encourage socially appropriate behavior. Obviously, those are massive generalizations, but the many variations and exceptions look almost insignificant from the perspective of the new order. Feelings have become the standard of judgment for family relations. Romantic love is often seen as a lodestar for life. For many people, entering into the social stability of marriage is no longer considered a typical part of growing up, and no marriage is expected to last any longer than the couple's romantic feelings. A vow of lifelong love is frequently considered a statement of current intention rather than a binding commitment. The parental role is often treated as less important than the couple's responsibility to follow their feelings.

For Christians, who believe in a religion of love, this focus on feelings rather than rules is welcome—in part. Insofar as love is a feeling that feeds and is fed by our divine calling, the greater modern attention paid to the "reasons of the heart" in the human sphere can help people love both neighbor and God more fully.[57] The new way can also bring dignity to sexual relations, in which love was often ignored in premodern societies, while physical lust was in practice too often given great sway. The expectation that children

---

57. The reference is to Blaise Pascal, *Pensées* (277 in the Brunschvicg numbering). Pascal was far from a romantic in his interest in the heart's logic. The feelings he cares about are mostly aimed at God—"this faith is in the heart, and makes us not say *scio* [I know], but *credo* [I believe]" (248)—and when the heart burns for other people, it is in deep friendship, not erotic love. Translation by W. F. Trotter from eBooks@Adelaide, 2014 [1670].

should be desired from the heart can be a spiritual improvement on the former dutiful approach to procreation. Perhaps most significantly, in comparison to the traditional idea of marriage as a social arrangement between or within families or tribes, the emotionally charged modern vision reflects more of the intensity of the biblical descriptions of God's almost desperate love of Israel and his almost desperate anger at her infidelity.

However, Christians, who are acutely aware of the power of sin, must also be wary of the new trust in feelings. Feelings that are not guided by moral considerations too easily move in immoral directions. Excessive respect for morally disordered feelings can easily lead away from the true flourishing of the full person. In particular, unguided feelings often distract people from their family responsibilities. From raising difficult children (and they are all difficult at least some of the time) to caring for ill and ill-tempered adult relatives, the responsible life of familial love often generates deeply unpleasant feelings. The virtuous life of familial love requires enduring, changing, or transcending those feelings. It requires "filling up what is lacking in Christ's afflictions"[58] and accepting Jesus' "invitation to manifest the moral greatness of man, his spiritual maturity," as John Paul II put it.[59]

Slow to Grow Up

The third challenging modern creation is the prevalence of an extended period of voluntary, nonconsecrated, noncelibate, nonparental adulthood. This state of life was almost unheard of in the old order. There were always people who neither married nor took up a celibate religious calling, but they were rarely happy about their social position and were generally attached to some family (for example as a servant or a maiden aunt). In the new era, it is standard practice to spend more than a decade between exiting the dependence of childhood and entering the responsibility of marriage. Two decades of life without either a permanent social position or a permanent personal commitment are not uncommon, and an increasing number of people never grow up, by the old standard. They often have active romantic and sexual lives, but these do not end up married, attached to a family, in holy orders, or with their own children.

---

58. Col 1:24.

59. John Paul II, Apostolic Letter *Salvifici Doloris* (February 11, 1984), 22.

332   CHAPTER 9

Again, Christians should have mixed feelings. The increased time available to mature and to develop a richer personality can increase true freedom. The unattached adult has more freedom to listen to God's call than does someone who has rushed into marriage or has been rushed into it. The unmarried and virtuous adult has more social dignity now than when this involuntary celibacy was socially denigrated. However, the lack of social pressure to take on adult responsibilities often seems to encourage an irresponsible approach to life. Sexual adventures, economic selfishness, pointless professional ambitions, and a shallow search for pleasures and excitement all too easily come to dominate lives. Modern freedom is too often the false freedom to sin.

Decline of Dependence

The fourth challenge to the family is posed by what can be called the socialization or "de-family-ization" of dependence. I mentioned some aspects of this topic in my discussion of domestic integral ecology in the previous chapter.

In the old way, families were generally expected to take care of their weak members. Anthropologists and historians can provide counterexamples, but the children, the ill, the feeble, and the old in most societies all usually relied almost entirely on some group of relatives for care. Sin being ubiquitous, these relatives always failed to show perfect love and were sometimes cruel. In some societies, especially in the late years of Christendom, other social organizations sometimes started to take on some of these responsibilities, but such institutions as orphanages for the young and special homes for the weak and old were generally considered inferior alternatives to care in the "bosom of the family."

The whole concept of family responsibility does not make much sense when personal ties are primarily based on feelings rather than on duties or responsibilities. The particular idea of a distinctly feminine sympathy with those in need makes no sense at all if a woman's place in society is considered identical to a man's. Also, the decline of subsidiarity has led to a greater social reliance on state-directed institutions and less on the most intimate grouping of all, the family. The Hegelian pattern is clear. As the family's role has become less prominent and more women have become employees much like

men, other institutions and arrangements, all of them more impersonal than almost any family, have taken up more of the responsibilities of care. Parents are generally still responsible for their children,
but they frequently entrust them to trained carers from infancy and
almost always to childcare centers and schools from an early age.
Similarly, old people and weak people are increasingly reliant on
institutions, whether "homes" or intrusive administrative systems.

Once more, Christians should have mixed feelings about this
trend. The positives of "de-family-ization" are significant. Universal
institutional schooling has promoted flourishing by bringing into
the world of learning many people whose own families would have
been unwilling or unable to provide a comparable education. The
institutions of social support have protected many weak people from
misery. Many families are so destructive that the supervision and
intervention by outside institutions improves the lot of their weakest
members. On the other side, the negatives may well be more significant. When families work well, as they often do, their support for
the weak is provided with more love than any institution can hope
to offer. In addition, responsibilities should be part of family life. For
example, adult children may be worse off morally and spiritually for
being able to shirk the commandment to honor their parents. The
contemporary permission granted to everyone to separate the feelings of love from the responsibilities of family relationships distorts
both love and family.

Families Lose Out to Individuals

The final challenging social change is the decline of the family as
a social unit, which I also touched on in the previous chapter. The
basic unit of society used to be the family, often an extended family
with some sort of chief, patriarch, or the occasional matriarch. Now
it is the individual adult. No longer can a father speak for his wife
and children in matters of law, religion, or culture. No longer does a
wife almost automatically consider herself bound to follow her husband's decisions, either inside or outside of the household. No longer
are children expected to follow almost unquestioningly the rules and
traditions of their families.

Yet again, this change is both welcome and unwelcome. It is bizarre
even to contemplate reversing women's suffrage and education. The

334   CHAPTER 9

strangeness of the notion reflects the fully justified social respect now granted to every woman, whether she is married or not. It is almost as bizarre to suggest that heredity really should determine children's destiny, even though it often actually does. The bizarreness arises in large part because children are less likely to be thought of as members of a family than as future autonomous adults. However, there are significant losses from the adoption of this new view. Family membership tends to be treated as just another optional commitment, like membership of a club or a religious denomination. This devaluation can easily introduce a harmful wedge between the socially valued feelings inside a family on one side and, on the other side, the genuinely valuable but socially mistrusted family responsibilities and the genuinely desirable but socially rejected subjection of individual willfulness to the family's good.

Before going on, I should say that the Catholic teaching about all these innovations—as about such other modern shifts as the new relationship between personal and professional life—is still being created. The general principles that I give at the end of this chapter can guide the discussions, but the social trends are moving too fast, and Catholic teaching is moving too slowly, to allow many firm rules. Without any authority, but with, I hope, some ability to *sentire cum ecclesia* (think with the Church), I can say that the social innovations have enough good in them that we would not want simply to reverse them and enough evil in them that we should not accept them uncritically.

I can also say that in fact that it is literally impossible to return to the premodern ideas of family. Once the experiment of new roles for women and new structures for families has been tried, the old world, in which these arrangements not only do not exist but are not even considered realistic possibilities, is gone forever. A postmodern society with premodern family structures would be something like a modern artist who paints in the nineteenth-century academic style—a conscious choice to go backward in history. That is quite different from the artist of the time who was simply following the then conventional rules of her trade.

The Modern Shift, in Theory

Christians often find that conversations with nonbelievers about family issues prove difficult and inconclusive. The parrying of

THE HUMAN FAMILY — I   335

supposed sociological facts resolves nothing, not only because all factual claims can be disputed but more significantly because any discussion of families is ultimately philosophical. For Christians to make any headway in these debates, they must understand their own philosophical grounding. They must also both understand and respond to the philosophies that motivate their opponents. These opponents are often not consciously aware of the principles their conclusions are based on, but Catholics cannot engage successfully unless they understand what is actually considered to be true about human nature on both sides of the intellectual gulf between them and the modern consensus. In this section, I try to bring to the surface the three schools of modern thought that, in my judgment, have most influenced the development of modern families: Hegel's universalism, Locke's individualism, and the Romantic cult of self-expression.[60] I also evaluate the familial implications of all three.

In this discussion I am relying on my own analysis rather than the magisterial texts. My excuse for such impudence and arrogance is simple—I believe that the wisdom of the Catholic teaching cannot be understood without conscious recognition of the seductive alternatives.

Hegel and the Vanishing Family

Hegel has come up several times in this book. Indeed, in my view the various strands of thinking that were developed in large part under his influence—most notably Marxist economics, big-government liberalism, and a retrospectively known historical determinism— provide the most impressive non-Catholic explanations and justification of many important modern changes and attitudes. In family matters, Hegel can be associated with five modern developments. None of them is entirely new or exclusively Hegelian, but I think they should be grouped together under his name because they fit so well with his understanding of the direction of history. (I am not referring here to his own writings on the family, which presented a

---

60.   The division is influenced by the subtler, broader, and more complex analysis of the various strains of modern thinking in Charles Taylor, *Sources of the Self, The Making of the Modern Identity* (Cambridge, Mass.: Harvard University Press, 1992). For both Hegel and Locke, the actual views of the founders of the school are less "advanced" than those presented here, but I believe the attributions are appropriate, because the contemporary ideas are implicit in the texts.

336 CHAPTER 9

remarkably conventional early nineteenth-century bourgeois vision, based on procreation, property, and social respectability.[61])

To start, there is the expansion of individual freedom. As discussed in the second chapter, in Hegel's view freedom increases as societies develop, because the progress of history inevitably first loosens and then entirely sweeps away the many tight, traditional strictures of family, tribe, and cult. Christianity originally promoted this development of Hegel's Spirit of history, because free Christians would "hate" their families for the sake of the gospel, putting conscience and Church before all lesser obligations.[62] History, however, has moved on while the Catholic Church had stayed still, so its family values are now regressive.

Hegelian freedom also takes the form of loosening family ties— the liberation from indissoluble marriage, from obligatory respect for elders, from most duties to children and relatives, and from the complex of emotional relations and practical expectations that can be described as loyalty. Family relations, customs, values, and honor inevitably become less important when the building blocks of societies are no longer quasi-families. Families are irrelevant to groups tied together by increasingly abstract considerations of religion, political expediency, and economic efficiency. In Hegel's model, the trend will culminate in the all-encompassing State, but the family has become socially secondary long before this State is fully developed. I mentioned one marker on this historical path earlier in this chapter—the definition and expansion of a succession of values and lifestyles that are distinctly not oriented to the family during an ever-lengthening period of adolescence. The youth culture is Hegelian.

Another milestone in the Hegelian historical narrative is the advent of modern bureaucratic governance, found in governments, whether democratic or more authoritarian, and in all types of nongovernmental organizations. These ruling and guiding rule-bound and meritocratic political-social systems have firmly supported the third Hegelian social development, an increasingly professional approach to all sorts of care (mentioned in the previous chapter). As the rules and ties of family become weaker, the interest of the government in what were formerly family matters becomes stronger. As

---

61. See the discussion in the historical appendix in Rocco Buttiglione, *L'uomo e la famiglia* (Rome: Dino, 1991), 202–38.

62. Lk 14:26.

society becomes more technocratic and less traditional, symbolic, and spiritual, the authorities increasingly support or mandate the substitution of the objective excellence of trained professionals for the subjective judgments of family members. For example, agents of the care bureaucracy replace the traditional wisdom and foolishness of kind aunts and firm matriarchs, while trained childcare workers replace mothers.

The professionalism of care can be seen as one aspect of the fourth Hegelian development: The State's assumption of ever more of the responsibilities traditionally assigned to families. To start, schooling has become predominantly a state affair. It is universal and starts at steadily younger ages. In most jurisdictions, the state's rules must even be followed by private schools and home-schooling parents. Then there is the welfare state. It is this administrative apparatus, not the family, which increasingly cares for the old and the ill. It intervenes freely whenever it decides families are dysfunctional. Its payments to people in need relieve the burden on family members, easing the paths to isolated old age, single motherhood, and divorce.

Finally, the Hegelian freedom of advanced societies includes freedom from all traditional religious ties and responsibilities. When modern social relations, emotional and administrative, supplant the primitive relations between people and God, the content of freedom changes. The transcendental ideal of Christian marriage, a bond made permanent by God, and the Christian notion of a family, a community sanctified by and created for God, are no longer ways to become free worshipers of God and free imitators of the fertile nuptial bond of Jesus and his Church.[63] Instead, these bonds look like the example of individual slavery, which is bad even if the slaves claim to be happy in their chains. In contemporary discussions of marriage and family, the freedom from religion is now assumed and references to divinely given family rules or responsibilities are commonly dismissed throwbacks to a darker age.

Christians should admit that history has basically vindicated the Hegelian narrative of the development of families. Families have indeed become less constraining, less socially important, less self-reliant, and less self-consciously spiritual. The first four of these developments has had both good and bad effects, while the last is overwhelmingly negative. However, as I have pointed out throughout

---

63. Eph 5:21–33.

338   CHAPTER 9

these chapters, the whole Hegelian vision is dangerous for Christians and all the more dangerous for its momentum and seductive charm. For example, Christians are supposed to feed the hungry and protect widows, but the welfare state does that well, perhaps as well as or even better than any Christian community in a preindustrial society ever managed (the comparison is difficult, since there is much more prosperity now to go around). Such secular accomplishments, though, often come with a high moral and social price.

In today's societies, Christians can usually protect their own families, but they should not be fooled. As the State takes on more of its Hegelian role of exclusive guardian of society, the old ties of family are obstacles to its universalizing historical task.

Locke's Adult Individualism

John Locke has been mentioned only a few times in this book, although many intellectual historians consider his understanding of society to be at least as influential as Hegel's. Perhaps I have slighted the British philosopher. After all, for the purposes of putting the Catholic Social Teaching in its intellectual context, Locke must be considered a founding father of modern individualism, which has come up several times.

In the individualistic view of the family life, there is no "human nature" that naturally binds people with effectively innate ties of love, family, obligation, and tradition. Rather, the Lockean "state of nature" is a presocial, solitary life. True, Locke and his followers admit that in practice all people have signed or inherited a "contract" to live together in society, so this primitive, almost prefallen individualism can never be seen in its pure form. However, Locke's individualism is not empirical but ontological. People are individuals by nature, in relationships only by accident or decision. This assumption is the polar opposite of the Christian claim that people are by nature social, as explained in chapter 1.

Locke's radical view of human nature led him to endorse some views on family matters that were far ahead of his time. Most notably, he expressed great respect for the wives' contribution to the family, he argued that there is no reason to ban divorce once the children are no longer young, and he endorsed a quite narrow definition

THE HUMAN FAMILY—I   339

of the mutual obligations of children and parents.[64] Those prescient recommendations show how relevant his vision of the world and of human nature is to the contemporary family. I identify four principles. (Just as Hegel was not fully Hegelian, Locke's own views were not fully Lockean, but in family matters the Englishman was more farsighted than was the Prussian.)

The first, which has already been mentioned, is the preeminence of contracts. If all social relations are fundamentally contractual, then people certainly do not live in and identify as families because their created nature is familial, because love durably and irresistibly attracts them to each other, or because they have obligations to their ancestors and their progeny. None of those reasons suggest a voluntary contractual arrangement. Locke's actual arguments are sometimes still stained by vestigial ideas of a preexisting human nature, but his fundamental principles point to a family life that is entirely guided by a collection of individual decisions that this or that family arrangement is currently advantageous. Of course, infants and children cannot make rational decisions, but in Locke's view this temporary problem can be rectified as soon as the little ones can reason for themselves.

The contractual view of the family has been very influential. In modern thinking, it is often assumed that people can define together what their family is (two fathers or two mothers, for example) and can leave their family whenever it suits them. They simply break one contract, pay the appropriate penalty, and move on to sign a new one.

The preeminence of contracts goes along with the second principle, which I have also mentioned—Locke's radical individualism. Each adult man (and woman, a contemporary Lockean would add) is free to think for himself, to use his property to buffer himself from other people, and to define his relationships with other people as he sees fit. Of course, he or she cannot make other people agree with the chosen definitions, but this impediment to perfect willfulness is merely practical. Lockeans declare that by nature people are not fundamentally in debt to their family, to their community, or to God.

Locke's individualism has also been influential on modern understanding of families in society. Society is seen not as a sort of

---

64.   John Locke, *Second Treatise on Government*, chap. 7, paragraph 82. Also see the essay by David Archard, "John Locke's Children" in *The Philosopher's Child: Critical Perspectives in the Western Tradition*, eds. Susan M. Turner and Gareth B. Matthews (Rochester, N.Y.: University of Rochester Press, 1998) and David C. Schindler, *Freedom from Reality: The Diabolical Character of Modern Liberty* (Notre Dame, Ind.: Notre Dame University Press, 2017).

340   CHAPTER 9

uber-family or as collection of families but as a collection of decision-making individuals. Families are not considered immutable structures that are oriented toward raising children and creating lasting intergenerational social ties. Rather, they are viewed as voluntarily formed groups of current and future adults whose mutual obligations are far less important than are the rights of each individual participant in family life. Like Hegel's increasing freedom, Locke's atomistic vision of human nature leads away from the traditional treatment of the family as a fixed social unit, let alone as the basic unit of society.

Locke's second principle leads to the third: children are not, as children, worthy creatures with their own dignity. Rather, they are only worthy because they will eventually be self-guided adults who will be able to own property and make contracts. While they are dependent, they are merely works-in-progress, temporarily in need of protection and guidance.

In this picture of childhood as imperfect adulthood, Locke is not much different from Aristotle and most of the Western philosophical tradition.[65] The full resonance of the love and spiritual respect that Jesus showed for little children was little recognized by premodern Christian thinkers or in the legal and social structures of Christendom.[66] What was new with Locke and his followers was the prominence of training children for autonomy, rather than for good citizenship, filial duty, or membership in a spiritual community. In Lockean logic, experience is crucial and tradition has no real value.

The current ideal of parenting in affluent societies is Lockean, aiming at creating autonomous individuals as quickly as possible. Children are expected to learn more at earlier ages, to fill more of their time with worthy activities, and to plan their adult life from as young an age as possible. In the rush to give them adult knowledge of sexual matters, their innocence and immaturity are underestimated or ignored. Many hours of distinctly childish labor of play and of joyful family life are sacrificed to these educational and pseudo-adult

---

65.   For some examples, see the essays in Turner and Mathews, *Philosopher's Child*.

66.   Perhaps the most remarkable aspect of the burgeoning literature of childhood studies is its novelty. Historians of childhood find that children were for the most part almost invisible until remarkably recently. That gap has been closing in psychology, sociology, history, and theology. For a beautiful theological appreciation of the true Christian attitudes toward children and childhood, see Hans Urs von Balthasar, *Unless You Become Like This Child*, trans. Erasmo Leiva-Merikakis (San Francisco: Ignatius, 1991 [1988]).

activities, which, not coincidentally, give children a more Hegelian social freedom and reduce the parents' Christian freedom to guide the formation of the children God has given them. Indeed, the Lockean parental duties can be performed, easily and often more professionally, by the organs of the Hegelian state, such as children's homes and "foster care" systems that are dominated by rules rather than by love.

The final Lockean principle is also negative: intergenerational family bonds deserve limited respect. These ties are not considered good in themselves. They are to be created and sustained only if and as long as they are mutually useful. In other words, adults can and should choose whether they will take care of their elderly parents or even of their children.

This sort of freedom is not yet firmly accepted. There is still a lingering sense of responsibility around both forward- and backward-looking intergenerational family relationships. However, some three hundred years after Locke sketched out this idea, a "me-centered" attitude has increasingly supplanted the traditional understanding of family relations.

For Christians, the Lockean view of families has some positive aspects. In particular, the emphasis on the equality of all individuals supports a fairer balance between men and women. Also, the treatment of children as future adults is an improvement on some even more adult-centric attitudes, for example considering children the property of their parents or treating them legally as almost nonpeople.

However, the balance is overwhelmingly negative. This idea that individual self-fulfillment should be preferred to family responsibilities is essentially anti-Christian. It is socially and psychologically incompatible with the Christian understanding that the participation in the family is a universal human vocation. Christians believe it is impossible to live a truly fulfilled life while ignoring family responsibilities. (Religious vocations are something of an exception, but, as Hegel understood, the Church is the family of God, which can supplant the family of blood.) More specifically, for Christians, who see the union of man and woman as central to God's plan for humanity, Locke's contractual understanding of marriage is basically inhuman. Set against the Catholic understanding of the family as a "domestic Church," a God-given sacred "place" for worship, love, and responsibility, Locke's

342   CHAPTER 9

calculating view of relationships looks almost diabolical. In addition, the Hegel-Locke separation of children from childhood and from the family is incompatible with any Christian society.

The Romantic Me-Culture

The cult of self-expression starts with the unquestioned belief that what is most important about me is exactly myself. I associate the cult with Rousseau, although, as with Hegelians and Lockeans, the intellectual association is approximate. Rousseau did not anticipate all the Romantic implications of his thought. Whatever the name given to this worldview, the founding principle is simple—my place before God and my relations with the rest of humanity, both in general and in the particular forms of my family or my society, are of interest only insofar as each of these relations helps me be my true self.

Self-expression can be seen as an extreme Lockean individualism. Certainly, a more individualistic approach to psychology is hard to imagine. However, the early proponents of this cult, the Romantics, emphasized the differences. They considered their interest in emotions and sensibility to be directly opposed to the cold calculations of Locke and especially to the utilitarians and other British empirical philosophers whom he inspired. The Romantic denigrated this worldview for its lack of feeling—for the natural world, for humankind, and for beauty of any sort. The expressive self is far from the rational or the utilitarian individual.

If the world were without sin, then the drive to be "my true self" would not undermine family responsibilities. On the contrary, since families are the God-given, natural, and primary "place" for the expression of love and commitment, true self-expression would naturally lead to strong family ties. However, in this sinful world, our desires, including our desire to find our real selves, are often not purely good. In practice, the obligations that come with membership in a family often appear to be impediments to self-discovery and self-development. Rousseau set a pertinent example by placing his own five children in a foundling home because he believed that the presence of illegitimate children would have damaged his own self-expression as a writer and as the lover of an unmarried woman.

Romantic literary heroes—grand, self-important, willful, passionate, and sensitive—exemplify the cult of self-expression. Again, this sort of heroism is, in theory or in a sinless world, not contrary to a Christian life. True self-discovery and self-expression help create saintly families. For example, a parent can show Christian heroism in the devotion to a child under trying circumstances. However, sanctity requires the self-work to be Spirit-guided and rightly ordered morally. In contrast, the Romantic quest for authentic self-expression is generally thought to move the hero beyond all externally imposed morality. The Romantic hero is more likely to discard than to cherish family ties.[67]

In the cult of self-expression, love is always a tremendous emotional experience. This idea, in its purest, sinless form, can easily be reconciled to the Christian ideal of love as the mutual total gift of the self to the other. Indeed, Christians should try to be romantic in their love; they should try to tie their families together with a love that is far nobler than mere social bonds of propriety and tradition, let alone than utilitarian bonds of mutual advantage. Once again, however, life and love are never pure. Sin always threatens to turn self-expression away from the good. Passionate romantic love, which blinds the lovers to their sacred commitments, all too often damages or even destroys families.

The cult of self-expression has been extended to children. They too are expected to find themselves, and society has created a panoply of tools to help them. A huge literature explores their view of the world, their appropriate development, and their dysfunctions. Trained experts and profitable businesses provide them with age-appropriate toys, books, games, music, activities, psychotherapy, and behavior-modifying drugs. For children, far more than for adults, self-expression is hostile to the agendas of Hegel and Locke. The freely expressive child clings to his or her family, not to society or the State. The free child has little desire for contractual autonomy. This child flourishes in childish activities, not in premature adulthood.

Christians can look with some bemusement on this conflict between modern strands of thinking, but they should appreciate, and learn from, the modern self-expressive cult's interest in child psychology. The sympathetic study of children has led to serious attempts to use love rather than discipline as the first principle of child-rearing. This is a significant cultural, as well as psychological, advance. Still, Christians should be wary of the expressivist cult's

---

67. Taylor, *Sources of the Self* provides a good overview of this development.

unwillingness to recognize children's inevitable serious moral struggles. Children should be happy, as the cult demands, but like adults, they can only be truly happy if their sinful desires are not satisfied. More than adults, they require instruction, example, and discipline to learn discernment and self-control. Self-expression is valuable, especially for children, but it also has quite severe limitations, also especially for children.

More generally, Catholics should admit that the Romantic quest for passion and intense emotion and its craving for deep self-knowledge present a helpful challenge to any lukewarm, timid, or rule-bound approach to family life. However, there is a discord that should never be forgotten. In the presence of sin, the authentic good cannot be found by simple introspection and cannot be expressed as mere willfulness.

This chapter is already too long, so I leave the more detailed Catholic answer to these modern views, and the explanation of the specific family teachings, to the next one.

CHAPTER 10

The Human Family—II

THE PREVIOUS CHAPTER ENDED with a discussion of how the family is understood in three sometimes overlapping and sometimes contradictory modern visions of society—the Hegelian idea of the overwhelming State, the Lockean notion of voluntary contracts made by free adults, and the Romantic cult of self-expression's search for every individual's true and authentic self. Each of these visions has some truth and has encouraged some good, but none of them is fully or fundamentally compatible with Catholic family teaching. In this chapter, I try to explain that teaching, emphasizing its social context and implications and showing its response to the claims of these three intellectual and spiritual antagonists.

The Catholic Response

I pointed out at the beginning of the previous chapter that the Catholic Church has been resoundingly defeated in every battle of the "culture war" over family matters. Even for most mass-attending Catholics, the Church's teaching (often dismissively referred to as its "official" teaching) looks out of touch and at least faintly ridiculous. This magisterial failure is regrettable, but it was probably inevitable. As I explained, the Catholic view of the family is basically opposed to all three of the most powerful modern approaches to family life. The Church cannot easily prevail against so many strong enemies. However, there is virtue in trying, so in this chapter I expound the teaching in terms that just might appeal to some of my contemporaries.

My initial approach is somewhat different from that used in other chapters. I sketch out a dialogue, citing few official documents. The rhetorical choice is based on experience and urgency. Experience has taught me that, by the time someone is ready to be impressed by papal wisdom verbatim, he or she is already almost persuaded of the rightness of Catholic family teaching. Before then, even the idea of offering magisterial quotes is likely to be alienating. The urgency comes from the need to insert family matters into the center of the Catholic Social Teaching. Without strong social support for the family, the rest of the teaching will be vain. Benedict XVI was clear: "It is thus becoming a social and even economic necessity once more to hold up to future generations the beauty of marriage and the family."[1]

The dialogue of apologetic evangelization can be imagined as taking place on a transatlantic flight. The friendly man in the seat next to me soon finds out that I am something of a Catholic apologist. He asks me, whether out of polite curiosity or in sneering mockery, to explain the teachings that sound too weird for any sane and intelligent person to take seriously. I start, as all discussions of Christian teaching should, by talking about love. I explain to my seatmate that the Christian understanding of love is almost as different from the fluid, Romantic, and passionate love of the authentic romantic self as it is from the Lockean individual's reversible contractual arrangements. Christian love is essentially supernatural. Its highest expression is the ultimate Christian mystery, the trinitarian revelation that God is love. Throughout the created world—the heavens and the earth, the plants and the animals—love is the divine force that offers its whole self to sustain fruitful unity, as the Father and Son offer themselves to each other to sustain the unity of the fruitful Spirit. Pagan fertility myths are veiled appreciations of this cosmic and supercosmic love, as is the cosmology of the ancient Greek philosopher Empedocles, who considered love to be one of the two driving forces of the universe, along with strife. Human love can only be understood fully if it is considered an expression or representation of this transcendental love.

This human representation or expression is almost never perfect, because sin mars almost all human relations. "Almost?" says my new friend. Indeed, I explain, human history does offer two examples of perfect love: the love of Jesus Christ for all humanity and the love of his mother Mary for Jesus and for all those whom Jesus loves.

---

1. Benedict XVI, Encyclical Letter *Caritas in Veritate* (June 29, 2009), 44.

THE HUMAN FAMILY—II   347

Without pausing to discuss how such perfect love works in practice, I move to the relevant point for families—both of the exceptions to love's imperfection are essentially familial. Mary loves her son and Jesus calls his true followers his real family.[2] Of course, I say, both admitting and explaining, both these models of perfect love are quite distant from the intense romantic-sexual affection that modern people usually assume is the standard type of love.

Indeed, the explanation is necessary because the cosmic and theological idea of love is so deeply countercultural that most people struggle to understand, let alone to accept, the idea that true love is quite different from passion. On our flight, perhaps the closeness to the heavens will encourage sympathy. If so, if the higher idea of love can be absorbed, then my new friend will accept my description of the conventional, passionate notion—it is small, dangerous, and selfish. It is small because it relies only on feelings, spurning reason, faith, and so much of what is noble in human nature. It is dangerous in two ways, socially because it rejects obligations and morally because it avoids all judgments of right and wrong. It is selfish because passion—whether for a person, a pet, a sports team, or a plate of pasta—has almost nothing to do with the recipient's response.

The Christian has something much better to offer: love as total gift of self. In true love, everything is given up for the sake of the beloved. At this point, I might venture a quotation from Benedict XVI. "Love is . . . a journey, an ongoing exodus out of the closed inward-looking self toward its liberation through self-giving, and thus toward authentic self-discovery and indeed the discovery of God."[3] The ultimate human expression of that love is not found in any romantic novel but in one innocent man's willing acceptance of his crucifixion for the sake of all humanity, that their sins be forgiven. If the plane trip is especially long, I might explain how this Christian love is perfectly, if mysteriously, expressed in the love of Christ for his spotless bride, the Church, but I fear that might confuse more than illume my nonbelieving fellow passenger. More promising is an explanation of the Christian belief that human beings are designed to express this self-offering love in all that they do, not merely in a narrowly defined "love life." Selfless love of the truth leads people to search for knowledge, selfless love of creation

---

2.   cf. Mt 12:47–50.

3.   Benedict XVI, Encyclical Letter *Deus Caritas Est* (December 25, 2005), 6.

helps them be better stewards of creation (I might say "of the environment" to avoid distractions), and selfless love of other people leads them not only into a couple bound by sexual passions but into all sorts of friendship and communities.

This preamble about love slides nicely into the observation that our physical bodies are designed for a particular sort of love. Bodies are not arranged to directly express the love of knowledge, of creation, or indeed of God—those are matters for soul, intellect, and spirit. Rather, the various ages and types of bodies—weak and strong, old and young, male and female—are made to flourish in the primordial community of the family. The love of men and women is expressed in a desire for each other that naturally leads to children. Children in their emotional neediness, bodily weakness, and intellectual immaturity crave the physical love, psychological care, and spiritual guidance of their parents. At the other end of life, old people need family members' loving physical care.

These characteristics of the various stages of life and of the two sexes, I explain to my slightly incredulous new friend, are not accidents of evolution. They are there by divine design. They are gifts from God that allow and encourage each person to give and to receive love in families. Love is always selfless. In families, it is self-giving and is offered and received at least from conception until death. "At least?," I am asked. Comforted that he is paying attention, I point out that Catholics believe that through the communion of saints the ties of familial love can extend past the grave or crematorium. However, I assure him that he does not have to understand all the details of the Catholic's cosmic and holy understanding of love.

This putative airplane discussion about love is certainly not the only way to introduce the Church's family teaching. My choice was directed at what I believe is the most common misconception, the small-minded view of love promoted by the cult of self-expression. The other two ideologies have their own confusions about love.

If I were flying next to an avowed Hegelian, I would have to deal with the master's belief that, although the voluntary unity of loving families was an advance over the forced unity based only on tradition and duty, the highest unity of being enfolded into the protective and domineering State would eventually transcend all sorts of intrafamily love. To counter that image, I would probably start with the relationship of truth and freedom, concluding that the family is a "place" where people can be truly free to be themselves, because marriage and family "correspond to the deepest needs and dignity of the person."[4] In contrast, the combination of the impersonal all-encompassing State with the isolated individuals who are under its sway can offer only slavery dressed up as a willful and often destructive liberty.

Proud and self-conscious Hegelians are scarce, despite the strongly Hegelian trends in modern history, including developments of family life. Believers in Lockean contractual individualism are much more common. If my seatmate were one of them, I would start with an explanation of how a community based on generosity is a better model of human relations than is one based the agreement of selfish people to get along for the sake of having fun, being happy, or protecting property. I would continue by pointing out the futility of thinking of my own self or my body as my property, since I am designed, whether by God or by some other higher force, to offer my self, not to possess it. I would suggest, politely but firmly, that it is dangerous nonsense to think the solitary life is somehow more essential or natural than is life built around loving mutual concern, between men and women and between adults and children. This anti-Lockean introduction would end with the familiar conclusion: that the family, the ultimate community, is the right "place" for human flourishing.

Whichever approach is chosen, sin has to be the next topic. I can easily warm to the topic, since sin lies behind all the problems of families. If people did not have trouble loving truly, living freely, or sharing their lives generously, then there would be no need for Catholic family teaching. Sin distorts judgment, hardens hearts, and leads people away from their created and redeemed nature. Sin is alluring, as Adam and Eve first discovered. It disguises itself as virtue, common sense, or reasonable compromise. It can be identified and fought against, but success in that battle requires serious attention and more than a touch of divine grace. My interlocutor might not be comfortable with all this. Sin may seem to him like an idea from long ago and God's grace an incomprehensible phrase from an old novel he once started but never finished. In response to his unease, I would ask him to think about his own experiences. Usually, he will admit that, if sin is as I say it is, then it not only exists but flourishes.

---

4. Benedict XVI, *Caritas in Veritate*, 44.

Grace is much more difficult for the secular mindset to understand, but that debate can be put off until another journey.

For this one, the next step in the evangelical explanation is to point out that sin cannot be abolished in family life. Even if, as Catholics believe, we are helped by divine grace, that grace will sometimes be refused. We can and do have helpful rules and customs about physical sexual relations, gender, and generations, but the rules will never be followed fully, by everyone, and from the heart. The family teaching, like all of the Catholic Social Teaching, will always be in some ways a counsel of imperfection. We can ask for families to be rightly ordered and can expect, given the right social environment, that they mostly will be. We cannot, however, hope that all families will always be good. One part of the Catholic family teaching is the obligation to show tender and active mercy to bad families, which can take such apparently harsh forms as punishing evil behavior and breaking up families to remove innocent people from harm's way.

This last point is important, because, as my seatmate will probably remind me, Catholic family teaching is frequently associated with the unquestioned acceptance of many sorts of cruelty. He might dimly recall tales of priests who told abused wives and children to accept their suffering humbly. He is unlikely to cite a biblical passage, but the priests in question could have quoted Paul who takes his own suffering as a way to make Christ's passion complete.[5] It is not exactly a cultural coincidence that women, rather than men, were expected to bear the brunt of this redemptive suffering.

I will not debate this issue on the flight, but the criticism of past Catholic practice is probably excessive. Certainly, such cruelty has not been the official teaching for many centuries. The Council of Trent in 1563 declared "for many causes, a separation may take place between husband and wife, in regard of bed, or in regard of cohabitation, for a determinate or for an indeterminate period."[6] Three centuries later, Leo XIII was more precise. "When, indeed, matters have come to such a pitch that it seems impossible for them to live together any longer, then the Church allows them to live apart . . . yet she never ceases to endeavor to bring about a reconciliation, and never despairs of doing so."[7]

---

5.   Col 1:24.

6.   Council of Trent. *The Canons and Decrees of the Sacred and Oecumenical Council of Trent.* J. Waterworth, ed. and trans. (London: Dolman, 1848), session 24, canon 8.

7.   Leo XIII, Encyclical Letter *Arcanum* (February 10, 1880), 41.

Unfortunately but inevitably, pastoral practice was not always in accord with the kindly intention of such declarations. I too have heard stories of priests sending abused wives back to their violently cruel husbands simply because the marriage vows supposedly required such sacrifices. However, if my companion insists on discussing the matter, I will graciously admit that, as is so often the case, the Church has learned from what is best in modern ways (or in this case perhaps recovered some lost wisdom). The good of the family remains paramount and humility in the face of suffering is still praised, but Christian counselors now understand that to tolerate sin is to encourage it and that humility does not excuse the failure to protect the most vulnerable members of families. Catholic teaching and most Catholic teachers now fully recognize that the family's good is sometimes best served by the exclusion of a harmful spouse or the placement of an abused child in a safer home.

Once the classic Christian picture has been drawn—families as part of God's wonderful plan, families as homes of virtue, families as stained by sin—I can move on to attack two modern ideas: the fluidity of roles within families and the absolute equality of all of these family roles. In truth, I will say, family roles are not actually fluid. Each has its own expected offering of joyous love and, in this sinful world, its own demands of sometimes hard duty. Husbands, wives, fathers, mothers, young children, adult children, grandparents, cousins, courting young adults, widows, and widowers—each family position comes with responsibilities, opportunities, limits, and potentials. The roles are not equal. There is always a hierarchy of parents over young children, for example, and—this part is tricky—a mutual hierarchy of men and women. These roles vary over time and among societies. Catholic family teaching attempts to identify some universal elements and then to articulate what those elements imply in the harsh contemporary world of abortion, contraception, divorce, and quasi-free love, as well as in the expressive modern world in which feelings are highly honored.

If my seatmate is alert, he will now bring up the most serious complaint about the teaching, the same reproach that I mentioned in introducing the entire Social Teaching—many of the counsels seem to have changed along with the standard practices of the rest of the world. I just mentioned the Church's more understanding approach to marital separation and the stronger concern for the psychological welfare of

children. I have hinted at the deeper appreciation of emotional closeness and spiritual flourishing in marriage and family life, for example
Leo XIII's already mentioned call for spouses "to have such feelings
for one another as to cherish always very great mutual love."[8] More
relevant to the airplane discussion is the evolution in the understanding of the position of women in families and societies. As late as 1930,
when Pius XI fulminated that for women to throw off "the burdensome duties properly belonging to a wife as companion and mother,"
the "burdensome" was meant to be obviously ironic. To him, such
behavior was not a true emancipation but a "debasing of the womanly
character and the dignity of motherhood."[9] The same pope expected
the horror of the communist approach to women to be self-evident.
In that system, "[s]he is withdrawn from the family and the care of her
children, to be thrust instead into public life and collective production
under the same conditions as man."[10] In direct opposition to this mindset, the past three popes have enthusiastically endorsed equal legal status of the sexes, equal educational and professional opportunities, and
the abandonment "once and for all" of "the forms of subordination that
have tragically marked the history of women."[11]

Considering this background of shifting teaching, my companion
might ask why he should take seriously any remaining outdated standards and rules. The Church, he could declare, has merely stalled.
Sooner or later, it will adopt modern standards on sexual behavior,
control of education, gender issues, contraception, and divorce.
Rather than wasting time and effort trying to swallow the current
unpalatable teaching, should he not simply ignore them while waiting for the Magisterium to find whatever high-minded arguments
it wants to concoct a tastier revision? He may even have read news
reports about bishops, or even the pope, seemingly preparing to
modernize the teaching.

I hope that this book has suggested the answer to this question.
Yes, the Church has learned from what is good in the modern world,

---

8. Leo XIII, *Arcanum*, 11. John M. Haas, "The Contemporary World," in Glenn Olsen, ed.,
Christian Marriage: A Historical Study (New York: Crossroad, 2001), 332–59, provides a helpful
summary of the magisterial and theological use and misuse of personalist psychology in discussing the goods, "meaning" and ends of marriage.

9. Pius XI, Encyclical Letter *Casti Connubii* (December 31, 1930), 74–75.

10. Pius XI, Encyclical Letter *Divini Redemptoris* (March 19, 1937), 11.

11. Francis, *Address to Participants in the General Assembly of the Pontifical Academy for Life*
(October 5, 2017), 3.

including the good aspects of modern family life. Yes, the modern challenges have helped clarify the distinction between the abiding truth and the imperfections of its expression in any society. No, none of the current teachings amount to a simple acceptance of contemporary mores. No, the Catholic understanding of the fundamental, underlying truth does not change, even as the doctrine is refined and purified and as the actual counsels of imperfection shift along with the dominant imperfections of families. Few bishops and no popes want to change the doctrine. At most, they want to present it in a more inviting way.

My seatmate may find it difficult to believe that the truth about families is inscribed in human nature. After all, there have been so many great changes in the actual look and feel of families and all their members. Women have indeed been liberated, to use a partially apt modern word. Their relations with men and children have altered significantly. However, I will explain that no novelties, whether welcome or not, can affect the fundamental truths, starting with the reality that all women are made by God in the model of Mary and Eve. They are constituted to offer spousal love, maternal love, and tender personal love to all in need. There are corresponding descriptions of the unchanging sexual nature of men and of children's dependence on and exuberant affection for their parents. As a result of these unchangeable truths about the different familial aspects of human nature, the Church's family teaching has probably changed less than have most other parts of the Social Teaching. I can assure my seatmate that the constancy will continue, because human nature does not change. The family teaching will always declare that the good of families requires respect for the unchanging nature of each of their members.

Still, I will admit, the flux in social roles has challenged and still challenges the Church. As the family revolution took form, the Magisterium has indeed refined its expressions and changed both some of its emphases and some of its practical counsel. This, I can point out to my skeptical companion, is a virtue. An evolving authority is much better than a stale one or than no authority at all. Individual families need relevant help because they are often too weak and confused to find their own ethical way without guidance and God's grace. The Catholic Church has an obligation to offer that grace in its sacraments and to expound, as best it can, God's laws in its

354   CHAPTER 10

grace-filled teaching. Whatever the current failings and confusions, the morally anchored Church can be an especially valuable guide for families in a society that has lost its moral compass.

The Catholic Response in More Detail

To start to explain where all this talk of nature and roles leads, I usually turn to children, the central concern of Catholic family teaching. For every parent and for the whole society, no activity is more important than nurturing children in body, mind, and soul. In this judgment, the Church follows Jesus, who blessed little children, saying that the kingdom of heaven belongs to them and that, "Whoever welcomes one such child in my name welcomes me."[12] Children are not merely the channel through which love and life extend through time. They are also theological models, because they exemplify the unconditional dependence, innocence, and acceptance shown by Jesus himself, the humble Son of the Father. Christians must treasure children and learn from them.

The contrast of the Christian view of children with the three modern theories of family life could hardly be sharper. Where Locke and his followers see children as incomplete individuals in need of intense training and development, Christians see infinitely valuable and already complete gifts from God, treasures entrusted to inevitably incompletely trustworthy parents. These children need loving support and supervision to flourish, but with this loving aid their God-given personalities and talents will basically develop on their own.

The Hegelian idea that children should be conformed to the realities of the world as soon and as extensively as possible through the wisdom of the State is rejected, on two counts. First, there is no hurry for children to gain worldly wisdom, since their innocence makes them powerful witnesses to the God-given beauty of being and their delight at the things of this world makes them embodied and ensouled statements of faith that our wicked valley of tears is not the final word in the human condition. Second, only families, not the state, can provide what children need most—the loving, personal mediation of their experiences of the world, from the unspeakably terrible to the unspeakably wonderful. The state, along with the many institutions of civil society, can help parents in many ways, not

---

12.   cf. Mt 19:14; Mt 18:5.

least in schooling and health care, but child-rearing is a fine example of subsidiarity. It is best done at the lowest, most intimate level of the family.

When it comes to romantic self-expression, the conversation is more delicate. In words, the expressivists are often enthusiastic about children. However, in deeds, the interest is often selfish. The young people are treated largely as objects of adult passions, which are expressed if and when it suits the adults in question. Christians, in contrast, understand that children do not thrive on sentiment. Rather, they need the sometimes-painful sacrificial love that always looks toward the future and toward eternity. Also, while the creed of self-expression has little recognition of the dangerous lure of sin for children, Christian childrearing is shot through with the loving discipline needed to train children to acquire the habits of virtue and the horror of sin.

The conclusion of my little speech is that Catholic family teaching aims to put children first. It promotes loving, disciplined, and morally and spiritually aware families in which children can live their lives to the fullest. In such families, the young are protected and the old, who should cherish and respect children, are themselves cherished and respected. These families are faithful in adversity. Sexuality is kept in its proper place. The last is particularly relevant to any presentation of the teaching, since within the family teaching the sexual teachings are the most opposed to the conventional wisdom of contemporary culture. I divide the main teachings into six parts, but the divisions are somewhat arbitrary. The Church has a single, unified ideal of a good family.

At this point in the chapter I am abandoning the imagined dialogue. I have not yet been on a flight long enough, or perhaps I have not yet found the right words, to persuade a skeptic that the Church has enough to offer to be worth discussing many of the details. I fear the rest of this chapter may be no more than a sermon for the already, or almost, converted.

Mothers and Fathers

Men and women differ in many ways. Until a few years ago, even firm secularists who denied the divine origin and spiritual meaning

356   CHAPTER 10

of sexual distinctions were willing to admit that there are nonphysical as well as physical differences between men and women. After that agreement, though, there was still much space for argument. Over the past century, the emancipation of women and, to a much lesser extent, the correlated "domestication" of men, have demonstrated that the two sexes are more alike in many ways than was widely assumed (by men, at least) in every premodern society, but how much more alike is still disputed.

Firm secularists today (and some Christians) are likely to take an extreme view, treating all binary men-women distinctions, including biological ones, as arbitrary cultural constructions. As Francis points out, this "ideology of gender . . . envisages a society without sexual differences, thereby eliminating the anthropological basis of the family."[13] Since, as Francis says, this approach denies that most basic anthropological fact about families, that a child is conceived by the union of mother and father and born from the body of his mother, it does not easily fit into a realistic discussion of sexual differences. In trying to understand the gains and limits of the modern experiment of sexual nondifferentiation, a more humble starting place is both more realistic and more helpful. It is fair to say that mothers and fathers are different, but that it is not yet clear what gender-based familial and social distinctions actually reflect or express the specific sexual natures of men and women.

The starting position of Catholics remains that of John Paul II. In his 1995 *Letter to Women*, he welcomed the "liberation" of women and apologized for the role of Christians in the "cultural conditioning which down the centuries have shaped ways of thinking and acting."[14] He observed that the damage has been great. "Women's dignity has often been unacknowledged and their prerogatives misrepresented; they have often been relegated to the margins of society and even reduced to servitude. This has prevented women from truly being themselves and it has resulted in a spiritual impoverishment of humanity."[15] However, the recognition of and recovery from past injustice should not lead to what might be considered the opposite error, refusing to respect what John Paul II had earlier called "the specific diversity and personal

---

13.   Francis, Post-synodal Apostolic Exhortation *Amoris Laetitia* (March 19, 2016), 56.

14.   John Paul II, *Letter to Women* (June 29, 1995), 6, 3.

15.   John Paul II, *Letter to Women*, 3.

THE HUMAN FAMILY—II   357

originality of man and woman." Indeed, the pope then warned that women should not "appropriate to themselves male characteristics contrary to their own feminine 'originality.'"[16]

Much of this broad social debate has become tangential to the family teaching. Although in the not so distant past many Catholics would have judged total "sex-blindness" in educational and professional opportunity, for example, as be contrary to the good of mothers, children, and families, the reversal of that judgment is now well accepted. The denial and denigration of the *maternal* nature of women, however, is another matter. The Catholic family teaching rejects the argument that "parenting" is essentially "gender-neutral." This new claim has rapidly gained almost universal acceptance in Western societies, but it is a distortion of the truth. Mothers are indeed very different from fathers.

The mother's childbearing and suckling are physical signs of the distinctly feminine gift of maternal love. In her created and redeemed nature, a mother's orientation of body, heart, and soul— exemplified in Mary's love for Jesus—is pervaded by a deep and encompassing love. Fathers have their own love for their children, for all children and for all in need. Still, in the era when sexual differences were accepted, that is for all of history and in every society until recent decades, most people would have said that paternal love is less intense and immediate than is the maternal variety, just as it is less physical. Although much of the old conventional wisdom on the sexes has been shown false, the Church teaches that this part remains true.

Contrary to today's enlightened consensus, the ineradicable, ontological feminine disposition to love and nurture children, and by extension everyone in need of care, not only exists but is a divinely given wonder. In the words of Francis, "For the grandeur of women includes all the rights derived from their inalienable human dignity but also from their feminine genius, which is essential to society. Their specifically feminine abilities—motherhood in particular— also grant duties, because womanhood also entails a specific mission in this world, a mission that society needs to protect and preserve for the good of all."[17] That women are more naturally inclined to caring labor than men are is not an inconvenient fact. It is an essential

---

16.   John Paul II, Apostolic Letter *Mulieris Dignitatem* (August 15, 1988), 10.

17.   Francis, Post-Synodal Apostolic Exhortation *Amoris Laetitia*, 173.

sexual difference that any good society will treasure and develop.

In his own theological language, John Paul II summarized this appreciation and judgment.

> "Motherhood involves a special communion with the mystery of life, as it develops in the woman's womb. The mother is filled with wonder at this mystery of life, and 'understands' with unique intuition what is happening inside her. In the light of the 'beginning,' the mother accepts and loves as a person the child she is carrying in her womb. This unique contact with the new human being developing within her gives rise to an attitude toward human beings—not only toward her own child, but every human being—that profoundly marks the woman's personality. It is commonly thought that women are more capable than men of paying attention to another person and that motherhood develops this predisposition even more."[18]

This understanding of sexual differentiation would seem to imply that mothers, rather than fathers, should normally be the primary carers for their small children. This understanding also points to marriages in which wives take the lead over husbands in all sorts of familial and caring labor and to societies that support the domestic feminine vocation. It also points to "maternal" vocations for all women, whether or not they have children of their own.

What does this maternal nature of women imply in practice? In many ways John Paul II was the right person to ask, because he was enthralled by what he often referred to as the "genius of women," the "sensitivity for human beings in every circumstance."[19] At least through the first years of his papacy, he seemed to have had some clear ideas about the social implication of the feminine-maternal vocation. In one of his early encyclicals he said, "It will redound to the credit of society to make it possible for a mother . . . to devote herself to taking care of her children." To compel mothers to take up paid work is "wrong from the point of view of the good of society and of the family." The needed "social re-evaluation of the mother's role"[20] would take the concrete form of ensuring that fathers received

---

18. John Paul II, *Mulieris Dignitatem*, 18.

19. John Paul II, *Mulieris Dignitatem*, 30.

20. John Paul II, *Address to Scientists and Representatives of the United Nations University* (February 25, 1981), 19.

a sufficiently large reward from their own labor to raise a family. The judgment presumably reflected his experience in communist Poland, the pope's homeland, where the obligation of mothers to leave their young children for paid work was widely resented.

However, that 1981 discussion of the feminine role was severely criticized by some Western Catholics.[21] Perhaps in response, the later *Letter to Women* included not only much praise for the special feminine "genius" but also a secular-sounding call for "real equality in every area: equal pay for equal work, protection for working mothers, fairness in career advancements, equality of spouses with regard to family rights and the recognition of everything that is part of the rights and duties of citizens in a democratic State."[22] Some economists might argue that it is difficult to reconcile equal pay for equal work with the protection and promotion of the unpaid labor of motherhood, but others would counter that the tax and benefit system of modern welfare states would allow both goals to be reached.

In any case, by 1995 John Paul had clearly fallen well behind the times when he argued, perhaps a little awkwardly, that the complementary nature of the two sexes has social implications. "[A] certain diversity of roles is in no way prejudicial to women, provided that this diversity is not the result of an arbitrary imposition, but is rather an expression of what is specific to being male and female."[23] His successors have repeated the message, falling even farther behind the times. Francis, for example, declared that "the utopia of the 'neuter' eliminates both human dignity in sexual distinctiveness and the personal nature of the generation of new life."[24] By admitting the existence of such socially meaningful differences, the Catholic Church stands well outside of the current Western secular consensus.

It is too early for a final judgment of every aspect of contemporary gender neutrality, but it is already clear, painfully so, that excessive biological reductionism ends up degrading the position of women in society. The sexual abuse of women, with varying degrees of social approval, is hardly a new manifestation of fallen human nature, especially fallen male nature, but the flourishing of fornication, pornography, and violence against women in the midst of

---

21.   See the discussion in Kenneth R. Himes, *Modern Catholic Social Teaching: Commentaries & Interpretations* (Washington, D.C.: Georgetown University Press, 2004).

22.   John Paul II, *Letter to Women*, 4.

23.   John Paul II, *Letter to Women*, 11.

24.   Francis, *Address to the Pontifical Academy for Life*, 3.

the contemporary liberation of women may seem anomalous. The simultaneous social respect for and biological denigration of women is not, however, necessarily contradictory. If the only relevant distinction between the sexes is biological, then men are free to view women as women—insofar as they are women and not fellow citizens, coworkers, or family members—as merely biological objects. This sexual objectification cannot logically be condemned as "objectively disordered" (as the *Catechism* says of "deep-seated homosexual tendencies"[25]), because it is a simply biological response to the stimuli provided by a merely biological difference. Since, however, sexual differences actually do extend to the whole person, as varying reflections of the divine in the human, the biological approach to sexual desire is indeed intrinsically disordered.

John Paul II understood that the Catholic family teaching's respectful approach to everything feminine precludes treating women as sexual objects, noting that modern societies had not come to the end of this "long and degrading history . . . of violence against women in the area of sexuality." He authoritatively condemned the distinctly modern threats to female dignity: "the widespread hedonistic and commercial culture which encourages the systematic exploitation of sexuality and corrupts even very young girls into letting their bodies be used for profit."[26]

In the succeeding decades, the professional equality of women has advanced steadily. More recently, there have been significant efforts to restrain sexual power games that degrade women in the workplace. However, the exploitative "hedonistic and commercial culture" remains as strong as ever, and Francis, as I mentioned, has called for an end to "[t]he forms of subordination that have tragically marked the history of women."[27]

In one crucial aspect, the contemporary crude social-biological logic really is inconsistent. Although Christians understand that nothing feminine should or even can be separated from the essential feminine role of carrying new life, modern societies give little respect to this distinctly feminine biological vocation. As far as fertility is concerned, the prime sexual responsibility for women is usually held to be avoiding pregnancy by using effective contraception. In

---

25. *Catechism of the Catholic Church*, 2358.

26. John Paul II, *Letter to Women*, 5.

27. Francis, *Address to the Pontifical Academy for Life*, 3.

THE HUMAN FAMILY—II   361

effect, in respect to sexual desire and activity, women are supposed
to accept a biological interpretation of their nature, a distinctly mas-
culine biological interpretation, but in respect to childbearing they
are expected to fight against what would seem to be indisputable
biological reality. From John Paul II onward, the Church has been
eloquent in condemning this double standard of femininity, which
springs from "that persistent mentality which considers the human
being not as a person but as a thing, as an object of trade, at the service of selfish interest and mere pleasure."[28]

Seuxal Relations in Their Proper Place

Both attacks on and defenses of Catholic sexual teaching are now
conducted almost exclusively in the domain of Locke—the good or
the happiness of the individuals involved. It is not surprising that
the attackers are imbued with individualism, but it is disappointing
that so many defenders argue on the same terrain. They rarely bring
families and societies into discussions of sexual activity. They write
as if they believe that sex is essentially a private matter for the people concerned. They are essentially wrong. Physical sexual relations,
contraception, marriage, adultery, and divorce are all social as well
as personal, because they all have profound implications on all of a
society's children, potential and actual. Any community must take an
interest in its future, so it necessarily has a legitimate and profound
interest in its members' sexual activity. The Church's teaching reflects
and responds to the intimate tie between the sexual life and the life of
families and society. The sexual teaching is intimately related to the
family teaching and is inherently part of the Social Teaching.

The core principles of the family teaching on sexual activity could
hardly be simpler. All relevant social customs and legal rules that by
their nature support children-oriented families are good. In practice,
this means that society should encourage marriage to be what it is
by nature—"an interior requirement of the covenant of conjugal love
which is publicly affirmed as unique and exclusive, in order to live in
complete fidelity to the plan of God, the Creator."[29] Covenantal love
is a lifelong, indeed an intergenerational, commitment to children,
a commitment that is central to Christian marriage. The faithful

---

28.   John Paul II, Apostolic Exhortation *Familiaris Consortio* (November 22, 1981), 24.

29.   John Paul II, *Familiaris Consortio*, 11.

monogamy of that most noble conception of marriage is in accord with created and redeemed human nature. It is also, with the help of God's grace, achievable by people in their fallen nature.

Conversely, all sexual customs and rules that by their nature undermine the good of families are bad. In practice, the most obvious bad customs and rules are those that permit or encourage any sort of sexual intimacy outside of marriage. Until about a century ago, extramarital sexual relations hardly needed condemnation in the lands of what used to be Christendom. Nearly everyone, including most of the very many people who in fact engaged in such socially destructive behavior, would have assumed its essential wrongness. Even when divorce, polygamy, concubinage, or prostitution were tolerated or endorsed, quite clear lines divided responsible and family-oriented sexual relations from irresponsible sexual behavior. In post-Christian cultures, all such boundaries have been blurred or erased. As a result of this "new thing," I do need to explain the damage to children and to society caused by violations of the principles of Christian marriage.

The damage from adultery is clear and immediate. The breaking of the vow of sexual fidelity directly undermines the adulterer's commitment to the family. He or she deprives the other actual or potential parent of the unique offering of body and soul, a deprivation that soils the mutual gift of selves that provides children with united and nurturing parents. Sexual relations between unmarried nonparents also damages the lives of children, although not as directly as adultery. The problem is that any willful and enthusiastic separation of sexual activity from the public and lasting commitment of marriage is implicitly disrespectful to children and families. To endorse that separation, as all post-Christian societies do, is to treat child-oriented marriage as just one sexual option among many. This "multiple choice" approach to sexual intimacy denigrates or even denies its inherent procreative meaning. In relegating children to the status of optional extras in sex, the social endorsement of nonmarital sexual activity expresses a moral judgment: that the good of a couple's commitment to children is less important than is the good of the search for romantic and physical sexual satisfaction.

The combination of divorce and remarriage is not simply opposed to the direct command of Jesus.[30] It is also antifamily and antichildren,

---

30. Mt 19:1–9.

even when the break-up of one couple eventually leads to the creation of another, possibly quite loving family. The disrespect of the initial bond of an actually or potentially childbearing couple destroys more than any new childbearing couple can create. Theologically, it destroys the sacramental tie that Paul identifies as the human embodiment of the mutual love of Christ and his Church.[31] Socially, it destroys the expectation of parental trust, commitment, and sacrifice that are essential to the nurture of psychologically secure children. The freedom to de-partner and re-partner deprives children of the nurturing experience of growing up in an environment oriented primarily to their welfare.

I wish it were not necessary to discuss the antichildren and antisocial nature of homosexual acts and relationships, let alone of the transsexual denial of physical reality. However, what were once almost universally considered moral and social problems are now generally treated as healthy manifestations of social, psychological, and physical diversity, so something must be said. In the family teaching, the argument against these sexual practices is the same as the argument against other types of extramarital sexual relation. Whatever the moral evaluation of same-sex attraction, same-sex erotic encounters, and gender dysphoria may be—the magisterial teaching is nuanced—it would remain true that the social approval of many sorts of sexual relations that cannot, by their nature, have the potential to produce children devalues responsible procreative love by reducing it to one alternative among many. The social endorsement of any "alternative lifestyles" effectively classifies families-with-children as nothing more than an ethically neutral "lifestyle choice." The vital social role of the people who create and nurture the community's future should be celebrated, not implicitly denigrated.

Contraception and Nature

By the standard of children-first family life, artificial contraception is at best suspect. There is an unavoidable antichildren tint to the desire for sexual relations without any possibility of pregnancy. The Catholic Church teaches that artificial contraception is worse than suspect. It is wrong. This judgment, widely dismissed as senseless and ridiculous, is actually good and beautiful. Conversely, artificial

---

31.   Eph 5:31–32.

contraception, widely accepted as a gift to women and to society, is actually bad for society as well as for the couples who use it. I will try to explain from the perspective of Catholic family teaching.

It is obviously true that men and women rarely or never have sexual intercourse solely for the purpose of procreation. Over the centuries, a fair number of Christian moralists, including some Catholics, have regretted this fact. At the extreme, some have treated the sexual act itself as an impure act that is unfortunately necessary for the continuation of humanity. The act's pleasure, they say, should be minimized and regretted. With slightly more moderation, some have condemned all erotic activity that primarily aims at physical pleasure or even at what might be called emotional closeness. The Second Vatican Council firmly condemned all such tendencies, endorsing the "actions within marriage by which the couple are united intimately and chastely" as "noble and worthy."[32] A few years later, Paul VI reiterated this appreciation of the goodness inherent to physical sexual love. The "uniting [of] husband and wife in the closest intimacy" gives the sexual act a "unitive significance."[33]

However, union can only be truly "signified" when the act is rightly ordered morally. Since children are supposed to come first in the ordering of society and in the life of couples, the act is disordered whenever the potential child-related aspect of sexual relations, the "procreative significance," is crushed.[34] Artificial contraception aims precisely at such a crushing of the procreative potential. This deviation from nature fundamentally warps the nature of each sexual act, the overall relations between husband and wife, and the vitality of society.

Indeed, artificial contraception causes at least as much social as psychological damage, because it attempts to remove the natural social context of sexual relations. Unlike potentially procreative sexual relations, contracepted intimacy has no possible implications for the future of the community. Such acts also escape the weight of the past, because the sterile union of bodies is not connected to the story of the generations. Cut loose from its social context, purpose, and responsibility, contracepted bodily union is entirely a matter of romantic love, lust, power, and the emotions of the moment.

---

32. Vatican Council II, Pastoral Constitution on the Church in the Modern World. *Gaudium et Spes* (December 7, 1965), 49.

33. Paul VI, Encyclical Letter *Humanae Vitae* (July 26, 1968), 12.

34. Paul VI, *Humanae Vitae*, 12.

Paul VI understood that the widespread use of artificial contraception would "open wide the way for marital infidelity and a general lowering of moral standards,"[35] weakening the basic familial intergenerational structures of all societies. He could have already seen the first flowerings of the new culture of sex without procreation in the enthusiasm of respectable adults for *Playboy* magazine, founded by Hugh Hefner in 1953. Or he conceivably could have seen an advance copy of the 1967 poem "Annus Mirabilis," although Philip Larkin did not publish this work until 1974. The poem declared that sexual intercourse was "discovered in 1963." The year is chosen for the rhyme scheme, but the reference is clearly to the then new contraceptive pill. This technology changed sexual intercourse from "A wrangle for the ring / A shame that started at sixteen / And spread to everything" to "A brilliant breaking of the bank / A quite unlosable game."[36]

Hefner, Larkin, and Paul VI all understood that the widespread use of effective contraceptive techniques both expressed and spread new ideas about what societies considered normal and natural sexual activity and attitudes. After shame connected with unrestrained sexual desire had been banished, first inside marriage and then in all relationships, responsible sex took on a new meaning. It was detached from marriage, children, and the social order.

This contraceptive understanding of sexuality has seduced most people in modern societies. It is certainly alluring to the modern sensibilities. For the expressive self, it brings pleasure and a certain sort of freedom. Detached from the societal moorings of parenthood, erotic intimacy can be emotionally rich for each person involved. For the protectors of the Hegelian state, contraception is prudent. It tends to separate courtship from familial considerations, encouraging people to live in neither their parents' families nor their own. Unmoored from these ties, the individual is freer (in the Hegelian sense) and more directly under the sway of the State. Contraception is also perfect for the Lockean adult individual who wants to treat his or her body as personal property, like a car or a house. From that perspective, an "unwanted pregnancy" is a violation of the fundamental right to control all the body's reproductive properties. Practical Hegelians and Lockeans also like the demystification of marriage created by contingent contracepted cohabitation and they approve

---

35. Paul VI, *Humanae Vitae*, 17.

36. Philip Larkin, "Annus Mirabilis" (1970).

of the ability of couples to precisely match the size of their families with their economic and emotional means.

However, appealing these arguments may be, the children-first principle is more powerful. The endorsement of antichildren sexual relations inevitably leads to an excessive elevation of the nonprocreative aspects of sexual relations and a corresponding denigration of the procreative implications. For those enthralled to the "contraceptive mentality," pregnancy is frequently something to be feared, even within marriage. It is hardly surprising that men and women with this attitude have so few children and often resort to abortion to avoid having them. Contraceptive sex is in practice an endorsement of children-last. As John Paul II explained, this conceptual devaluation of motherhood reflects a deep disorder in what his successor would call human ecology. The Polish pope wrote of child-resisting couples "refusing the spiritual riches of a new human life. The ultimate reason for these mentalities is the absence in people's hearts of God."[37]

I should perhaps note that my social criticism of contraception is different from the personalist argument against the practice made in John Paul II's "theology of the body."[38] He argued that the sexual act, which by nature is a total mutual gift of self, is necessarily a sinful lie when an integral part of that gift, its procreative potential, is intentionally withheld. Contraceptive sex may be accompanied by overwhelming feelings identified as love, but the ontological incompleteness of the act disqualifies the emotions that accompany it. My approach complements his. Socially as well as morally, artificial contraception violates the true nature of sexual relations.

Objectors to the teaching on contraception often argue that the children-first principle absurdly requires total sexual abstinence when the couple has no real procreative potential, whether because of age or some physical impediment. They are confused. The natural potential gift of reproduction is in fact present in any sexual act whenever that act's procreative potential is not thwarted. The moral and social nature of the act is the same, whether a pregnancy would be miraculous, unlikely, or extremely likely.

Thus, the entire procreative potential of the two bodies is given freely and fully in sexual relations during the infertile phase of a

---

37.   John Paul II, *Familiaris Consortio*, 30.

38.   John Paul II, *Man and Woman He Created Them: A Theology of the Body*, Michael Waldstein trans. and introduction (Boston, Mass.: Pauline Books, 2006 [1986]).

woman's monthly cycle. The voluntary limiting of sexual relations to this time of the month is a sort of contraception but does not involve an artificial or unnatural withholding of the procreative significance of sexual love. Indeed, rather than undermine the unitive significance of the sexual act, as contraceptive sex does, the attention to the cycle of fertility enhances this meaning. John Paul II explained, "The choice of the natural rhythms involves accepting the cycle of the person, that is the woman, and thereby accepting dialogue, reciprocal respect, shared responsibility, and self-control. To accept the cycle and to enter into dialogue means to recognize both the spiritual and corporal character of conjugal communion and to live personal love with its requirement of fidelity."[39] From the perspective of children first, the physical and spiritual discipline required for periodic abstinence from sexual relations is an expression of "true and authentic love,"[40] a sign of respect for the unbreakable tie of sexual relations with procreation.

There is an important proviso to this endorsement of natural family planning. If the mentality that motivates the timing of sexual relations is sufficiently distant from children-first thinking, then the attention to timing is basically a quasi-artificial method of contraception—maximizing the sex while minimizing the "danger" of pregnancy. John Paul II warned against the "reduction to mere biological regularity, detached from the 'order of nature,' that is, from the 'Creator's plan.'"[41] The purity of motivation can be tested easily. If the couple responds to an unexpected pregnancy as if the new life were an unmitigated disaster, then their married love is still more in tune with the current mores of society than with the right order of men, women, and children.

Divorce and Grace

I have already said that divorce is by its nature a violation of the children-first principle. In modern societies, in which as many of half the children do not spent all their minor years living with both parents,[42] that claim is widely considered to be retrograde, shock-

---

39.   John Paul II, *Familiaris Consortio*, 32.

40.   Paul VI, *Humanae Vitae*, 16.

41.   John Paul II, *General Audience* (August 29, 1984).

42.   A 2013 UK government study estimated that 47 percent of sixteen-year-olds were not living with both birth parents. UK Department for Work and Pensions, "Percentage of Children

ing, unrealistic, and cruel. Surely, it is said, it is better for parents who no longer love each other to separate than to "live a lie," which only surrounds the children with hostility and coldness. As is usually the case, there is some truth to the modern argument. Psychological studies suggest that the good of the children is not invariably served by the unity of the family. If one parent is dangerously insane, horribly brutal, or deeply harmful in some other way, any actual or potential children are better off without him (or, much more rarely, without her). As I mentioned earlier, the Church has responded to this evidence by taking a kinder view of separation. The separated parents can still show full respect for the principle of children first, as well as for the Catholic understanding of marriage as an unbreakable sexual and social bond, by not introducing quasi-parents into their children's lives.

However, there is much more fiction than fact in the argument that the couple's emotional satisfaction should take priority over the good of the children. Modern psychological evidence does not only suggest that separation is sometimes helpful to children. It strongly indicates that in most cases children do much better when their two parents raise them together.[43] This makes sense, especially if both parents are firmly committed to the children-first principle. Then the two parents can shape their married lives around the family, trying to ignore or overcome their own conflicts and coldness of heart. With that attitude, maternal and paternal love will be allowed to take precedence over the usually much more troubled sexual love of the parents, so the tensions of the parental romance will seem less important to both mother and father. Then the couple can better support the social order—which is always strengthened when love overcomes sin—by living out their own particular sacrifices of the heart and spirit for the sake of the common good of the family. With grace, married love can be an example of self-giving and forgiving, a benefit to the children involved and to the whole community. Of

---

Living with Both Birth Parents, by Age of Child and Household Income; and Estimated Happiness of Parental Relationships" (April 2013). In 2014, 47 percent of all children in the United States under seventeen lived in single-parent, no-parent or, blended-parent households, according to Pew Research Center, "Parenting in America: Outlook, Worries, Aspirations Are Strongly Linked to Financial Situation (December 17, 2015), 15.

43.   For a clear and balanced summary of the numerous clinical studies, see the relevant chapters of Alison Clarke-Stewart and Cornelia Brentano, *Divorce: Causes and Consequences* (New Haven, Conn.: Yale University Press, 2006). The articles on children in Robert E. Emery, ed., *Cultural Sociology of Divorce: An Encyclopedia* (Los Angeles: Sage, 2013) reinforce the conclusions.

course, in our sinful world, family harmony requires hard work. "There is no family that does not know how selfishness, discord, tension, and conflict violently attack and at times mortally wound its own communion."[44] No couple can show perfect love for each other or their children all the time, but the unshakable fidelity of a divorce-free marriage provides the best possible introduction into the good life, the life of total commitment to God and neighbor.

The essentially familial nature and social responsibility of marriage are not changed when there are no children or when all the children have grown up. Marriage is defined by the total mutual sexual gift of the couple, a gift that is by its nature fecund in the multiplication of love, only sometimes taking the form of the creation and nurturing of new life. Just as the procreative nature of sexual intercourse is not lost when it cannot end in pregnancy, the familial nature of marriage is not compromised by the lack of children. "[E]ven when procreation is not possible, conjugal life does not for this reason lose its value."[45] The husband and wife should love each other with the same sacrificial love, the same commitment to the future, and the same reliance on God as if children were actually present. The childless couple is still a social unit whose rupture damages the whole society's integrity. Divorce also violates the principle of children first, even if in practice no children are affected directly.

Love, Life, and Death

The children-first principle of the family teaching can be considered a special case of a general Christian moral rule—human life should be promoted and protected most fervently when it is weakest. This preferential option for the vulnerable is a social principle that should guide families through each member's life, from conception to natural death.

The vulnerable-first principle starts at the moment of conception. Abortion, which is directly antichild, antifamily, and antisocial, is a murderously direct violation, an "unspeakable crime."[46] An abortion kills a totally vulnerable and completely innocent person in absolute need of his or her parents' protection; it destroys the respect of father

---

44. John Paul II, *Familiaris Consortio*, 21.

45. John Paul II, *Familiaris Consortio*, 14.

46. Vatican Council II, *Gaudium et Spes*, 51.

and mother for each other's good intentions toward their children; and it supports a social intolerance for the difficulties of raising children. John Paul summoned up his strongest language to condemn it. "[B]y the authority which Christ conferred upon Peter and his Successors, in communion with the Bishops—who on various occasions have condemned abortion and who in the aforementioned consultation, albeit dispersed throughout the world, have shown unanimous agreement concerning this doctrine—I declare that direct abortion, that is, abortion willed as an end or as a means, always constitutes a grave moral disorder, since it is the deliberate killing of an innocent human being. This doctrine is based upon the natural law and upon the written Word of God, is transmitted by the Church's Tradition and taught by the ordinary and universal Magisterium."[47]

The vulnerable-first principle also promotes the care of the ill. Their weakness can teach the well how to be children of God, because the sick person's reliance on other people's generosity offers their carers the possibility of giving unselfish love. The principle should also guide the treatment of these facing the "mystery of death."[48] When these people prepare to meet their loving, judging, and merciful God, they should be surrounded by love, especially and ideally by the love of their family. As I discussed in chapter 8, euthanasia, which puts death in human hands, is an insult to the divine gift of life. John Paul II declared that "euthanasia is a grave violation of the law of God, since it is the deliberate and morally unacceptable killing of a human person."[49] It is also an insult to the family, because the decision to end a life before God decides it is over is a decision to spurn the last moments—whether years or hours—of the family's love. It is particularly shocking when the decision is made by family members, who should show sacrificial love from the very beginning until the very end of life.

Obviously, serious debates are required to determine the right care of the ill and the definition of euthanasia (to distinguish it from the withdrawal of heroic medical care). Those debates do not belong in this book, as they are not part of the Social Teaching, but the basic principles most certainly do. The strong members of any family, from the smallest household to the entire human race,

---

47. John Paul II, *Evangelium Vitae*, 62.

48. John Paul II, *Evangelium Vitae*, 64.

49. John Paul II, *Evangelium Vitae*, 65.

THE HUMAN FAMILY—II 371

should always try to help the weak, and no weakness can erase the God-given goodness of life. On the contrary, the weak can often teach the strong the beauty of humility and of dependence on the love of others, ultimately on the love of God. "For when I am weak, then I am strong."[50]

Parents and Children

To put the vulnerable-first principle in action is to demonstrate what John Paul II called the "spiritual fecundity of the family."[51] The family is indeed meant to be fertile in love. Created by God to foment mutual love, divine worship, and divinely inspired service, its mission is to spread God's love to every member, through the generations and into the whole world. With the grace of God, the family's unity in love—of mother and father, parents and children, past and future united in the present, this life looking toward the next—can create a true domestic church, offering to all within and without a foretaste of the eternal banquet of the kingdom of heaven.

Of course, sin wounds all families, so they never fully live up to their calling. Of course, the divine mission can be lost sight of in the daily worries about what to feed the fussy little one, what curfew to set for the teenager, and just how to treat Grandma now that she is losing her memory. However, the underlying reality of the high calling is quite real. The divine gifts to the family are substantial, as are the accompanying responsibilities.

The gifts start with procreation, when God allows a man and a woman to work with him in the creation of a new beloved person. Then there is the wonder of watching and helping a child grow up. The physical, intellectual, and moral development is the gift of God, the work of the child, and the responsibility of the parents and other family members. "[B]y begetting in love and for love a new person who has within himself or herself the vocation to growth and development, parents by that very fact take on the task of helping that person effectively to live a fully human life."[52] There is much to be said about both the wonder and the responsibility, but I mention only three particular aspects.

---

50. 2 Cor 12:10.

51. John Paul II, *Familiaris Consortio*, 41.

52. John Paul II, *Familiaris Consortio*, 36.

First, "the parents have been appointed by God Himself as the first and principal educators of their children."[53] The assertion of parental priority in education is aimed directly at the Hegelian claim that the wise state should take control of education, along, eventually, with all other child-related matters. As I hope I have made clear by now, this claim is false, even when the state deigns to delegate some tasks to the parents and even when the authorities do not actually mis-educate children or inculcate them with pernicious moral standards. The Hegelian claim is false because education should be an expression of love—of the world, God, learning, and beauty—and parents are uniquely able to show and spread love to their offspring.

Parents can delegate their children's formal schooling to public or private institutions, but they cannot abdicate their "unrenounceable authority" over their children's upbringing.[54] The responsibility is particularly grave for "[s]ex education, which is a basic right and duty of parents." The teaching on these intimate and morally important matters "must always be carried out under their attentive guidance."[55] From a Christian perspective, it is hard to think of a topic less suitable for the government than the procreative and unitive sexual relations of men and women. Conversely, from a Hegelian perspective, education in socially approved sexual behavior is far too important be left to mere parents.

The assignment of ultimate responsibility for education is a solid teaching. Unfortunately, the Magisterium does not actually provide much helpful guidance for either parents or local church authorities on how to find or create worthy schools, on how to supplement and correct the errors of state-run schools, on how to deal with unworthy institutions, or on the aptness of home schooling and other parent-guided alternatives to conventional institutions. The least bad choice will of course vary with circumstances, but a bit more magisterial guidance would certainly be welcome, as would, in many countries, a greater effort to make existing nominally Catholic schools more truly Catholic.

Second, Christian parents are obliged to bring their children up as Christians. "[B]y means of the rebirth of baptism and education in the faith the child is also introduced into God's family, which is the

---

53. John Paul II, *Familiaris Consortio*, 40.

54. John Paul II, *Familiaris Consortio*, 21.

55. John Paul II, *Familiaris Consortio*, 37.

Church."[56] This formation in faith should go well beyond dragging the kids along to church on Sunday, teaching them some prayers, and getting them through First Holy Communion and Confirmation, although all of these are enjoined or strongly recommended. In this hostile secular age, spiritually and intellectually empty religious practice in childhood is unlikely to anchor a durable adult faith. The best way to keep children close to God and the church is for the family to be a true Christian community in which the children are instructed and inspired by their parents' sacrificial and forgiving love, both within the family and out into the world. The Church's fervor for a God-centered, explicitly Christian family is a denial of the Lockean argument that parents should not impose their will on future adults in the private matter of religion. The Magisterium explains that, on the contrary, without a religious formation children will never acquire "a truly responsible freedom."[57]

Finally, the Magisterium emphasizes that both raising and being children requires a "great *spirit of sacrifice* . . . , a ready and generous openness of each and all to understanding, to forbearance, to pardon, to reconciliation."[58] In other words, the domestic church, like any Christian community, is built by countering all of our sins. God will provide the needed grace, but we have to cooperate. With the appropriate spiritual discipline, children can learn joyful obedience and parents can avoid unjust anger, selfishness, laziness, and all thoughts and deeds that detract from their children's dignity. This psychological realism invalidates any idea that the family is primarily a "place" for self-expression of Romantic selves, untempered by objective moral standards.

The challenge of raising a Christian family is particularly great today. Already in 1981, John Paul II provided a list of social signs of a "disturbing degradation of some fundamental values: a mistaken theoretical and practical concept of the independence of the spouses in relation to each other; serious misconceptions regarding the relationship of authority between parents and children; the concrete difficulties that the family itself experiences in the transmission of values; the growing number of divorces; the scourge of abortion; the ever more frequent recourse to sterilization; the appearance of

---

56. John Paul II, *Familiaris Consortio*, 15.

57. John Paul II, *Familiaris Consortio*, 21.

58. John Paul II, *Familiaris Consortio*, 21, emphasis added.

374 CHAPTER 10

a truly contraceptive mentality"[59] Forty years later, all of these problems have worsened almost everywhere. Christian parents today are far more threatened than they are supported by their societies.

A Brief Cheerful Conclusion

The family teaching can be considered the core and culmination of all the Social Teaching. Without it, the counsels on the economy, government, and everything else would not merely be imperfect (they are, after all, counsels of imperfection by nature). Without the family teaching, the rest of the Social Teaching would be stranded and incomplete. Unless the family, properly understood as the basic human community of overflowing and sacrificial love, is socially respected and sexually well ordered (at least in intention), every other aspect of society will be distorted by the inevitable sadness, distorted power structures, and hope-deprived structures of the spiritually disordered domestic life. No modern challenge to the Catholic understanding of human nature and the nature of human experience in society is as great the three-fold (Hegelian, Lockean, and Romantic) challenge to the Catholic understanding of the family. My use of the word "Catholic," instead of "Christian," shows that how successful this undermining modern challenge has been. Many devout Christians have willingly accepted significant portions of the deeply disordered modern understanding of the family.

For Catholics on the defensive, the situation can look desperate. They are besieged by a particularly wrongheaded approach to sexuality, marriage, and intergenerational relations. Since the popular dedication to these distorted ideas and practices is especially firm, the Catholic teachings are commonly rejected with special vehemence, and the vast majority of Catholics, including many priests and quite a few bishops, do not really understand the teachings of the Church. They are so imbued with Hegelian, Lockean, and Romantic notions that they cannot see how families can actually best reflect the "splendor of truth [that] shines forth in all the works of the Creator and, in a special way, in man, created in the image and likeness of God."[60]

Reeducation will be hard work and progress is likely to be slow. However, it is quite wrong to end this rather gloomy summary of a

---

59. John Paul II, *Familiaris Consortio*, 6.
60. John Paul II, Encyclical letter *Veritatis Splendor* (August 6, 1993), 1.

despised teaching with anything like despair. God has good things in mind for humanity, for each society, and for every family. While a great effort is required to live the Church's family teaching to the fullest, the rewards are tremendous. The teaching offers an escape from family wretchedness and sexual disorder. Better still, it provides a visible example—a light that "shines in the darkness"[61]—of how men and women, children and adults, can truly live out their calling to family love.

---

61. Jn 1:5.

CHAPTER 11

Three Concluding Thoughts

Light and Shadows

John Paul II may well have been the wisest observer of the culture of Western countries in the late twentieth century. His experience of life in Poland under both Nazi and communist rule left him with a profound understanding of godless societies at their most brutal. He also had great insight into the characteristics, both good and bad, of the societies of what was sometimes called the free world. He readily and skillfully applied the tools and wisdom of both Christian and post-Christian thinkers to the postcolonial, postcommunist, and post-Christian globalized and "technologized" societies of his time. He appreciated what moderns had accomplished, explained what had been lost by the dismantling of Christendom, and demonstrated that ultimately only Christianity could fill the huge and inevitable hole at the center of societies that had thrown off their religious heritage.

What did all this wisdom teach the pope about the "new things" of contemporary society? He drew no simple lesson. He neither blindly adored nor unequivocally condemned the efforts of modern people to find the fullness of life. The result of more than two centuries of effort, he said, were neither simply good nor simply bad, but a mix of "much light, [and] not a few shadows."[1]

I think that image provides an apt way to summarize all that I have talked about—economics, government, various aspects of society, the environment, and family life. There is much light and there are many shadows. The mixed judgment is merited, but it can be

---

1. John Paul II, Apostolic Letter *Tertio Millennio Adveniente* (November 10, 1984), 36.

deeply frustrating. As I have pointed out several times, it would be so much easier for good Catholics if they could either just say either no or yes to everything modern.

A simple "no" would make for a splendid morality tale, of the sort found far more often in didactic literature than in real life. In such a preternaturally clear world, the wicked societies that turned away from Catholicism would have found that this apostasy had made life worse for everyone in every way. The prophetic message from God would be clear: "You were and are bad, evil, and wrong. Such a betrayal has been, is being, and will be clearly punished! The further people turn away from Catholicism, Christianity, and religion of all sorts, the worse everything—absolutely everything—will get."

Such a jeremiad may eventually be justified, for example if nuclear war breaks out, but for now it is vastly exaggerated. Post-Catholics and other post-Christians in the West have accomplished good things that Christians did not do but should have done or at least made a serious effort to do, in their fifteen or so centuries of running Europe. Religious people have helped create many of the good things in the post-Christian world, but most of the credit belongs to largely secular ideas, people, and institutions. It is the post-Christian culture that has fed the hungry, clothed the naked, and educated the ignorant. That culture has prevented illnesses and healed the sick in ways that would have been considered practically miraculous in all the years of Christendom. The moderns also did many things that Catholics and many other Christians at first thought were against the faith, but that were eventually deemed acceptable or even praiseworthy. They established democratic governments, narrowed the economic and social gaps between the privileged and the masses, ensured a dignified economic life for most of the poor, rationalized and softened criminal punishments, integrated the Jews into the broader society, and offered previously unimaginable opportunities to women.

In short, it is simply not true that the old, predominantly Christian societies of Europe and its settlements were obviously superior to the non-Christian arrangements that have succeeded them. That assumption has been disproven as fully as the rise of Islam discredited the early mediaeval Christian assumption that God clearly demonstrated his favor to the one true religion by thwarting all

378 CHAPTER 11

rivals.[2] Whatever the final judgment on the modern world may be, it has undoubtedly brought lights, sometimes quite Christian lights, in many places where Christian societies had lived in darkness.

The light can make Christians uncomfortable. To see non-Christians and anti-Christians doing so much good undermines confidence in the value and universality of Christian truth. Why is God so generous to our enemies? Various explanations are possible. Perhaps the accomplishments of non-Christian societies are in fact trivial in comparison to the damage done by the loss of faith and religious practice. Perhaps the successes should really be credited to the Christian account, because they are actually built on the modern worldview's now nearly forgotten Christian foundation. Perhaps these accomplishments are a punishment or lesson for the Church, a reminder that the worldly and sinful Christianity of Christendom was deeply inadequate. Perhaps they are a trial of the faithful, to test and tempt believers with especially appealing idols. Perhaps it is purification, a lesson to Christians that the City of Man is not really that important, since, after all, the wicked servants can manage it so well.[3] Perhaps the moderns are bringing with them the Antichrist, and the end times are approaching. Perhaps their successes show the generosity of God, who plants seeds of truth in every place and at all times.

I will not offer any grand explanation of the workings of divine providence in bringing so much post-Christian light into the world, because I do not have one. I will only say that Christians look foolish when they rage against the whole of modern society, industrial economies, the cult of progress, and the welfare state. These things cannot be entirely the work of the devil. To reject them completely not only denies the incontrovertible good that post-Christian ideas and arrangements have accomplished. Such a rejection also maligns the good intentions of most the people who developed both the ideas and the arrangements.

On the other side, a simple "yes" to modern society is also unacceptable. Many Catholics would prefer it otherwise. The enthusiasts would like the Church to say that the shadows of the modern experiment are neither dark nor extensive enough to require anything more

---

2. For a classic account of that interesting story, see R. W. Southern, *Western Views of Islam in the Middle Ages* (Cambridge, Mass.: Harvard University Press, 1962). For some refinements, see the essays in John Victor Tolan, ed., *Medieval Christian Perceptions of Islam* (New York: Routledge 2000 [1996]).

3. Lk 16:1–13.

THREE CONCLUDING THOUGHTS 379

critical than a few cautions in an overall endorsement of the new ways. As with the naysayers, it would be easier if the yeasayers were actually right. In that case, the atheistic society could be baptized as Christian in some hidden sense, so every resident would join the ranks of what the theologian Karl Rahner called anonymous Christians.[4] All could or would be saved. Catholics could pursue justice hand-in-hand with nonbelievers. When the faithful campaigned for a better world, they might be inspired by their religious belief, but faith would not be a prerequisite for good works. Just as Hegel predicted and Locke recommended, religious matters would be entirely relegated to private life. Catholics could pray at home and then jump on the train of history, accepting a resolutely secular society without any substantial reservations.

It is not that way either. The shadows are numerous and dark. Atheistic governments have done some terrible things, starting with the slaughter of millions of people in the wars and persecutions of the twentieth century. Defenders of modernity often dismiss these horrors as either aberrations from the true spirit of the age or as tragic mistakes that have now been overcome and will never be seen again. Let us hope they are right. Even if they are, almost all post-Christian, post-Stalin-and-Hitler governments have legalized abortion, often with the support of many people who called themselves Christians. The result of that change of social values has been the slaughter of millions of children in the wombs of their mothers. The social response to the massive death-on-demand may be even worse than the horrible fact. Many people consider the spread of "reproductive rights" to be a sign of progress. Even people who are uncomfortable with the idea of abortion for themselves are often reluctant to criticize other people's choices.

The spread of abortion is an extreme example of a widespread and profound spiritual poverty, as the popes have proclaimed with increasing urgency and sadness. There is a distressing emptiness at the core of even the most successful modern societies, those prosperous liberal democracies with their generous welfare states and their self-consciously modern understandings of justice, gender, education, and so much more. Speaking broadly, all these societies have lost touch with many of the noblest aspects of the common

---

4. Karl Rahner, Paul Imhof, and Hubert Biallowons, *Karl Rahner in Dialogue: Conversations and Interviews 1965–1982* (New York: Crossroads 1986), 207.

good. They do not know what to strive for, they are not inspired by virtue or sacrifice, and they are largely blind to beauty. The poverty can be seen in the spiritual numbness of numerous individuals. It also has many social manifestations, including economic injustice, environmental abuse, crass materialism, political apathy and corruption, fervor for authoritarian leaders, disrespect for the dignity of women in family life, the uglification of cities, and the disintegration of families. Despite all these signs of social failure, practical atheism has become so deeply entrenched that many people do not even recognize their spiritual poverty. The superficially happy ignorance only testifies to the depth of their deprivation.

No simple evaluation of the modern world is possible, so we are condemned to complexity and ambiguity. Catholics, like everyone else, live in this land of lights and shadows. They should appreciate the light and fight against the darkness. The latter responsibility, the obligation to spread the gospel in an uncomprehending world, is a heavy one for Christians. It is a call to evangelize that renders inadequate any simple retreat into individual, self-regarding piety. A full Christian life must include a willingness to bear witness to the truth when society offers lies, confusion, and injustice. In modern societies, believers have to reject many leading ideas, because those ideas are intrinsically opposed to the truths of the faith, the truths that reflect, illuminate, and express the transcendental reality of human nature.

All Christians are called to reject the debased idea of freedom as mere choice or the lack of restraint. They must always remember that true freedom, both personal and social, cannot be separated from truth. They should fear the power of the modern state and the insidious damage of moral relativism. They should reject both the cult of supposedly scientific reasoning and its modern rival, the cult of emotional self-expression.

In these tasks, the Catholic Church and its members must try to emulate the Creator who separated light from darkness. Each modern idea and development should be studied repeatedly and weighed carefully. In the course of this book I have tried to show, among other things, that the Catholic Social Teaching has a long and reasonably successful history of doing just that. The practical judgments have often shifted, but the process of holding everything up to the touchstone of timeless truth has remained constant. The labor is always challenging and mistakes will be made, but, really, there is no alternative.

From Frightened Pride to Confident Humility

At the beginning of this book, I said that the Catholic Social Teaching is aimed at the whole world and not just at loyal sons and daughters of the mother church. That catholicity (small "c") was implicit from the beginning of the modern teaching and has been explicit for the past half century. It will not go away, since the truth is itself universal. However, there are different ways of telling the truth. The rhetoric of the Social Teaching—the tone of the Catholic dialogue with the world and of the Magisterium's dialogue with Catholics—has changed greatly over the 125 or so years of the modern Catholic Social Teaching. I identify three periods—the combative but cautiously open beginning, a middle time of full-on cooperation, and the current epoch of prophetic isolation.

In the first document of the new teaching, Leo XIII wrote as if he expected the world to listen. "We approach the subject with confidence, and in the exercise of the rights which manifestly appertain to Us, for no practical solution of this question will be found apart from the intervention of religion and of the Church."[5] Leo did not seem to worry that the world might bristle at or simply reject a rhetorical tone more appropriate to great emperors than to someone carrying the traditional title of the servant of the servants of God. It is not just the tone that lacks humility and an openness to dialogue. The content was also sometimes quite imperious, for example in Leo's declaration, from a different encyclical: "To wish the Church to be subject to the civil power in the exercise of her duty is a great folly and a sheer injustice."[6]

When Leo was writing, at the end of the nineteenth century, his presumptuous tone was probably more anachronistic than he realized. Still, some of his intentions somewhat belie the assertive rhetoric and arrogant statements. To a large extent, Leo was actually recognizing the practical and cultural losses suffered by the Vatican in the wake of the fall of Christendom. His arguments, which showed a serious effort to understand and then help the many people who had strayed from the Catholic teaching, were in some ways a peace offering to the world's new political and economic powers. For example, after haughtily declaring that "[t]he Church . . . deems it unlawful to place the various forms of divine

---

5. Leo XIII, Encyclical Letter *Rerum Novarum* (May 15, 1891), 16.
6. Leo XIII, Encyclical Letter *Immortale Dei* (November 1, 1885), 33.

worship on the same footing as the true religion', he pragmatically continued, 'but [it] does not, on that account, condemn those rulers who, for the sake of securing some great good or of hindering some great evil, allow patiently custom or usage to be a kind of sanction for each kind of religion having its place in the State."[7] Such temporizing separated him from his predecessor Pius IX, who had unequivocally rejected a large collection of modern ideas in the 1864 *Syllabus of Errors*. While Pius basically refused to sully the Church by participating in the great social debates of his time, Leo was anxious that the Magisterium speak in ways that its opponents would be able to understand. In *Rerum Novarum*, for example, he presented his defense of private property and the demand of better treatment for workers in terms that many non-Catholics could accept fairly easily.

Pius X, Leo's successor, reverted to the tradition of anathemas. A typical example was his 1911 attack on Portugal's "vicious and pernicious Decree for the Separation of Church and State." The description was not unfair, but it is hard to see what Pius expected to gain by writing that "[w]e by our Apostolic authority denounce, condemn, and reject the Law for the Separation of Church and State in the Portuguese Republic. This law despises God and repudiates the Catholic faith."[8] The words of the encyclical's opening condemnation help explain his arrogance. Pius denounced "to all Christendom the heinousness of this deed." That was silly, since by then nothing was left of any "universal Christianity" (a more literal rendering of the Latin words translated by the Vatican as "Christendom").[9]

However, Pius X was the last pope who expected Christendom to return. Each of his successors were more realistic than the last. Benedict XV fully reversed Pius IX's ban on "official visits of the Heads of Catholic states to Rome," a big step on the road to reconciliation with post-Christendom. Still, there was a long way to go. Benedict also ignored the paucity of "Catholic states" and reiterated that this was a surrender only in practice, not in theory. It was not, he said, "a tacit renunciation of its sacrosanct rights by the Apostolic See, as if it acquiesced in the unlawful situation in which it is placed."[10]

---

7. Leo XIII, *Immortale Dei*, 36.

8. Pius X, Encyclical Letter *Iamdudum* (May 24, 1911), 9.

9. Pius X, *Iamdudum*, 2.

10. Benedict XV, Encyclical Letter *Pacem, Dei Munus Pulcherrimum* (May 23, 1920), 16.

THREE CONCLUDING THOUGHTS 383

Pius XI, the next pope, moved much farther. He did not fully abandon papal presumption, but he often acted and wrote like a leader who was in danger of losing a great historic battle of ideas. His fairly quick abandonment of the Vatican claim to any temporal power in Italy reflected the recognition that this already-lost battle was no more than a skirmish in the great struggle of the day. He identified the ultimate enemy as "atheistic communism, which aims at upsetting the social order and at undermining the very foundations of Christian civilization."[11] The mention of Christian civilization is backward-looking, but his approach was new. The division of the world was no longer between the Us of the Pope and his Catholic supporters and a hostile Them that included everyone else, even other Christians. Rather, Pius XI wrote of a "battle joined by the powers of darkness against the very idea of Divinity." In that apocalyptic struggle, he said, "it is Our fond hope that, besides the host which glories in the name of Christ, all those . . . who still believe in God and pay Him homage may take a decisive part."[12] This is a dramatic plea for help from outsiders—from Protestants, the traditional enemies of the Catholic Church, and from Muslims and members of other religious, the traditional enemies of the true faith. Pius was also painfully and humbly aware that Catholics themselves were partly responsible for the Church's problems. "It is unfortunately true that the manner of acting in certain Catholic circles has done much to shake the faith of the working-classes in the religion of Jesus Christ."[13]

The repositioning of the Catholic hierarchy in the battles that shaped the modern world was gradual. In the writings of Pius XI, the willingness to call on non-Catholic allies still sounded somewhat forced. Under his successors, Pius XII and especially John XXIII, the new approach entered fully into the mainstream of magisterial thinking. The popes came to believe that Christians could gain much more by working in a friendly and respectful partnership with the flawed secular world than by dismissively condemning it. John hoped to revivify the fading Christian heritage of some regions and to contribute to the debates on justice and peace in all places and on all issues.

The new attitude set the tone for what I just identified as the second period, the era of cooperation. In the first few decades after

---

11. Pius XI, Encyclical Letter *Divini Redemptoris* (March 19, 1937), 3.

12. Pius XI, *Divini Redemptoris*, 72.

13. Pius XI, *Divini Redemptoris*, 50.

the Second World War, the almost two-millennia-old Church often looked like a natural ally with the much newer powers of the non-communist parts of the post-Christian world. Catholic-educated leaders were common in newly decolonized countries. Almost all the most important architects of peace and prosperity in Western Europe were guided by their Christian faith and influenced by the Catholic Social Teaching. Christian Democracy and Christian Social-ism, largely Catholic endeavors, were important European political movements. Labor unions connected to the Catholic Church were powerful in several countries. In the United States, Catholics rose into the political and intellectual mainstream, culminating with the 1960 election of President John Kennedy, a practicing Catholic.

The Social Teaching broadened out during the decades of friend-ship. While non-Catholics had always been welcome to read and learn from the earlier documents, they were not the target audience. Their welfare was often not a central concern. Indeed, as I mentioned in the discussion of anti-Semitism in chapter 6, the almost exclusive papal focus on distinctly Catholic interests often, and in that case disastrously, had taken precedence over more universal demands for active charity. John XXIII was quite different. He looked benignly toward the non-Church world, addressing his 1963 encyclical *Pacem in Terris* to "all men of Good Will" and completely removing the long-standing magisterial caution about Catholics working too closely with non-Catholics. Instead, he called for "extensive co-op-eration" with other Christians and also with "men who may not be Christians but who nevertheless are reasonable men, and men of natural moral integrity."[14] It is impossible to imagine Pius IX, or even Pius XII, writing in such a respectful way about people who had cho-sen to reject the Church of Christ.

Paul VI, who followed John, reinforced the new openness. The main goal of his first encyclical, *Ecclesiam Suam*, was to show "how vital it is for the world, and how greatly desired by the Catholic Church, that the two should meet together, and get to know and love one another."[15] The mix of confidence, friendship, and humility both reflected and influenced the tone of the Second Vatican Council, which was taking place when the document appeared.

On the Church's side, the change has endured. Since Paul VI's time, Catholic leaders have tried to stay close to the world. The

---

14.   John XXIII, Encyclical Letter *Pacem in Terris* (April 11, 1963), 157.

15.   Paul VI, Encyclical Letter *Ecclesiam Suam* (August 6, 1964), 3.

Catholic Social Teaching is now deeply concerned with, and always addressed to, the whole of humanity. However, while the Church has remained open, the world has increasingly spurned its approaches. Few of the modern people who Paul said "run the risk of becoming confused, bewildered, and alarmed" have found comfort in Christian faith—and even fewer in the Magisterium's Catholicism. Far more of them have adopted what the pope called the "most outlandish views." As he noted, these "secular philosophies and secular trends" have tended "to vitiate the true teaching and discipline of the Church of Christ."[16]

The publication of Paul's *Humanae Vitae* in 1968 can be considered a turning point. The numerous shocked and hostile responses to his restatement of the traditional teaching on contraception showed just how far the world, including many Catholics, had already traveled from that "true teaching and discipline."[17] Since then, the Magisterium's influence has steadily diminished. It now has hardly any effect on popular mores, social debates, non-Catholic intellectual life, or political developments. The Church-inspired Solidarity movement's leading role in the liberation of Poland from communism illustrates the extent of the decline. Not only was the 1989 revolution the last display of significant direct Christian political influence in Europe, but, even then, most residents of the country's Western neighbors looked on the Church's role in that struggle as bizarre and anachronistic.

Today, even though Soviet communism has disappeared, as Pius XI had so fervently hoped, the Church and its religious allies are almost everywhere losing the larger combat, the fight against all the "enemies of religion."[18] The post-Christian governments of the traditional lands of Christendom have moved ever further into a non-Christian or even an anti-Christian worldview. Elsewhere, there are countries where religion remains a significant social and political force, but contrary to Pius's hope, the religion in question is almost never Catholic Christianity. More controversially but more significantly, I believe that secular values are in the ascendant in almost every country in the world, whatever the level of religious practice and stated belief. It is not only in the United States and not only

16. Paul VI, *Ecclesiam Suam*, 26.
17. Paul VI, *Ecclesiam Suam*, 26.
18. Pius XI, *Divini Redemptoris*, 72.

among Christians that, in the words of Benedict XVI, "[f]aith becomes a passive acceptance that certain things 'out there' are true, but without practical relevance for everyday life. The result is a growing separation of faith from life: living 'as if God did not exist.'"[19]

For Catholics intent on living out the full Social Teaching of the Church, the result of these historical developments points to a hostile forced separation from the rest of society. In the debates that shape policies and popular attitudes, the audience for Catholics speaking as Catholics is now almost entirely Catholic. Few non-Catholics read any of the documents of the Social Teaching. Few secular writers bother to look into what the popes and the Magisterium are saying about any social issue. No leading politician would dream of saying that he or she follows any aspect of this teaching simply out of the believer's duty to follow the Magisterium. Quite the reverse—even in traditionally Christian countries, Catholic politicians who are suspected of respecting the Church's authority often deny vociferously that they want to impose any of its unpopular teachings. Outside of politics, it is surprising when any popular commentator discusses an idea from the Catholic tradition, let alone actually mentioning the Catholic source. As for the family teaching, it takes great bravery to stand up for it publicly and often great "endurance and patience" to live it out privately.[20]

The predominant tone of the teaching has changed to suit this new, more hostile era. Benedict XVI emphasized calm defiance. "This mission of truth is something that the Church can never renounce. Her social doctrine is a particular dimension of this proclamation: it is a service to the truth which sets us free."[21] Francis has adopted a more excited, prophetic voice, for example in his declaration that '[m]oney must serve, not rule! The Pope loves everyone, rich and poor alike, but he is obliged in the name of Christ to remind all that the rich must help, respect, and promote the poor."[22] Either way, the Church is becoming a voice crying in the wilderness.

As the relations with the modern word have become more distant, the Church's actual recommendations have become both more and less accommodating to it. The compromises come out whenever the Church still hopes to have some effect, however tiny. Catholic leaders

---

19. Benedict XVI, *Address at Celebration of Vespers and Meeting with the Bishops of the United States of America* (April 16, 2008), 1.

20. Col 1:11.

21. Benedict XVI, Encyclical Letter *Caritas in Veritate* (June 29, 2009), 9.

22. Francis, Apostolic Exhortation *Evangelii Gaudium* (November 24, 2013), 58.

are willing to be grateful for very small steps toward, for example, in the social support of families or openness to migrants. Also, they will fight hard and pragmatically for legal exemptions from unjust laws, rather than, say, call for the witness of civil disobedience. On the other side, exalted principles tend to emerge most strongly when the world is least likely to listen. No one with any power is going to ask Francis for a practical economic agenda.

Catholics certainly do not need to live in full isolation from their secular neighbors or in full resistance to every value and practice of secular societies. They should, as bishops often tell them, vote in elections, participate in community activities, and work with non-Catholics and maintain warm social contact with people of all faiths and none. However, as I hope I have shown, the cooperation must be careful and should often be limited. In many parts of life, Catholics *are* increasingly called to stand outside of normal society, sometimes in their daily activities and quite often in their thinking.

Indeed, ever more of the Catholic Social Teaching is becoming a guide for a Catholic resistance. Believers should prepare to make sacrifices for the sake of the liberating truth, because both the authorities of this world and the social consensus of modern society are moving against them. Believers can expect ridicule for refusing to live out the new ideas of the family. They court economic pain by rejecting much of the economic orthodoxy on profit maximization. Ideological tests are likely to limit political careers. Catholic parents often find that schools, even nominally religious institutions, are fundamentally hostile to Catholic family teaching. Catholic would-be public intellectuals have almost no public to argue with.

The Catholic isolation and opposition should not be exaggerated. It is far too early to speak of anything like widespread persecution in formerly Christian countries. Unlike the too many greatly suffering Christians in too many parts of the world, Catholics in post-Christendom still enjoy freedom of religious practice and, with a few exceptions, enough political and social freedom to express their unpopular views openly.

Still, there is more than a little irony in new Catholic isolation, in both its physically dangerous and its socially shunned forms. This distance from the non-Catholic consensus, which has been created against the will of the six most recent popes, is a sort of twisted mirror of the Church's eighteenth- and nineteenth-century separation, which was enthusiastically maintained by many more of their predecessors. For much of the earlier period, a more open Church might have been able to use the lingering Christian sympathies of many social and intellectual leaders to influence the shape of post-Christian Europe. They might even have managed to maintain more support for Christian values and spur less disrespect for the Catholic Magisterium. Throughout that period, many Catholics worked for exactly that sort of openness. However, the popes largely scorned all new thinking as impious and insolent, while the bishops mostly told Catholics to stay far away from any and all of the new secular ideas and practices. Catholics who tried to bring in the best of modern ideas and purify the Church from the worst of its own sins were generally either ignored or punished.

Now that the Church is historically humbled, its leaders make every effort to share the wisdom of its rich tradition with a modern world that even that world's defenders often admit has lost its way. Now, though, the intellectual and cultural heirs to the potentially Christian-friendly secular reformers of the nineteenth century reject the Catholic offer with an indignant blind dogmatism that is all too reminiscent of the papal rejection of those early reformers. In effect, the Church-World drama continues with the roles reversed, but with sadly similar results. Once again, the Catholic faithful find themselves isolated.

Progress and Its Discontents

I am sometimes asked to summarize the difference between the kindly secular and the orthodox Catholic understandings of the social good. My answer varies. When I am thinking morally, I discuss the relationship of freedom and truth. Catholics reject the secular claims that truth is relative and freedom, defined as choice, is absolute. When I am thinking sociologically, I discuss the Catholic recognition of the value of tradition, authority, and hierarchy. In my economic moments, I discuss the preference for the common good and the social solidarity that supports it over any sort of individualism. If the discussion starts with government, I talk about the distinctly Catholic view of human nature—inherently religious and simultaneously good, fallen, and redeemed—and about the Catholic acceptance of the goodness and necessity of social hierarchies of respect and responsibility.

THREE CONCLUDING THOUGHTS   389

These numerous answers are all reasonable. Perhaps the only fair response to the question is another chapter. However, as I look back over this already long book and contemplate the topics that I decided to leave out, I am struck by another broad theme, the Catholic response to progress. Progress, the forward movement of history, has been cherished by modernizers since at least the Enlightenment of the eighteenth century. Of course, the idea that history has a direction was hardly new then. The Old Testament's narrative of the travails of Israel is almost always teleological, although the actual end depends on the chosen people's response to the Lord's love and demands. Many Christian thinkers have also seen some providential direction in history. The biblical book of Revelation has led many of them to expect a narrative of increasing woe. Others have been attracted to the essentially progressive three-age view of Joachim of Fiore. The twelfth-century monk announced the beginning of the last period, in which the liberated and liberating Holy Spirit would supplant the constraining authority of the Son's Church, the Church having already supplanted the Father's harsher justice in guiding the people of Israel. Joachim's idea was declared heretical, as the Church is the Holy Spirit working through history. However, his image of a last, better age helped shape the modern idea that, roughly speaking, progress itself is the goal of history, rather than merely a description of the path to that goal.[23]

This modern idea of all-encompassing progress is encapsulated, in the words of Paul VI, in "man's effort to free himself in face of the demands of nature and of social constraints."[24] Progress is seen not only in the desire for new and better technologies but also in the willingness, even the desire, to overthrow well-established but faulty ideas about society. Like most modern innovations, the cult of progress is not totally misguided. The untiring and all-encompassing search for progress has indeed produced genuine progress in many things. Even the most pious Christian can only sound ridiculous in objecting to absolutely everything that been made new over the past few centuries. Appropriately enough, the documents of the Catholic Social Teaching have numerous expressions of acceptance and gratitude for many types of progress—from the modern business economy and advanced technology to new types of prisons, new roles

---

23.   See Henri de Lubac, *La postérité spirituelle de Joachim de Flore.* (Paris: Éditions Lethielleux, 1979), especially vol. 2, chap 17.

24.   Paul VI, Apostolic Letter *Octogesima Adveniens* (May 14, 1971), 41.

390   CHAPTER 11

for women, and new possibilities for education and travel. The technical progress continues unabated with the internet and the digital manipulation, transfer, and storage of information. So do some types of desirable non-technological progress, for example the changing social attitudes toward the handicapped. This last deserves special mention, because it belies claims that the secular imagination is totally inhumane or has run out of good new ideas. In the past few decades there has been a clear increase in the respect for the dignity of some of the least of Jesus' brothers.

However, I would echo the comment of John Paul II, in his first encyclical, about the modern fascination with, desperate search for, and remarkable success at finding what is called progress. "[T]his progress cannot fail to give rise to disquiet on many counts. . . . Does this progress, which has man for its author and promoter, make human life on earth 'more human' in every aspect of that life? Does it make it more 'worthy of man'? . . . [T]he question keeps coming back with regard to what is most essential—whether in the context of this progress man, as man, is becoming truly better, that is to say more mature spiritually, more aware of the dignity of his humanity, more responsible, more open to others, especially the neediest and the weakest, and readier to give and to aid all."[25]

The answer to the John Paul's essential question is undoubtedly at least partly negative. The regress can even be seen in the just-mentioned treatment of the people most in need of help to thrive. Scientific "progress" has led not only to kindness but also to the unprecedented cruelty off killing many of the weakest people before they are even born. The "progress" in weapons of destruction, tools of popular manipulation, and the equipment of intoxication are equally repellent. As Benedict XVI explained, "We have all witnessed the way in which progress, in the wrong hands, can become and has indeed become a terrifying progress in evil."[26] The blind modern idolatry of progress has to be rejected.

This at least partial magisterial rejection of the cult of modern progress is certainly not new. The 1864 *Syllabus of Errors* of Pius IX includes the claim that the pope must "come to terms with progress, liberalism, and modern civilization."[27] He was only thinking

---

25. John Paul II, Encyclical Letter *Redemptor Hominis* (March 4, 1979), 15.

26. Benedict XVI, Encyclical Letter *Spe Salvi* (November 30, 2007), 22.

27. Pius IX, *Syllabus Errorum*, annex to Encyclical Letter, *Quanta Cura* (December 8, 1864), 80.

THREE CONCLUDING THOUGHTS 391

of claimed but not genuine progress. His successors have all tried to explain the difference between destructive change and genuine advances. Indeed, I believe that this discernment is at the heart of the Catholic Social Teaching.

The work is important because progress cannot be the "condition for and the yardstick of human freedom."[28] No amount of technical or social change can ever overcome the limits of the human condition. The idolatrous belief that it can eventually do exactly that will lead only to disaster, sooner or later. The unquenchable thirst for worldly progress ties people, who have a heavenly calling, too tightly to the world of sin and death. Indeed, as that world shakes off more of its Christian heritage, the cult of progress will lead humanity to embrace blindly all that is new. Such so-called progress is, in the words of Paul VI, "a two-edged sword. It is necessary if man is to grow as a human being; yet it can also enslave him, if he comes to regard it as the supreme good and cannot look beyond it. When this happens, men harden their hearts, shut out others from their minds, and gather together solely for reasons of self-interest rather than out of friendship; dissension and disunity follow soon after."[29] Without moral progress, the objects of evil desires will become ever more awesome and dangerous. Benedict is clear: "If technical progress is not matched by corresponding progress in man's ethical formation, in man's inner growth, then it is not progress at all, but a threat for man and for the world."[30]

Such moral progress is both possible and desirable. Paul VI called for a "genuine progress" in the "development of moral consciousness, which will lead man to exercise a wider solidarity and to open himself freely to others and to God." Solidarity is justly included in the list of key principles of the Catholic Social Teaching (as discussed back in chapter 2). However, Paul warned that "for a Christian, progress necessarily comes up against the eschatological mystery of death. The death of Christ, his resurrection, and the outpouring of the Spirit of the Lord help man to place his freedom, in creativity and gratitude, within the context of the truth of all progress and the only hope which does not deceive."[31]

---

28. John Paul II, *Redemptor Hominis*, 15.

29. Paul VI, Encyclical Letter *Populorum Progressio* (March 26, 1967), 19.

30. Benedict XVI, *Spe Salvi*, 22.

31. Paul VI, *Octogesima Adveniens*, 41.

Those sentences are clumsy in English. Still, if I had to summarize the Catholic Social Teaching in a few words, those are the ones I would choose. They express the breadth, the ambition, and the fundamental unity of the teaching, along with the accomplishments and limits of the entire modern experiment. I close the whole book with a paraphrase of this magisterial wisdom.

God's saving grace, shown in the person of Jesus, should shape everything in our societies. We must always recognize that the City of God can never be built in this world, where the shadow of death can never be lifted, but we must try our best to promote virtue and combat sin in society, just as in our personal lives. The modern world has enhanced some virtues and strengthened some sins. It desperately needs all the Christian love that we can offer.

Bibliography

A. Papal Texts

Unless otherwise noted, texts are taken from the Vatican website (Vatican.va). Quotes from John Paul II's catechesis on human sexuality are taken from the Michael Waldstein translation (in the bibliography). References are always to sections, as marked on the website. When the section numbers are not the same in different languages (as sometimes happens in relatively early documents), I have followed the English numeration. When the English text was confusing, I have cross-checked the Italian, Latin or, for Benedict XVI, the German, to help elucidate the meaning. I have noted all my changes from the Vatican's English versions.

Benedict XIV. *A Quo Primum*. Encyclical Letter. June 14, 1751. Accessed at http://www.papalencyclicals.net/ben14/b14aquo.htm.

Benedict XV. *Ad Beatissimi Apostolorum*. Encyclical Letter. November 1, 1914

———. *Pacem, Dei Munus Pulcherrimum*. Encyclical Letter. May 23, 1920.

———. *To the Peoples Now at War and to Their Rulers*. Apostolic Exhortation. July 28, 1915.

Benedict XVI. *Address at Celebration of Vespers and Meeting with the Bishops of the United States of America*. Speech. April 16, 2008.

———. *Address to Participants in the Plenary Assembly of the Pontifical Council for Culture*. Speech. November 13, 2010.

———. *Address at Welcome Ceremony and Meeting with Authorities of State*, Paris, September 12, 2008.
———. *Caritas in Veritate*. Encyclical Letter. June 29, 2009.
———. *Deus Caritas Est*. Encyclical Letter. December 25, 2005.
———. *Homily (Holy Saturday)*. Homily. April 7, 2012.
———. *Jesus of Nazareth*. Pt. 2, *Holy Week: From the Entrance into Jerusalem to the Resurrection*. London: Catholic Truth Society, 2011.
———. *Meeting with the Clergy of the Diocese of Bolzano-Bressanone*. Speech. August 6, 2008.
———. *Message for the Celebration of the 2010 World Day for Peace: If You Want to Cultivate Peace, Protect Creation*. January 1, 2010.
———. *Message for the 42nd World Communications Day*. January 24, 2008.
———. *Spe Salvi*. Encyclical Letter. November 30, 2007.
———. *Visit to the Bundestag*. Speech. September 22, 2011.
Boniface VIII. *Unam Sanctam*. Papal Bull. November 18, 1302. Accessed at https://www.ewtn.com/library/PAPALDOC/B7UNAM.HTM.
Francis. *Address at the Second World Meeting of Popular Movements*, Santa Cruz de la Sierra, Bolivia. Address. July 9, 2015.
———. *Address to Participants in the General Assembly of the Pontifical Academy for Life*. Speech. October 5, 2017.
———. *Address to the Participants in the Congress on Child Dignity in the Digital World*. Speech. October 6, 2017.
———. *Address to the Pontifical Academy of Sciences*. May 2, 2019.
———. *Address to the 2016 Annual Meeting of the Executive Board of the World Food Programme (WFP)*. Speech. June 13, 2016.
———. *Amoris Laetitia*. Post-synodal Apostolic Exhortation. March 19, 2016.
———. *Evangelii Gaudium*. Apostolic Exhortation. November 24, 2013.
———. *Laudato Si'*. Encyclical Letter. May 24, 2015.
———. *Message for the First World Day of the Poor*. November 19, 2017.
———. *Message for the 104th World Day of Migrants and Refugees 2018*. August 15, 2017.
———. *Message for the World Day of Migrants and Refugees 2016*. September 12, 2015.

BIBLIOGRAPHY   395

———. Morning Meditation, *The Way of Peace*. Daily Meditations. November 19, 2015.

Gregory XVI. *In Supremo Apostolatus*. Papal Bull. December 3, 1839. Accessed at http://www.papalencyclicals.net/greg16 /g16sup.htm.

———. *Mirari Vos*. Encyclical Letter. August 15, 1832. Sourced from http://www.papalencyclicals.net/greg16/g16mirar.htm.

John XXIII. *Mater et Magistra*. Encyclical Letter. May 15, 1961.

———. *Pacem in Terris*. Encyclical Letter. April 11, 1963.

John Paul II. *Address to the Fiftieth General Assembly of the United Nations*. Address. October 5, 1995.

———. *Address to Scientists and Representatives of the United Nations University*. Speech in Hiroshima, Japan. February 25, 1981.

———. *Centesimus Annus*. Encyclical Letter. September 1, 1991.

———. *Discorso ai partecipanti al congresso internazionale di teologia morale*. Speech. April 10, 1986.

———. *Evangelium Vitae*. Encyclical Letter. March 25, 1995.

———. *Familiaris Consortio*. Apostolic Exhortation. November 22, 1981.

———. *General Audience*. October 8, 1980.

———. *General Audience*. August 29, 1984.

———. *Homily in Regina Caeli Prison*. July 9, 2000.

———. *Incontro con la comunità ebraica nella sinagoga della città di roma*. Speech. April 13, 1986. Available in English at https: //www.nytimes.com/1986/04/14/world/text-of-pope-s-speech -at-rome-synagogue-you-are-our-elder-brothers.html.

———. *Laborem Exercens*. Encyclical Letter. September 14, 1981.

———. *Letter to Artists*. April 4, 1999.

———. *Letter to Women*. June 29, 1995.

———. *Man and Woman He Created Them: A Theology of the Body*. Translated and introduced by Michael Waldstein, Boston, Mass.: Pauline Books, 2006 (1986).

———. *Meeting with Mexican Indios*. Speech in Cuilapan, Mexico. January 29, 1979.

———. *Message for the Celebration of the World Day for Peace, Peace with God the Creator, Peace with All of Creation*. January 1, 1990.

———. *Message for World Day for Peace, Peace on Earth to Those Whom God Loves!*, January 1, 2000.

———. *Message for the Celebration of the World Day for Peace 2003, Pacem in Terris: A Permanent Commitment.* January 1, 2003.

———. *Message for the Celebration of the World Day for Peace 2004, An Ever Timely Commitment: Teaching Peace.* January 1, 2004.

———. *Message for the 89th World Day of Migrants and Refugees 2003.* October 24, 2002.

———. *Message for the First Annual World Day of the Sick.* October 21, 1992.

———. *Message for the 90th World Day of Migrants and Refugees 2004.* December 15, 2003.

———. *Mulieris Dignitatem.* Apostolic Letter. August 15, 1988.

———. *Redemptor Hominis.* Encyclical Letter. March 4, 1979.

———. *Redemptoris Rmissio.* Encyclical Letter. December 7, 1990.

———. *Salvificis Doloris.* Apostolic Letter. February 11, 1984.

———. *Sollicitudo Rei Socialis.* Encyclical Letter. December 30, 1987.

———. *Tertio Millennio Adveniente.* Apostolic Letter. November 10, 1984.

———. *Visit to the "Favela Vidigal."* Speech in Rio de Janeiro. July 2, 1980

———. *Veritatis Splendor.* Encyclical Letter. August 6, 1993.

Leo XIII. *Arcanum.* Encyclical Letter. February 10, 1880.

———. *Aux milieux des sollicitudes.* Encyclical Letter. February 16, 1892.

———. *Graves de Communi Re.* Encyclical Letter. January 18, 1901.

———. *Immortale Dei.* Encyclical Letter. November 1, 1885.

———. *Libertas Praetantissimum.* Encyclical Letter. June 20, 1888.

———. *Quamquam Pluries.* Encyclical Letter. August 15, 1889.

———. *Rerum Novarum.* Encyclical Letter. May 15, 1891.

Paul VI. *Address to the United Nations.* October 4, 1965.

———. *Ecclesiam Suam.* Encyclical Letter. August 6, 1964.

———. *Humanae Vitae.* Encyclical Letter. July 26, 1968.

———. *Octogesima Adveniens.* Apostolic Letter. May 14, 1971.

———. *Populorum Progressio.* Encyclical Letter. March 26, 1967.

———. *Regina Caeli.* Angelus Message. May 17, 1970.

———. *Visit of Pope Paul VI to the FAO on the 25th Anniversary of Its Institution.* Speech. November 16, 1970.

Pius IX. *Syllabus Errorum.* Annex to *Quanta Cura.* Encyclical Letter. December 8, 1864. Accessed at http://www.papalencyclicals.net/pius09/p9syll.htm.

BIBLIOGRAPHY

Pius X. *E Supremi.* Encyclical Letter. October 4, 1903.

———. *Iamdudum.* Encyclical Letter. May 24, 1911.

———. *Notre charge apostolique.* Encyclical Letter. August 25, 1910. In English at http://www.papalencyclicals.net/pius10/p10notre.htm.

Pius XI. *Casti Connubii.* Encyclical Letter. December 31, 1930.

———. *Divini Redemptoris.* Encyclical Letter. March 19, 1937.

———. *Quadragesimo Anno* Encyclical Letter. May 15, 1931.

Pius XII. *Address to the First International Congress of Histopathology of the Nervous System.* September 14, 1952. In English at https://www.ewtn.com/library/PAPALDOC/P12PSYCH.HTM.

———. *Christmas Radio Message of 1944.* December 24, 1944.

———. *Christmas Message of 1953.* December 24, 1953.

———. *Christmas Message of 1956.* December 23, 1956.

———. *Discorso ai giuristi cattolici circa l'aiuto ai carcerati.* Speech. May 26, 1957.

———. *Exsul Familia Nazarethana.* Apostolic Constitution. August 1, 1952. In English at http://www.papalencyclicals.net/pius12/p12exsul.htm.

———. *Letter to American Bishops.* December 24, 1948.

B. Other Church Documents

Catechism of the Catholic Church. Vatican City: Libreria Editrice Vaticana, 1993 (for Latin text; English text revised in 1997).

———. "New Revision of Number 2267 of the Catechism of the Catholic Church on the Death Penalty—Rescriptum 'Ex Audientia SS.MI.'" August 2, 2018.

Catechism of the Council of Trent (The Roman Catechism). "Manutian Text as Reflected in the Maredsous Edition of 1902, the Fourth Roman Edition of 1907 and the Turin Edition of 1914. Translation and Preface by John A. McHugh, O.P. and Charles J. Callan, O.P. (Circa 1923)." Accessed at http://www.saintsbooks.net/books/The%20Roman%20Catechism.pdf.

Congregation for the Doctrine of the Faith. "Instruction on Certain Aspects of the 'Theology of Liberation.'" Rome, August 6, 1984.

———. "Notificatio" and "Decretum" [Concerning the *Index of Prohibited Books*]. *Acta Apostolicae Sedis* 58 (1966), 445 and *Acta*

Apostolicae Sedis 58 (1966), 1186. June 14, 1966, and November 15, 1966. Accessed at https://catholicherald.co.uk/how-paul-vi-abolished-the-index-of-prohibited-books-50-years-ago-today/.

Commission for Religious Relations with the Jews. *We Remember: A Reflection on the Shoah.* January 25, 1998.

Council of Trent. *The Canons and Decrees of the Sacred and Oecumenical Council of Trent.* Translated and edited by J. Waterworth. London: Dolman, 1848. Accessed at http://www.documentacatholicaomnia.eu/03d/154 5–1545,_Concilium_Tridentinum,_Canons_And_Decrees,_EN.pdf.

Holy Office, *Index Librorum Prohibitorum.* Vatican City: Typis Polyglottis, 1938.

———. "Statement by the Holy Office approved by Pius XII on 28 July 1949," cited in Letter from Cardinal F. Marchetti-Selvaggiani to the Cardinal Archbishop of Boston. August 8, 1949. Accessed at https://www.catholicculture.org/culture/library/view.cfm?recnum=1467.

Holy See Permanent Observer at the FAO. *Intervention at the 31st Regional Conference of the FAO in Europe.* Voronezh, Russian Federation. May 16, 2018.

International Theological Commission. *Human Development and Christian Salvation.* September 1977 (summary of meetings held October 4–9, 1976).

———. *La libertà religiosa per il bene di tutti: approccio teologico alle sfide contemporanee.* March 21, 2019.

———. *Memory and Reconciliation: The Church and the Faults of the Past.* December 1999.

Pontifical Council for Justice and Peace. *Compendium of the Social Doctrine of the Church.* Vatican City: Libreria Editrice Vaticana, 2004.

Pontifical Council for Pastoral Care of Migrants and Itinerant People. *Pilgrims of Beauty and Faith.* No date. Accessed at http://www.vatican.va/roman_curia/pontifical_councils/migrants/s_index_tourism/rc_pc_migrants_sectiontourists.htm.

Synod of Elvira. *Canons.* c305. Accessed at https://earlychurchtexts.com/public/elvira_canons.htm.

Vatican Council II. *Dignitatis Humanae.* Declaration on Religious Freedom. December 7, 1965.

———. *Gaudium et Spes.* Pastoral Constitution on the Church in the Modern World. December 7, 1965.

———. *Inter Mirifica*. Decree on the Media of Social Communications. December 4, 1963.

———. *Lumen Gentium*. Dogmatic Constitution on the Church. November 21, 1964.

———. *Nostra Aetate*. Declaration on the Relation of the Church to Non-Christian Religions. October 28, 1965.

———. *Perfectae Caritatis*. Decree on the Adaptation and Renewal of Religious Life. October. 28, 1965.

———. *Sacrosanctum Concilium*. Constitution on the Sacred Liturgy. December 4, 1963.

C. Books and Articles

Agamben, Giorgio. *Homo sacer: Il potere sovrano e la nuda vita*. Turin: Einaudi, 1995.

———. *Pilate and Jesus*. Translated by Adam Kotsko. Stanford, Cal.: Stanford University Press, 2015 (2013).

Allen, Robert C. "Economic Structure and Agricultural Productivity in Europe, 1300–1800." *European Review of Economic History*, 4, no. 1 (2000): 1–25.

Anderson, Gary A. *Sin: A History*. New Haven, Conn.: Yale University Press, 2009.

Angier, Tom. "Aristotle on Work." *Revue international de philosophie* 278, no. 4 (2016): 435–50.

Anscombe, G. E. M. "War and Murder." In *Nuclear Weapons and Christian Conscience*, edited by Walter Stein, 45–62. London: Merlin Press, 1961.

Aquinas, Thomas. *Selected Writings*. Edited by Ralph McInerny. London: Penguin, 1998.

———. *Summa theologica*. Translated by the Fathers of the English Dominican Province. 5 vols. London: Sheed & Ward, 1920 (1274). Cited by part, question, and article.

Arblaster, Anthony. *The Rise and Decline Western Liberalism*. Oxford: Basil Blackwell, 1984.

Archer, Margaret S., and Pierpaolo Donati, eds. *Pursuing the Common Good: How Solidarity and Subsidiarity Can Work Together*. Vatican City: The Pontifical Academy of Social Sciences. Accessed at http://www.pass.va/content/dam/scienzesociali /pdf/actapass14.pdf.

Arendt, Hannah. *The Human Condition*. Chicago: University of Chicago Press, 1971.

Aubert, Roger, et al. *History of the Church*. Vol. 8, *The Church in the Age of Liberalism*, edited by Hubert Jedin and John Dolan and translated by Peter Becker. London: Burnes & Oates, 1981 (1971).

Augustine, *City of God*. Translated by Marcus Dods. Edinburgh: T&T Clark, 1871. Accessed at https://www.gutenberg.org /files/45304/45304-h/45304-h.htm.

Bainton, Roland. *Christian Attitudes towards War and Peace: A Historical Survey and Critical Re-evaluation*. London: Hodder and Stoughton, 1960.

Balthasar, Hans Urs von. *Dare We Hope "That All Men Be Saved."* Translated by David Kipp and Lothar Krauth. San Francisco: Ignatius Press, 1988 (1986).

———. *Theo-Drama: Theological Dramatic Theory*. Vol. 4, *The Action*, translated by Graham Harrison. San Francisco: Ignatius Press, 1994 (1980).

———. *Theologie der Geschichte: Ein Grundriss*. Einsiedeln, Germany: Johannes, 2004 (1959).

———. *Unless You Become Like This Child*. Translated by Erasmo Leiva-Merikakis. San Francisco, Ignatius Press, 1991 (1988).

Bandow, Doug, and David Schindler, eds. *Wealth, Poverty and Human Destiny*. Wilmington, Del.: ISI Books, 2003.

Baron, Jane B. "Rescuing the Bundle-of-Rights Metaphor in Property Law." *University of Cincinnati Law Review* 82. no. 1 (2014): 57–101. Accessed at http://scholarship.law.uc.edu/uclr/vol82 /iss1/2.

Beestermöller, Gerhard. "Thomas Aquinas and Humanitarian Intervention." In *From Just War to Modern Peace Ethics*, edited by Heinz Gehard Justenhoven and William A Barbieri, 71–99. Berlin: de Gruyter, 2012.

Beetham, David. *Bureaucracy*. 2nd ed. Buckingham, UK: Open University Press, 1996.

Bellamy, Richard. *Rethinking Liberalism*. London: Pinter, 2000.

Benestad, J. Brian. *Church, State and Society: An Introduction to Catholic Social Doctrine*. Washington, D.C.: The Catholic University of America Press, 2010.

Bess, Gabby. "Reuse, Reduce, Reproductive Rights: How Abortion Can Help Save the Planet." *Vice*. October 6, 2015. Accessed at https://www.vice.com/en_us/article/vv5kj9/reuse-reduce -reproductive-rights-how-abortion-can-help-save-the-planet.

Bloch, Marc. *Les rois thaumaturges: Étude sur le caractère surnaturel attribué à la puissance royale particulièrement en France et en Angleterre, nouvelle édition.* Paris: Gallimard, 1982 (1924).

Blume, Michael A. "Migration and the Social Doctrine of the Church." *People on the Move* (December 2002): 88–89. Accessed at http: //www.vatican.va/roman_curia/pontifical_councils/migrants /pom2002_88_90/rc_pc_migrants_pom88–89_blume.htm.

Blythman, Joanna. *Swallow This: Serving Up the Food Industry's Darkest Secrets.* London: Fourth Estate, 2015.

Bohman, James, and William Rehg, eds. *Deliberative Democracy: Essays on Reason and Politics* Cambridge, Mass.: MIT Press, 1997.

Bokenkotter, Thomas. *Church and Revolution: Catholics in the Struggle for Democracy and Social Justice.* New York: Doubleday, 1998.

Borsay, Peter, and Jan Hein Furnée. *Leisure Cultures in Urban Europe, c. 1700–1870: A Transnational Perspective.* Manchester: University of Manchester Press, 2016.

Boswell, James. *The Life of Samuel Johnson.* Edited by George Birkbeck, Norman Hill, and L. F. Powell. Oxford: Oxford University Press Scholarly Editions Online, 2014 (1791).

Braudel, Fernand. *Les structures du quotidien: Le possible et l'impossible* Paris: Armand Colin, 1979.

Brenkert, George G. "Freedom and Private Property in Marx." *Philosophy & Public Affairs* 8, no. 2 (1979), 122–47.

Breuer, Thomas. "Die Haltung der katholischen Kirche zur Judenverfolgung im Dritten Reich." PSM Geschichte, May 22, 2003. Accessed at https://www.zum.de/psm/ns/k_kirche.php.

Bromberg, Howard. "Pope John Paul II, Vatican II, and Capital Punishment." *Ave Maria Law Review* 6, no. 1 (2007): 109–54.

Bullivant, Stephen. *Faith and Unbelief, A Theology of Atheism.* London: Canterbury Press Norwich, 2013.

Buttiglione, Rocco. *L'uomo e la famiglia.* Rome: Dino, 1991.

Capizzi, Joseph E. *Politics, Justice, and War: Christian Governance and the Ethics of Warfare.* Oxford: Oxford University Press, 2015.

Carens, Joseph H. *The Ethics of Immigration.* Oxford: Oxford University Press, 2013.

Castles, Francis G., Stephan Leibfried, Jane Lewis, Herbert Obinger, and Christopher Pierson, eds. *The Oxford Handbook of the Welfare State*. Oxford: Oxford University Press, 2010.

Cavanaugh, William T. *The Myth of Religious Violence: Secular Ideology and the Roots of Modern Conflict*. Oxford: Oxford University Press, 2009.

Chadwick, Henry. *The Church in Ancient Society: From Galilee to Gregory the Great*. Oxford: Oxford University Press, 2001.

Chatzkel, Jay. *Intellectual Capital*. Oxford: Capstone Publishing, 2002.

Christiansen, Drew, and Walter Gracer, eds. *"And God Saw That It Was Good": Catholic Theology and the Environment*. Washington, D.C.: United States Catholic Conference, 1996.

Clarke, Peter B., ed. *The Oxford Handbook of the Sociology of Religion*. Oxford: Oxford University Press, 2009.

Clarke-Stewart, Alison, and Cornelia Brentano. *Divorce: Causes and Consequences*. New Haven, Conn.: Yale University Press, 2006.

Collins, Irene. *Liberalism in Nineteenth-Century Europe*. London: Historical Association, 1957.

Coman, Peter. *Catholics and the Welfare State*. London: Longman, 1977.

Condorcet [Nicolas de Caritat, Marquis de Condorcet]. *Des progrès de l'esprit humain*. Edited by Monique Hinker and François Hinker. Paris: Éditions Sociales, 1971.

Conklin, Carli N. "The Origins of the Pursuit of Happiness." *Washington University Jurisprudence Review* 195 (2015): 195–262. Accessed at http://openscholarship.wustl.edu/law _jurisprudence/vol7/iss2/6.

Connelly, John. *From Enemy to Brother: The Revolution in Catholic Teaching on the Jews, 1933–1965*. Cambridge, Mass.: Harvard University Press, 2012.

Constitution of the United States of America (1791). Accessed at https://billofrightsinstitute.org/founding-documents/bill-of -rights/.

Corrin, Jay P. *Catholic Intellectuals and the Challenge of Democracy*. Notre Dame, Ind.: University of Notre Dame Press, 2002.

Council of the European Communities. *Treaty on European Union*. Maastricht, the Netherlands, 1992. Accessed at https: //europa.eu/european-union/sites/europaeu/files/docs/body /treaty_on_european_union_en.pdf.

BIBLIOGRAPHY 403

Coyle, Diane. *GDP: A Brief but Affectionate History*. Princeton, N.J.: Princeton University Press, 2015.

Critchlow, Donald T. "Birth Control, Population Control, and Family Planning: An Overview." In *The Politics of Abortion and Birth Control in Historical Perspective*, edited by Donald T. Critchlow, 1–21. University Park, Penn.: Pennsylvania State University Press, 1996.

———. *Intended Consequences: Birth Control, Abortion and the Federal Government in Modern America*. New York: Oxford University Press, 1999.

Crooks, Peter, and Timothy H. Parsons. *Empires and Bureaucracy in World History: From Late Antiquity to the Twentieth Century*. Cambridge: Cambridge University Press, 2016.

Crüsemann, Frank. *The Torah: Theology and Social History of Old Testament Law*. Translated by Allan W. Mahnke. Edinburgh: T&T Clark, 1996 (1992).

Cunningham, Hugh. *Time, Work, and Leisure: Life Changes in England since 1700*. Manchester: University of Manchester Press, 2014.

Dahl, Robert A. *Democracy and Its Critics*. New Haven, Conn.: Yale University Press, 1989.

Davies, Oliver. *The Creativity of God: World, Eucharist, Reason*. Cambridge: Cambridge University Press, 2004.

d'Avray, David. *Medieval Marriage: Symbolism and Society*. Oxford: Oxford University Press, 2005.

Daniélou, Jean, and Henri Marrou. *Nouvelle histoire de l'*Église. Vol. 1, *Des origines à saint Grégoire le Grand*. Paris: Éditions de Seuil, 1963.

Davies, W. D., and Dale C. Allison Jr. *A Critical and Exegetical Commentary on the Gospel According to Saint Matthew*. Vol. 3, *Commentary on Matthew XIX–XXVIII*. London: Bloomsbury, 2004 [1997].

Deady, Carolyn W. "Incarceration and Recidivism: Lessons from Abroad." Newport, R.I.: Pell Center for International Relations and Public Policy, 2014. Accessed at https://salve.edu/sites/default/files/filesfield/documents/Incarceration_and_Recidivism.pdf.

Deane-Drummond, Celia. "Joining in the Dance: Catholic Social Teaching and Ecology." *New Blackfriars* 93, no. 1044 (2012): 193–212.

de Lauzun, Pierre. *Finance, un regard chrétien*. Paris: Editions Embrasure, 2013.

Department for Work and Pensions (UK), "Percentage of Children Living with Both Birth Parents, by Age of Child and Household Income; and Estimated Happiness of Parental Relationships." April 2013. Accessed at https://assets.publishing.service.gov.uk/government/uploads/system/uploads/attachment_data/file/223251/Children_both_parents_income_FINAL.pdf.

de Roover, Raymond. "The Concept of the Just Price: Theory and Economic Policy." *The Journal of Economic History* 18, no. 4 (1958): 418–34.

de Ruggiero, Guido. *The History of European Liberalism.* Translated by R. G. Collingwood. Oxford: Oxford University Press, 1927.

Duff, R. A., and David Garland, eds. *A Reader on Punishment.* Oxford: Oxford University Press, 1994.

Dulles, Avery. "Catholicism & Capital Punishment." *First Things* 112 (April 2001): 30–35. Accessed at https://www.firstthings.com/article/2001/04/catholicism-capital-punishment.

———. *Magisterium: Teacher and Guardian of the Faith.* Naples, Fla.: Sapientia Press, 2007.

Dummett, Michael. *On Immigration and Refugees.* London: Routledge, 2001.

Dupré, Louis. *Transition to Modernity: An Essay in the Hermeneutics of Nature and Culture.* New Haven, Conn.: Yale University Press, 1993.

Eadie, Edward N. *Understanding Animal Welfare: An Integrated Approach.* Berlin: Springer, 2012.

Elegido, Juan Manuel. "The Just Price: Three Insights from the Salamanca School." *Journal of Business Ethics* 90, no. 1 (2009): 29–46.

Emery, Robert E, ed. *Cultural Sociology of Divorce: An Encyclopedia.* Los Angeles: Sage, 2013.

Eppstein, John. *The Catholic Tradition of the Law of Nations.* London: Burns Oates & Washbourne, 1935.

Esping-Andersen, Gøsta. *The Three Worlds of Welfare Capitalism.* Princeton, N.J.: Polity & Princeton University Press, 1990.

EUR-lex. "The Principle of Subsidiarity." European Union, 2015. Accessed at https://eur-lex.europa.eu/legal-content/EN/TXT/?uri=LEGISSUM:ai0017.

Finnis, John. *Natural Law & Human Rights.* 2nd ed. Oxford: Oxford University Press, 2011.

Follett, Richard R. *Evangelicalism, Penal Theory and the Politics of Criminal Law Reform in England, 1808–30*. Basingstoke, UK: Palgrave, 2001.

Fortin, Ernest L. "On the Presumed Medieval Origin of Individual Rights." *Communio: International Catholic Review* 26, no. 2 (1999): 55–79.

Foucault, Michel. *Surveiller et punir: naissance de la prison*. Paris: Gallimard, 1975.

Franco, Paul. *Hegel's Philosophy of Freedom*. New Haven, Conn.: Yale University Press, 1999.

Franks, Angela. "A Body of Work: Labor and Culture in Karol Wojtyła and Karl Marx." In *Leisure and Labor: Essays on the Liberal Arts in Catholic Higher Education*, edited by Anthony P. Coleman, chapter 12. Lanham, Md: Lexington, 2019.

Frenkel, Michael. "Is Migration Good for an Economy? A Survey of the Main Economic Effects." *Journal for Markets and Ethics/ Zeitschrift für Marktwirtschaft und Ethik* 5, no. 1 (2017): 13–22. Accessed at https://www.degruyter.com/downloadpdf/j/jome .2017.5.issue-1/jome-2018–0002/jome-2018–0002.pdf.

Furet, François. *Penser la révolution française*. Paris: Gallimard, 1978.

Furet, François, and Denis Richet, *La révolution française*. Paris: Hachette, 2001.

Gaillardetz, Richard R. *Teaching with Authority: A Theology of the Magisterium in the Church*. Collegeville, Minn.: Liturgical Press, 1997.

Gårdlund, Torsten. *The Life of Knut Wicksell*. Translated by Nancy Adler. Cheltenham, UK: Edward Elgar, 1996 (1958).

Gibellini, Rosino. *The Liberation Theology Debate*. Translated by John Bowden. London: SCM Press, 1987 (1986).

Girard, René. *The Girard Reader*. New York: Crossroad, 1996.

Godelier, Maurice. *The Metamorphoses of Kinship*. Translated by Nora Scott. London: Verso, 2011 (2004).

Goethe, Johann Wolfgang von. "Der Zauberlehrling" (1799). Accessed at http://germanstories.veu.edu/goethe/zauber_dual. html.

Goodwin, Neva R. "Five Kinds of Capital: Useful Concepts for Sustainable Development." Global Development and Environment Institute Working Paper Number 03–07, Tufts University, Medford,

Mass., 2003. Accessed at http://www.ase.tufts.edu/gdae/ /publications/working_papers/03–07sustainabledevelopment .PDF.

Gordon, Christian Joseph K. "*Ressourcement* Anti-Semitism? Addressing an Obstacle to Henri de Lubac's Proposed Renewal of Premodern Christian Spiritual Exegesis." *Theological Studies* 78, no. 3 (2017): 614–33. Accessed at https://doi .org/10.1177/0040563917714621.

Gotcher, Robert F. "Henri de Lubac and *Communio*: The Significance of His Theology of the Supernatural for an Interpretation of *Gaudium et Spes*." PhD diss., Marquette University, 2002.

Gottlieb, Robert. *Forcing the Spring: The Transformation of the American Environmental Movement*. Rev. ed. Washington, D.C.: Island Press, 2005.

Green, T. H. *Lectures on the Principles of Political Obligations and Other Writings*. Edited by Paul Harris and John Morrow. Cambridge: Cambridge University Press, 1986.

Grewel, David Singh. "The Political Theology of Laissez-Faire: From *Philia* to Self-Love in Commercial Society." *Political Theology* 17, no. 5 (2016): 417–33.

Grimes, Katie Walker. "From Slavery to Incarceration." *Church Life Journal*: March 7, 2019. Accessed at http://churchlife .nd.edu/2019/03/07/from-slavery-to-incarceration/.

Gross, Jan T. *Fear: Anti-Semitism in Poland after Auschwitz*. Princeton, N.J.: Princeton University Press, 2006.

Guardini, Romano. *Letters from Lake Como: Explorations on Technology and the Human Race*. Translated by Geoffrey W. Bromiley. Edinburgh: T&T Clark, 1994 (1927).

Gutiérerrez, Gustavo. *A Theology of Liberation*. London: SCM Press, 1988 (1974).

Hadas, Edward. *Human Goods, Economic Evils: A Moral Look at the Dismal Science*. Wilmington, Del.: ISI Books, 2007.

Hamilton, Carol V. "The Surprising Origins and Meaning of the 'Pursuit of Happiness.'" History News Network, 2008. Accessed at http://historynewsnetwork.org/article/46460.

Hamilton, Victor. *The Book of Genesis: Chapters 1–17*. Grand Rapids, Mich.: Eerdmans, 1990.

Hanby, Michael. "Absolute Pluralism: How the Dictatorship of Relativism Dictates." *Communio International Catholic Review* 40 (2013): 542–76.

BIBLIOGRAPHY

———. "Technology and Time." *Communio: International Catholic Review* 43, no. 3 (2016): 342–64.

Hegel, G. W. F.: *The Letters.* Translated by Clark Butler and Christine Seiler. Bloomington, Ind.: Indiana University Press, 1984.

———. *The Philosophy of History.* Translated J. Sibree. Kitchner, Ont.: Batoche Books, 2001 (1840).

———. *Philosophy of Right.* Translated T. M. Knox. Oxford: Oxford University Press, 1942 (1821).

Heidegger, Martin. *Basic Writings.* rev. ed. Edited by David Farrell Krell. London: Routledge, 1993.

Hallebeek, Jan. "Thomas Aquinas' Theory of Property." *Irish Jurist* New Series 22, no. 1 (1987): 99–111.

Held, David. *Models of Democracy.* 3rd ed. Cambridge: Polity, 2006.

Hennelly, Alfred T. ed. *Liberation Theology: A Documentary History.* Maryknoll, N.Y.: Orbis Books, 1990.

Himes, Kenneth B., ed. *Modern Catholic Social Teaching: Commentaries & Interpretations.* Washington, D.C.: Georgetown University Press, 2004.

Hirschman, Albert O. *The Passions and the Interests: Political Arguments for Capitalism before Its Triumph.* Princeton, N.J.: Princeton University Press, 1997 (1977).

Hittinger, Russell. "The Coherence of the Four Basic Principles of Catholic Social Doctrine—An Interpretation." In *Pursuing the Common Good: How Solidarity and Subsidiarity Can Work Together,* edited by Margaret S. Archer and Pierpaolo Donati, 75–123. Vatican City: The Pontifical Academy of Social Sciences, 2008. Accessed at http://www.pass.va/content/dam/scienzesociali/pdf/actapass14.pdf.

Hobbes, Thomas *Leviathan.* Edited by Edwin Curley. Indianapolis, Ind.: Hackett, 1994 (1660).

Hoffman, Andrew J. *From Heresy to Dogma: An Institutional History of Corporate Environmentalism.* Stanford, Calif.: Stanford University Press, 2001.

Hollenbach, David. *The Common Good and Christian Ethics.* Cambridge: Cambridge University Press, 2002.

Holland, Joe. *Modern Catholic Social Teaching: The Popes Confront the Industrial Age 1740–1958.* Mahwah, N.J.: Paulist Press, 2003.

Horkheimer, Max, and Theodor Adorno. *Dialectic of Enlightenment.* Translated by Edmund Jephcott. Stanford, Calif.: Stanford University Press 2002 (1947).

Humboldt, Alexander von. *Kosmos: The Physical Phenomena of the Universe.* London: Hippolyte Baillière, 1845.
Hütter, Reinhard. *Dust Bound for Heaven: Explorations in the Theology of Thomas Aquinas.* Grand Rapids, Mich.: Eerdmans, 2012.
Jamieson, Dale, ed. *A Companion to Environmental Philosophy.* Oxford: Blackwell, 2001.
Jenkins, Willis. *Ecologies of Grace.* Oxford: Oxford University Press, 2008.
Jennings, Jeremy. "Liberalism and the Morality of Commercial Society." In *The Cambridge Companion to Liberalism*, edited by Steven Wall, 42–56. Cambridge: Cambridge University Press, 2015.
Johnson, James Turner. *Ideology, Reason, and the Limitation of War: Religious and Secular Concepts, 1200–1740.* Princeton, N.J.: Princeton University Press, 1975.
Jonas, Hans. "Toward a Philosophy of Technology." *Hastings Center Report 9/1*, 1979. Reprinted in *Philosophy of Technology: The Technological Condition*, 2nd ed., Robert C. Scharff and Val Dusek. Chichester, UK: Wiley Blackwell, 2014.
Jonkers, Peter. "Hegel on the Catholic Religion." In *Hegel's Philosophy of the Historical Religions*, edited by Bart Labuschagne and Timo Slootweg, 177–206. Leiden: Brill, 2012.
Kaftan, Oliver J. "Ora et labora—(k)ein benediktinisches Motto, Eine Spurensuche." *Erbe und Auftrag* 14, no. 4 (2014): 415–42.
Kant, Immanuel. *Groundwork of the Metaphysic of Morals.* 3rd ed. Translated by H. J. Paton. London: Hutchinson's University Press 1956 (1785).
———. *Perpetual Peace: A Philosophical Sketch.* Translated by Mary Campbell Smith. London: George Allen & Unwin, 1904 (1795). Accessed at https://www.gutenberg.org/files/50922/50922 -h/50922-h.htm.
Keeley, Laurence. *War before Civilization: The Myth of the Peaceful Savage.* New York: Oxford University Press, 1996.
Kelly, Michael. "Catholicism and the Left in Twentieth Century France." In *Catholicism, Politics, and Society in Twentieth Century France*, ed. Kay Chadwick, 142–69. Liverpool: Liverpool University Press, 2000.
Keslassy, Elsa. "Global Broadcasters Score Big with Live World Cup Final Ratings." *Variety*, July 18, 2018. Accessed at https://variety .com/2018/tv/global/world-cup-final-ratings-1202876383/.

Keys, Mary. *Aquinas, Aristotle, and the Promise of the Common Good*. Cambridge: Cambridge University Press, 2006.

Klein, Herbert S. "Anglicanism, Catholicism and the Negro Slave." *Comparative Studies in Society and History* 8, no 3 (1966): 295–327.

Knowles, David. "Church and State in Christian History." *Journal of Contemporary History* 2, no. 4 (1967): 3–15.

Koshar, Rudy. *Histories of Leisure*. London: Bloomsbury, 2002.

Kuznets, Simon. *Economic Growth of Nations*. Oxford: Oxford University Press, 1971.

Laidler, Harry W. *Social-Economic Movement: An Historical and Comparative Survey of Socialism, Communism, Co-operation, Utopianism, and Other Systems of Reform and Reconstruction*. London: Routledge & Kegan Paul, 1948.

Lambert, Yves. "Trends in Religious Feeling in Europe and Russia." *Revue française de sociologie* 47, no. 5 (2006): 99–129. Accessed at https://www.cairn.info/revue-francaise-de-sociologie-1-2006-5-page-99.htm.

Langholm, Odd. *The Legacy of Scholasticism in Economic Thought: Antecedents of Choice and Power*. Cambridge: Cambridge University Press, 1998.

Larkin, Philip. "Annus Mirabilis." (1970). Accessed at https://www.thelondonmagazine.org/archive-philip-larkin-two-poems-to-the-sea-annus-mirabilis/.

Lederhendler, Eli, ed. "Jews, Catholics, and the Burden of History." *Studies in Contemporary Jewry* XXI (2005). Oxford: Avraham Harman Institute of Contemporary Jewry, Hebrew University of Jerusalem.

LeVasseur, Todd, and Anna Peterson, eds. *Religion and Ecological Crisis: The "Lynn White Thesis" at 50*. Abingdon, UK: Routledge, 2017.

Levine, Daniel H. "Religion and Politics in Comparative and Historical Perspective." *Comparative Politics* 19, no. 1 (1986): 95–122.

Locke, John. *The Works of John Locke. A New Edition, Corrected, In Ten Volumes*. Vol. 5, *Second Treatise on Government*. London: Printed for Thomas Tegg, 1823 (1690). Accessed at http://www.yorku.ca/comninel/courses/3025pdf/Locke.pdf.

Long, D. Stephen, and Nancy Ruth Fox. *Calculated Futures: Theology, Ethics and Economics*. Waco, Tex.: Baylor University Press, 2007.

Lubac, Henri de. *Le drame de l'humanisme athée*. Paris: Éditions du Cerf, 2000 (1959).

———. *Le mystère du surnaturel.* Paris: Aubier, 1965.

———. *La postérité spirituelle de Joachim de Flore.* Paris: Éditions Lethielleux, 1979.

———. "Note Historique." *Oeuvres Complètes.* Vol. 4, *Affrontements Mystiques*, 336–46. Paris: Cerf, 2006 (1950).

Luz, Ulrich. *Matthew 21–28; A Commentary.* Translated by James E. Crouch. Minneapolis: Fortress Press, 2005.

Macina, Menahem R. "Essai d'élucidation des causes et circonstances de l'abolition, par le Saint-Office, de l'"Opus sacerdotale Amici Israel"(1926–1928)." *Travaux Recherches de l'Université*: 87–110. Lille: l'Université Charles-de-Gaulle, 2003. Accessed at https: //www.academia.edu/4612959/Essai_d_%C3%A9lucidation_ des_causes_et_circonstances_de_l_abolition_par_le_Saint -Office_de_l_Opus_sacerdotale_Amici_Israel_1926–1928_.

MacIntyre, Alasdair. *After Virtue: A Study in Moral Theory.* 2nd ed. London: Duckworth, 1985.

Maestro, Marcello. *Cesare Beccaria and the Origins of Penal Reform.* Philadelphia: Temple University Press, 1973.

Malinvaud, Edmond, ed. *Forum on the Meaning of the Priority of Labor, 5 May 2003, Miscellanea 4.* Vatican City: The Pontifical Academy of Social Sciences, 2004.

Malinvaud, Edmond, and Mary Ann Glendon, eds. *Conceptualization of the Person in Social Sciences. Acta 11.* Vatican City: Pontifical Academy of Social Sciences, 2006.

Maloni, Michael J., and Michael E. Brown, "Corporate Social Responsibility in the Supply Chain: An Application in the Food Industry" *Journal of Business Ethics* 68, no. 1 (2006): 35–52.

Malthus, Thomas. *An Essay on the Principle of Population.* Electronic Scholarly Publishing Project, 1998 (1798). Accessed at http://www.esp.org/books/malthus/population/malthus.pdf.

Manent, Pierre. *La cité de l'homme.* Paris: Fayard, 1994.

———. *Cours familier de philosophie politique.* Paris: Gallimard, 2001.

Mandeville, Bernard. "The Fable of the Bees or Private Vices Publick Benefits." Edited by Irwin Primer. New York: Capricorn Books, 1962 (1714). Accessed at https://archive.org/stream /fableofthebeesor027890mbp/fableofthebeesor027890mbp _djvu.txt

Manuel, Paul Christopher, and Margaret MacLeish Mott. "The Latin European Church: 'Une Messe Est Possible.'" In *The Catholic*

Church and the Nation-State: Comparative Perspectives, 53-68. edited by Paul Christopher Manuel, Lawrence C. Reardon, and Clyde Wilcox. Washington, D.C.: Georgetown University Press, 2007.

Maritain, Jacques. *Les droits de l'homme et la loi naturelle*. Paris: Paul Hartmann, 1945 (1942).

———. *Man and the State*. London: Hollis & Cater, 1954.

———. *La personne et le bien commun*. Paris: Desclée de Brouwer, 1947.

Marx, Karl, and Friedrich Engels. *Marx/Engels Selected Works*. Vol. 1, *The Communist Manifesto*, translated by Samuel Moore, 98–137. Moscow: Progress Publishers, 1969 (1848). Accessed at https://www.marxists.org/archive/marx/works/download/pdf/Manifesto.pdf.

Mathews, Kenneth A. *New American Commentary: An Exegetical and Theological Exposition of Holy Scripture*. Vol 1A, *Genesis 1–11:26*. Nashville, Tenn.: B&H Publishing Group, 1996.

Maxwell, John Francis. *Slavery and the Catholic Church: The History of Catholic Teaching Concerning the Moral Legitimacy of the Institution of Slavery*. Chichester, UK: Barry Rose Publishers, 1975.

McCall, Brian M. *The Church and the Usurers: Unprofitable Lending for the Modern Economy*. Ave Maria, Fla.: Sapientia Press, 2013.

McCann, Dennis P., and Patrick D. Miller, eds. *In Search of the Common Good*. New York: T&T Clark, 2005.

McMullin, Ernan, ed. *The Church and Galileo*. Notre Dame, Ind.: University of Notre Dame Press, 2005.

Meeks, Wayne. "Social and Ecclesial Life of the Earliest Christians." In *The Cambridge History of Christianity*, edited by M. Mitchell and F. Young. Cambridge: Cambridge University Press, 2006.

Minnerath, Roland. "The Fundamental Principles of Social Doctrine. The Issue of their Interpretation." In *Pursuing the Common Good: How Solidarity and Subsidiarity Can Work Together*, edited by Margaret S. Archer and Pierpaolo Donati, 45–56. Vatican City: The Pontifical Academy of Social Sciences, 2008.

Minnerath, Roland, Ombretta Fumagalli Carulli, and Vittorio Possenti. *Catholic Social Doctrine and Human Rights, Acta 15*. Vatican City: The Pontifical Academy of Social Sciences, 2010.

Misner, Paul. *Social Catholicism in Europe: From the Onset of Industrialisation to the First World War.* London: Darton, Longman and Todd, 1991.

Mokyr, Joel. *A Culture of Growth: The Origins of the Modern Economy.* Princeton, N.J.: Princeton University Press, 2017.

Momigliano, Arnaldo. "A Note on Max Weber's Definition of Judaism as a Pariah-Religion." *History and Theory* 19, no. 3 (1980): 313–18.

Murray, John Courtney, "Leo XIII: Separation of Church and State." *Theological Studies* 14 (1953): 145–214. Accessed at https://www.library.georgetown.edu/woodstock/murray/1953c.

Mussolini, Benito. "Discorso del 28 Ottobere 1925 ai cittadini milanese." Accessed at http://www.mussolinibenito.it/discorsodel28_10_1925.htm.

Musto, Ronald G. *The Catholic Peace Tradition.* Maryknoll, N.Y.: Orbis Books, 1986.

Nash, Roderick. *Wilderness and the American Mind.* 3rd ed. New Haven, Conn.: Yale University Press, 1982.

Nolan, Patrick, and Gerhard Lenski. *Human Societies: An Introduction to Macrosociology.* 10th ed. Boulder, Colo.: Paradigm, 2004.

Noonan, John T., Jr. *The Scholastic Analysis of Usury.* Cambridge, Mass.: Harvard University Press, 1957.

Novak, Michael. *Spirit of Democratic Capitalism.* New York: Simon & Schuster, 1982.

OECD Migration Policy Debates, "Is Migration Good for the Economy?" May 2014. Accessed at https://www.oecd.org/migration/OECD%20Migration%20Policy%20Debates%20Numero%202.pdf.

O'Loughlin, Thomas, "A Half-Century after *Ecclesiam Suam* and '*The 1964 Instruction*': The Practice of Historical Disciplines with the Practice of Theology." *New Blackfriars* 99 (May 2018): 312–31.

Olsen, Glenn W., ed. *Christian Marriage: A Historical Study.* New York: Crossroad, 2001.

Parry, Jonathan. "The Gift, the Indian Gift and the 'Indian Gift.'" *Man* New Series, 21 no. 3 (1986): 453–73.

Pascal, Blaise. *Pensées.* Translated by W. F. Trotter. Adelaide: eBooks@Adelaide, 2014 (1670). Accessed at https://ebooks.adelaide.edu.au/p/pascal/blaise/p27pe/complete.html.

BIBLIOGRAPHY 413

Patrick, Dale. *Old Testament Law*. London: SCM Press, 1986.

Paul, Mark. "The Catholic Church and the Kielce Tragedy." In *Kielce - July 4, 1946: Background, Context and Events*. Toronto: Polish Educational Foundation in North America, 1996.

Perreau-Saussine, Emile. *Catholicism and Democracy: An Essay in the History of Political Thought*. Translated by Richard Rex. Princeton, N.J.: Princeton University Press, 2012.

Petersen, William. "The Malthus-Godwin Debate, Then and Now" *Demography* 8, no. 1 (1971): 13–26.

Pew Research Center. "Parenting in America: Outlook, Worries, Aspirations Are Strongly Linked to Financial Situation." December 17, 2015. Accessed at http://www.pewresearch.org /wp-content/uploads/sites/3/2015/12/2015–12–17_parenting - in-america_FINAL.pdf.

———. "Religion in Latin America: Widespread Change in a Historically Catholic Region." November 13, 2014. Accessed at http: //www.pewforum.org/2014/11/13/religion-in-latin-america/.

Phayer, Michael. *Pius XII, the Holocaust, and the Cold War*. Bloomington, Ind.: Indiana University Press, 2008.

Pierson, Christopher, and Francis G. Castles. *The Welfare State Reader*. Cambridge: Polity Press, 2000.

Pilling, David. *The Growth Delusion: The Wealth and Well-being of Nations*. London: Bloomsbury, 2018.

Pistone, Michele R., and John J. Hoeffner. *Stepping Out of the Brain Drain: Applying Catholic Social Teaching in a New Era of Migration*. Lanham, Md.: Lexington Books, 2007.

Pollard, John F. *The Unknown Pope: Benedict XV (1914–1922) and the Pursuit of Peace*. London: Geoffrey Chapman, 1999.

Pope, Hugh. *A Manual for Dominican Lay-brothers*. Woodchester Priory, UK, 1926.

Pritchett, Lant. "Alleviating Global Poverty: Labor Mobility, Direct Assistance, and Economic Growth." Center for Global Development, CGD Working Paper 479, Washington, D.C., 2018. Accessed at https://www.cgdev.org/publication/alleviating -global-poverty-labormobility-direct-assistance-and-economic -growth.

Purdy, Jedediah. "Environmentalism's Racist History." *The New Yorker*. August 13, 2015. Accessed at https://www.newyorker .com/news/news-desk/environmentalisms-racist-history.

Rahner, Karl, Paul Imhof, and Hubert Biallowons. *Karl Rahner in Dialogue: Conversations and Interviews 1965–1982*. New York: Crossroads 1986.

Ratzinger, Joseph. "Eucharist, Communion, and Solidarity." Lecture given at the Bishops' Conference of the Region of Campania in Benevento, Italy. June 2, 2002. Accessed at http://www.vatican.va/roman_curia/congregations/cfaith/documents/rc_con_cfaith_doc_20020602_ratzinger-eucharistic-congress_en.html.

———. *God and the World: A Conversation with Peter Seewald*. San Francisco: Ignatius Press, 2002.

———. "Liturgy and Church Music." Lecture given at the Eighth International Church Music Congress, Rome on November 17, 1985. Accessed at https://media.musicasacra.com/publications/sacredmusic/pdf/liturgy&music.pdf.

———. "Mass 'Pro eligendo romano pontifice.'" Homily. April 18, 2005. Accessed at http://www.vatican.va/gpII/documents/homily-pro-eligendo-pontifice_20050418_en.html.

Ravallion, Martin. *The Economics of Poverty: History, Measurement, and Policy*. Oxford: Oxford University Press, 2016.

Renault, Emmanuel. "Hegel et le paradigme du travail." *Revue internationale de philosophie* 278, no. 4 (2016): 469–90.

Rhonheimer, Martin. "The Holocaust: What Was Not Said." *First Things* 137 (November 2003): 18–27. Accessed at https://www.firstthings.com/article/2003/11/the-holocaust-what-was-not-said.

Riordan, Patrick. *A Grammar of the Common Good: Speaking of Globalisation*. London: Continuum, 2008.

Rodin, David, and Richard Sorabji, eds. *The Ethics of War: Shared Problems in Different Traditions*. Aldershot, UK: Ashgate, 2006.

Rose, Carol M. "Canons of Property Talk, or, Blackstone's Anxiety." *The Yale Law Journal* 108, no. 3 (1998): 601–32.

———. *Property and Persuasion: Essays on the History, Theory, and Rhetoric of Ownership*. Boulder, Colo.: Westview Press, 1994.

Rothschild, Emma. *Economic Sentiments: Adam Smith, Condorcet, and the Enlightenment*. Cambridge, Mass.: Harvard University Press, 2001.

Rousseau, Jean-Jacques. *Du contrat social, ou Principes du droit politique*. Paris: Union Générale d'Éditions, 1963 (1762). Accessed at http://classiques.uqac.ca/classiques/Rousseau_jj/contrat_social/Contrat_social.pdf.

Ryan, Alan. "Liberalism 1900–1940." In *The Cambridge Companion to Liberalism*, edited by Steven Wall, 59–84. Cambridge: Cambridge University Press, 2015.

Sachs, Aaron. *The Humboldt Current: A European Explorer and His American Disciples*. Oxford: Oxford University Press, 2007.

Scheid, Daniel P. *The Cosmic Common Good: Religious Grounds for Ecological Ethics*. Oxford: Oxford University Press, 2016.

Schindler, David C. *Freedom from Reality: The Diabolical Character of Modern Liberty*. Notre Dame, Ind.: Notre Dame University Press, 2017.

Schindler, David L. "Freedom, Truth, and Human Dignity: An Interpretation of *Dignitatis Humanae* on the Right to Religious Liberty." *Communio: International Catholic Review* 40 no. 2–3 (2013): 209–316.

Sharpless, John. "World Population Growth, Family Planning, and American Foreign Policy." In *The Politics of Abortion and Birth Control in Historical Perspective*, edited by Donald T. Critchlow, 103–127. University Park, Penn.: The Pennsylvania State University Press, 1996.

Sheils, W. J., ed. *The Church and War: Papers Read at the Twenty-First Summer Meeting and the Twenty-Second Winter Meeting of the Ecclesiastical History Society*. Oxford: Basil Blackwell, 1983.

Shelley, Percy Bysshe. "Prometheus Unbound: A Lyrical Drama in Four Acts." London: C & J Ollier, 1820. Accessed at http://knarf.english.upenn.edu/PShelley/prom2.html.

Silver, B., et al. "Substantial Changes in Air Pollution across China during 2015–2017." *Environmental Research Letters* 13 (2018): 114012. Accessed at http://iopscience.iop.org/article /10.1088 /1748–9326/aae718/pdf.

Snyder, Susanna. "Biblical and Theological Perspectives on Migration." In *Fortress Britain: Ethical Approaches to Immigration Policy for a post-Brexit Britain*, edited by Ben Ryan, 94–113. London: Jessica Kingsley, 2018.

Schuck, Michael J. *That They Be One: The Social Teaching of the Papal Encyclicals 1740–1989*. Washington, D.C.: Georgetown University Press, 1991.

Siedentop, Larry. *The Origins of Western Liberalism*. London: Allen Lane, 2014.

Simon, Julian. *The Ultimate Resource*. rev. ed. Princeton, N.J.: Princeton University Press, 1996.

Skotnicki, Andrew. *Criminal Justice and the Catholic Church*. Lanham, Md.: Rowman & Littlefield, 2008.

Smith, Adam. *An Inquiry into the Nature and Causes of the Wealth of Nations*. Sao Paolo: Metalibri, 2007 (1776). Accessed at https://www.ibiblio.org/ml/libri/s/SmithA_WealthNations_p.pdf.

———. *The Theory of Moral Sentiments*. London: Henry G. Bohn, 1853 [1759]. Accessed at https://oll.libertyfund.org/titles/smith-the-theory-of-moral-sentiments-and-on-the-origins-of-languages-stewart-ed.

Soltis, Kathryn Getek. "Can Justice Demand Prison Abolition?" *Church Life Journal*. March 12, 2019. Accessed at https://churchlife.nd.edu/2019/03/12/can-justice-demand-prison-abolition/.

———. "The Christian Virtue of Justice and the U.S. Prison." *Journal of Catholic Social Thought*, 8, no. 1 (2011): 37–56.

Southern, R. W. *Western Views of Islam in the Middle Ages*. Cambridge, Mass.: Harvard University Press, 1962.

Spencer, Herbert. *Social Statics*. London: John Chapman, 1851. Accessed at https://oll.libertyfund.org/titles/spencer-social-statics-1851.

Spring, David, and Eileen Spring, eds. *Ecology and Religion in History*. New York: Harper & Row, 1974.

Stepelevich, Lawrence S. "Hegel and Roman Catholicism." *Journal of the American Academy of Religion* 60, no. 4 (1992): 673–91.

Taylor, Charles. *A Secular Age*. Cambridge, Mass.: Harvard University Press, 2007.

———. *Sources of the Self, The Making of the Modern Identity*. Cambridge, Mass.: Harvard University Press, 1992.

Thomson, Augustine. *Dominican Brothers: Conversi, Lay, and Cooperator Friars*. Chicago: New Priory Press, 2017.

Tierney, Brian. "The Idea of Natural Rights: Origins and Persistence." *Northwestern Journal of International Human Rights* 2, no. 1 (2004): Article 2. Accessed at http://scholarlycommons.law.northwestern.edu/njihr/vol2/iss1/2.

———. *The Idea of Natural Rights: Studies on Natural Rights, Natural Law, and Church Law 1150–1625*. Atlanta: Scholars Press, 1997.

Tolan, John Victor, ed. *Medieval Christian Perceptions of Islam*. New York: Routledge 2000 (1996).

Tucker, May Evelyn, and John A. Grim, eds. *Worldviews and Ecology: Religion, Philosophy and the Environment*. Maryknoll, N.Y.: Orbis Books, 1994.

Turner, Susan M., and Gareth B. Matthews, eds. *The Philosopher's Child: Critical Perspectives in the Western Tradition*. Rochester, N.Y.: University of Rochester Press, 1998.

United Nations. "The Universal Declaration of Human Rights." New York: United Nations, 1948. Accessed at https://www.ohchr.org/EN/UDHR/Documents/UDHR_Translations/eng.pdf.

United Nations Department of Economic and Social Affairs, Population Division. *Population Facts*. December 2018. Accessed at https://population.un.org/wup/Publications/Files/WUP2018-PopFacts_2018-1.pdf.

Virginia, Commonwealth of. *Declaration of Rights*. Yale Law School: Avalon Project, 2008 (1776). Accessed at http://avalon.law.yale.edu/18th_century/virginia.asp.

Voas, David. "The Rise and Fall of Fuzzy Fidelity in Europe." *European Sociological Review* 25, no. 2 (2009): 155–68.

Vorgrimler, Herbert, ed. *Commentary on the Documents of Vatican II*. Volume 5, *Pastoral Constitution on the Church in the Modern World*. Translated by W. J. O'Hara. London: Burns & Oates, 1969.

Walzer, Michael. *Just and Unjust Wars*. New York: Basic Books, 2006 [1977].

Weber, Max. *Economics and Society: An Outline of Interpretive Sociology*. Edited by Guenther Roth and Claus Wittich. Berkeley, Calif.: University of California Press, 1968 (1914–1920).

Weigel, George. "*Caritas in Veritate* in Gold and Red." *National Review*, July 7, 2009. Accessed at https://www.nationalreview.com/2009/07/caritas-veritate-gold-and-red-george-weigel/.

Welby, Justin. "Building the Common Good." In *On Rock or Sand? Firm Foundations for Britain's Future*, edited by John Sentamu. London: SPCK, 2015.

White, Lynn, Jr. "The Historical Roots of Our Ecologic Crisis." *Science* 155 (1967): 1203–7, reprinted in *Ecology and Religion in History*, edited by David Spring and Eileen Spring, 15–31. New York: Harper & Row, 1974.

Wilhelm I. "Address to German Parliament 17 November 1881." Accessed at http://ghdi.ghi-dc.org/docpage.cfm?docpage_id=2644.

BIBLIOGRAPHY

Wills, Susan E. "Ten Legal Reasons to Reject Roe." Washington D.C.: United States Conference of Catholic Bishops, 2003. Accessed at http://www.usccb.org/issues-and-action/human-life-and -dignity/abortion/ten-legal-reasons-to-reject-roe.cfm.

Winch, Donald. "Secret Concatenations: Mandeville to Malthus." Carlyle Lectures delivered at Oxford, 1995, no. 5. Accessed at https://arts.st-andrews.ac.uk/intellectualhistory/islandora /object/intellectual-history%3A36/datastream/OBJ/view.

Witherington, Ben, III. *The Acts of the Apostles: A Socio-Rhetorical Commentary.* Grand Rapids, Mich.: William B. Eerdmans, 1998.

Witte, John Jr., and Frank S. Alexander, *The Teachings of Modern Roman Catholicism on Law, Politics, and Human Nature.* New York: Columbia University Press, 2007.

Wohlstetter, Albert. "The Delicate Balance of Terror." RAND Working Paper 1472, Washington, D.C., 1958.

Wolf, Kenneth Baxter. *The Poverty of Riches: St. Francis of Assisi Reconsidered.* New York: Oxford University Press, 2003.

Woodcock, Andrew. "Jacques Maritain, Natural Law and the Universal Declaration of Human Rights." *Journal of the History of International Law* 8, no. 2 (2006): 245–66.

World Bank. "Impact of Migration on Economic and Social Development: A Review of Evidence and Emerging Issues." 2010. Accessed at http://siteresources.worldbank.org/TOPICS/ Resources/214970–1288877981391/Migration&Development -Ratha-GFMD_2010a.pdf .

———. "Trends in Migration and Remittances." 2017. Accessed at http://www.worldbank.org/en/news/infographic/2017/04/21 /trends-in-migration-and-remittances-2017.

Wulf, Andrea. *The Invention of Nature: Alexander von Humboldt's New World.* London: John Murray, 2015.

Yardley, Jim, "Pope Francis Takes 12 Refugees Back to Vatican After Trip to Greece." *New York Times,* April 16, 2016. Accessed at https://www.nytimes.com/2016/04/17/world/europe/pope -francis-visits-lesbos-heart-of-europes-refugee-crisis.html.

Zakaria, Fareed. "The Rise of Illiberal Democracy." *Foreign Affairs* 76, no. 6 (1997): 22–43.

Zamagni, Stefano. "Catholic Social Thought, Civil Economy, and the Spirit of Capitalism." In *The True Wealth of Nations: Catholic Social Thought and Economic Life,* edited by Daniel K. Finn, 63–94. New York: Oxford University Press, 2010.

D. Websites Cited:

Acton Institute website. https://acton.org/
Death Penalty Information. https://deathpenaltyinfo.org/executions
-year
Disney parks attendance. https://disneynews.us/disney-parks
-attendance/ .https://disneynews.us/disney-parks-attendance/
Federal Bureau of Investigation (United States). https://ucr.fbi.gov
/crime-in-the-u.s/2015/crime-in-the-u.s.-2015/tables/table-1
Necrometrics (death tolls). http://necrometrics.com/20c5m.htm
Organization for Economic Co-operation and Development. https:
//www.oecd.org
Our World in Data. https://ourworldindata.org/
Under Caesar's Sword Project, Notre Dame University. http://ucs
.nd.edu/assets/233538/ucs_report_2017_web.pdf

Index

abortion: and artificial contraception, 208, 215, 366; Christians being required to perform, 159; and families, 327, 351, 369, 373; feelings about, 201; and paganism, 146; as sin, 170, 370; and the state, 149, 162, 201, 208, 262–63, 283, 379

Adam and Eve: created in divine image, 203; curse on, 248–49; in garden of Eden, 49, 236; and Jesus, 251; as men and women, 314–17; and original sin, 39, 164, 274 , 277

adultery, 319, 323–24, 326, 363

Agamben, Giorgio, 134, 194n, 232n

alienation: and consumerism, 112; from labor, 104, 109; as loneliness in society, 78, 223, 293–94

animal rights, 206, 265

anti-Semitism: Catholic condemnation of, 227; modern, 227–35; in Poland, 230;

theology of, 231–35. *See also* Jews; Magisterium: on anti-Semitism

Aquinas, Thomas: on the advance of reason, 4; on creation's nature and purpose, 254; on God's sovereign dominion, 60; grace perfects nature, 260; on justice, 57; on just war, 177, 181–82; on natural and supernatural, 19; on private property, 58–59; on scientific caution, 270

aristocracy. *See* hierarchy

Aristotle: in Christendom, 191; on children, 340; on justice, 118; as political philosopher, 128; on social hierarchy, 44n

atheism: and communists, 86, 111, 214, 383; and human rights, 206; humanism, 279; on manual labor, 46n; moral striving in, 285; and penal reform, 221; "practical," 156, 380; secular, 117, 141, 154; semi-official, 158, 379;

socialist, 33; suppression of, 157

Augustine of Hippo, 4, 26, 136–37, 175, 177, 182, 190

Balthasar, Hans Urs von, 135n, 232n, 285, 340n

Beccaria, Cesare, 221, 225

Bentham, Jeremy, 221

birth control. *See* contraception, artificial

bishops: dissent of, 352–53; moral authority of, 35, 154; relations to modern governments, 199–202, 387; relations to Nazis, 230, 234; relations to pope, 144; response to Second Vatican Council, 32; responsibility against heresy, 156; secular authority, 139, 147; silence of, 142; and subsidiarity, 82; and war, 163, 176, 180; and welfare state, 89, 211–13

Buddhism, 136, 154, 243

bureaucracy: and capital, 74; and Christian beliefs, 161; in corporations, 30; and free markets, 117, 273; in governments, 33–34, 195; magisterial response to, 89; and the proto-Hegelian state, 79–80, 309, 336–37; and subsidiarity, 83–86; and the welfare state, 212–15

capital punishment, 145, 224–27

capitalism: Catholic evaluation of, 113, 196; in economic theory, 72–74; and environmentalism, 273; freedom in, 114; human essence of, 74–75; John Paul II on, 61, 111; recent trends, 76; in *Rerum Novarum*, 33–34, 42, 63; socialist judgment of, 108; vs. oppressive governments, 117

Catholic Social Teaching: in the Bible, 10; Catholic doctrinal foundations, 36; call to perfection, 40; contribution to secular debate, 383; degree of authority, 13–14; development of, 381–88; future of, 245, 386–87; in history, 11, 192; inherent imperfections of, 37–38, 39–40; impracticality, 257; influence, 14–15; scope 35–36; sources, 4–5; universal nature of, 35–37; unpopularity of, 2, 162, 312–13, 345

children: Catholic education of, 38–39, 371–72; Christian teaching on, 354–55; and divorce, 323; Locke on, 339; modern ideas about, 34, 305–6, 312, 327–28; and mothers, 50; obligation to parents, 316, 317, 319, 339; and ordered families, 25, 333; as property, 341; and pornography, 299; rights of, 208–9, 318; Romantic appreciation of, 343–44; and subsidiarity, 83; technocratic care of, 308, 333, 337; and war, 186; and the welfare state, 211, 214

China, 136, 144, 279, 283, 309

Christendom: audience for Social Teaching, 35; capital punishment in, 225; children in, 340; church and state in, 139, 332; conflicts within, 149; defined, 23; evaluation of, 147–51, 378; Jews in, 233; justice in, 204, 217, 224; and outsiders, 191–92; and the modern world, 27, 196, 245, 376, 382; war in, 175

Church: as bride of Christ, 318–19, 363; family of God, 318; separation of church and state, 140–42; theological role of, 18, 40, 93

cities, 291–96; beauty in, 294; Catholic role in, 296; nineteenth-century development of, 33, 44; material wealth and poverty, 292–93; pollution in, 246–47; premodern size of, 286n; spiritual decay, 293–95, 380; variety, 291; and wilderness, 267

climate change, 267–70, 272, 309

common good: defined, 12–13; environmental, 246, 259; and GDP, 76, 104; human rights and, 206; importance of, 388; and markets, 109, 113, 116; migration and, 241; natural and supernatural, 139; non-Catholics and, 285; penal system and, 217; and private property, 63; and profits, 75; and religion, 156, 158; secular government and, 230;

and solidarity, 81–92, 94; and subsidiarity, 83; and unions, 77; and war, 171, 184; and the welfare state, 211

communism: atheistic, 86, 148; Catholic response to, 202, 383, 385; and democracy, 195; and human rights, 207; popular appeal of, 214; and private property, 63; revolutionary requirement of, 108, 274; and women, 352

Comte, Auguste, 2

Condorcet, Marquis de, 106–7

Confédération Française des Travailleurs Chrétiens (CFTC, French labor union), 77

consumerism, 58, 75, 98, 100–2, 112, 272, 274, 309

contraception, artificial, 363–67; Church's teaching rejected, 313, 385; "contraceptive mentality," 366–67; as human right, 206, 208; and marriage, 322; and sexual relations, 360; social implications of, 364–66; as technocratic, 282–83

creation: and the common good, 12; environmentalist devaluation of human role in, 264–65; and the Fall, 23, 50; human body in, 260–64; human stewardship and domination of, 36, 48, 72, 249–52, 254; human use and misuse of, 49, 257–59, 283; and materialism, 193; original harmony of, 248–49; restored harmony of, 250–52;

424 INDEX

sacramental meaning, 255; secularists' interest in, 161; triple harmony (human, world, God), 251, 254–56, 258, 270; unity of, 60; universal destination of, 61, 256
crime and legal punishment. *See* penal system

David (biblical king), 45, 130–33, 166, 231, 318
Declaration of Independence (U.S.), 205
democracy, 193–202; anti-Catholicism in, 197–98; bureaucracy in, 79, 336; Catholic responses to, 148, 153, 161, 196–202, 377; Hegelian trends in, 85; Lockean hopes for, 85–86, 379; historical novelty of contemporary forms, 194–95; and sin, 222; and truth, 195–96, 200; and tyranny, 87, 196
development (economic): authentic, 68–69; and autonomy, 71–72, 100; Benedict XVI on, 98; and integral ecology, 256; and migration, 243; and population, 282–83
dignity: of children, 340, 373; of nonhuman creation, 253, 255, 275, 289; of women, 323–24, 326, 329, 356–57, 359, 380
dignity, human: and abortion, 208; all labor having equal, 45–46, 54–56; and capital punishment, 225–27; and consumerism, 101; of

criminals, 217, 221; and democracy, 196; as economic principle, 57, 112; and human rights, 203–5, 207; of laborers, 77, 119; and migration, 244; modern idea of, 192; and peace, 188; of people with disabilities, 390; and political authority, 238; and property, 62–63; and religious freedom, 156–58; and secularism, 160; and subsidiarity, 82–83; universal recognition of, 35
divorce: in the Bible, 314, 317, 319; Catholic teaching on, 321, 326, 369; and liberation of women, 326–27; Locke on, 338; and psychology, 367–69 sociology of, 305, 312, 327, 362–63, 373; and the welfare state, 215, 337
domestic ecology, 302–9; challenges for children, 306; challenges for parents, 304–5; modern material improvements, 303; modern spiritual deterioration, 303–4; separation of old, 307–8; and technocracy, 308; treatment of the ill, 306–10

ecology. *See* climate change; creation; pollution
economics: gross domestic product (GDP), 76; *Homo economicus*, 115–16; as invisible hand, 105–6; markets, 61, 76, 93, 104–17, 118–21, 124. *See also* capitalism;

development; injustice (economic); labor; prices and wages; *individual economists*
education: Catholic and state, 38–39, 151; parents' role in, 371–73
environmentalism. *See* climate change; creation; pollution
Empedocles, 346
England, 27, 109, 150, 185, 198, 294
Enlightenment, 26, 105–6, 108, 179, 207, 211, 225, 277, 389
Erasmus, 179
eschatology, 26, 134–37, 164, 259, 285, 391; and the created world, 252; and peace, 178, 180; and second coming of Christ, 251
eugenics, 265
Europe: as Christendom, 147–51, 377; Christian Democrats in, 384–85; interwar, 109, 195; Jews in, 231; migration to, 238, 242; post-Christian, 385; settlers in North America, 172; secularization in, 154; source of modern ideas, 30, 65; subsidiarity in, 84; unification of, 172, 179; Vatican influence in, 144, 197; war in, 179, 185. *See also individual countries*
euthanasia, 170, 262, 263, 370

families: antifamily culture, 304–5; in the Bible, 313–20; of criminals, 219; and euthanasia, 370; and food, 289–90; importance to Social Teaching, 346, 386; and migration, 239–40, 243; modern changes in, 327–34; in the modern experiment, 312; nature of, 353–56; parents and children in, 371–74; primordial organization of, 320; and private property, 60; right to found, 208; and sexual relations, 361–63; sin in, 368–69; as social group, 21, 210, 211, 213–14, 317–19, 333; summary of Catholic teaching on, 355; and technocratic paradigm, 284, 295; universal human family, 188, 239, 253. *See also* marriage
Ferry, Jules, 38
Fletcher, Colin, 266
food: agriculture, 42; and animal mistreatment, 289; as basic human good, 56, 70, 255; industrial, 286–88; integral ecology of, 286–91; in paradise, 248; shortages of, 65, 106, 186, 303; spiritual value of, 289–91; sufficiency of, 213, 377
France, 66, 77, 84, 152, 172–73, 196; Catholic schools in, 38; and Leo XIII, 199; political movements in, 202; secularization of, 148. *See also* French Revolution
Francis of Assisi, 43, 64, 252
freedom: Christian understanding of, 18, 26, 192; of the Church, 40; of conscience,

130, 157–58; and contraception, 365; and divorce, 363; economic, 33, 68; and families, 312; free elections, 201; free markets, 111–15; Gregory XVI on, 196–97; Hegelian idea of, 79–81, 92, 336–37; in human nature, 16; and human rights, 203, 206; liberal idea of, 86–87, 107, 201, 312, 320, 341; and migration, 239–40, 243; in marriage contract, 325; "modern liberties" rejected, 152; and peace, 188; political, 133; of the press, 197; and progress, 391; and property, 59; and sin, 68, 332; and subsidiarity, 85; and technology, 97, 111; and truth, 31, 196, 348, 380, 388; of women, 326, 329. *See also* freedom of religion
freedom of religion, 106, 151, 155–59, 161, 199, 201, 208, 373, 387
French Revolution, 44, 87, 93, 106, 148, 150, 198
Friends of Israel (Catholic organization), 229–30
Freudian thinking, 29, 93

gender. *See* sexual differences
Germany, 172–73, 185, 198, 212, 229, 234
gifts: and exchange, 120–21; taxes as, 123
Goethe, Johann Wolfgang von, 273
Guardini, Romano, 269, 281

Hanby, Michael, 281–82
Hefner, Hugh, 365
Hegelians (followers of G. W. F. Hegel): on Catholicism, 81, 87, 336; on conflict and war, 92; on contraception, 365; and control of families, 283, 341, 348, 372; and democracy, 85; dialectical view of history, 26; direction of history, 79–81; and family decline, 335–38; influence, 78; liberal-Hegel convergence, 87, 89; and subsidiarity 82–84; on war, 173–74; on women's role, 332
Heidegger, Martin, 281n, 295
hierarchy: bureaucracy and, 93; in capitalism, 74; in Christendom, 65; decline of, 33, 44–45, 47, 197; in families, 316–17, 351; injustice in 25; justice of, 123; liberalism and 93, 108; in marriage, 324; need for, 24, 388; obedience to, 132; in premodern governments, 194; and subsidiarity, 82; in war, 184. *See also* bishops
Hitler, Adolf, 202, 234, 379
Hobbes, Thomas, 22
Holy Family, 45, 81, 238
homosexuality, 89, 159, 201, 215, 328, 360, 363
human nature: and authority, 24–25; in the Christian economy, 118; as created, fallen, and redeemed, 15–18; dignity of, 16, 20; and families, 353; liberal idea of, 89; love in,

21–23; sin's effects on, 23–24; social, 20–21; supernatural calling, 19–20. *See also* sexual differences
human rights, 202–9; anti-Catholic, 208–9; in the Bible, 202–3; Catholic response to, 94, 205–9; and duties, 206; and God-given human nature, 205–6; and human dignity, 203; and individualism, 203–4; and migration, 239; and religion, 204; reproductive rights, 208; and sin, 206, 222; and solidarity, 92
humanism, 56, 69, 278–79, 310
Humboldt, Alexander von, 264, 267, 268; and deep ecology, 265

Index of Prohibited Books, 32, 301
individualism: Catholic response to, 30, 31, 85, 86; as distortion of Christian thinking, 193; and families, 339; and Hegelians, 90; and human rights, 204, 206; liberal vs. economic, 109, 114, 115; and pollution, 274, 277; and private property, 59; psychology of, 22, 24
infertility, 369; in vitro fertilization, 262–63
injustice, economic, 57, 103, 109, 113–14, 118–26, 310, 380; biblical, 52–53, 55; for the poor, 44, 65, 71; of private property, 63. *See also* justice

integral ecology, 276–310; "book of nature" 284; breadth of concerns, 264, 269; of cities, 291–96; and families, 311; of food, 285–91; human attitude to creation, 283; indolence of affluence 103–4; of leisure, 296–302; light and shadows in, 285
Islam, 170, 377
Israel. *See* Jews
Italy: and Jews in Second World War, 230; and migrants and refugees, 238–40; secularization of, 148, 150; unification of, 151, 198; Vatican claims on, 382–83

Japan, 65, 136, 185, 198
Jesus Christ: on abundance of life, 13; on adultery, 319; betrayal of, 321; Caesar and God, 9; on children, 340, 354; crucifixion, 127, 218, 224; demand for perfection, 4; on divorce, 317, 323, 362; economic teachings, 51–55; evangelical technique, 157; on family, 314, 347; on forgiveness, 173, 218, 225, 319; gratuitous love of, 124, 189; humanist model, 279; and Jews, 231; life of, 45, 124; as logos, 191; as migrant, 237–38; multiplication of talents, 97; peace and war, 133, 164–68; and Pilate, 134; on the poor, 65, 126; as prisoner and liberator, 219; reveals "man to man

428 INDEX

himself," 140; on the rich, 100, 296; sacrificial love of, 251; two great commandments, 217–19; washing feet, 160; the way, truth, and life, 40. *See also* theological concepts

Jews: in Christendom, 147, 156–57, 228; and early Christians, 132; as chosen family of God, 319; civil rights for, 228, 377; and creation, 255; historical purpose, 389; intermarriage with Christians, 146; Israelite infidelity to God, 318, 331; Israelite government, 194; Israelite standard of justice, 52; Israelite war, 165–68; as priestly people, 129–31; in secular societies, 154. *See also* anti-Semitism

Joachim of Fiore, 389

Johnson, Samuel, 27

Jonah (prophet), 272–75

Jonas, Hans, 281

Joseph (husband of Mary), 45

Judas Iscariot, 52–53

justice: and the atheistic state, 142; global, 94; and human rights, 204; just war criteria, 181–85; in liberation theology, 67–68; migrants' search for, 239; and the penal system, 218–21; social, 21, 23, 47; solidarity and injustice, 92; in subsidiarity, 82; unjust authority, 132–33; and war, 163, 166, 169, 171–81; and the welfare state, 211, 216. *See also* injustice, economic

Kant, Immanuel, 20, 179

Kennedy, John, 384

Kolbe, Maximilian, 192

labor: and affluence, 103; agricultural, 286, 288; and alienation, 104; and capital. 72–75; dignity of the worker, 44–48, 77; domestic and caring, 290, 303–5, 307, 357–59; globalization of, 188; in the human condition, 49–50, 121; John Paul II on, 55–56, 112; of love, 126; and markets, 110, 112; and mass production, 88; priority over capital, 72–78; regulation of, 274; and responsibility to creation, 257; and universal destination of goods, 62

Lamennais, Félicité de, 196–97

Larkin, Philip, 365

Latin America, 67–68, 154, 177, 202, 204, 238, 245, 265

Lauzun, Pierre de, 116

leisure, 296–302; definitions of, 296–97; modern significance of, 297–98, 302; modern squandering of, 298–99; popular culture, 300–1; and spiritual life, 302; tourism, 300

liberalism: on capital punishment, 225; and Catholicism, 28–29, 196, 390; classical liberals, 85–87, 154; and conflict, 92; government, 48, 195; and Hegelians, 90; Hitler on, 234; and Leo XIII, 33, 108; meaning shift, 87; Pius XI on,

109; and property, 59; and
royalty, 92; spiritual poverty
in, 379; and subsidiarity, 79
liberation theology, 48, 67–68
Libertarians, 113
life (human): modern care for,
261; modern disrespect of,
262; sacredness of, 261
Lockeans (followers of John
Locke): on Catholics, 197; on
contraception, 365; on family,
317, 338–42, 373; individualist, 90, 338; on property, 59;
for small government, 85–86

Mabillon, Jean, 220
Magisterium: on abortion, 370;
admission of error, 231; on
anti-Semitism, 228, 230; on
authoritarian governments,
202; binding, 14, 138; on capital and labor, 75; on capital
punishment, 226–27; changes
of Social Teaching, 3–4, 41,
47; defined, 6; on democracy,
199–201; dissent from, 138,
162; on domestic ecology,
308–9; on education, 373;
on environmental concerns,
89, 270, 272; on families,
302, 311–12, 353; on migration, 235, 240; on modernity,
30–32, 152, 198; on penal
system, 221–22; on poverty,
99; on private property, 62;
on religious freedom, 156–57;
on science and technology,
97–98, 257, 282–83; secular
response to, 155, 388; social

concerns in, 10; on solidarity
and subsidiarity, 95; on the
state's role, 117; on welfare
state, 211–12, 215; wisdom
of, 15
Mandeville, Bernard, 105, 115
Maritain, Jacques, 207
marriage: in the Bible, 314, 317,
319; Catholic understanding
of, 321–25, 337, 346, 349, 368;
childless, 369; contractual
understanding of, 341; declining popularity of, 331–32;
emotional closeness in, 352;
redefinition of members,
161; without religious foundation, 336–37; Romantic
idea of, 330–31; separation,
351; sexual shame in, 365;
social nature of, 361–62; in
the welfare state, 215. *See also*
divorce; family
martyrs, 145
Marxism: anti-Catholic, 197;
on capital, 73; and history,
27, 93; on labor and capital,
89; and liberation theology,
48, 68; on necessity of revolution, 74; and preferential
option for the poor, 66; and
private property, 59. *See also*
socialism
Mary (mother of Jesus), 17,
45, 132, 162, 330; and the
Annunciation, 231; as model
woman, 353; as refugee, 238;
and perfect love, 346–47
materialism: Catholic rejection
of, 192–93; in communism,

111; dualism with spiritual, 285; Francis on, 75; and jealousy, 103; John Paul II on, 101; in popular culture, 300, 301; and material poverty, 69; and secular values, 68; and spiritual poverty, 380

migration, 235–44; Catholic debate on, 2, 387; difficulty of accepting migrants, 244; economic arguments about, 242–43; and economic development, 70–71; effects, 34; and Muslims, 242–43; and solidarity, 92, 242

Mill, John Stuart, 85, 90

modern world: Catholic response to, 29–33, 380; changes in, 33–34; defined, 27–28; "enemies of religion," 385; evaluated, 376–80

motherhood: delayed, 304–5; dignity of, 352; distinctly feminine role, 104, 305–6, 352; and sexual relations, 263, 327; and welfare state, 215, 308; and work-life balance, 305, 328, 352. *See also* sexual differences

Muir, John, 265

music, 153, 281, 300–1, 343

Mussolini, Benito, 84, 202

Napoleon, 84, 179

nationalism, 94–95, 110, 148, 310

nuclear weapons, 34, 180–81, 185, 186, 187, 189, 282, 377

OECD (Organization for Economic Cooperation and Development), 77

Ora et labora, 46

Ozanam, Frédéric, 192

pacifism, 168–69, 176, 179

Papal States, 151, 180, 186, 196, 202

Pascal, Blaise, 330n

penal system, 216–27; in the Bible, 216–19; bureaucracy in, 222; in Christendom, 219–20; modern reform of, 220–22, 224; prison abolition movement, 223–24; and sin, 222. *See also* capital punishment; justice

Poland, 228, 230, 359, 376, 385

pollution: Catholic responsibility for, 253; Catholic–secular agreement on, 259–60, 268; as economic issue, 111; government responsibility for, 63, 89; magisterial pessimism about, 271–72; religious and environmental, 246, 252; in rich and poor countries, 247; secular humanist interpretation of, 279–80; social response to, 274; and solidarity, 91; as solvable technical problem, 267–68; ultimate moral source of, 251, 252, 268–69

popular culture, 300–1

population growth, 106, 253, 265, 271–72, 282–83

poverty, material: agricultural, 287; and autonomy, 86–88; Church response to, 33–34, 99–100; decline of, 65–71, 99–100, 111, 213; domestic, 303; local and global, 71, 91, 95; and migration, 238, 242–44; and pollution, 247, 272, 274; and tourism, 300; urban, 292–93

poverty, spiritual: of affluence, 103, 126, 379–80; and charity, 216; in Christendom, 150; and Francis of Assisi, 43; isolation, 91; of labor, 104; renunciation of property, 4, 53

preferential option for the poor, 44, 63–72; in distributive justice, 123; "ecological debt," 258; in global agriculture, 287; global dimension, 122, 310; pre-Constantinian, 146; prophetic concern, 386; and welfare state, 212–13

preferential option for the vulnerable, 369–71

prices and wages: for caring labor, 104; fair and just, 43, 71, 119, 273; of food, 290; and markets, 74, 75, 108–9, 113, 120; and migration, 242; unjust, 121; and the welfare state, 212

progress, 388–92; Aquinas on, 270; in Christendom, 148; false, 101; as good, 257; Hegelian, 87, 336; moral responsibility for, 256, 282–83, 391; "myth of," 271; philosophy of

history, 26, 320, 378; toward peace, 180; in the penal system, 224; on pollution, 271–72; technological, 97, 391; in urban development, 292; through war, 173–74

property: body as, 349, 365; children as, 341; Christian idea of, 60; Hegel on, 80; and individualism, 339–40; John Paul II on, 60–61; Leo XII on, 42, 60, 63, 382; private, 58–63; right to, 205; social mortgage on, 61; socialists on, 63; in war, 173; in welfare state, 214; women's owning, 326

Protestants: and Catholics, 30, 149; and divorce, 326; and Hegel, 81; and Hitler, 234; reformers, 150; and welfare states, 213

race, 2, 21, 242; Jewish "race," 228, 230, 234

Rahner, Karl, 379

Rawls, John, 90, 128

Romanticism: and children, 343–44; and Christianity, 31, 344; in the family, 373; as guide to life, 330–31, 380; and individualism, 342; and love, 343, 346–48, 351, 355; and responsibility, 157, 332; and sexual desire, 362, 364, 365; and sin, 342

Rome, ancient, 136, 194. *See also* Italy

Rousseau, Jean-Jacques, 197–98, 317, 342

royalty. *See* hierarchy

Russia, 85, 108, 170, 225

same-sex marriage. *See* homosexuality.

Schmitt, Carl, 93

Second Vatican Council: hierarchical subsidiarity, 82; natural and supernatural in, 134; reform of religious orders, 47; religious freedom, 155–58; response to modern world, 32, 153

secularization: Catholic response to, 159–62; and Catholic Social Teaching, 2, 3; as crucial to modernity, 31; government responsibility, 134–36; and materialism, 68; rising, 154; tolerance of religion, 155

self-expression. *See* Romanticism

sexual differences and relations, 355–61; in the Bible, 313–16; biological gender, 262–63, 356, 359–60; feminine genius and vocation, 305–6, 357–58; implications of, 358–59, 361; liberation of women, 326–30, 353; oppression of women, 356, 360

Shelley, Percy Bysshe, 28

sin: and authority, 25; in cities, 292; as creating conflict, 93; and duty, 123; in the economy, 57–58, 74, 77, 118, 121, 128; in education, 355; in the environment, 50, 268, 274; and fallen human nature 17–18, 319; in families, 332, 349–51, 371; and forgiveness, 189; in free markets, 115; and human rights, 205–6; in liberation theology, 67–69; and love, 21, 368; no overcoming without grace, 108; no technical answer to, 99; and sacrifice, 22–23; secular disbelief in, 160; and self-expression, 343–44; of sexual disorder, 315; in society, 23, 26, 36, 143; structures of, 24, 66, 134, 150, 257, 290, 293, 325; vigilance against, 310–11; of war, 163, 168, 179–80

slavery, 43

Smith, Adam, 105–6

social assistance state. *See* welfare state

socialists and socialism: and Catholics, 196, 199; Christian version of, 384; and communism, 109; Leo XIII on, 33, 44, 211; and liberalism, 108; and liberation theology, 67; and private property, 59, 63; in the welfare state, 214

solidarity, 89–95; in consumption, 101; in economic exchanges, 118, 121; global, 91, 93–94; and leisure, 298; and migration, 215, 239–42; and preferential option for the poor, 70; and progress, 391; and subsidiarity, 95; technology and, 99; and unions, 78; and the welfare state, 188, 212

Spinoza, Baruch, 29
Stein, Edith (Benedicta of the Cross), 192
subsidiarity, 78–89; Catholic response to its decline, 89; and centralization, 309; and the family, 332, 355; and freedom of religion, 157; and solidarity, 95; and the welfare state, 210, 213, 215
Summa theologica. See Aquinas, Thomas
survival of the fittest, 34, 110

technology: in the Bible, 53–54; Christian response to advances of, 96–99, 111–12, 257–59; in cities, 293–96; and consumerism, 100; contraceptive, 282–83, 365; enslaving workers, 74; in the food chain, 286–88; and leisure, 298–99; and loving care, 307–8, 337; and migration, 238; and moral responsibility, 283; and pollution, 273, 278; and progress, 389; Romantic opposition to, 280; secular use of, 280; and social change, 268, 271; and social problems, 290; and solidarity, 94; spiritual meaning of, 280–82; and subsidiarity, 88; technocratic paradigm, 280–85; in war, 171, 174, 179
Thérèse of Lisieux, 192
theology: antimodern theology, 32; atonement for sin, 189; childhood, 354; Christ's natures, 10, 140, 165, 279;

conscience, 156–57; creation, 60, 247, 254, 257, 270, 273; divine response to sin, 236, 249–50; "food indeed," 250; grace, 19, 120, 260 (perfects nature), 392; of history, 26–27, 129, 378; Incarnation, 237, 260–61; kenosis (self-emptying) 22–23, 41, 64; logos, 191; lord of life and death, 261; love, 347; of marriage, 322–34, 337; migration, 239–40; original sin, 36, 277, 315; peace and war, 165–66, 176; perfect love of Jesus and Mary, 346; redemption, 17–19, 26; salvation for the poor in spirit, 219; salvation outside of the Church, 35; scriptural authority, 49; sexual relations (including contraception), 364, 366–67; Trinity, 12, 20, 24, 114, 281; universal truth of Christianity, 191; wealth and God's blessing, 50–52. *See also* Church; Jesus Christ; liberation theology; theology of the body
theology of the body, 314, 324, 366
Thucydides, 173
Tiridates III (King of Armenia), 147
Tourism, 300
Trump, Donald, 246

unions (labor), 77–78, 110. *See also* labor

United Nations, 91, 179, 188, 203, 207

United States of America: abortion in, 208; anti-abortion campaign, 164; anti-Catholicism in, 198, 207; big government liberalism, 87; capital punishment in, 226; Catholic parishes, 296; Catholic schools, 39; church and state in, 139; Declaration of Independence, 205; freedom of religion in, 199, 207; holy war in, 170; hunger in, 65; migration in, 238, 242; politics and Catholics, 384; regulation in, 88; responses to *Centesimus Annus*, 5; in Second World War, 185; secularization in, 154–55

Universal Declaration of Human Rights, 203, 207

universal destination of goods, 58–63, 123, 212, 256

usury, 43, 64

Utilitarians/Utilitarianism, 111, 115, 118, 154, 180, 205n, 214, 221, 288, 342–43

Vitoria, Francisco de, 177

Walt Disney's Magic Kingdom, 297

war, 163–90; appeal of, 169–71; change in Catholic teaching on, 178–80; conscientious objection to, 176, 178; current teaching about, 185–87; divine blessing on, 170, 177; and duty of peace, 188; and forgiveness, 189; goal of, 171; just, 169, 177, 181–85; and murder, 170; path to peace, 172–73; path to progress, 173–74; preference for peace, 175; technology in, 171, 180–81

wealth (material), 51, 64, 69, 72

Weber, Max, 93

welfare state, 210–16; anti-Christian, 212–15; and the Bible, 210; borders of, 240; Catholic responses to, 48, 62, 88–89, 95, 153, 161, 193, 211–14; and charity, 215–16; effectiveness of, 71, 213; and families, 337–38; Hegelian, 82–83, 85, 151, 210–11; migration and, 238, 242; paying mothers, 359

Wicksell, Knut, 107

wilderness, 264–65; Catholic response to, 266–67

Wilhelm I (emperor of Germany), 212

work. *See* labor

women. *See* families; motherhood; sexual differences

Lightning Source UK Ltd.
Milton Keynes UK
UKHW012136291220
375860UK00001B/6